CRUSADERS AND PRAGMATISTS

*Movers of Modern
American Foreign Policy*

ALSO BY JOHN G. STOESSINGER:

Henry Kissinger: The Anguish of Power
Why Nations Go to War
Nations in Darkness: China, Russia, America
The United Nations and the Superpowers
Power and Order
Financing the United Nations System
The Might of Nations: World Politics in Our Time
The Refugee and the World Community

CRUSADERS AND PRAGMATISTS

Movers of Modern American Foreign Policy

JOHN G. STOESSINGER

The City University of New York

W · W · NORTON & COMPANY
New York   London

W. W. Norton & Company, Inc., 500 Fifth Avenue, New York, N.Y. 10110
W. W. Norton & Company Ltd., 25 New Street Square, London EC4A 3NT

Library of Congress Cataloging in Publication Data

Stoessinger, John George.
  Crusaders and pragmatists.

  Bibliography: p.
  Includes index.
    1. United States—Foreign relations—20th century.
  2. Presidents—United States—History.   I. Title.
  E744.S89   1979   327.73   79–16698
  ISBN 0–393–01284–0
  ISBN 0–393–95063–8

2 3 4 5 6 7 8 9 0

To my mother

Acknowledgments

In this quest, my friends have been a fountainhead of strength. Ralph Buultjens, Norman Cousins, Walter Kaufmann, Hans J. Morgenthau, and Elie Wiesel read the entire manuscript and shared their thoughts with me. Though engaged in their own research and writing, these friends gave their time unstintingly. Their reflections deepened my perspectives and made my search less lonely. I shall always be grateful for their gift.

Acknowledgment is also due to five colleagues in the profession who made valuable suggestions for improvement: Professor Franz Bax of the University of Virginia; Professor Thomas Bierstecker of Yale University; Professor Frederick Turner of the University of Connecticut; Professor Richard Walker of the University of South Carolina; and Professor Dina Zinnes of Indiana University.

My editor, Donald S. Lamm, the president of W. W. Norton, deserves special appreciation. His sensitivity, thoughtfulness, and care turned a burden into a joy. No writer could be more fortunate. My secretary, Deborah Monsen, was of enormous help in the preparation of the manuscript for publication. Finally, my year as Presidential Professor at the Colorado School of Mines opened up quite unsuspected vistas. New friendships broadened my horizons and energized my spirit. I learned in the American West that an individual life can still make a difference. That year restored to me the inner strength that is the precondition of all creative work.

J. G. S.

June 1979

CONTENTS

Foreword

CRUSADERS
AND PRAGMATISTS

This book will focus on the human element in American foreign policy. It will examine the *personalities* of leading figures and their impact on their nation and the world.

In our time, we have been led to think of states almost as living actors on the world scene. How often we hear a phrase such as "the *United States* decided" or "the *United States* agreed." The question we must ask, however, is "*who* decided for the United States and *who* agreed." To speak of "actors," "powers," or of "systems" merely beclouds the basic truth that human beings, made of flesh and blood, make these decisions on behalf of collectivities called states. States have no existences apart from the lives of men and women. They are creatures of the human will.

While this book will focus on personalities, it is *not* meant to be a single-factor analysis. Clearly, personality does not explain everything. But like any effort at theoretical innovation, mine will emphasize *that* conceptual insight which is original and new. Unlike a photograph, the analysis will not attempt to reproduce every detail of the truth; more like a portrait, it will try to uncover a new truth.

The body of the book will consist of eight major case studies, all taken from the twentieth century. These cases will explore the interplay between personality and foreign policy at crucial turning points in recent American history. The case studies will be held together by interchapters—narrative connecting tissue and personality vignettes—that will provide continuity.

The personalities and turning points we shall examine are the following:

Woodrow Wilson and the League of Nations;
Franklin Roosevelt and Yalta;
Harry Truman and Korea;
John Foster Dulles and Suez;
John Kennedy and the Cuban missile crisis;
Lyndon Johnson and Vietnam;
Henry Kissinger and the Soviet Union and China;
Jimmy Carter and the human-rights initiatives.

In our time, a person who makes foreign policy may hold our future in his hands. *His* personality may be *our* destiny. A leader's character may spell the difference between war and peace, destruction and survival. The United States is a government of laws and not of men in its relations to its citizenry. But in its foreign relations in this century, the United States has been a government of men—a handful of men.

The first fact that the eight cases in this book illuminate is how *few* men have made the crucial decisions in recent American foreign policy. Beginning with Woodrow Wilson, most of these decisions were made by a single man, who at times, but by no means always, consulted with a small group of advisers.

The League of Nations was Wilson's personal crusade and its defeat the direct result of his character flaws. Nobody was able to persuade him to make the necessary compromises. Roosevelt's major foreign policy decisions were reached in almost total secrecy by himself and a handful of advisers. Truman's decision to repel the North Korean attack in 1950 was made by him, in consultation with Dean Acheson and a small group of top officials. The Congress was not involved in any significant way in the "police action" that was to become a major American war. Dulles's handling of the Suez crisis in 1956 stemmed from his personal judgments, which he shared only with President Eisenhower. Kennedy's decision to quarantine Cuba in 1962 was reached in complete secrecy after several days of brainstorming with a dozen government officials. Lyndon Johnson's move in the 1960s to send half a million men into combat to Vietnam and to Americanize the war was his own, buttressed by the support of half a dozen men. The American people and the Congress generally acquiesced in this massive escalation. The peace movement only became effective when *American* casualties rose in alarming numbers and the futility of the war had become obvious. In 1971, Richard Nixon sent Henry Kissinger on a secret trip to China that reversed more than two decades of American foreign policy. And during the last year of the Nixon presidency and the two years of Gerald Ford's administration, Henry Kissinger was in fact the foreign policy of the United States. Only during the presidency of Jimmy Carter did Congress rouse itself from its long torpor. Yet even Carter made a personal decision to mediate between the leaders of Israel and Egypt and another to recognize formally the government of mainland China. Hence, over the span of more than half a century, the pivotal decisions affecting the Republic were made by a small elite of men.

It follows from the above that a leader's *personality* is a decisive element in the making of a foreign policy. Whether a leader uses his power for good or evil is secondary to the fact that this power exists as an objective reality. Such a leader is a historical *fact* at least as much as a state or "system." Differences in leaders' personalities thus may make or break a nation's foreign policy. It matters very much, in short, *who* is there at a given moment.

Two basic personality types have characterized decision makers in twentieth century America. First, there has been the *crusading* type whose hallmark is a missionary zeal to make the world better. The crusader tends to make decisions based on a preconceived idea rather than on the basis of experience. Even though there are alternatives, he usually does not see them. If the facts do not square with his philosophy, it is too bad for the facts. Thus, the crusader tends toward rigidity and finds it difficult, if not impossible, to extricate himself from a losing posture. He does not welcome dissent and advisers will tend to tell him what he wants to hear. He sets out to improve the world but all too often manages to leave it in worse shape than it was before.

The second basic type is the *pragmatic* one. The pragmatist is guided by the facts and his experience in a given situation, not by wishes or unexamined preconceptions. He is generally aware of the alternatives to his chosen course of action and explores the pros and cons of each as objectively as possible. He encourages advisers to tell him what he ought to know, not what they think he wants to hear. Always flexible, he does not get locked into a losing policy. He can change direction and try again, without inflicting damage to his self-esteem. Neither hope nor fear but evidence alone governs his decisions. And when there is no evidence as yet, there is always common sense.

Naturally, these two basic types are not to be considered as mutually exclusive. A pure crusader would be a saint or a fanatic, while a pure pragmatist would be an efficient machine. Usually both types are present to some degree in each personality, but one tends to *predominate*. Over the years, crusading and pragmatic leaders have tended to alternate in cycles. The crusading spirit has dominated American foreign policy in times of protracted crisis or prolonged national trauma while the pragmatic mode has been more in evidence during periods of relative calm and consolidation. Like a pendulum, America has tended to swing between two moods: Sunday evangelism and weekday realism.

In any analysis that focuses on personalities, a crucial question must, of course, be asked: Did the presence of a particular leader make a decisive difference or was he merely present at the right place and at the right moment? In short, was he endowed with a particular gift or was he merely lucky—or unlucky—to be there?

Perhaps a conceptual distinction might be helpful here. We may distinguish between two types of decision makers—whether they are crusaders or pragmatists: the first type is a *player* on the stage of history; the other is a *mover*. In its pure form, the player type would be the legendary little Dutch boy who stuck his finger in the hole of the dike and saved the town. Without depriving the boy of his glamour, it is clear that almost anybody in the situation could have done the job. All that was required was a boy, a finger, and the lucky chance of passing by. But the event itself had a tremendous impact on the life of the Dutch town. The little boy stumbled upon greatness and, for a moment, became a player in a larger play. The mover, on the other hand, is an exceptional person. He does not only *find* the turning point on the historical road; he also helps *create* it. He increases the odds of success or failure for the alternative he chooses by virtue of the extraordinary qualities he brings to bear upon it. Whether these qualities are creative or destructive is not the basic point. The mover's distinctive quality is that he leaves his personal imprint upon history—*for better or for worse*. And this imprint does not stem primarily from luck or circumstance. It stems from the very nature of the mover's personality. The player, thus, is not necessarily exceptional. The mover, on the other hand, enters history not only because of what he does, but more importantly, through what he *is*.

In this book, we shall study *eight movers* in modern American foreign policy. All appeared at dramatic turning points in recent history. Some were crusaders and some were pragmatists. We shall analyze the impact of these personalities on the watersheds of our recent history. Perhaps we can then determine which leaders in our past might serve as inspirations and which as warnings. Perhaps blindness in the past can sharpen *our* sight today. And perhaps past wisdom can give *us* courage for tomorrow.

CRUSADERS AND PRAGMATISTS

*Movers of Modern
American Foreign Policy*

Introduction

YOUNG AMERICA
AND THE WORLD

"My fellow immigrants," Franklin Delano Roosevelt once addressed the Daughters of the American Revolution. In essence, he was correct. Save for the native Indians and the black slaves imported in chains from Africa, America was a nation of immigrants. Most of them had fled from other continents in search of opportunity and freedom. The world's first modern democracy was to be man's great experiment in human liberty. The Old World was a world of darkness; the New World beckoned to the children of light.

In its foreign policy, too, the United States would be different. It would divorce itself from the power politics of Europe that had always led to wars and it would remain aloof from the senseless quarrels among European despots. George Washington's warning to his countrymen not to become involved in entangling alliances became the guideline of the nation's foreign policy. The Monroe Doctrine, proclaimed in 1823, echoed this belief. It declared essentially that the New World wanted nothing more to do with the Old World. America would quarantine itself. It would be isolationist or, in more contemporary language, nonaligned. Let the corrupt Europeans continue to devour each other. America would be a morally superior "city on a hill."

These early American beliefs, needless to say, were naïve.

During most of the nineteenth century the United States owed its isolation from "power politics" to the balance of power on the European continent. Ever since the Congress of Vienna of 1815, which restored peace in Europe after the defeat of Napoleon, Britain had always made sure that no one state or coalition of states had ever conquered most of Europe. By throwing its weight on the weaker side, regardless of the moral merits of the case, Britain had been able to preserve a rough equilibrium and balance. This balance of power had protected Britain's own security, but also quite inadvertently, had prevented a would-be world conquerer such as Napoleon, from menacing the United States. Hence, paradoxically, the American "city on the hill" was protected by the very power balance it despised.

All this began to change however, when at the turn of the century, Germany began to challenge Britain. Great Britain in the late nineteenth century was a vast colonial empire on which "the sun never set." But Germany, too, wanted colonies and "a place in the sun." A powerful German navy began to threaten Britain's control of the seas and even an Anglo-French alliance could not contain German ambitions of European conquest. At that point, America, too, became ambitious to expand. In the wake of the Spanish-American War in 1898, the United States annexed the Philippines and, soon thereafter, Puerto Rico, Guam, Hawaii, and the Samoan Islands became American territories. These new possessions were never called colonies, however. Expansion was justified by another slogan: manifest destiny. In its essence, however, manifest destiny was colonialism, although with an exceedingly bad conscience.

During World War I, when a German victory became a possibility, the United States was drawn ever more tightly into the vortex of world politics. After three years of terrible bloodletting, Britain and France were near exhaustion. Their ally, the czarist regime in Russia, was tottering and German submarines took a terrible toll on Britain's navy. For the United States, a German victory would have meant a serious threat. A hostile German empire would have dominated European Russia and, together with Austria-Hungary and the Ottoman Empire, would have extended its influences over the Balkans and the Middle East as far as the Persian Gulf. Thus, the United States had every reason to ally itself with Britain and France to safeguard its own security. But even then, in the face of real danger, the American people were so unaware of the role of power in international affairs that the United States probably would not have intervened. What finally triggered American intervention in the war was a German campaign of unrestricted submarine warfare, which claimed American lives and destroyed American property. In the end, the German high command forced President Woodrow Wilson's hand.

When Wilson took the United States into the First World War in April 1917, the American people were not particularly interested in the alliances on the European continent. Rather, they believed that they were fighting a war for freedom and democracy, a "war to end all wars," a crusade that would destroy German despotism and banish power politics forever. American power must be used only in a struggle against evil and thus be transformed into a crusade for a righteous cause. But once this mechanism was set in motion, America's "righteous power" [1] would have to punish sinner and eliminate evil. Hence, American wars were often total wars aimed at the complete destruction of the enemy. There could be no compromise with evil, for compromise meant contamination. The embattled democracy thus became a terrible avenger. It fought to punish the power that was rash enough to provoke it and then fought to the bitter end.

George Kennan described this American attitude in an evocative metaphor:

> I sometimes wonder whether a democracy is not uncomfortably similar to one of those prehistoric monsters with a body as long as this room and a brain the size of a pin: he lies there in his comfortable primeval mud and pays little attention to his environment; he is slow to wrath—in fact, you practically have to whack his tail off to make him aware that his interests are being disturbed; but once he grasps this, he lays about with such blind determination that he not only destroys his adversary but largely wrecks his native habitat. You wonder whether it would not have been wiser for him to have taken a little more interest in what was going on at an earlier date and to have seen whether he could not have prevented some of these situations from arising instead of proceeding from an undiscriminating indifference to a holy wrath equally undiscriminating.[2]

[1] John Spanier, *American Foreign Policy Since World War II*, 7th ed. (New York: Praeger, 1977), p. 16.

[2] George F. Kennan, *American Diplomacy* (Chicago: University of Chicago Press, 1951), p. 66.

This attitude had far-reaching consequences for the evolution of America's place in the world. In the first place, foreign policy developed as a reaction to external challenges to America's survival. Seldom, if ever, did the young nation take the initiative. Second, America's moralistic attitude toward "the old country" led to an "all-or-nothing approach to war—either to abstain from the dirty game of power politics or to crusade for its complete elimination." [3] Even more important, this moralism caused American foreign policy to swing from isolationism to intervention and back again. All-or-nothing swings thus became a common pattern. After the First World War, the United States retreated once more into its shell. And when Germany again provoked the United States—this time with the mortal threat of nazism—Franklin Roosevelt, like Woodrow Wilson a quarter century before, had to arouse the nation from its torpor. In that sense, 1939 was 1917 all over again.

Perhaps at the bottom of the belief in American "exceptionalism" was a unique perception of international politics. Americans tended to regard human institutions as improvable and even as perfectible. Thus peace was normal and conflict was an aberration. In the European state system, on the other hand, conflict had always been perceived as a natural condition and harmony was the exception. Hence, the United States, so long isolated from Europe, did not accept the objective reality of conflict among nations. Differences among states were not considered natural. Such obstacles could be removed and peace and harmony restored, given sufficient patience and goodwill. Americans did not see power as merely the raw material of international politics or as an instrument of classical diplomacy. They saw it as inherently evil and—most of the time—as unnecessary. It could only be employed legitimately in a crusade against evil. Otherwise, the guilt over its use would be too great. In short, for most Americans, power was either good or bad, while for most Europeans, it simply was a fact of life in world politics.

In the conduct of a nation's foreign policy, realism might be more compassionate than romanticism. The American national style, rooted as it unquestionably was, in a desire to do away with violence, tended to make violence more enduring, more terrible, and more destructive to political stability than did the old chessboard power politics of Europe. As George Kennan has said, "a war fought in the name of high moral principle finds no early end short of some sort of total domination." [4] The moralist approach to foreign policy thus became closely linked to the concept of total war or total isolation. What it did *not* allow was a practical and consistent participation in world politics.

Woodrow Wilson embodied these early American attitudes to an extraordinary degree. During his presidency, American foreign policy was directed personally by him, at times in consultation with a trusted adviser such as Colonel Edward House. To a large extent, the foreign policy decisions of the United States in those years were the reflections of Wilson's personality. A study of Woodrow Wilson thus reveals the strengths and weaknesses of the American national style "writ large."

Wilson tried to keep his country out of war as long as possible, but once in it, turned it into a crusade and led the embattled democracy to victory. He hoped to replace "power politics" with collective security and a world rule of law through the League of Nations Covenant. He tried to persuade his allies to place world order above their national interests, and failed. He could not talk Britain, France, Italy, and Japan out of their territorial demands at Versailles in 1919. He also failed in his efforts to replace the balance of power and the state system. His League of Nations was stillborn, without American participation. Shortly after this collision with reality, Wilson died, a broken and defeated man. The state system had absorbed the United States at last. Woodrow Wilson's struggle had been the struggle of a man who had fought a war not only to make the world better, but to make it over. In this attempt he failed, but his failure was heroic. The United Nations Charter, ratified a generation later, was his vindication.

[4] Kennan, op. cit., p. 101.

1

WOODROW WILSON
Crusader for a Better World

THE MAKING OF A CRUSADER

"How blessed I am in my home!" Woodrow Wilson once wrote in his diary when he was a student at Princeton University. And he did, indeed, have much to be thankful for. As long as they lived, his parents showered him with love and concern. His mother, who came from a religious Scottish family, was totally devoted to him. His father, whom Wilson called "that incomparable man" was a highly respected and learned Presbyterian minister. Dr. Joseph Ruggles Wilson believed in the Calvinist doctrine that man was an innately corrupt sinner whose only chance for salvation lay in being elected by God to a state of grace and eternal life. Young "Tommy" Wilson was not a promising student. He was eleven before he could read well and had trouble with his catechism. Dr. Wilson undertook to remedy this situation and, on Sunday afternoons would lecture him on history, literature, science, and above all, theology. These tutorials were severe, at times an agony. Dr. Wilson would assign his son long compositions as homework. If a passage was not clear, the elder Wilson would snap: "Suppose you try again and see if you can say what you mean this time, and if not, we'll have another talk and a third go at it." [1] Dr. Wilson did his best to impart his stern Christian

---

[1] Alexander L., and Juliette L. George, *Woodrow Wilson and Colonel House* (New York: John Day, 1956), p. 7.

8

values to his son. The end of all individual and national action
for the minister was "the fixed and eternal standard" of judgment
expressed in the Bible. "Fear God and work hard," Dr. Wilson told
his son. He also advised him to avoid introspection: "In short,
dearest boy, do not allow yourself to dwell upon *yourself*—concentrate your thoughts upon *thoughts* and *things* and *events*." [2] In
an essay he wrote at nineteen, "Tommy" warned of the need to
"overcome evil desires with the strong weapon of prayer, and by
cultivating those heavenly desires which are sure to root out the
evil one." [3] Before he was twenty, Woodrow Wilson had a faith
too high to be questioned. The Christian life for him was a war,
a perpetual striving upward toward perfection that did not permit
ambiguity or doubt and certainly not *compromise*.

While still at Princeton, Wilson revealed his political personality. He became a skilled debater and was elected editor of the
Princetonian. In that position, he alone determined policy and
content. The college newspaper became a one-man show. The
quality of leadership was high but it was also completely authori-
tarian. After graduation, Wilson went to law school and from
there to Johns Hopkins University where he earned a doctorate in
political science. His book, *Congressional Government*, was a significant success and landed him a job at Princeton, where in 1890,
he began a twenty-year career, twelve years as professor and eight
as president of the university.

Wilson's leadership as president of Princeton foreshadowed
in microcosm the strengths and weaknesses he would reveal later
as president of the United States. He instituted an imaginative
program of undergraduate tutorials, which was ahead of its time
but brought him into conflict with Dean Andrew West, who
wanted to expand the graduate school. Wilson turned the conflict
into a crusade, called for Dean West's resignation, and appealed
to alumni across the country for his cause. He refused to back
down or compromise in the slightest, even though a compromise
would have been quite possible. Finally, it was Wilson who lost
out and, in the end, had to resign. His rigidity had backfired and
cost him the Princeton presidency. In 1910, however, he ran a

2 James D. Barber, *The Presidential Character* (Englewood Cliffs, N.J.: Prentice-
Hall, 1972), p. 104.
3 Ibid.

successful campaign for governor of New Jersey and his determined leadership in that post soon brought him into the national political arena. In 1912, he was elected president of the United States.

Fifty-six years old when he reached the presidency, Wilson's religious, crusading faith was firmly in place. Shortly after his election, he said to a supporter: "I wish it clearly understood that I owe you nothing. Remember that God ordained that I should be the next President of the United States." [4] Life would not be worth living, Wilson said, "if it were not for the driving power of religion. The way to success is to show you are not afraid of anybody except God and His judgment." [5] Wilson's God was not a passive spectator, but one actively at work in the affairs of mankind. He would lead humanity toward salvation. There would be difficulties along the way, but the ultimate outcome was not in doubt. And God's men, his disciples dedicated to His service, would lead the people along the righteous path. Wilson *knew*, as surely as he knew God's will, that the American people were with him. "I have never had a moment's doubt," he said, "as to where the heart and purpose of this people lay." [6] He was a messenger of God to the people of America and the nations of the world. "God above, the people below, were joined by Woodrow Wilson." [7]

Not surprisingly, Wilson's closest friend and associate in the White House was a man of unquestioning obedience and loyalty. "My faith in you is as great as my love for you," Colonel Edward House wrote to Wilson, "without your leadership God alone knows how long we will wander in the darkness." [8] "You are the only one in the world," Wilson in turn told House, "to whom I can open my mind freely." [9] The president was quite open in explaining why he valued House: "What I like about House is that he is the most self-effacing man that ever lived." [10] But when, after many years of friendship, House finally ventured some independent thoughts about Wilson's handling of the Senate on the

[4] Ibid., p. 62.
[5] Ibid., p. 63.
[6] Ibid., p. 64.
[7] Ibid.
[8] Ibid., p. 62.
[9] Ibid.
[10] Ibid.

question of the League of Nations, Wilson broke off the relationship. He alone knew what was best and God was with him. Arthur Link, a leading Wilson scholar, admirably summarized Wilson's lonely faith:

> Mankind, he felt, lived not only by the providence of God but also under His immutable decrees; and nations as well as men transgressed the divine ordinances at their peril. He shared a Calvinistic belief, held in his day mainly by Southern Presbyterians and members of the Reformed churches in Europe, in predestination—the absolute conviction that God had ordered the universe from the beginning, the faith that God used men for His own purposes. From such beliefs came a sure sense of destiny and a feeling of intimate connection with the sources of power.[11]

Wilson saw himself as a man destined to make the world's salvation part of his own. In this relentless struggle, he would yield nothing and crush his enemies with righteous power. And if he could not win, he would die in the attempt.

THE STRUGGLE AGAINST EVIL: WAR AND BOLSHEVISM

In 1908, when Woodrow Wilson was still at Princeton, he wrote *Constitutional Government in the United States.* "One of the greatest of the President's powers," Wilson wrote in a key passage, was "his control, which is very absolute, of the foreign relations of the nation. The initiative in foreign affairs, which the President possesses without any restriction whatever, is virtually the power to control them absolutely." [12] When, four years later, the political scientist became president of the United States, he soon began to practice what he had written. When coupled with his sense of messianic mission, Wilson's conception of the presidency made that office into a formidable fountainhead of power. But that power was never to be used without a moral purpose. It was to become a major instrument in the struggle against evil. Three of Wilson's crucial foreign policy decisions all serve to illustrate this point: the intervention in Mexico; the American entry

---

[11] Arthur S. Link, *Wilson: The New Freedom* (Princeton: Princeton University Press, 1956), p. 64.

[12] Woodrow Wilson, *Constitutional Government in the United States* (New York: Macmillan, 1908), p. 138.

into World War I; and the decision not to recognize the Bolshevik regime in Russia nor participate in an attempt to achieve its overthrow.

The darker side of Wilson's crusading spirit appeared quite early in his presidency. In 1913, he became convinced that brigands and bandits were endangering the lives of American citizens in Mexico. Besides, he was convinced that the Huerta regime was immoral and a threat to the liberty and security of the Western Hemisphere. Accordingly, Wilson decided to intervene with American troops hoping to restore law and order. He felt additionally justified in doing so because the United States did not recognize Huerta, which made the Mexican regime in Wilson's eyes a nongovernmental organization. For the next seven months, American troops occupied Veracruz. Wilson thought he knew what was best for Mexico and was prepared to impose an American solution. "I am going to teach the Latin American republics to elect good men," declared the author of *Congressional Government* and advocate of government by the consent of the governed. Thus, amid proclamations of goodwill and high moral purpose, Wilson sponsored American military intervention on a scale never seen before in Latin America. And when, two years later, Pancho Villa killed American citizens in Mexico and sent raiding parties into Texas and New Mexico, Wilson dispatched a punitive expedition into Mexico, led by General John J. Pershing. Thus, an intervention, justified by moral imperatives, had aroused fierce national resentments, embroiled the United States in Mexican politics, and brought the two nations to the brink of war.

During approximately the same period—from 1914 to early 1917—Wilson used his formidable energies to keep the United States out of the First World War. During these years, Wilson acted as national leader and spokesman and made all major decisions. Like most Americans, Wilson expected that the United States would take no part in the conflict. Though Wilson's sympathies were with Britain and her allies, he was determined to preserve American neutrality. Mediation, he believed, seemed the best way to provide Christian service and assure that the United States would remain at peace. He made repeated overtures and twice sent Colonel House on "peace missions" to Europe, only to conclude sadly that the belligerents wished to end the war their own way.

Commerce, however, was not quite consistent with neutrality. American businessmen began to trade with Europe and looked for the new business the war would bring. Wilson supported this activity, which he regarded as a legitimate—not to mention profitable—expression of neutral rights. Thus guns and ammunition became an important part of the war traffic. And since Britain controlled the seas, it seemed only natural, and not at all objectionable, that the bulk of American commerce would go to the Allies. But what Wilson had failed to anticipate was the emergence of the submarine as Germany's primary means of economic warfare. The United States gradually became caught between German and British efforts to strike at each other on the seas. Wilson strenuously protested the activity of both nations, but he threatened only Germany, partly because of a growing relationship with Britain and partly because he regarded the use of submarines as a savage infringement of neutral rights. Torn between a desire to keep the United States at peace and the need to protect its honor, he personally agonized over each decision regarding a submarine incident. When, in May 1915, for example, the British liner *Lusitania* was sunk, drowning more than 1,000 people of whom 128 were Americans, Wilson declared: "There is such a thing as a nation being too proud to fight." Wilson's protests against submarine warfare made the German government more circumspect, but each German concession further aligned the United States with Britain and made demands for an unrestricted U-boat campaign more appealing in Berlin. But Wilson's delicate course between belligerency and pacifism managed to keep the United States out of the war for two and a half years.

Wilson showed little interest in the nature of the European war. "With the objects and causes of the war," he declared in 1916, "we are not concerned. The obscure foundations from which its stupendous flood has burst forth we are not interested to search for or explore." [13] There was no real recognition that anything transpiring on the other side of the Atlantic really concerned the United States. Instead, Wilson couched American policy in terms of moral principle, lecturing the belligerents on their responsibilities as civilized nations. The European leaders, in turn, began to regard Wilson as a phrase-making evangelist who showed little appreciation of their problems.

As late as January 22, 1917, less than three months before

---

[13] George F. Kennan, op. cit., p 63.

the American intervention, Wilson's attitude toward the warring European powers was loftily noncommittal. In a speech to the Senate on that day, the president expressed the hope for a "peace without victory. Only a peace among equals can last," he declared. He also proposed that, after the war was over, "there must be not a balance of power, but a community of power, backed by the organized force of mankind." It was the first hint of his future plans for a League of Nations.

War finally came to the United States not because Wilson pursued it, but because he reluctantly concluded that the nation would suffer less loss of life, property, commerce, and prestige by going to war than by remaining the victim of the unrestricted submarine warfare that the Germans had launched in the spring of 1917. But when, in April, the U-boat campaign precipitated America's entry, Wilson, in typical crusading fashion, made a complete about-face. Once in the war, the president used his oratorical gifts to create a national consciousness of common effort "to fight a war to end all wars, and to make the world safe for democracy." It now became "a war for freedom and justice and self-determination amongst all the nations of the world . . . the German people themselves included." On January 8, 1918, in his famous Fourteen Points speech, Wilson expressed his belief that the war was an opportunity for the world to affirm its belief in Christian principles and to conform to moral laws. He also expressed his commitment to self-determination: the right of people to rule themselves. He was convinced that the United States was destined to lead the world spiritually and politically to create a just and lasting peace. Secret deals and power politics would be abolished. Covenants would be open, he declared, and openly arrived at. And, in the fourteenth point, he made clear that the peace would have to be protected by an international organization that would embody the ultimate moral authority: a league of nations. The battleground had moved from Princeton University to the nation, and now to the world. At long last, the crusader had found a cause great enough to match the depth of his conviction.

As the war approached its end, Wilson undertook the major responsibility for the armistice, insisting as a precondition that Germany renounce its military government. To lead the American delegation to the Paris peace conference, the president, not surprisingly, chose himself.

But before the war was finally over, Wilson had to confront another kind of crusader: V. I. Lenin, who, in November 1917, had led the Bolsheviks to victory in Russia. How would the American president respond to this new and totally unexpected challenge?

The great majority of Americans from the president down to the rank-and-file saw the overthrow of czarist Russia in March 1917, as the triumph of freedom and democracy, American style. The unanimous reaction of statesmen, businessmen, labor leaders, editors, and politicians to the events in Petrograd was truly extraordinary. Wilson and the American public shared this view virtually without dissent. George Kennan, Sr., then widely regarded as the leading authority on Russia, proclaimed "the complete triumph of democracy" in March 1917.[14] Other commentators were equally enthusiastic. The *New York Times,* referring to the provisional government of Prince Lvov, stated editorially that "democracy [was] the very soul of the Russian revolution, the sustaining principle of the new Government." Wilson, in his war message to Congress on April 2, 1917, not only pronounced the new Russian government as "a fit partner for a league of honor", but despite Russia's czarist past, continued to describe that nation as "democratic at heart, in all the vital habits of her thought, in all the intimate relationships of her people that spoke their natural instinct, their habitual attitude towards life." Religious groups were lavish in their praise. The reaction of *Zion's Herald,* a Boston Methodist weekly, was typical: "Autocracy has received its death blow; democracy has triumphed. All of America rejoices in the dawn of the new day for Russia." [15] And the *Washington Star* editorialized: "A free people naturally wants all the other peoples of the world to be free." [16] Russia was thus perceived as a Slavic version of the United States and Russian "democracy" as a replica of the American model.

The facts, well known in retrospect, were quite different. Prince Lvov and his government were wealthy landowners with strongly aristocratic tastes. The majority of the population were peasants with little or no experience in self-government, who har-

[14] *New York Times,* 16 March 1917.

[15] *Zion's Herald,* 21 March 1917.

[16] Cited in Leonid I. Stakhovsky, *American Opinion About Russia* (Toronto: University of Toronto Press, 1961), p. 6.

bored bitter resentments against the landholding classes. The political situation in Russian in the spring of 1917 was hardly ripe for
democratic government. Alexander Kerensky, who followed Prince
Lvov, was not much better. Out of touch with the peasants, he
failed to see their yearning for an end to the war and for a little
land to call their own.

In Wilson and most of America, the wish inspired the
thought. In March 1917, the United States was about to declare
war on Germany and help to "make the world safe for democracy."
It would have been embarrassing, to say the least, to be allied
with the czarist autocracy in this crusade. The Russian Revolution was nothing less than providential. It removed the embarrassing czar just in time for Wilson's war message and, in Wilson's
view, reinstated the Russian people as fellow belligerents in the
democratic cause against the German kaiser. Russia had not only
become a democratic nation, she would now also become a formidable military ally. In Wilson's mind, democracy in Russia and
continuing the war were inextricably linked. This misperception of
the March Revolution was destined to bear bitter fruit when the
real nature of the revolutionary process in Russia began to reveal
itself.

When the Bolsheviks seized power in November 1917, Wilson and most Americans reacted as if the impossible had happened. And since it was impossible, it would soon cease happen-
ing. Again, a distinction was drawn in the American mind between
the Russian people and the "usurping gang" of Bolshevik leaders.[17] The American missionary spirit asserted itself in the pages
of the influential *New York World:* "Russia canot be abandoned,
either to Germany or to anarchy." [18] The predominant belief in
the United States was that the Bolsheviks were a small minority
whose crazy ideas would soon topple them from power, where-
upon the democratic instincts of the Russian people would again
rise to the surface. The *New York Times,* according to a study
made by Walter Lippmann during the period from November
1917 to November 1919, predicted the fall of the Bolsheviks from
power no fewer than ninety-one times.[19] It also reported four
times that Lenin was planning flight and three times that he had

---

[17] *Literary Digest,* 8 December 1917, p. 15.
[18] Cited in ibid.
[19] Cited in *The New Republic,* 4 August 1920.

already fled. Three times it announced Lenin's imprisonment and once even his death.[20]

Lenin's separate peace with Germany in March 1918 at Brest-Litovsk convinced Wilson that the impossible might last a little longer than had been anticipated. Most Americans reacted to Brest-Litovsk as an act of Bolshevik perfidy and regarded the Russians as cowardly quitters at best or German agents at worst. Lenin was awarded the "ignoble peace prize" by several American newspapers, and one paper, the *Kansas City Star*, with a strong suggestion of sour grapes, stated: "Well, if Russia is lost to us, all right. We never did want to make the world safe for the Bolshevik kind of democracy anyway." [21]

President Wilson's perceptions of Russia were fairly typical of those of the American public-at-large. The president had been critical of the czar and the victory of the Bolsheviks did not outrage him. He even made some conciliatory gestures toward the new Soviet government in early 1918, although he decided to withhold formal recognition. On the occasion of the Brest-Litovsk Treaty, the American president sent the following statement to the Soviet government: "The whole heart of the people of the United States is with the people of Russia in their attempt to free themselves forever from autocratic government and become the masters of their own life." But he added, regretfully, that the United States would not be able to offer either economic aid or recognition.

The All-Russian Congress replied to Wilson's message in kind, thanking "the toiling and exploited classes of the United States of North America" and expressing

> its warm sympathy and its firm confidence that the happy time is not far distant when the toiling masses of all bourgeois countries will throw off the yoke of capitalism and will establish a socialist order of society, which alone is capable of assuring a firm and just peace as well as the cultural and material well being of all the toilers.[22]

In the words of a leading scholar of the period, "Suddenly, Americans were hearing their own gospel, in Bolshevik translation, re-

---

[20] Ibid.

[21] Cited in *Literary Digest*, 12 January 1918.

[22] Quoted in Kennan, *Russia Leaves the War* (Princeton: Princeton University Press, 1956), pp. 512–513.

turning to them like an ironic and ominous echo. Two missionaries were now competing for the souls of the peoples of the world." [23]

Even after Brest-Litovsk, Wilson still believed that the Russians were democratic at heart and anxious to defeat the German autocrats. The myth of the Bolsheviks as a transient phenomenon died hard. The *Saturday Evening Post* told its two million subscribers that Germany practiced despotism by an elite, but Lenin represented a "despotism by all the lowest." [24] The Bolsheviks were an evil that the Wilson administration boycotted diplomatically and the vast majority of Americans opposed vehemently. Thus, when Japan, Britain, and France prepared for intervention against the Bolsheviks in April 1918, and when the simultaneous counterattacks of white Russian anti-Bolshevik generals had reduced the areas under Soviet control to the size of medieval Muscovy, the demand for American military intervention mounted. Wilson resisted these pressures for several months, even though he had come to believe that "the new dictatorship in Russia was just as selfish, ruthless, and pitiless as that of the Czars, and his heart went out to the ill-starred masses." [25] What finally forced Wilson's hand was a marooned contingent of some forty-five thousand Czechoslovak soldiers in eastern Russia who caught the popular fancy and whose thousands of relatives in America put pressure on Congress and the president. A force of thirteen thousand Americans was sent to Russia, and the resulting loss of lives in battles with Bolshevik contingents embittered both sides even further.

New myths about Bolshevik Russia sprang up in the United States during the interventionist phase. The Bolsheviks now became veritable monsters who had ordered the nationalization of Russian women. In October 1918, the *New York Times* reported that, in certain Russian provinces under Soviet control, every eighteen-year-old girl had to register at a "bureau of free love" and was then given a husband without her consent.[26] Such reports appeared in numerous American papers until late 1919.

---

[23] Peter G. Filene, *Americans and the Soviet Experiment, 1917–1933* (Cambridge: Harvard University Press, 1967), p. 37.

[24] *The Saturday Evening Post*, 6 July 1918.

[25] R. S. Baker and W. E. Dodd, *The Public Papers of Woodrow Wilson, 1917–1924* (New York: Harcourt, Brace, 1927), vol. II, p. 70.

[26] *New York Times*, October 26, 1918.

After the Allied armistice with Germany in November 1918, American intervention simply no longer made sense. The Czechoslovaks had been evacuated; the war was over; and the parents of the American soldiers in Russia brought great pressure to bear on their representatives in Congress to bring their sons home. Enthusiasm for intervention turned to bitterness that Americans were still suffering and fighting in Russia despite the armistice in Europe. The public clamor against the intervention was now as vociferous as it had been six months earlier in favor of it. But not until June 1919, after hundreds of casualties, were American troops withdrawn from northern Russia, and the last troops did not leave Siberia until April 1920.

During the intervention, American attitudes toward Russia froze into an almost bizarre hostility. As one observer put it: "Bolshevism means chaos, wholesale murder, the complete destruction of civilization." [27] According to *Current History*, the issue was "Bolshevism Against Civilization." As late as November 1919, Secretary of State Robert Lansing was still in favor of extending diplomatic recognition to the White general, Kolchak. When the Bolsheviks had clearly won the civil war, Wilson finally despaired about the "democratic spirit" of Russia. There now developed considerable support for making Russia a trusteeship under the League of Nations and thus to supervise her gradual entry into civilization.[28]

The "red scare" of 1919 exposed the darker side of the missionary spirit. The emotions of the two crusades against Germany and Bolshevism, not yet dissipated, frantically sought new objects. Vindictiveness and xenophobia now took command. Strikes in Seattle and Boston and a Communist coup in Hungary provided additional fuel for the mounting hysteria. In November 1919, Attorney General J. Mitchell Palmer arrested 450 supposed Communists in twelve cities and one month later seized 4,000 more suspects in thirty-three cities. On December 21, 1919, 249 persons were actually deported on the "Soviet Ark" to the Soviet Union. As one supporter of the attorney general put it, "My motto for the Reds is S.O.S.—ship or shoot. I believe we should place them

---

[27] Lincoln Steffens to Allen H. Suggett, *Letters* (New York: Harcourt, Brace, 1938), vol. I, p. 466.

[28] *New York Times*, 12 January 1919.

all on a ship of stone, with sails of lead, and their first stopping
place should be hell." [29] The "red scare," in the words of one
thoughtful observer, was "Wilsonianism turned inside out, confident messianism become paranoid, intolerant Americanism seeking to purify the nation of alien and disturbing elements." [30]

Thus, President Wilson and most Americans by 1920 perceived
a Russia that had merely changed chains. After a few brief glimpses
of liberty, she was now enslaved by a despotism far more diabolical
and cunning than that of the czars. Czarism, though objectionable, was a least content to oppress its own people. The Bolsheviks, however, were determined to impose their fearful philosophy beyond their own borders onto the rest of the world.

This was the way in which two great peoples collided in the
cauldron of world war and revolution. And this was how they
started on a road that was to lead them to the brink of war. Neither Wilson nor Lenin was able to transcend his experience or to
expand his vision. Each remained within his universe, and neither
developed a sense of empathy for the other's destiny. Thus, neither could teach his people to reach out across the gulf that was
to separate Americans and Russians for generations.

Concrete policy decisions flowed from these perceptions. On
the American side, the March Revolution was seen as the triumph
of democracy and the birth of a powerful new ally in the war.
This linkage between democracy and war proved fatal; it led to
Wilson's expectation that Russia would continue the war even
though her people were desperately longing for peace.

On the Soviet side, Lenin viewed the United States through
the lenses of Marxism. The empirical reality of America remained
inaccessible to him. This peculiar perception led to a policy of a
priori rejection of America as a political presence in the world.
Any meaningful modus vivendi or partnership was foreclosed by
Lenin. There was simply not enough room for both systems in the
world for very long.

Thus, each side came to perceive the other as its mortal enemy. And since both sides believed this with growing intensity

[29] Quoted in Foster R. Dulles, *The Road to Teheran* (Princeton: Princeton
    University Press, 1944), p. 164.
[30] Quoted in Filene, op. cit., p. 63.

and deepening conviction, by 1920 they had come very close to being right.

The League of Nations was the most important crusade in Woodrow Wilson's life. It was *his* league, *his* unique contribution to history. He saw himself as the leader of an afflicted humanity longing for peace: "I am speaking for the silent mass of mankind everywhere who have as yet had no place or opportunity to speak their real hearts out." [31] His struggle for the league was an ordeal in two phases: first, he had to convince his fellow victors at the Paris peace conference; and second, he had to convince the American people.

When Wilson arrived in Paris, he astounded the European diplomats with his sense of messianic mission:

> Why has Jesus Christ so far not succeeded in inducing the world to follow his teachings in these matters? It is because he taught the ideal without devising any practical means of attaining it. That is why I am proposing a practical scheme to carry out His aims.[32]

Even though he was ill much of the time at Paris, Wilson insisted on personally supervising every detail of the negotiations. He had only taken three advisers with him: his personal aide, Colonel House, Secretary of State Robert Lansing, and an army general, Tasker Bliss. All three men were often left completely in the dark. Wilson had not even shown the secretary of state his draft for the league covenant. When he finally did and Lansing tried to help, Wilson snapped that he did not intend to have lawyers drafting the treaty. Not a single senator or congressman had been invited to attend. Wilson wanted to be Christ's sole messenger during the peace negotiations.

On Memorial Day 1919, Wilson gave an address at the American army cemetary in France. Its climax invoked the spirit of Martin Luther:

[31] Barber, op. cit., p. 44.
[32] George and George, op. cit., p. 230.

I beg you to realize the compulsion that I myself feel I am under. . . . I sent these lads over here to die. . . . Here I stand, consecrated in the spirit of the men who were once my comrades and who are now gone, and who left me under eternal bonds of fidelity.[33]

Over and over again, Wilson denied that he had any self-interest in the league. "I would be glad to die that it might be consummated," he declared, "I thank God that the whole issue has nothing to do with me. The facts are marching and God is marching with them. You cannot resist them. You must either welcome them or subsequently, with humiliation, surrender to them. It is welcome or surrender." [34]

He lectured Georges Clemenceau of France and David Lloyd George of Britain for hours. On one occasion, when they asked him several logical questions, he called them madmen. "Logic! Logic! I don't give a damn for logic!" Wilson shouted.[35] He infuriated the Europeans by repeatedly comparing his mission to that of Christ. "I never knew anyone to talk more like Jesus Christ and act more like Lloyd George," said Clemenceau. "God had ten commandments but Wilson has fourteen," the French leader added caustically. Finally, however, Wilson prevailed upon the European diplomats to accept his idea of a league of nations. Besides, Clemenceau and Lloyd George had gotten what they wanted most: harsh peace terms to be imposed upon Germany including heavy reparation payments. The league, to them, was of secondary importance.

Wilson was not happy with the peace terms, but there was little he could do about them. The French insisted on a part of the Rhineland, the Italians on Fiume, and the Japanese on Shantung. Germany not only had to cede territory and pledge to pay crushing reparations but was forced to take full responsibility for wars of the past. The Germans even had to return trophies and works of art captured from France by the Prussian army in the war of 1870. Lloyd George and Georges Clemenceau called the Treaty of Versailles, which resulted from the Paris peace confer-

---

[33] Gene Smith, *When the Cheering Stopped* (New York: Morrow, 1964), p. 52.
[34] George and George, op. cit., p. 295.
[35] Barber, op. cit., p. 44.

ence, "a stern and just treaty." But to the German people, Versailles became a symbol of injustice and later fueled Adolf Hitler's engine of destruction. The seeds of World War II were planted in the settlement of World War I.

Wilson was pleased, however, with the principle of national self-determination that was embodied in the peace settlement. The nationalists that had yearned for independence under the Austro-Hungarian monarchy now received their freedom. Czechoslovakia was a typical example. The Czechs had had their own culture and language under the Austrian kaiser, but not their sovereignty. Now they became a nation, and their first president, Tomáš Masaryk, was a close friend of Woodrow Wilson's.

Thus, with very mixed emotions, Wilson signed the Versailles treaty and then embarked for the United States. He was worn to the bone, but felt that he had salvaged a workable treaty. Most important of all, the League of Nations would now become a reality. The moral power of mankind would, at long last, be harnessed in a collective security organization. Any aggressor would be deterred by the overwhelming power of world law. Article Ten, the heart of the league covenant, provided that each member state would pledge to help, with military force, if necessary, in such a common effort. It was to be "one for all and all for one." As he set sail for home, Woodrow Wilson believed that he stood on the threshold of a new and better world.

Wilson's tragic struggle with the United States Senate over the League of Nations was his final battle. Much has been written about this drama and about the reasons for Wilson's defeat. Wilson's partisans have blamed the Senate for its refusal to ratify, while critics have pointed to the president's tactical mistakes and political obtuseness in dealing with the legislators. There is a third interpretation, however, that comes even closer to the truth: *Wilson's crusading personality made it impossible for him to make the compromises that would have been necessary for the acceptance of the league.* The problem was not that Wilson made political mistakes and intellectual misjudgments. The problem was that his personality was such that *any* compromise was anathema to him. There is little doubt that a more pragmatic leader could have lived easily enough with most of the reservations demanded by the Senate. But, to Woodrow Wilson, it was all or nothing.

The situation Wilson faced in July 1919 was difficult but not insurmountable. He needed two-thirds of the Senate on his side, or sixty-four votes. Republicans controlled the Senate with a majority of two. The chairman of the Senate Foreign Relations Committee was Henry Cabot Lodge, Wilson's archenemy and the leader of fifteen "irreconcilable" opponents of the league. Forty-nine senators had declared themselves, shortly before Wilson's return from Paris, in favor of a league treaty *with reservations*. There was a strong support both within the Senate and in the country as a whole for *some* form of league. In the words of one thoughtful scholar, "the President faced an implacable enemy in Lodge, a very difficult proposition in the Foreign Relations Committee, a near stand-off in the Senate as a whole, and a generally favorable climate of opinion in the American public." [36] Rarely was there a situation that called more clearly for adroit and sensitive political leadership.

From the very first day of his encounter with the Senate, however, Wilson revealed a messianic attitude. "The stage is set, the destiny disclosed," he proclaimed in placing the treaty before the Senate. "It has come about by no plan of our conceiving, but by the hand of God who led us in this way." He challenged the Senate on moral grounds. "Accept or reject." That was the way Wilson posed the question.

Senator Henry Cabot Lodge, himself a skillful orator, was a formidable opponent. He began the deliberations on the league covenant by reading aloud its entire text of 268 pages. This took two weeks and often he read to a clerk alone as the senators drifted away. Lodge's strategy was to wreck the league by insisting on a barrage of reservations that, he believed, Wilson would never accept. These covered a variety of topics ranging from the control of immigration to the right of withdrawal from the league. Above all, Lodge attacked the league as an unconstitutional device to deprive the United States of its sovereign powers, particularly in the field of foreign policy. He also ridiculed Wilson personally. Speaking of the league covenant, he said: "As an English production, it does not rank high. It might get by at Princeton, but certainly not at Harvard." The following episode shows to what degree Lodge and Wilson had *personalized* their struggle over the League:

[36] Ibid., p. 19.

Once Senator James Watson said to Lodge, "Senator, suppose that the President accepts the treaty with your reservations. Then we are in the League, and once in, our reservations become purely fiction." Lodge replied, "But my dear James, you do not take into consideration the hatred that Woodrow Wilson has for me personally. Never under any set of circumstances in this world could he be induced to accept a treaty with Lodge reservations appended to it." Watson said, "But that seems to me to be a rather slender thread on which to hang so great a cause." To which Lodge exclaimed: "A slender thread! Why, it is as strong as any cable with its strands wired and twisted together." [37]

Wilson despised his opponents. To one of his allies who warned that the treaty was in grave danger he said: "Anyone who opposes me, I'll crush." In the end, Lodge could say with satisfaction, "We can always count on Mr. Wilson. He has never failed us."

Wilson's attitude alienated the "mild reservationists" more and more. Most of these men would have been quite prepared to go along with the league if Wilson had accepted some amendments which, in their opinion, would have protected the American national interest. But Wilson's rigidity toward them was as unbending as that vis-à-vis the "irreconcilables." When Colonel House, his trusted aide of many years, urged him to be more conciliatory with the "mild reservationists," Wilson ignored his counsel and the two men parted company.

In his debates with the "mild reservationists," Wilson stuck to the position that no word of the covenant could be changed without resubmitting it to the European powers. He frequently lectured the senators in the style of a schoolmaster. Actually, he never even asked the British and French leaders whether they would have accepted reservations. Later, it became clear that they wanted America in the league and were not very much concerned with what Georges Clemenceau called "a few harmless compromises."

In September, as the hostility against him in the Senate mounted steadily, Wilson abruptly left Washington to launch a nationwide speaking tour on behalf of the League of Nations. He delivered forty addresses in twenty-two days before he collapsed with a stroke in Colorado. He was sick and isolated after his col-

[37] George and George, op. cit., p. 279–280.

lapse, and his wife kept vigil by his bedside. On one occasion, she pleaded with him: "For my sake, won't you accept these reservations and get this awful thing settled?"

> He turned his head on the pillow. He took her hand. "Little girl, don't you desert me; that I cannot stand. Can't you see that I have no moral right to accept any change in a paper I have already signed? It is not *I* who will not accept it; it is the Nation's honor that is at stake," his eyes were gleaming. "Better a thousand times to go down fighting than to dip your colors to a dishonorable compromise." [38]

On March 19, 1920, the Senate defeated the League of Nations by a margin of seven votes. The tragedy had run its course. Wilson, however, until his dying day, was unable to see reality. In his last speech, delivered in December 1923 a few weeks before his death, on the front porch of his home, he aimed one final blast at the opponents of the league: "I have seen fools resist Providence before, and I have seen their destruction as it will come upon these again—utter destruction and contempt. That we shall prevail is as sure as God reigns."[39]

A pragmatic leader, if confronted with the growing signs of failure, would have respected facts and changed his strategy. The crusader, however, was unable to see the warning signals. He was compelled to stay on the same destructive course even though it meant ruination.

Wilson's personality collided with the conditions of his time. A deep emotional need for his league, unsullied by imperfections, tore Wilson apart and killed him in the end. In his dream was his greatness, in his rigid personality his tragedy. And his personal disaster became the prelude to the catastrophe of the Second World War.

One sensitive historian has described the fate of Wilson well:

> The demon that Woodrow Wilson vainly fought was within himself. Tragedy, if it be not noble is not tragedy, and no one will deny to Woodrow Wilson the elements of nobility. Yet . . . the very essence of statesmanship lies not in the grim endurance of preordained defeat, but rather in the wisdom to know when to

[38] Smith, op. cit., p. 120.
[39] "The American Presidents," *Time* magazine, special report, March 1976, p. 40.

take occasion by the hand and by yielding the shadow to substance.[40]

Woodrow Wilson was perhaps the classical crusader. The defeat of the League of Nations certainly did not stem from a want of objective possibilities. But Wilson's rigid crusading personality did not permit him to explore these opportunities. A more pragmatic man might have compromised with the "mild reservationists" in the Senate and the United States might have joined the league. With the United States as a member, Mussolini and Hitler might not have been able to kill the league quite so easily. Perhaps Harry Truman was right when he told the Senate in 1943 that the Second World War was the result of the refusal of the United States to join the League of Nations. True, the league was structurally weak and had no teeth. But without the United States it was certainly doomed to total failure. Born in an American cradle, it was buried in an American grave.

Woodrow Wilson did not fail because of what he did or did not do. He failed because of what he was.

[40] Cited in George and George, op. cit., p. 20.

Interchapter

THE WORLD
BETWEEN TWO WARS

The two decades between the world wars can hardly be described as a period of peace. At best, it was an armistice during which the shadow of dictatorship gradually lengthened across the face of Europe. The Treaty of Versailles had left the Germans chafing under the burden of heavy reparation payments. A nightmarish inflation almost wiped out the middle class and placed Germany on the auction block between the political extremes of Left and Right. Britain and France, though the victors in the war, were themselves in dire economic straits and heavily indebted to the United States. The expansionary thrust of Bolshevism in Russia acted as an additional destabilizing influence. Two right-wing dictators capitalized on the growing chaos and unrest: Benito Mussolini in Italy and Adolf Hitler in Germany. By the early 1930s, the Great Depression engulfed the Western world, adding immeasurably to Europe's economic misery and to the appeal of the dictators. When Hitler seized power in Germany in 1933, and shortly afterward, marched into the Rhineland, Britain and France did not resist. Nor had the League of Nations been equipped with the necessary "teeth" to repel a Japanese assault on Manchuria in 1931. And it appeared equally helpless in the face of Mussolini's attack on Ethiopia in 1936 and Hitler's annexation of Austria in 1938. A few months later, at Munich, in a fateful act of appeasement, Britain and France showed their weakness, and Czechoslovakia was sold out to Hitler. Shortly afterward, Joseph Stalin, the ruler of the Soviet Union, signed a nonaggression pact with

Nazi Germany. Everywhere in Europe, democracy was on the defensive and tyranny was on the rise. In September 1939, the armistice was over. Germany invaded Poland and the Second World War had broken out. These shattering events and their impact on the United States are deserving of attention.

It is impossible to assert conclusively that American participation in the League of Nations would have prevented the fatal drift toward the Second World War. Quite possibly, if the United States had taken a determined stand, Japanese, Italian, and German aggression might have been stopped or, at least, discouraged. However, it must be conceded that President Warren G. Harding's "back to normalcy" program of isolationism did not argue well for the "one-for-all" and "all-for-one" collective security ideal. Be that as it may, the league without the United States was a weak and largely ineffectual body. No member state was willing to give up a single particle of sovereignty and questions involving conflicts between states had to be decided by a unanimity that was almost impossible to obtain. There was not even a clear prescription for military action against an aggressor state. Whatever useful work the league achieved was largely attained in the technical and economic spheres. But on anything necessitating a forcible response, the league was simply powerless. Germany and the Soviet Union were excluded in the early years, the former because of its role in starting the war, the latter because of its Bolshevik regime. Even when these two states finally joined—in 1926 and 1934 respectively—they did so primarily to strengthen their own political positions, rather than in support of the collective security ideal. For a few years, during the late 1920s, France had an ardent league advocate in its foreign minister, Aristide Briand. In 1928, most of the league's members signed a pact renouncing the use of war. This pact had resulted from negotiations between France and the United States. Significantly, however, the Kellogg-Briand Pact did not provide for sanctions against violators. The league's "moment of truth" arrived in 1931, when the Japanese militarists invaded Manchuria. The only action the league was able to take was the appointment of a study commission, which concluded, not surprisingly, that the Japanese had, indeed, attacked Manchuria. When Mussolini followed suit with his brutal assault on Ethiopia in 1936, that nation's emperor, Haile Selassie, gave a moving and prophetic speech from the league's rostrum, pleading for help from civilized mankind. "It is us today; it will be you tomorrow," he warned the assembled delegates. His plea was useless. By the time Hitler had marched into Austria and Czechoslovakia two years later, the league's life had virtually ended. Its last meeting took place in 1939.

The seeds of the Second World War, however, were sown as early as 1919, at Versailles. The new German republic, established at Weimar, was doomed from the start, largely due to the shortsightedness of the victorious allies. The war reparations imposed upon Germany were gigantic: 31.5 billion dollars, to be paid in annual installments of 500 million. All the German political parties were convinced that their country could not pay this sum. The Allies insisted, however, and thus made an economic recovery impossible. An unimaginable inflation followed and, five years after the war, one American dollar bought a trillion German marks. The middle-class burgher, the main supporter of the Weimar Republic, saw his savings wiped out almost overnight. Foreigners with dollars or pounds sterling lived like kings in elegant Berlin hotels. The government made reparation payments with worthless currency and with loans from the United States. But the middle class was driven to fury and despair and began to look for panaceas from the Left and the Right.

The coming of the Great Depression only hastened the catastrophe. Stalin welcomed it as "the first swallow of the coming spring." He was sure that Germany would soon go Communist. And he had good reason to rejoice. Loans from America had suddenly dried up. Factories were silent as six million unemployed German workers joined the bread lines. Thousands of small businesses went under. President Herbert Hoover established a moratorium on German war reparations in order to strengthen the tottering republic. But by 1930, the ranks of the German Communist Party had swelled by 50 percent.

Yet, there was an even greater threat: Adolf Hitler. The future führer had been an obscure corporal in the German army in the First World War. When he was informed that Germany had lost the war, "all went black before his eyes." In 1919, he joined the National Socialist German Workers' Party (NSDAP) and four years later he led the abortive beer hall putsch against the Weimar Republic, which landed him in prison for nine months. While in prison, Hitler dictated a book to his faithful disciple Rudolf Hess.

The book was *Mein Kampf*. In it, Hitler wrote of his burning passion for German nationalism, his hatred for the "November 1918 criminals," Communists and Jews. He declared that Providence had chosen the Aryans as the master race. He would purify the German people; he would make them strong again; he would repudiate the "Versailles Diktat"; he would make the Germans conquer until they were the lords of the earth.

When Adolf Hitler emerged from prison in 1924, the German currency had become worthless. This helped Hitler in his agitation against the Weimar Republic, since it was linked to the hated Versailles treaty and to the reparation payments. But Hitler reserved his greatest fury for Communists and Jews. He accused the German Communist Party of being an agent of the Soviet Union and repeated again and again that German workers did not have to be Communists to better their lot. Hitler's party, after all, was also a socialist workers' party; but above all, it was national and German. He would see to it that every German had a job and bread. And he would discipline the Jewish "money barons."

"Never in my life have I been so well disposed as in these days," Hitler wrote in 1930, in the depth of the depression, "for hard reality has opened the eyes of millions of Germans to the unprecedented swindles, lies, and betrayals of the Marxist deceivers of the people." Wherever Nazis encountered Communists, they tried to destroy them, and club them to death in innumerable street wars. Finally, caught between two tyrannies, the Weimar Republic gave up the ghost. On January 30, 1933, the former army corporal became chancellor of the German Reich. The German people had imposed the Nazi holocaust upon themselves. Hitler was inaugurated as the führer in peacetime, by Germans.

With Hitler's triumph, the inexorable march to war began. In October 1933, Hitler took Germany out of the League of Nations. In March 1935, he declared the Treaty of Versailles null and void and announced a massive military buildup, including general conscription. One year later, Hitler ordered his troops to march into the Rhineland, in clear violation of the Treaty of Versailles. Britain and France, fatefully, did not respond with counterforce, largely because of their internal weakness. Britain had been seriously weakened by a general strike in the mid-1920s and the Great Depression had turned the economic slump into a national catastrophe. Besides, a large segment of the British public was of the opinion that one could "do business with Hitler." This was also true of Neville Chamberlain, who was to become prime minister in 1937. France, too, had suffered a severe economic decline. By 1935, the number of unemployed had reached half a million. A bitter internal struggle over power that was to bring a socialist, Léon Blum, to the premiership in 1936, consumed the nation's energies. Thus, both France and Britain, the leading democracies of Europe, were too beset by their domestic problems to resist the Nazi tide.

The democracies' failure to respond was crucial. In 1936, Hitler helped his fellow dictator in Spain, Francisco Franco, win a civil war. In that war, Hitler tested not only his new weapons, but engaged in the terror bombing of the little Spanish town of Guernica, later immortalized by Picasso's famous painting. In 1938, the führer effected Anschluss with Austria, incorporating Austria into the Reich. In September 1938, Neville Chamberlain agreed that Hitler could take over the Sudeten area in exchange for a promise that this was to be the führer's "final territorial demand." Two weeks later, however, at Munich, Chamberlain agreed to Germany's absorption of all of Czechoslovakia, even though Britain and France had signed defense treaties with the Czech republic. The Munich conference was attended by Hitler, Mussolini, Chamberlain, and the French prime minister, Edouard Daladier, with the Czechs being informed only after the decision to sell them out had been agreed upon. Czechoslovakia's president, Eduard Beneš, stunned by the betrayal, abdicated and shortly afterward, Nazi tanks rumbled into Prague. Chamberlain, returning home from Munich, expressed his faith in "peace in our time," but Winston Churchill, shortly to become the British prime minister, described the conference as "a disaster of the first magnitude."

The effects of Munich became quickly manifest. Stalin, dismayed by the weakness of the two democracies and impressed by Hitler's strength, formed an alliance with the German dictator. The British and French, guilty over Munich, now extended an unconditional guarantee to Poland. And when, in September 1939, Hitler invaded that Eastern European country, Britain and France declared war on Nazi Germany.

The United States during the interwar period was generally

aloof toward foreign affairs; only in the early 1920s was there a brief flurry of interest. In 1922, as a result of American initiative, a naval disarmament agreement, which established definite ratios controlling the tonnage of the battleships of the five great naval powers, was signed in Washington, D.C. Britain abandoned its claim to having the strongest navy in the world, and agreed to an equal American navy. Britain and the United States were each allowed 525,000 tons of capital ships, Japan 350,000 tons, and France and Italy 175,000 tons each. Thus, as a consequence of the First World War, the power of the United States had increased considerably.

Yet, after 1922, the United States withdrew once more into its insularity. Since America was unwilling to use its power, that power, for purposes of foreign policy, did not really exist. Americans again turned their backs on European power politics. Their energies turned inward, first in the scramble for prosperity and then, after 1929, in the desperate struggle to endure the Great Depression. Presidents Harding and Coolidge evinced virtually no interest in foreign affairs and Herbert Hoover, who did pay some attention, quickly became absorbed in the quicksand of the economic crisis. In 1931, the United States announced the Hoover-Stimson doctrine in response to Japan's attack on Manchuria, which denied the recognition of any forcible conquest. The doctrine did nothing to change Japan's imperialist course. Franklin Roosevelt's inauguration in March 1933, almost coincided with Hitler's emergence as führer, but Roosevelt's energies, too, were absorbed by the priorities at home. Americans believed again that the turbulence in Europe would not really touch them. In America's relationship with Europe, the years 1938–1941 bear an eerie resemblance to the years 1914–1917. Once again, an American president hoped to keep the nation out of war. Once again, he tried to remain neutral, yet edged ever closer to America's traditional allies. Once again, in 1941, as in 1917, Americans believed that a war had been thrust upon them. And once again, once they were in it, they turned the war into a national crusade to make the world over.

2

FRANKLIN D. ROOSEVELT

Prophet and Prince

THE ROOTS OF SELF-CONFIDENCE

The personality of Franklin D. Roosevelt demonstrates the difficulty of fitting human beings into categories. This most complex and elusive of modern American presidents was *both* a crusader and a pragmatist in his foreign policy. He was equally capable of lifting up Woodrow Wilson's fallen banner and of behaving like Machiavelli's Prince. In order to understand this apparent paradox, we must remember that Roosevelt's foreign policy had two overriding goals: to win the war and to save the peace. The former required a relentless and uncompromising realism, but the second enabled him to resurrect Wilson's vision in the form of the Atlantic Charter and the United Nations. Roosevelt was a warrior, but he was a warrior for peace.

No short vignette can do justice to the extreme complexity of Roosevelt's "heavily forested" interior. Here was a man who invested enormous energies in a wide range of policies, both foreign and domestic. Yet, he was also one of the least self-revealing of presidents, especially with regard to the emotional thrust behind his actions. James Barber describes him aptly as a prime example of an "active-positive" president, but beyond the obvious connotations of this phrase, it tells us relatively little.[1] Most of Roosevelt's biographers have had similar difficulties. One is in

[1] Barber, op. cit., p. 209.

the presence here of one of the great movers of the twentieth century, and yet there are few clues. Until early manhood, there was no drama, no upheaval in young Franklin's life. Among the hundreds of biographies of American presidents one would search in vain for the story of a childhood more secure or more serene.

Yet it is precisely the absence of early drama and upheaval that gives us an important clue to the evolution of Roosevelt's personality. His parents, James and Sara Roosevelt, had infused in Franklin a profound sense of self-esteem, a confidence so strong that he could even overcome the apparent end of his career when he was crippled by polio at the age of thirty-nine.

Young Franklin's identity was formed in a stable and harmonious home. He moved securely from the pedestal of the only child of doting parents into the later but equally untroubled environments of Hyde Park, Groton, and Harvard friendships. His references to his Hyde Park home were always loving. Not surprisingly, throughout his entire presidency he had a habit of describing his foreign policies in metaphors of home and family: the Good Neighbor policy; the Big Four policemen of the world; his idea that new institutions like the United Nations must toddle like a child for a few years before gaining strength; and his repeated references to heads of state sitting around the conference table like members of the same family, or like neighbors. On one occasion, in a reference to the strained relationship between himself and General de Gaulle, he declared that the best way to keep peace in the family was to keep the members of the family apart.[2]

At the age of sixteen, Franklin owned his own sailboat. But when, shortly afterward, he announced to his parents that he intended to go to Annapolis and become a naval officer, his father took him aside and told him that a nautical life was out of the question.

> An only child who expected to inherit an estate, James explained, could not choose the navy, for it would take him too far from home. Franklin must remain on dry land—if possible, the land of Dutchess County. "Study law as I did," James advised. "It prepares a man for any profession."[3]

[2] James MacGregor Burns, *Roosevelt: The Soldier of Freedom* (New York: Harcourt Brace Jovanovich, 1970), p. 604.

[3] Allen Churchill, *The Roosevelts* (New York: Harper and Row, 1965), p. 180.

Eventually, Franklin did indeed study law. But he also became a naval officer. His talent for combining opposites developed early. By the time he entered Groton, Franklin had substantial self-esteem, a talent for charming and even mastering people, and the gift of laughter.

Two men influenced Franklin's developing world view, both in much the same direction. One was Dr. Endicott Peabody, headmaster of Groton, and the other was "cousin" Theodore Roosevelt. Peabody was a rather formidable Yankee who was out to develop "manly Christian character." He intended to make the well-off Groton boys agents of social betterment. His motto was "service" and he preached that a man's faith should be put into work for a larger integrating cause. Franklin made the headmaster into his model. Much later, as president, Roosevelt recalled to the aging Peabody that,

> More than forty years ago you said, in a sermon, in the Old Chapel, something about not losing boyhood ideals in later life. These were Groton ideals—taught by you—I try not to forget and your words are still with me.[4]

At graduation time, Theodore Roosevelt, then governor of New York, gave a stirring speech. "If a man has courage, goodness, and brains," TR declared, "no limit can be placed to the greatness of the work he may accomplish—he is the man needed today in politics." The message was similar to Peabody's: "Serve the Lord with gladness, and do it through action in the practical world."

If, at Groton, Franklin learned how to get along with his contemporaries, at Harvard, he learned how to lead them. He became editor-in-chief of the Harvard *Crimson*, but his stewardship of that newspaper, unlike Wilson's of the *Princetonian*, was relaxed and democratic. He managed the *Crimson* staff effectively and gracefully. His coeditor remembered that "in his geniality there was a kind of frictionless command." His sophomore year, 1901, was a watershed, however. That year Franklin's father died; President McKinley was assassinated; and "cousin" Theodore became president of the United States.

Two years later, Franklin stunned his mother by announcing that he had decided to marry his cousin Eleanor. In 1905, at the

---

4 Barber, op. cit., p. 218.

age of twenty-three, Franklin married the twenty-year-old Eleanor who unlike himself, had had a lonely and unhappy childhood and had been told by her mother "never cry where people are, cry by yourself." Years later Franklin had a love affair with Eleanor's vivacious social secretary, Lucy Mercer, a relationship that was to last until the end of Roosevelt's life. In his private life, too, Roosevelt had a talent for combining opposites.

In 1910, at President Theodore Roosevelt's urging, Franklin went into politics. His name, handsome appearance, and wealth helped him to win a seat in the New York State Assembly, and subsequently in the State Senate. At 31, Franklin was offered the post of assistant secretary of the Navy by the president. Franklin loved the job. "I now find my vocation combined with my avocation in a delightful way," he wrote. As yet, however, there was little depth. The Washington elite liked Roosevelt, and considered him to be an easygoing, bright, amusing young man, in short, a charming "lightweight."

The great test of Roosevelt's character occurred in 1921: the terrible bout with polio that left him a cripple for life. His mother wanted him to retire from public life, but Eleanor disagreed. Her courage and persistence finally won out and Roosevelt resumed his career, going on to the governorship of New York and ultimately to the White House. As Nietzsche might have said, "What did not kill him, made him stronger." The illness also deepened his personality. Once Eleanor answered a cruel question—"Mrs. Roosevelt, do you think your husband's illness affected his mind?" —with a perceptive answer: "Yes, I think it did. I think it made him more sensitive to the feelings of people."

FDR's political personality was set after his victory over polio. His self-confidence remained intact, as did his charming way of dominating those around him. An element of duplicity that came in handy when seeking compromises or combining opposites never left him. A deep abiding faith that the path to godliness led through the world of action and of service always remained a part of him. The terrible illness that might have broken a less resilient spirit gave FDR a new dimension: a depth and a compassion that made him, in James MacGregor Burns's telling phrase, "democracy's aristocrat." And finally, there was that irrepressible, infectious laughter that made Winston Churchill say that meeting Roosevelt was like opening a bottle of champagne.

THE WAR LEADER

No two men could have been more different than Franklin Roosevelt and Adolf Hitler. Roosevelt had loved his parents and had a strong feeling for home and family; Hitler had hated his father, had become a drifter, and had felt at home only in the army. Roosevelt liked liquor, tobacco, meat, and laughter; Hitler spurned all four. Roosevelt dealt with realities that were concrete and practical; Hitler was attracted to the metaphysical and the apocalyptic. Roosevelt conducted a love affair with life; Hitler was fascinated by violence, hate, and death. A man like Hitler was almost beyond Roosevelt's ken.

At first, like Woodrow Wilson a quarter of a century before, Roosevelt tried to ignore the storm that was gathering on the other side of the Atlantic. His first response to Hitler was the "quarantine" speech of October 5, 1937. While expressing his dismay at the lawlessness and aggressive tendencies that were on the rise in Germany, Roosevelt promised a policy of American neutrality. "When an epidemic of physical disease starts to spread," he declared, "the community approves and joins in a quarantine of the patients in order to protect the health of the community against the spread of the disease." It seemed like Wilson in 1914 all over again. Even two years later, in September 1939, when Hitler had invaded Poland, and only Britain and France stood between Hitler and the countries of Europe, Roosevelt still responded to the press, wanting to know whether the United States could stay out of the war: "I not only sincerely hope so, but I believe we can and every effort will be made by the Administration to do so." [5]

It quickly became clear, however, that Hitler was a far more terrible danger than the kaiser.

The collapse of France in 1940 and the successful Nazi blitzkrieg in Western Europe sent a tremor of fear through the American people. Britain now stood alone against Hitler. Obviously, a Nazi-dominated Europe posed a mortal threat to the security of the United States. In September 1940, Congress approved the Selective Service Act, the first peacetime draft in American history.

[5] Joseph P. Lash, *Roosevelt and Churchill* (New York: Norton, 1976), p. 21.

Roosevelt has been severely criticized for his foreign policy between 1939 and 1941. But, not surprisingly, critics have descended upon him from both sides. Some have maintained that he consciously and deliberately led the nation into war while others have accused him of waiting too long and thus gambling with the national security of the United States. The facts seem to indicate that he was ambivalent and that this ambivalence was based on a correct reading of the contradictory attitudes of the American public. In late 1940, 75 percent of the American people approved helping the British, but 85 percent indicated a desire to avoid war at all costs. Hence, Roosevelt made up his mind to supply the British with material aid but decided not to send American boys to die on foreign soil. Renouncing the spirit of neutrality, he began to funnel aid—munitions, raw materials, and dollars—to Britain. Most important among these aid programs was the "destroyer deal" of September 1940. This was Roosevelt's first "executive agreement" in foreign policy. Done secretly and without congressional approval, it set the tone for Roosevelt's later war policy: complete personal control of the conduct of the war, until the unconditional surrender of the enemy.

By May of 1940, almost half of Britain's one hundred destroyers had been sunk or damaged by the Germans. That month, Winston Churchill asked Roosevelt for "the loan of forty or fifty of your older destroyers" to help the Royal Navy hold the channel. In June, as more British ships were put out of action, Churchill's tone became more urgent: "Nothing is so important for us . . . we must ask therefore as a matter of life and death to be reinforced with these destroyers." [6] By July, Churchill was desperate: "Mr. President, with great respect I must tell you that in the long history of the world this is a thing to do now. The worth of every destroyer that you can spare is to be measured in rubies." [7]

Roosevelt was deeply sympathetic to Britain's lonely stand. But he responded to Churchill's first request by saying that "a step of that kind could not be taken except with the specific authorization of Congress, and I am not certain that it would

---

[6] Arthur M. Schlesinger, Jr., *The Imperial Presidency* (Boston: Houghton Mifflin, 1973), p. 105.
[7] Ibid.

be wise for that suggestion to be made to the Congress at this moment." [8] Not only was Roosevelt's assessment of Congress accurate, but the chief of naval operations, when approached on the matter, objected vigorously. The old destroyers, in his opinion, were absolutely essential to the American navy.

When, by September eleven more British ships had been destroyed and Churchill had dispatched yet another desperate personal cable, Roosevelt chose to act. He knew that congressional approval would be required for a sale or loan. But what about a trade? If Churchill could be persuaded to lease British bases to the United States in exchange for the destroyers, the deal might be closed by executive order. And, moreover, by emphasizing the value of the bases, it might be presented as an advantageous horse trade to the American public.

Basic to an understanding of Roosevelt's decision to barter away the American destroyers was his empathy for Winston Churchill and the plight of Britain. The two men had not yet met as president and prime minister but there had been extensive correspondence between them. They had already recognized that they were kindred spirits. Both men had come to power in times of national emergency; both had enormous courage when confronted with adversity; both were pugnacious, resilient, and optimistic. And even though Churchill represented the tradition of an empire while Roosevelt had been much less respectful of tradition, the two men were to form a lasting bond of friendship that was to transcend the dictates of a strategic and political alliance.

Armed with a memorandum from his legal advisor, Benjamin V. Cohen, asserting that executive action would be legal if it could be shown that such action would strengthen rather than weaken American defenses, the president set out to sell the deal to the American public. Having secured Churchill's enthusiastic approval for ninety-nine-year leases of several British air and naval bases in the Western Hemisphere, Roosevelt scheduled a press conference for August 16. At that conference, he announced that he was holding conversations with the British for the acquisition of air and naval bases. Was this a quid pro quo for destroyers? he was asked. "I do not know what the quid pro quo is going to be"

[8] Ibid.

was the carefully calculated replay. "The emphasis is on the acquisition of the bases for the protection of the Hemisphere." [9] Roosevelt knew that there was broad support for the acquisition of such bases and therefore he wanted that part of the deal to sink into the public consciousness first. Only on the following day did he announce the transfer of the destroyers. Two days later, a public opinion poll disclosed that 62 percent of those polled approved of the transaction, apparently perceiving it as a good deal for the United States. The president's message to Congress described the destroyer deal as "the most important action in the reinforcement of our national defense that has been taken since the Louisiana Purchase." Even the *Chicago Tribune*, the most violently isolationist newspaper in America, commented:

> Any arrangement which gives the United States naval and air bases in regions which must be brought within the American defense zone is to be accepted as a triumph. If the bases could be obtained in no other way, they are to be taken on the terms offered. [10]

Thus Roosevelt, acting on the basis of his executive authority and circumventing Congress, came to the help of Britain in her hour of greatest need. Had he gone to Congress, the destroyers would probably never have reached Britain and Hitler might have decided to invade England, with disastrous consequences for the democracies. By placing the emphasis on the bases rather than the destroyers, Roosevelt made it appear that the United States had gotten the better part of the bargain. In fact, the bases were of only peripheral importance for the United States, but the destroyers were a life-and-death matter for Britain. In the destroyer deal, Roosevelt first showed his hand: a highly personal style, based on deep loyalties and convictions, yet shrewdly masked, in order to circumvent, rather than directly challenge, the strictures of the legislature and the public. His personal decision to accede to Winston Churchill's desperate plea played a crucial role in the Battle of Britain. Hitler screamed with rage when he was informed of the deal and declared that he was going to turn everything he had on England. But on September 17, less than two weeks after the announcement of the deal, Hitler postponed Operation Sea Lion—the planned invasion of England—indefinitely.

[9] Lash, op. cit., p. 212.
[10] Ibid., pp. 219–220.

The destroyer deal had edged the United States closer to Britain. This trend continued throughout most of late 1940 and 1941. By then, Roosevelt had been elected to a third term and enjoyed a freer hand. In December 1940, the president declared that it was the task of the United States to serve as "the arsenal of democracy." Congress responded by passing, in March 1941, the Lend-Lease Act, which permitted the president to provide war materials to those states whose survival was vital to the United States.

During the spring of 1941, Hitler pondered a crucial decision: whether to invade Britain after all or attack the Soviet Union. Never in modern history did the fate of the world depend so much on the arbitrary decision of a single man. Would he carve his path of blood and terror in the East or in the West? Finally, on June 22, 1941, the die was cast as Nazi Panzers rolled across the Soviet border. "Duce!" the führer wrote his ally Mussolini, "the decision has been made. Now I feel spiritually free. With hearty and comradely greetings. Yours, Adolf Hitler."

Churchill responded immediately. "No one has been a more consistent opponent of Communism than I have for the last twenty-five years," the British leader said. "But all this fades away before the spectacle which is now unfolding. We shall give whatever help we can to Russia and the Russian people." [11] Roosevelt, however, hesitated.

Most Americans, Roosevelt knew, were less willing than the British to walk with Satan. A Communist victory, Senator Robert Taft had said flatly, "would be far more dangerous than a fascist one." Senator Harry Truman had struck a common note: "If we see that Germany is winning we ought to help Russia and if Russia is winning we ought to help Germany and that way let them kill as many as possible, although I don't want to see Hitler victorious under any circumstances." [12]

Roosevelt believed that Hitler was a greater threat to American security than Stalin. Yet Roosevelt and Stalin were virtually polar opposites. Stalin was hard and cynical, Roosevelt flexible and supple. Stalin was the product of poverty-ridden Russian Georgia; Roosevelt of a graceful Hyde Park culture. Stalin had risen to

[11] Burns, op. cit., p. 96.
[12] Ibid., pp. 111–112.

power through the Soviet Party structure jockeying for power, finally isolating and destroying his opponents; Roosevelt had risen through the loose interstices of an open society. Stalin was a supreme practitioner of realpolitik; Roosevelt's realism was leavened by an idealist's vision. Thus, the American president did not rush to Stalin's aid. He was quite prepared to leave the lead to Churchill. Though he did persuade the Congress to extend the Lend-Lease Act to Soviet Russia, the fate of Britain remained uppermost in his mind.

By the summer of 1941, Roosevelt's problem resembled Wilson's even more. His policy was to help Britain as much as possible, short of war. But it had become clear that lend-lease would not be enough. The British simply did not have the resources to win the war by themselves. It had also become clear that the conversion of the United States into the "arsenal of democracy" could not take place without a full-scale mobilization, which, in turn, required a declaration of war. These grim calculations plunged Roosevelt into a deep depression. Harry Hopkins, Roosevelt's personal assistant, who knew him well, was of the opinion that the president was loath to get into the war and thus would rather follow public opinion than lead it. But, in August 1941, his first personal meeting with Churchill on warships off the coast of Newfoundland lifted the American president out of his gloom. At that meeting was born the Atlantic Charter, which provided the first glimpse of the two leaders' notion of a postwar world: a United Nations with the power to enforce the peace.

The meeting on the *Augusta* was one the president and prime minister had long hoped for, but they had been forced to wait on the tumultuous events of 1940 and 1941. When the encounter finally came about, it revealed a great deal about Roosevelt's diplomatic style. The president demanded that the conference transpire in total secrecy. He had excluded even his secretary of state, Cordell Hull, and had not informed him of the conference until it was almost over. Grace Tully, his private secretary of many years, had no hint of the rendezvous. Roosevelt wanted to meet Churchill at last, establish a personal relationship, and achieve a sense of unity. "At last we've gotten together," Roosevelt exclaimed as Churchill clambered aboard the *Augusta*. The Atlantic Charter became one of the most compelling statements of the war. The two men invoked the spirit of Wilson when they expressed their hopes for "a wider and permanent system of general security." The United Nations was born on these warships off the coast of Newfoundland. And it was born out of the initiative of the two war leaders whose *personal* command of foreign policy was by then virtually absolute.

Yet, far from easing his difficulties, the Atlantic conference suspended Roosevelt even more painfully on the horns of the isolationist-interventionist dilemma. Only the Japanese assault on Pearl Harbor in December 1941 resolved his inner conflict. "They have attacked us at Pearl Harbor" he informed Churchill, "we are all in the same boat now." The leadership of the Allied cause now passed from Britain to the United States. During the next three and a half years, Roosevelt made the most brilliant use of the enormous resources at his command. All his formidable energies were bent toward the single goal of total victory.

In his State of the Union address, the president struck a crusading Wilsonian note: "This is the conflict that day and night now pervades our lives. There never has been—there never can be—successful compromise between good and evil. Only total victory can reward the champions of tolerance, and decency, and freedom and faith."

But there was also in Roosevelt's war leadership, unlike Wilson's, an almost complete acceptance of "power politics" as a fact of international life. Certainly, no desire to "make the world safe for democracy" was apparent in Roosevelt's compromises with Franco's Spain, Vichy France, Stalin's Russia, and Badoglio's regime after Italy's surrender. His quick adoption of the most "modern" means of warfare, including population bombing and unrestricted submarine operations, also exhibited this strong realist strain, as did his decisions to postpone a second front in Europe from 1942 to 1943 to 1944. The end—total victory and the security of the United States—justified these means. He was prepared to walk in the company of lesser devils in order to defeat Satan. Thus, Roosevelt, in Burns's words, became "both realist and idealist, both fixer and preacher, both a prince and a soldier." [13]

Roosevelt's policy of unconditional surrender encapsulates the realist-idealist dilemma and deserves particular emphasis. Even though his chiefs of staff had urged him to modify the doctrine,

[13] Burns, op. cit., p. 550.

Roosevelt insisted on it to the end. It probably hardened the resistance of the German people, discouraged the opposition against Hitler inside the armed forces, and quite possibly, prolonged the war. The policy also prevented Roosevelt from saving Jews from the gas ovens of Auschwitz because such an initiative would have forced him to negotiate with Hitler.

Roosevelt, of course, was not unaware of the power of these arguments. Yet, Hitler was anathema to him and his moral credo did not permit a compromise. Nor, in all likelihood, would the majority of Americans have tolerated it. Besides, if the war had come to a negotiated end, another "stab-in-the-back" legend might have arisen in Germany, as it had in 1918. Thus, Roosevelt the war leader turned the conflict into a crusade. He moralized and dramatized, personalized and simplified in order to adhere to the unconditional· surrender policy. It became a *personal* commitment from which he never wavered. Winning the war always took precedence. In essence, he saw the war against Hitler as a struggle for the survival of civilization itself. In that ultimate sense, Roosevelt's perception of the war was very much like Wilson's after April 1917. And in the service of that gigantic effort, Franklin Roosevelt sacrificed his life.

THE PEACEMAKER: YALTA

There is a cliché that Roosevelt won the war for the United States but lost the peace. It is a trivial comment, based on the oft-repeated criticism that Roosevelt "sold out" the interest of the United States to Stalin at the Yalta conference in February 1945. The facts about Roosevelt's role at Yalta reveal a far more complex picture.

In order to understand Yalta, one must understand Roosevelt's belief in his personal charisma. He was convinced that he could establish a personal relationship with Stalin that could bridge the differences between the two countries and usher in an "era of good feeling." As early as March 1942, Roosevelt wrote to Churchill that he could handle the Soviet leader better than anyone else:

> I know you will not mind my being brutally frank when I tell you
> that I think I can personally handle Stalin better than either your
> foreign office or my State Department. Stalin hates the guts of all

your top people. He thinks he likes me better, and I hope he will continue to do so.[14]

Roosevelt met Stalin for the first time at the Teheran conference in November 1943. His approach to Stalin was characteristic. When on the second day of the conference, Churchill asked Roosevelt for lunch, the president declined because he feared that Stalin would suspect that he and Churchill were hatching a plot if they met privately. But that afternoon, Roosevelt refused to commit the United States to the opening of a second front in Europe. Instead, he proposed an ad hoc committee to consider the matter. Stalin disagreed and stridently demanded such a front in order to take the pressure off the Soviet Union. And after the war, the Soviet leader added, fifty thousand German officers had to be rounded up and liquidated. Churchill retorted that he and his country would not stand for such butchery. The president spoke up and proposed a "compromise": only forty-nine thousand Germans should be shot. Churchill walked out of the room but still, Stalin could not be deflected—he kept asking for a second front.

The next morning, the three leaders met again. Roosevelt continued to work on Stalin. His own description of that effort is revealing:

> I said, lifting my hand to cover a whisper (which of course had to be interpreted), "Winston is cranky this morning, he got up on the wrong side of the bed." A vague smile passed over Stalin's eyes, and I decided I was on the right track. I began to tease Churchill about his Britishness, about John Bull, about his cigars, about his habits. It began to register with Stalin. Winston got red and scowled, and the more he did so, the more Stalin smiled. Finally, Stalin broke out with a deep heavy guffaw and for the first time in three days I saw light. I kept it up until Stalin was laughing with me and it was then that I called him "Uncle Joe." He would have thought me fresh the day before, but that day he laughed and came over and shook my hand.
>
> From that time on our relations were personal, and Stalin himself indulged in an occasional witticism. The ice was broken and we talked like men and brothers.[15]

[14] Winston Churchill, *The Hinge of Fate* (Boston: Houghton Mifflin, 1950), p. 201.

[15] This was Roosevelt's account of the episode, as told later to his secretary of labor, Frances Perkins. Quoted in Burns, op. cit., p. 412.

That evening Roosevelt broached the sensitive question of Poland with Stalin. He explained that there were in the United States from six to seven million Americans of Polish extraction and he did not wish to lose their votes. He would like to see the Polish state restored, but he proposed that the eastern border be moved farther to the west and the western border be moved even to the Oder River. Stalin answered that now that the president had explained, he understood.

The picture of Roosevelt that emerges from Teherán is that of an extremely manipulative man. Through cajolery and flattery, he not only deflected Stalin from the subject of the second front, which was paramount in the Soviet leader's mind, but he even received a tentative agreement from Stalin that the Soviet Union would not simply absorb Poland. As for Churchill, Roosevelt observed laconically: "I must say he behaved very decently afterward."

Yet, the manipulation was not to work for long. Stalin bitterly resented the postponements of a second front that, he suspected, were prompted by an Anglo-American desire to see the Nazi and Soviet armies bleed each other to death. Stalin's hardened attitude at Yalta was the result of this suspicion.

Roosevelt, on the other hand, was convinced, as the end of the war came into view, that he could work with Stalin. He was confident that an "era of good feeling" between the Soviet Union and the United States would characterize the postwar world of reconstruction. "Uncle Joe," as Roosevelt affectionately referred to Stalin in private conversations, would surely cooperate in a common effort to rebuild a shattered world. Besides, Roosevelt did realize that the West had not treated the Soviet Union completely fairly. After all, there had been the West's rejection of Soviet efforts in the late 1930s to build an alliance against Hitler. There had been the Munich Pact of 1938, which, by selling out Czechoslovakia to Hitler, had in effect opened a gateway to the East for the Nazi dictator. And most important, there had been the postponements of the second front that had forced the Soviet Union to take the brunt of the war against the Nazis. But if Roosevelt could demonstrate his good intentions and his friendliness, Stalin would eventually come around. Thus, in February 1945, Roosevelt staked everything on another face-to-face encounter with Stalin. The trip to the Soviet Union would be an ordeal for the aging, crippled man. But nothing could deter Roosevelt from his aim to meet again with Stalin. The Soviet Union was rapidly absorbing its Eastern European neighbors in a relentless quest for security and power. Stalin seemed to have forgotten his promise about Poland made at Teheran. Yalta, in Roosevelt's opinion, was to be the supreme test of his personal diplomacy.

At Yalta, Roosevelt, Churchill, and Stalin sat down to remake a good part of the world map and to reshape the structure of world power. The American president focused on three major issues: the new United Nations organization, about to be born at San Francisco; the future of Poland; and Soviet participation in the war against Japan.

This time, Stalin was not to be disarmed by pleasantries. When Roosevelt mentioned to him that he and Churchill called him "Uncle Joe," Stalin flared up in anger. And when Roosevelt declared that he was more bloodthirsty than a year ago and that he hoped that Stalin would again propose a toast to the execution of fifty thousand Germans, the Soviet leader was unmoved. Everyone was more bloodthirsty than a year ago, he answered simply.

The United Nations was at the top of Roosevelt's agenda. The president was deeply aware of Wilson's tragedy. He knew that Wilson's admirers believed that the great crusader for the League of Nations had been dramatically vindicated. Twenty years after the Senate's rejection of the league, Wilson's warnings had come true. The Wilsonians believed that the very defeat of the league had now made possible an American commitment to a new international organization. Roosevelt did not share this view. He had no wish to be a martyr, to be vindicated only a generation later. He would not reenact the Wilson drama. He would make sure to temper his crusading zeal with a generous dose of realism. Thus, when we examine Roosevelt's attitudes toward the United Nations, we find *both* the Prophet and the Prince.

Roosevelt's Wilsonianism was evident in his general statements about the United Nations. Covenants were to be open once again, and "openly arrived at." In the words of Secretary of State Cordell Hull, "there [would] no longer be need for sphere of influence, for alliances, balances of power, or any other of the special arrangements through which, in the unhappy past, the nations strove to safeguard their interest." Sound moral principles and good fellowship would take their place. Roosevelt's Advisory Commission on Postwar Foreign Policy had been even more emphatic in its stress on the subordination of power politics to principles: "The vital interests of the United States lie in following a diplomacy of principle—of moral disinterestedness instead of power politics." Woodrow Wilson might easily have been the author of these statements.

But then there was Roosevelt the pragmatist. The president was just as eager as Stalin and Churchill to safeguard the national interest by insisting on a Great Power veto in the United Nations on all questions of substance. Stalin even demanded the extension of the veto principle to procedural matters and to the peaceful settlements of disputes. At Yalta, Roosevelt used all his persuasive powers to change Stalin's mind and finally succeeded. The veto would apply only to substantive questions. Then Roosevelt and Stalin bargained fiercely over the UN voting formula. Stalin, pointing to the "autonomous republics" within the Soviet Union, demanded sixteen votes in the proposed UN General Assembly. Roosevelt, after several arduous sessions, bargained the Soviet leader down to three: one for the Soviet Union, one for the Ukraine, and one for Byelorussia. At that point, Stalin would no longer budge and was supported by Churchill who had an eye on the British empire and its dominions. Roosevelt realized that, if he refused to compromise, his entire dream of the United Nations might be imperiled. Mindful of the Wilson precedent, he acquiesced in the Soviet Union's two extra votes, on the understanding that the United Nations conference itself would approve them, with the support of the Big Three. Later, he told his friend, Adolf Berle, Jr., who expressed unhappiness with the Yalta voting formula: "I didn't say it was good. I said it was the best I could do."

On the question of Poland, Roosevelt told Stalin that he was "more interested in Poland's sovereign independence and freedom than in any particular frontier lines." Specifically, he requested a government of national unity, to be based on free elections in which all five major political parties would participate. Churchill agreed, asserting that Britain had declared war on Germany in order to preserve a free Poland. Stalin, who defended the existing pro-Soviet government at Lublin, finally agreed to reorganize that government on a "broader democratic basis" and to permit free elections on the basis of open suffrage and secret ballot. Crucially, however, there would be no way for the United States or Britain to monitor the conduct of the elections. Stalin would not permit an American or British presence in Poland.

In retrospect, it is difficult to see how Roosevelt could have done much better. The Soviet Union, after all, was in physical occupation of Poland. There was nothing the United States could have done to prevent the Soviet Union from entering Poland except to get there first, and this it was not prepared to do. Thus, Roosevelt's position on the Polish question did not stem from naïveté, or from a "sellout" mentality, but simply from an acceptance of the facts. He knew that Stalin was absolutely determined about Poland, which he considered vital to the Soviet Union's security. Thus, Roosevelt had probably reached the limits of his bargaining power over Poland. After two German invasions in less than thirty years, Stalin's view was not surprising. To the Soviet leader, a democratic government meant a Communist government and "free elections" meant elections from which parties not "friendly" to the Soviet Union would be barred. The model Roosevelt had in mind when he spoke of free Polish elections was Czechoslovakia, a democracy with ties to both the Soviet Union and the West. But, as it turned out, to Stalin, a "friendly" state meant a completely Communist state. Given these conditions, it does not appear likely that any other Western leader could have improved much on Roosevelt's performance.

The matter of the Balkan states was settled relatively simply. Here Churchill took the initiative. He suggested that the Soviet Union's interest predominate in 90 percent of Rumania and 75 percent of Bulgaria, and that Britain should have a 90 percent "say" in Greece. Finally, he recommended that both "go fifty-fifty" in Yugoslavia and Hungary.[16] Churchill pushed a piece of paper in Stalin's direction and Stalin checked his approval with a mark. As Churchill described the occurrence: "After this there was a long silence. The penciled paper lay in the center of the table. At length I said: 'Might it not be thought rather cynical if it seemed we had disposed of these issues, so fateful to millions of people, in such an offhand manner? Let us burn the paper.' 'No, you keep it.' said Stalin." [17]

Roosevelt faced a problem on the matter of Soviet participa-

---

[16] Diana Shaver Clemens, *Yalta* (New York: Oxford University Press, 1970), p. 71.

[17] Winston S. Churchill, *Triumph and Tragedy* (Boston: Houghton Mifflin, 1950), pp. 227–228.

tion in the Pacific war. He hoped that Stalin would enter the war against Japan. His military chiefs had told him that an American invasion of Japan would be immensely costly if the Soviet Union were to stand aloof. Thus, Roosevelt had to ask Stalin for a second front against Japan. In view of the fact that Roosevelt had delayed a second front in Europe for two years, his hand at Yalta was not particularly strong. The tables were now turned. Under the circumstances, Roosevelt's agreement that the Soviet Union should receive some Manchurian ports and railroads was quite understandable. Stalin, in fact, did not ask for as much at Yalta as Soviet power in Asia would have enabled him to do. Actually, Roosevelt did reasonably well.

The decisions taken by Roosevelt at Yalta, then, were neither naïve concessions nor cynical sellouts. They flowed from the military power realities that existed at the time. And so far as Roosevelt's efforts to establish a relationship with Stalin were concerned, these efforts were important for the historical record. If the attempt had not been made, it would have been all too easy for historians to say later: "Perhaps cooperation with Stalin *was* possible. But it was never tried." We do know today that Roosevelt tried, and that he gave his last energies to that attempt. He was convinced that, through patience, fairness, and goodwill, Stalin's mistrust could be conquered. To this purpose, he held to the last breath.[18] And from his efforts there did emerge a structure of peace. The structure was flawed but it reflected the realities of power. Impure by ideal standards, it nonetheless gave new hope to mankind exhausted by "the scourge of war." The United Nations was a product of many compromises, including those of Roosevelt. But at least it did not die, as did Woodrow Wilson's league, in an American grave. *Roosevelt's crusade, unlike Wilson's, was tempered by reality.*

Perhaps the most striking observation to be made about Roosevelt's diplomacy was its highly personal character. His major foreign policy decisions, both before and during the Second World War, were strictly his own and were reached in secrecy. The destroyer deal, the Atlantic Charter, the unconditional surrender policy, and Yalta are all cases in point. In the crunch, "democ-

---

[18] Herbert Feis, *Churchill, Roosevelt, Stalin* (Princeton: Princeton University Press, 1957), p. 596.

racy's aristocrat" acted on his own. The wellspring of these four decisions was his supreme self-confidence. On the whole, history has vindicated Roosevelt. If he had appealed to Congress on the destroyer deal, no ships might ever have reached England and Hitler might have crossed the English Channel. The Atlantic Charter, drafted in utmost secrecy with Winston Churchill, laid the foundations for the United Nations. On the matter of unconditional surrender, it is not likely that an aroused American public would have found any other formula acceptable. And at Yalta, Roosevelt probably did as well as the strategic realities allowed. In retrospect, the quality of these four decisions was extremely high. And Roosevelt reached them essentially alone.

Finally, Franklin Roosevelt was unique among American leaders in the sense that he combined the qualities of the crusader with those of the pragmatist in equal measure. In his war policy, FDR was a crusader. He was completely single-minded in his aim to win the Second World War. But in his quest for the reconstruction of the postwar world, he became a pragmatist. With his consummate political skills, FDR sensed that the crusading spirit was appropriate in times of war, but that the subtle diplomacy of reconstruction required the talents of a pragmatist. FDR had always shown a formidable gift for reconciling opposites. This talent, when coupled with his supreme self-confidence, made Franklin Roosevelt a statesman for all seasons.

---------- *Interchapter* ----------

THE ORIGINS
OF THE COLD WAR

Harry S. Truman was sixty years of age when he assumed the presidency of the United States on April 12, 1945. On that day, Soviet and American forces met in the heart of Europe, near the German town of Torgau. Adolf Hitler, who had exulted at the news of Franklin D. Roosevelt's death, had only two more weeks to live.

"I am not big enough for this job," Truman had groaned just before he was sworn in as president.[1] Actually, he was better prepared than he thought. He had had a great deal of practical experience including that of leadership in crisis situations. While most of the men who had shaped the nation's foreign policy had come from relatively narrow backgrounds in business, law, or academe, Harry Truman brought to the presidency an unusually broad, if somewhat shallow, range of experience.

Truman's parents had been too poor to send their son to college, but training in the Missouri National Guard had earned the young man an officer's commission. During World War I, Harry Truman had commanded an artillery battery in France. His determination and capacity for leadership were already apparent in the war. Years later, he recalled how he shaped his troops into line:

> When I first took command of the battery I called all the sergeants and corporals together. I told them I knew they had been

[1] Robert J. Donovan, *Conflict and Crisis: The Presidency of Harry S. Truman, 1945–1948* (New York: Norton, 1977), p. 15.

55

making trouble for the previous commanders. I said, "I didn't
come over here to get along with you. You've got to get along
with me. And if there are any of you who can't, speak up right
now and I'll bust you right back. . . ." We got along.[2]

On one occasion, under German fire, Truman rallied his retreating
troops by insulting them with choice Missouri invective. The experience of command gave Truman confidence in his ability to
lead men. It also reinforced a belief, possibly inherited from his
blunt and outspoken parents, that the best way to deal with re-
calcitrant opponents was to "talk tough."

Yet despite his inclination to belligerent rhetoric, Truman
was a strong believer in the virtues of accommodation. After the
clothing store he and a wartime friend had opened in Kansas City
went bankrupt in 1922, Truman went into politics. His rise to
national prominence stemmed largely from the support that he
received from the powerful Pendergast machine. His path to
power was paved with compromises. He had to work through the
unsavory Pendergast organization to succeed in Kansas City politics and to be elected to the position of a county judge. Only
much later, as senator from Missouri, did Truman manage to
build an independent political base. This he did by reconciling
diverse interest groups within the Democratic party. His nomina-
tion for the vice-presidency in 1944 was also a compromise, in this
case between the party's liberal and conservative wings. Thus, while
Truman had his principles, he also believed that conciliation and
adjustment were the very lifeblood of the political process.

One principle to which Truman attached particular weight
was the importance of keeping one's word. A man who did not
carry out his obligations was not to be trusted. After the failure
of his clothing store, Truman insisted on paying off his creditors
even though it took him years to do so. "When I say I'm going
to do something, I do it, or bust my insides trying to do it," he
declared. Loyalty to friends he regarded as a sacred duty. One of
the embarrassments of his administration was Truman's refusal to
disassociate himself from some of his more disreputable Missouri
cronies. Truman judged men by their reliability in keeping agree-

---

[2] John Lewis Gaddis, "Harry Truman and the Origins of Containment,"
Makers of American Diplomacy. Frank J. Merlin and Theodore Wilson, eds.
(New York: Scribner's, 1974), pp. 191–192.

ments and this was the standard by which he, too, wanted to be judged.

Truman's conception of loyalty as a personal matter also characterized his later approach to the witchhunts of Senator Joseph McCarthy. As president, he fiercely defended Dean Acheson and George Marshall against the ludicrous charge that they were "soft on communism," but he never took the case against McCarthy to the American public. He did try to establish procedures that would guarantee the rights of the accused. Yet, by the middle of 1952, more than one million Americans had been investigated. The cost in terms of breakdown of social trust was immense. No stratum of American society remained immune. Truman's behavior was not exemplary. He decided to stand by his own, but did not go much further. Loyalty, to him, was not, primarily, a matter of abstract principle. It was, first and foremost, a personal emotion.

Despite his lack of formal education, Truman was an avid reader and developed an astounding knowledge of history. He liked to draw lessons from it and there is little doubt that this tendency influenced some of his later decisions in the White House. His belief, however, that historical parallels offered reliable guides for dealing with current problems occasionally led him to make simplified comparisons between past and present.

By temperament, Truman was an optimist. Harmony among nations was possible, he believed, provided there was a collective organization to sustain and enforce the peace. World War I had convinced him that such a structure was essential and that Woodrow Wilson had found the right formula in the League of Nations concept. He was convinced that the failure of the United States to join the league had had tragic consequences for the world. "I am sure as I can be," he told the Senate in 1943, "that this World War is the result of the 1919–1920 isolationist attitude, and I am equally sure that another and worse war will follow this one, unless the United Nations and their allies decide to work together for peace as they are working together for victory." [3] While in the Senate, Truman labored hard to commit the United States to membership in the United Nations, and after becoming president, he never wavered in his support for the world organization. Dur-

[3] Ibid., p. 193.

ing most of his life, he carried in his wallet a copy of Alfred
Lord Tennyson's poem "Locksley Hall," which predicted a "Parliament of Man, The Federation of the World." "We're going to
have that someday," Truman once commented. "I guess that's
what I've really been working for ever since I first put that poetry
in my pocket." Harry Truman had strong ideals, but he did not
have the rigidity of a crusader.

Throughout most of his life, Truman remained unusually
humble. He took pride in the fact that power had sought him
rather than the other way around. Yet, his experience had taught
him that an executive, to be effective, must not hesitate to use his
authority and must guard it from all challenges. The fact that
he had not aspired to the presidency probably made it possible
for Truman to wield his awesome power without guilt, but his
broad and practical experience gave him the necessary confidence.
Thus, when lightning struck on that April day in 1945 and Truman became president of the United States, he would soon con-
found the skeptics. Insofar as any human being could be prepared
for such a job, Truman had that preparation: experience with crisis,
a quick, pragmatic mind, and confidence tempered with humility.

Upon entering the White House, Truman seized the reins of
power with vigor and decisiveness. Subordinates noticed this at
once. One of them said: "When I saw him today, I had fourteen
problems to take up with him and got through them in less than
fifteen minutes with a clear directive on every one of them. You
can imagine what a joy it is to work with a man like that." This
brisk approach to decision making quickly established the new
president's authority. It was consistent with a lifelong habit:
whether rallying frightened troops in France, dealing with can-
tankerous politicians in Kansas City, or running for office in seemingly hopeless elections, Truman had always responded to crisis
situations by taking the offensive. Now, in the biggest crisis of his
life, he responded characteristically by rising to the challenge with
courage and determination.

Thus, he grew quickly in his job. Soon the famous triangular
block inscribed with the motto "The buck stops here" made its
appearance on his desk. He developed a capacity for making extremely tough decisions without tormenting afterthoughts. As he
wrote in a letter to his mother shortly after he assumed office:
"I have to take things as they come and make every decision on

the basis of the facts as I have them and then go on from there; then forget that one and take the next." [4] At the time he made the decision to drop the atomic bomb on Japan, he wrote to his sister: "Nearly every crisis seems to be the worst one, but after it's over, it isn't so bad." [5] His advisers admired his readiness to accept full responsibility; historians, however, will regard most of Truman's foreign policy decisions as controversial for decades to come.

Harry Truman believed in a strong chief executive. In his view, whenever a president weakly deferred to the Congress, the public interest was the real loser. A decade of experience as senator had made Truman wary of the power of special interests in the passage of legislation. He had always admired "strong liberal presidents," and had singled out for his particular affection Thomas Jefferson, Andrew Jackson, Abraham Lincoln, Theodore Roosevelt, and Franklin D. Roosevelt. He saw himself as the champion of the common man and was deeply committed to the liberal tradition in American politics. Foreign policy decisions, in Truman's view, could only be made by the president in a strictly bipartisan manner. There was a core of iron in the man. Admirers lauded it as strength of character and detractors blamed it for the congealing of the cold war.

The defeat of Germany in April 1945 was the prelude to the cold war. Soon thereafter, the process of dividing Germany and most of Europe into American and Soviet spheres of influence gathered momentum. While the United States demobilized its fighting forces, the Soviet Union established control over seven Eastern European countries whose absorption had been prepared during the last year of the war: Albania, Bulgaria, Hungary, Poland, East Germany, Rumania, and Yugoslavia.

During his initial months in office, Harry Truman tried to continue Roosevelt's policy of cooperation with the Russians. His style, however, was very different from that of his predecessor. While FDR had attempted to woo Stalin and had observed an impeccable politeness toward the Soviet leader, Truman believed that negotiations would be more fruitful if he "talked tough."

---

[4] Harry S. Truman, *Memoirs* (New York: Doubleday, 1955), vol. 1, p. 293.
[5] Ibid., p. 433.

When the Soviet foreign minister, V. M. Molotov, stopped off in Washington on his way to San Francisco where the United Nations was about to be established, Truman lectured him in a manner not unlike his handling of Battery D. He wanted cooperation with the Russians, he snapped, not a one-way street. Molotov emerged from the meeting badly shaken. "I gave it to him straight," Truman bragged later, "one-two to the jaw."

Nevertheless, Truman adhered to the agreements Roosevelt had hammered out at Yalta. Even though he personally disapproved of the UN voting formula, he agreed at Potsdam in July and August 1945, that the Russians could have three seats in the UN General Assembly. He turned down Winston Churchill's proposal that Allied troops in central Europe remain in the advanced positions they had attained by V-E Day. And he made no changes in the Far Eastern agreements between Roosevelt and Stalin. Thus, the new president's tough talk was designed to facilitate, not impede, negotiations. Any appearance of weakness, Truman thought, would encourage Stalin to ask for more. He had developed a grudging respect for the Soviet dictator. "Stalin," Truman obseved once, "is as near like Tom Pendergast as any man I know." Truman liked to say of his old Kansas City boss that, whatever his other faults, he had always kept his word.

When, in Truman's view, Stalin broke his word, the policy of accommodation died abruptly. Soviet troops had occupied Iran during World War II, but Stalin had promised their withdrawal by March 2, 1946. His failure to keep his pledge was no small matter. "I held Stalin to be a man of his word," Truman stated shortly thereafter. "Troops in Iran after March 2, upset that theory." His sense of honor was outraged. "They understand one language," he fumed, "and that is the language they are going to get from me from this point." Thus were sown the seeds of the containment policy. Churchill's "Iron-Curtain" speech, delivered that same month in Fulton, Missouri, in Truman's home state, only strengthened the presidential resolve. Thus, when one year later, Greece and Turkey were threatened by a Communist takeover, containment became official American policy.

In February 1947, Great Britain notified the United States that she was no longer able to protect Greece and Turkey, both of which were near collapse. Britain, the traditional holder of the balance of power on the European continent, abdicated her responsibility. The United States would have to shoulder Britain's burden. There was no one else who could step in. All other European powers had suffered too grievously to stand up to the Soviet Union. Communist penetration of Greece and Turkey would give the Soviet Union a strong base in the eastern Mediterranean that would further threaten American interests. The United States would have to defend itself without a European buffer nation. From the debris of the Second World War, a bipolar world had emerged.

On March 12, 1947, Harry Truman addressed a joint session of Congress and declared that "it must be the policy of the United States to support free peoples who are resisting attempted subjugation by armed minorities or by outside pressures." Through this "Truman Doctrine," the United States took over from Britain the responsibility of protecting Greece and Turkey. In June, Secretary of State George Marshall proposed a vast European recovery program at a commencement address at Harvard University. The aim of the Marshall Plan was the ultimate restoration of the economies of Europe through American aid. This aid was also offered to Eastern Europe, but Stalin refused to accept it. Relations between the Soviet Union and the United States now deteriorated rapidly. The negotiations over a German peace settlement bogged down. In July, George F. Kennan, head of the State Department's policy-planning staff, writing under the pseudonym "X" in the journal *Foreign Affairs*, asserted: "The main element of any United States policy toward the Soviet Union must be that of a long-term patient but firm and vigilant containment of Russian expansive tendencies."

The containment policy was not conceived in global terms. Its goal was the considerably less ambitious one of stopping Soviet expansion in Europe and thereby to restore the balance of power on that continent. Further Communist victories would have placed Europe under the domination of a single hostile power, the very thing Americans had fought two world wars to prevent. Truman's belief was that economic assistance, not military force, was the best way to resist Soviet expansion. "Communism succeeds only when there is weakness, or misery, or despair," he argued. "It cannot succeed in a strong and healthy society." This belief, however, Truman was soon to learn, was mistaken.

In February 1948, the Soviet Union electrified the West by absorbing the eighth European country, Czechoslovakia, into the Soviet orbit. Unlike the other countries the Soviet Union had taken over, Czechoslovakia had been a vital democracy. Its first president, Tomáš Masaryk, had been a close friend of Wilson's. It seemed to Truman that the Czech nation had been raped twice: first by the Nazis and now by the Communists. Stalin's latest gambit galvanized Harry Truman into action. The president prevailed upon the leader of the Republican opposition in the Senate, Arthur H. Vandenberg, to draft a resolution that was to become the basis of the North Atlantic Treaty Organization. Truman's bipartisan approach was good politics because NATO was to set a new precedent. For the United States, membership in a peacetime alliance was a drastic reversal of its foreign policy. And yet, a year later, Truman had achieved his goal. In April 1949, Belgium, Canada, Denmark, France, Great Britain, Iceland, Italy, Luxembourg, the Netherlands, Norway, Portugal, and the United States signed the North Atlantic Treaty. The U.S. Senate ratified the treaty in July. Europe had become America's first line of defense. The premise of Europe's economic recovery was her military security. Harry Truman now perceived himself as the defender of a democratic Western Europe. And he determined to stand fast.

It seemed that the United States would have to depend for its security on a regional military alliance. The United Nations, still in its infancy, was already in deep trouble. Collective security in the UN Security Council was not working well. The Soviet Union had cast a string of vetoes and paralyzed the council. The world's policemen had fallen out among themselves. The spirit of Yalta had been replaced by the icy winds of cold war.

The showdown came in Germany. In Berlin, the former capital, the cold war reached a point of rigidification. In 1945, Germany had been occupied by the four major victorious powers, the United States, Britain, France, and the Soviet Union. The Yalta and Potsdam agreements of 1945 had divided Germany into four zones, three Western and one Soviet. Berlin was situated in the Soviet zone but was itself divided into four sectors. Under the agreements, none of the four occupation powers was to have the right to change the status quo without the consent of the three others. In 1948, however, shortly after the absorption of Czechoslovakia, Stalin began to put pressure on the Western garrisons in Berlin. The Soviet administration suspended all communications between West Berlin and the Western zones of Germany. The object of this blockade was to turn West Berlin into an island and to starve it into submission. The American response was the famous Berlin airlift, which effectively countered the Soviet move by supplying the population of West Berlin from the air. In May 1949, the blockade was lifted.

By this time, the division of Germany had begun to be accepted as a long-term condition. Both superpowers attempted to absorb their zones of occupation into their respective orbits. The three Western zones emerged as the Federal Republic of Germany, with its capital at Bonn, and the Eastern zone was turned into a Soviet dependency. The deadlock over Germany intensified the cold war because, by that time, all maneuverability in Europe had disappeared. The Soviet Union and the United States, in J. Robert Oppenheimer's words, had begun to resemble "two scorpions in a bottle."

In September 1949, United States intelligence discovered that the Russians had exploded their first atomic bomb. Truman received this information calmly. He had never expected the American nuclear monopoly to last indefinitely. In January 1950, the president announced that the United States would build a hydrogen bomb. The race for nuclear superiority was on. The cold war had become a fact of life.

It is tempting to explain the genesis of the cold war purely in terms of the expansionary zeal of Communist ideology. Indeed, a fairly good case can be made for such a position. Marxism, with its prediction that the "expropriated" would expropriate the "expropriators" on an international scale, envisaged world revolution as its ultimate goal. Leninism fashioned a network of Communist parties—the Comintern—to "give history a push" and hasten the day of communist victory. This inherent aggressiveness of the Communist ideology, emanating from the Soviet Union as its citadel and directing center, elicited protective countermeasures in the West. These, in turn, generated suspicions of "capitalist encirclement" in the Soviet Union. Suspicion begot countersuspicion, gradually drawing East and West into a vicious circle, and thus, the cold war was launched.

A moment's reflection shows that this description of the cold war, though tempting, is all too simple. It does not explain the fact that the Soviet Union on many occasions pushed forward its frontiers for reasons other than ideology. For example, it could hardly be said that the Nazi-Soviet pact of 1939 was the result of Communist ideology. Nor could it be assumed without question that the extension of American influence in Europe and Asia during World War II was purely a countermove to Communist expansion. Even a cursory inspection suggests that the cold war may have some of its roots in geographic, historical, or cultural factors. This is not to say that Communist ideology is not important. But it does not explain everything.

It is a striking fact that Russian expansion can often be explained without reference to Marxist-Leninist ideological factors. For example, in the Second World War the Soviets could scarcely have permitted their Anglo-American partners to extend Western influence into all sections of the power vacuum created by the Axis defeat. American expansion in both Europe and Asia has often been hesitant and reluctant. Nevertheless, the war ended with an American general in Berlin and another in Tokyo. This the Soviets could hardly afford to neglect. After all, Soviet suspicions had been aroused when the Americans had twice postponed the establishment of a second front against Hitler.

The temptation to explain American world strategy after World War II purely in terms of countermoves to Soviet expansionism is almost as great as the temptation to explain the latter exclusively in terms of Marxist-Leninist ideology. Yet here again we must beware of the pitfall of the single factor analysis. No doubt there is much truth in such an interpretation of American policies, but it explains only part of the story. Over a century before the cold war developed, the great French philosopher, Alexis de Tocqueville, predicted its coming. And well before 1945 the map of the world suggested the primacy of America and Russia. Already by 1850 the United States formed one of the greatest land empires of the globe, stretching from the Atlantic to the Pacific and from the Canadian frontier to the Gulf of Mexico and the Caribbean Sea; already by 1800 the Russian empire, stretching from Manchuria to Warsaw, covered over one-sixth of the entire land of our globe. Already by 1850 there were as many Russians as there were Frenchmen and Englishmen and Germans; already by 1890 there were more Americans than Frenchmen and Englishmen together; already by 1900 the United States produced more steel than any other country in the world; already during the First World War the financial wealth of the world shifted to America. Well before 1945 the United States and Russia were becoming the two largest empires in the history of mankind.

It is true that the United States had liquidated many of its possessions by the end of World War II. By 1946 the Philippines were given their independence and the remaining American possessions were being steadily prepared for self-government or statehood. On the other hand, it is quite clear that World War II had broadened the United States's perception of its strategic interests. Soon after hostilities had ended in Europe, the entire North Atlantic, from the Azores to Iceland and Greenland, had come within the sphere of American influence. And as a result of the occupation of Japan, the Pacific was transformed into what was virtually an American strategic lake. Indeed, World War II had created several power vacuums which the United States had decided to fill long before the cold war actually crystallized.

Hence, American expansion, too, was a complex phenomenon. Reaction to Soviet expansionism, while very important, was not the only factor in the picture. The cold war had multiple roots and both sides share the responsibility for its origins.

3

KOREA 1950

In 1949, the Chinese Communists came to power on the Chinese mainland after a bitter civil war with Generalissimo Chiang Kai-shek's Nationalists. By promising land reform, the Communists had gained the support of the peasants whom Chiang Kai-shek had virtually ignored. Mao Tse-tung, the leader of the new China, described himself as a Communist, but had in fact developed an ideology sharply at variance with the orthodox, Moscow-directed creed. He had organized Chinese communism on a peasant rather than an urban, industrial basis. What this meant for Stalin was that, shortly after Marshall Tito's defection in Yugoslavia the year before, he found himself confronted with a second and far more serious challenge. There were now two major centers of communism: Moscow and Peking. The alliance between them was to last less than a decade.

In Europe, the cold war had rigidified since the Berlin crisis of 1948. Power there confronted concerted counterpower. There was no further room for maneuver. Thus, it was no accident that during the late 1940s, the major arena of the cold war shifted away from the European continent. And the rise of China as a formidable and independent power in the Communist world helped move this arena to East Asia. Thus was the stage set for the Korean War.

The actual outbreak of the war remains shrouded in mystery. We can only speculate about the motivations for the North Korean attack of June 1950. Four possibilities, in descending order of probability, suggest themselves.

The most likely explanation is that it was a probing action by Stalin against the West. Secretary of State Dean Acheson, in a speech before the National Press Club in Washington on January 12, 1950, had outlined the "military defense perimeter" of the United States. In Europe, the perimeter was NATO; in Asia, it extended to Japan and the Philippines. There was one notable omission—Korea. It is reasonable to assume that Stalin, thus encouraged, ordered the North Koreans to attack the South.

A second possibility is that Stalin sought to create problems not for the United States but for China. Mao Tse-tung had come to power in China without the help of Stalin and since, at that time, the Soviet leader was engaged in major purges of Communist parties everywhere, it is not likely that he was untroubled by Mao's ascendancy. Perhaps, it might be argued, Stalin's pact with Mao in February 1950 was merely a facade and Stalin's order to absorb South Korea an attempt to place China in a Soviet nutcracker. In short, Stalin might not have told the Chinese about the imminent attack. It might have come as much of a surprise to them as it did to the Americans. And if the war did involve the United States, then Stalin would succeed in ruining any possibility of reconciliation between mainland China and America. A Machiavellian plan indeed, but certainly not one that was beyond the Soviet leader's ken.

A Chinese initiative in North Korea represents a third, though unlikely, possibility. Mao Tse-tung had been in power for less than a year and was fully occupied with problems of domestic consolidation. Besides, North Korea was clearly in the Soviet orbit and China had little, if any, influence there. Finally, it is most improbable that the North Korean attack was an internal affair, as has been contended by the Soviet Union: that it was precipitated by an independent decision of Premier Kim Il-sung. Kim had been placed in power in P'yŏngyang by Stalin. He had come to Korea with the Soviet army and had lived in Russia for years. His government in 1950 was, for all practical purposes, a dependency of Moscow; independent North Korean action was almost impossible.

What does seem certain is that Stalin was behind the North Korean attack. His motives seem less certain. At any rate, he was sure of a speedy military victory. The North Korean leadership announced that it would win the war before the anniversary of V-J Day in September.

Harry Truman considered Korea the toughest decision of his presidency. History's shadow hovered over him. If he failed to rally the democracies, Korea would become another Munich and yet another world war was sure to follow. In this case study we shall examine the responses to the North Korean assault by President Truman and General Douglas MacArthur. The following crucial phases will be examined: (1) Truman's decision in June 1950 to commit American forces and to initiate a United Nations "police action"; (2) MacArthur's crossing of the thirty-eighth parallel; and (3) MacArthur's drive toward the Chinese border at the Yalu River, which precipitated China's military intervention. Finally, we shall assess the significance of these decisions in the larger perspective of recent history.

TRUMAN'S DECISION TO REPEL THE NORTH KOREAN ATTACK

At 4 A.M., Korean time, on Sunday, June 25, 1950, more than 100,000 North Korean troops charged across the thirty-eighth parallel into South Korea. This event presented the United States with two classic challenges of a genuine crisis: danger and opportunity.

At the time of the North Korean attack, Harry S. Truman was sixty-six years old and had served as president for more than five years. During those years, he had made some crucial foreign policy decisions. He had also developed a deep commitment to the United Nations. "As long as I am President," he had declared on May 10, 1950, "we shall support the United Nations with every means at our command."

Secretary of State Dean Acheson, fifty-seven years old at the time of the Korean crisis, had been in office for almost a year and a half. His relationship with the president was excellent. He thought of himself as "the senior member of the Cabinet" and was completely loyal to the president. Truman, in turn, had great confidence in Acheson's judgment and, in case of disagreements between the secretary of state and other members of the cabinet, almost always ruled in Acheson's favor.

This happy partnership between Harry Truman and his secretary of state deserves attention. Not only did Acheson respect the absolute authority of the president in matters of foreign policy, but he also found Truman's unpretentious and open manner in dealing with subordinates entirely acceptable. Truman was clear and precise in his instructions and quite prepared to delegate authority without relinquishing responsibility. Roosevelt, on the other hand, under whom Acheson had served as undersecretary, had not been above allowing a great deal of confusion in administrative ranks before finally reaching a decision, but had occasionally been devious and secretive in the relations with his staff. Acheson had regarded Roosevelt with admiration, but without much affection. He felt much more strongly toward Truman.

Dean Acheson, by anybody's standards, was rather a learned man, an author of several books. Truman, too, however, was an avid reader and a closet intellectual. Acheson respected the former haberdasher who had a love for books. Long after their retirement from active service, the two men would share their impressions about books they had both read. And right up to Truman's death in 1973, strollers who passed the iron-gated Victorian house in Independence, Missouri, late at night, could see the reading light in the upstairs study of the aged president. Many of the books the old man read had been recommended to him by his former secretary of state.

Both men had a stoic attitude toward misfortune. Truman seldom complained when things went wrong. He acted. Acheson, too, believed that "much in life could not be affected or mitigated and, hence, must be borne. Borne without complaint, because complaints were a bore and a nuisance to others and undermined the serenity essential to endurance." [1]

Acheson shared Truman's tendency to look for "lessons in history." His support of the president's decision to repel the North Korean invasion was rooted, like Truman's, in the conviction that the failure of the democracies to resist German and Japanese aggression a dozen years earlier must not be repeated. Like Truman, however, Acheson knew little about Asia in general, and China in particular. The carelessness with which both men later viewed China's interests and power stood in marked contrast to their concern for European policy and care not to provoke the Soviet Union. Both men, in fact, shared a monumental blind spot on the nature and challenge of Mao Tse-tung's China.

[1] Dean Acheson, *Morning and Noon* (Boston: Houghton Mifflin, 1965), p. 18.

Given Acheson's convictions about the nature of the presidency, it is not surprising that he disapproved profoundly of MacArthur's later insubordination. Acheson's courage in defending Truman's unpopular policy of limited war before a hostile Congress earned him the devotion of the president. And when, in turn, Acheson came under fire from Senator McCarthy, the president defended him with a fierce and tenacious loyalty. Each knew that McCarthy was a demagogue and neither had the intention of caving in under his attacks. Not only were the two men in essential agreement on basic policy, but they also became joined together in adversity.

Seldom have two men from such different social backgrounds respected one another as much or worked as well together as Harry Truman and Dean Acheson. The underlying reason for this is not particularly mysterious: their differences in manners and appearances, so obvious for everyone to see, were superficial. Much more profound though less visible was an abiding harmony that made the two men kindred spirits.

Most important, Acheson deeply admired his president's ability to make difficult decisions. "The decisions are his," he wrote, "the President is the pivotal point, the critical element in reaching decisions on foreign policy. No good comes from attempts to invade the authority and responsibility of the President." [2] A secretary of state, in Acheson's view, should be the "principal, unifying, and final source of recommendation" on foreign policy matters to the president. Acheson's admiration for Truman was rooted in his belief that the more difficulty a problem presented, the rarer was the capacity for decision. As he put it:

> The choice becomes one between courses all of which are hard and dangerous. The "right" one, if there is a right one, is quite apt to be the most immediately difficult one. . . . In these cases the mind tends to remain suspended between alternatives and to seek escape by postponing the issue.[3]

Acheson saw it as his duty to give the president the "real issues, honestly presented, with the extraneous matter stripped away." [4]

[2] Dean Acheson, "Responsibility for Decision in Foreign Policy," *Yale Review*, Autumn 1954, p. 12.
[3] Ibid., p. 7.
[4] Ibid.

The decision was the president's; ultimately, he must decide. Like his chief, Acheson was committed to the United Nations. On June 22, 1950, only two days before the North Korean attack, he had declared before a Harvard commencement audience that the United States would give its "unfaltering support to the United Nations."

At 11:20 P.M., Saturday night, June 24, Dean Acheson telephoned President Truman at his home in Independence, Missouri, where he was spending a quiet weekend with his wife and daughter. "Mr. President, I have very serious news," the secretary of state reported, "the North Koreans have invaded South Korea." He explained that, a few minutes earlier, a cable had been received from John J. Muccio, the United States ambassador in South Korea, advising that North Korean forces apparently had launched "an all-out offensive against the Republic of Korea." [5]

Acheson recommended that an emergency meeting of the United Nations Security Council be called immediately. The president concurred and expressed his strong feeling that the issue of the invasion must be brought before the United Nations. A few minutes later, Assistant Secretary John D. Hickerson telephoned the home of Ernest A. Gross, the United States deputy representative to the United Nations, and, failing to reach him, telephoned the home of the secretary general of the United Nations, Trygve Lie.

Trygve Lie, the first secretary general, had been active in Norwegian labor politics for many years before his election to the UN post. He was known to be a man of conviction who would not hesitate to take positions on explosive issues. Only a few months before the Korean crisis he had provoked the extreme displeasure of the American government by publicly supporting the application of the People's Republic of China for membership in the United Nations. By summer, his relations with the host country had deteriorated even further because of Senator Joseph McCarthy's probe for disloyal Americans in the United Nations Secretariat. [6] Now the other superpower was reproached. "My God," Lie exclaimed on hearing the news, "that's a violation of the

[5] Department of State, *United States Policy in the Korean Crisis*, Far Eastern Series, no. 34 (Washington D.C.: Government Printing Office, 1950), p. 1.

[6] For a full treatment of this subject, see John G. Stoessinger, *The United Nations and the Superpowers*, 3rd ed. (New York: Random House, 1973), chap. 3.

United Nations Charter!" [7] He decided to cable immediately a request for full information to the United Nations commission on Korea whose observers were actually on the scene. In the meantime, Acheson and a small group of State Department officials in Washington considered possible courses of action.

The most striking observation to be made about these early American responses was the unanimous agreement that the United States would have to respond to the North Korean challenge through the United Nations. As Ambassador Philip C. Jessup summarized these first reactions: "We've got to do something, and whatever we do, we've got to do it through the United Nations." [8] At 2 A.M. on Sunday, Secretary Acheson again telephoned the president and informed him that a group of officials in the State Department had drafted a resolution that charged North Korea with a "breach of the peace" and an "act of aggression" and asked the UN Security Council to end the fighting. President Truman approved the draft, and, at 3 A.M., Ambassador Gross telephoned Secretary General Lie requesting a meeting of the Security Council by early afternoon.

During the early hours on Sunday morning, top officials at the United States Mission to the United Nations, under the guidance of Ambassador Gross, planned the American strategy for the Security Council meeting. Gross, greatly worried about a possible Soviet veto, which would paralyze the council, made contingency plans for initiating an emergency session of the General Assembly within twenty-four hours. The delicate problem of whether the operative paragraph of the resolution should take the form of an "order" or of a "recommendation" to the Security Council was sidestepped when Gross suggested that the phrase "call upon" be employed. This language was diplomatically strong, but kept the precise legal status of the resolution somewhat in doubt. Another problem was resolved by midmorning when a message from the United Nations commission on Korea became available. The commission reported a "serious situation which [was] assuming the character of a full-scale war." Since sole reliance on American sources would have created difficulties in the

[7] Cited in Glenn D. Paige, *The Korean Decision* (New York: Free Press, 1968), p. 95.
[8] Ibid., p. 100.

Security Council, this United Nations source provided a most welcome basis for factual information. By noon, the Americans were ready for the meeting.

Shortly after 11 A.M., Dean Acheson arrived coatless at the State Department. For Acheson, who had been named "Best Dressed Man of the Year" in 1949, this was unusual behavior. Reporters deduced from it that the situation was most serious. Acheson, indeed, had just learned from military intelligence sources at General Douglas MacArthur's headquarters in Tokyo that the North Korean attack seemed like an "all-out offensive" and that "the South Koreans seemed to be disintegrating." [9] At 2:45 P.M., he telephoned the president who now decided to return to Washington without delay. At the Kansas City airport, the president was described by reporters as "grim-faced" and one of his aides privately told a reporter: "The boss is going to hit those fellows hard." [10]

According to his *Memoirs*, the president spent most of the journey to Washington alone in his compartment, reflecting on the "lessons of history." The North Korean attack, in his view, was reminiscent of the aggressive acts unleashed by the German, Italian, and Japanese military adventurers that had led to World War II. There was no doubt in the president's mind that a Soviet probing action was behind the North Korean invasion. Unless Communist belligerency was deterred promptly and effectively, a third world war between Communist and non-Communist states would inevitably ensue. Finally, the principles of the United Nations, ratified with such high hopes in 1945, would have to be affirmed through a collective response to aggression.[11] He would act through the United Nations if possible, but without it if necessary. While still in flight, the president sent a message to his secretary of state instructing him to arrange a dinner conference at Blair House to which leading State and Defense Department officials were to be invited. At that very moment, the UN Security Council was beginning its emergency session. Present in the council chamber were the representatives of China, Cuba, Ecuador, Egypt, France, India, Norway, the United Kingdom, the United States,

[9] *New York Herald Tribune*, 26 June 1950.
[10] *New York Times*, 2 July 1950.
[11] Truman, op. cit., vol. 2, pp. 332 ff.

and Yugoslavia. The Soviet Union, conspicuous by its absence, was boycotting the Security Council in order to express its opposition to the presence of Nationalist China.

Secretary General Lie informed the council that, on the basis of information submitted by the United Nations commission on Korea, it was his belief that North Korea had violated the Charter. He then went on to say that he considered it "the clear duty of the Security Council to take steps necessary to re-establish peace and security in that area." [12] Immediately after the secretary general had made his statement, Ambassador Gross proceeded to read the American draft resolution to the assembled delegates. He "called upon" North Korea to cease hostilities and to withdraw to the thirty-eighth parallel; he also "called upon" all member states "to render every assistance to the United Nations in the execution of this resolution." [13]

While no mention was made of the Soviet Union, American officials were convinced that it was behind the North Korean move. As Edward W. Barrett, assistant secretary of state for political affairs, put it, "the relationship between the Soviet Union and the North Koreans [was] the same as that between Walt Disney and Donald Duck." [14] At 5:30 P.M., the council was ready to vote on the American draft resolution. The final vote would have been unanimous save for a single abstention: Yugoslavia. Several delegates, believing that the United Nations was fighting for its very life, actually risked their political futures by deciding to vote in the absence of instructions from their governments.[15] Independent voting of this nature was most unusual.

Despite strong UN support, neither President Truman nor his secretary of state had any illusions about the situation. Both men knew that the United States would have to take unilateral military initiatives if the North Korean attack was to be successfully stemmed.

President Truman landed in Washington in a determined frame of mind. "That's enough," he snapped at reporters who crowded around him to take pictures, "we've got a job to do!" [16]

[12] United Nations Security Council, Fifth Year, *Official Records*, no. 15, 473rd meeting, 25 June 1950, p. 3.
[13] *New York Times*, 26 June 1950.
[14] Ibid.
[15] Paige, op. cit., p. 120.
[16] *Chicago Tribune*, 26 June 1950.

Before departing for Blair House, he stated that he was not going to let the North Korean attack succeed and that he was going to "hit them hard." [17] Thirteen of the nation's top diplomatic and military leaders, including the Joint Chiefs of Staff, awaited the president at Blair House and by dinner time, Truman and Acheson were in complete agreement on the main proposals to be presented at the meeting.

After dinner, the president opened the discussion by calling upon the secretary of state to advance suggestions for consideration by the conference. He encouraged all those who were present to voice their opinions freely. Acheson then proceeded to make four specific recommendations: (1) that General MacArthur be authorized to furnish South Korea with generous supplies of military equipment; (2) that the air force be authorized to cover and protect the evacuation of American civilians; (3) that consideration be given to strengthening the role of the UN Security Council; and (4) that the Seventh Fleet be interposed between Formosa and the Chinese mainland. [18]

There was complete agreement on Acheson's first recommendation. As General Omar Bradley put it: "This is the test of all the talk of the last five years of collective security." [19] In view of the sparsity of information from the battle area, however, no one recommended that American ground forces be committed at that moment. "No one could tell what the state of the Korean army was on that Sunday night," the president later noted in his *Memoirs*. [20] Accordingly, as an interim measure, General MacArthur was authorized to give the South Koreans whatever arms and equipment he could spare. There was no disagreement whatsoever over the second recommendation, which was Ambassador Muccio's main concern. As Defense Secretary Louis A. Johnson put it, the measure was more of an "assumption" than a "decision." So far as the role of the United Nations was concerned, the president emphasized that, in this crisis, the United States was "working for" the world organization. He added that he would wait for the Security Council resolution to be flouted before taking any additional measures. He instructed the Joint Chiefs of Staff, how-

[17] Ibid.
[18] Paige, op. cit., p. 127.
[19] Truman, op. cit., vol. 2, p. 334.
[20] Ibid., p. 335.

ever, to "prepare the necessary orders" to make American forces available should the United Nations request them.[21] Finally, there was full agreement to use the Seventh Fleet in order to restrain the Chinese Communists as well as the Chinese Nationalists from military operations that might widen the theater of war. The conference closed with a strong sense of resolve that the United States was prepared, under the United Nations banner, to take whatever measures were required to repel the invasion.

On Monday morning, Ambassador Gross reported from the United Nations that there seemed to be growing support among the delegates for sterner measures to enforce North Korean compliance with the Security Council resolution of June 25. In Washington, President Truman pointed out Korea to reporters on a large globe in his office and said to an aide: "This is the Greece of the Far East. If we are tough enough now, there won't be any next step." [22] Members of the White House staff commented upon the president's mood of grim resolution. By 2 P.M., the military situation in South Korea had grown so desperate that President Syngman Rhee placed a personal telephone call to Washington to plead with President Truman to rescue his government from complete disaster. The president and secretary of state met in seclusion during the afternoon in order to plan the next steps. By evening they had agreed that the situation had become serious enough to warrant another full-scale conference at Blair House at 9 P.M.

"There was no doubt! The Republic of Korea needed help at once if it was not to be overrun," President Truman recalled in his *Memoirs* about the second conference.[23] Unless such help was immediately forthcoming, no further decisions regarding Korea would be necessary. Accordingly, the president proposed that the navy and air force be instructed to give the fullest possible support to the South Korean forces south of the thirty-eighth parallel. In addition, the president recommended stepped-up military aid to the Philippines and the French forces engaged in fighting Communist Viet Minh troops in Indochina. No mention was made

[21] Ibid.

[22] Beverly Smith, "The White House Story: Why We Went to War in Korea," *Saturday Evening Post*, 10 November 1951, p. 80.

[23] Truman, op. cit., vol. 2, p. 337.

of ground troops in Korea, but it was clear that American sea and air cover were logical preludes to such a commitment. That strong naval and air support would give the South Koreans sufficient superiority to render a ground commitment unnecessary was deemed unlikely. Ambassador Gross believed that the Security Council resolution could be "stretched" to cover the president's recommendation. The problem of possible Soviet or Chinese countermoves was discussed and the conclusion reached that neither the Soviet Union nor China was likely to intervene directly in Korea. Once again, the conferees drew historical analogies, this time from the Greek crisis of 1947 and the Berlin crisis of 1948. There, too, resolute American resistance had been successful. Support for the president's position was unanimous. As Defense Secretary Johnson was to recall later:

> If we wanted to oppose it, then was our time to oppose it. Not a single one of us did. There were some pointing out the difficulties . . . and then the President made his decision which . . . I thought was the right decision.[24]

Ambassador Jessup recalled that he "felt proud of President Truman" and General Bradley explained that "we did it so we wouldn't have one appeasement lead to another and make war inevitable." [25] The president confided to Acheson that "everything I have done in the last five years has been to try to avoid making a decision such as I had to make tonight." [26] In his *Memoirs*, he later recalled that "this was the toughest decision I had to make as President." [27]

By Tuesday, June 27, General MacArthur had been notified of the president's decision. His reaction was one of pleasant surprise since he had not expected such forceful action. At noon, the president and Acheson briefed a group of congressional leaders on the most recent developments. The responses in both the Senate and House were overwhelmingly favorable. While a few congressmen and senators questioned the president's authority to make these decisions without prior congressional approval, not a single legislator directly opposed the wisdom of the decision.

[24] Cited in Paige, op. cit., p. 179.
[25] Ibid.
[26] Smith, op. cit., p. 80.
[27] Truman, op. cit., vol. 2, p. 463.

During the afternoon, attention shifted from Washington to the United Nations. At 3 P.M., the Security Council met in one of the most dramatic sessions of its short history. There was considerable apprehension in the United States Mission that Ambassador Yakov A. Malik of the Soviet Union would be present in order to cast yet another veto. A great deal of thought had been given to this possibility and a contingency procedure, which would mobilize the General Assembly in the event of Security Council paralysis, was under active consideration. Just before the council meeting, Ambassadors Gross and Malik were lunching with Secretary General Lie and other UN delegates. As the delegates rose from the table, Lie approached Malik and told him that the interests of the Soviet Union demanded his participation in the meeting. "No, I will not go there," the Soviet delegate replied. Outside the restaurant Ambassador Gross heaved a huge sigh of relief.[28]

The Soviet absence from the council on that fateful afternoon has been the subject of a great deal of speculation. Most likely, it was a blunder. The cumbersome Soviet process for reaching decisions probably had left Malik without instructions on what to do in the Security Council. Hence, his only option was to be absent from the council altogether.

The American position was stated by chief delegate Warren R. Austin. The text of the resolution had been approved personally by President Truman. Its operative paragraph recommended "that Members of the United Nations furnish such assistance to the Republic of Korea as may be necessary to repel the armed attack and to restore international peace and security in the area." [29] The council had before it another report from the United Nations commission on Korea that stated that the North Korean regime was carrying out a "well-planned, concerted, and full-scale invasion of South Korea." [30] The council postponed a vote twice because the delegates of India and Egypt were waiting for instructions. Finally, just before midnight, the Security Council passed the American-sponsored resolution with the United Kingdom, France, China, Cuba, Ecuador, and Norway

[28] Paige, op. cit., p. 203.
[29] United Nations Document S/1508, 26 June 1950.
[30] United Nations Document S/1507, 26 June 1950.

supporting the United States; Egypt and India abstaining; Yugoslavia in opposition; and the Soviet Union absent. The Security Council had recommended military measures in order to stem the North Korean assault. At almost precisely the time of the voting, Seoul, the capital of South Korea, was taken by the North Korean army.

On the following morning, President Truman chaired a meeting of the National Security Council in Washington. The council had before it a report from General MacArthur stating that "the United States would have to commit ground troops if the thirty-eighth parallel were to be restored." [31] The president signed a bill to extend the Selective Service Act, but stopped short of ordering American ground forces into combat in Korea. That afternoon, amid loud acclaim by the press, General MacArthur flew to Korea to conduct a personal reconnaissance of the military situation. The *New York Times* commented editorially that:

> Fate could not have chosen a man better qualified to command the unreserved confidence of the people of this country. Here is a superb strategist and an inspired leader; a man of infinite patience and quiet stability under adverse pressure; a man equally capable of bold and decisive action.[32]

The president decided to wait for the general's report from the scene of battle before taking the crucial step of committing ground forces.

MacArthur, with a small group of advisers, surveyed "the dreadful backwash of a defeated and dispersed army" during a convoy ride toward Seoul. Thousands of southbound refugees clogged the roads, probably unaware that MacArthur was passing by. The South Korean army seemed to be in a state of complete and disorganized rout.[33] During his flight back to Tokyo, the general drafted a report to the president in which he made his position absolutely clear:

> The only assurance for holding the present line and the ability to regain the lost ground is through the introduction of United

[31] Roy E. Appleman, *South to the Naktong, North to the Yalu* (Washington, D.C.: Government Printing Office, 1960), p. 34.

[32] *New York Times*, 29 June 1950.

[33] Courtney Whitney, *MacArthur: His Rendezvous with History* (New York: Knopf, 1956), p. 327.

States ground combat forces into the Korean battle area. . . . Unless provision is made for the full utilization of the Army-Navy-Air team in this shattered area, our mission will at best be needlessly costly in life, money and prestige. At worst, it might even be doomed to failure.[34]

Specifically, the general declared that, if the president gave the authorization, he could "hold Korea with two American divisions." [35]

At the same time that MacArthur was drafting his report, the president held a press conference in Washington. One reporter wanted to know whether the United States was at war or not. "We are not at war," the president replied. When another reporter queried the president whether "it would be possible to call the American response a police action under the United Nations," Truman responded that this was exactly what it was. The action was being taken to help the United Nations repel a raid by a "bunch of bandits." [36] Later that evening, President Truman and Acheson considered an offer by President Chiang Kai-shek to send 33,000 Chinese Nationalist troops to Korea. The president was not inclined to accept the offer but delayed making a final decision.

General MacArthur's urgent recommendation to commit American ground forces in Korea reached Washington at dawn on June 30. "Time is of the essence and a clear-cut decision without delay is essential," the general insisted. At 5 A.M., Secretary of the Army Frank Pace, Jr., communicated MacArthur's recommendation to the president. Truman, without hesitation, approved the commitment of one regimental combat team. During the morning he met with the secretary of state and top military officials. At that conference it was decided to decline politely the Chinese Nationalist troop offer and to give General MacArthur "full authority to use the troops under his command." [37]

On the afternoon of June 30, Ambassador Austin informed the UN Security Council of the latest American decision. He emphasized again that the American action was being taken under

[34] Ibid., pp. 332–333.
[35] Marguerite Higgins, *War in Korea* (New York: Doubleday, 1951), p. 33.
[36] Paige, op. cit., p. 243.
[37] Truman, op. cit., vol. 2, p. 343.

the United Nations banner. Other members, however, would have to contribute if the Korean police action was going to be a genuine collective security measure. The United States had taken the lead in protecting the UN Charter. Now it was up to the others to assume their share of the responsibility.

In response to the Security Council resolution of June 27, Secretary General Lie had sent a cable to all member states asking for information on the nature and amount of assistance each member state was prepared to give. Of the fifty-nine replies, he felt fifty-three were generally favorable.[38] In concrete and specific terms, however, actual military contributions were slow in arriving. Within two weeks of the request, naval and air units from the United Kingdom, Australia, and New Zealand were actively involved and units from the Netherlands and Canada were on their way. By the middle of September, Lie reported that fourteen members other than the United States had contributed ground forces. From the beginning, the United States bore the main brunt of the fighting, with the Republic of Korea in second place. By services, the American contribution was 50 percent of the ground forces, 85 percent of the naval forces, and 93 percent of the air forces. The respective contributions of South Korea were 40 percent, 7 percent, and 5 percent.[39] From these figures it is evident that the contributions of other UN members remained small indeed. While the military contributions were disproportionate throughout the Korean War, it must be noted that thirty governments decided to render supplementary assistance in the form of field hospitals, blood plasma, rice, and soap. Iceland, for example, made a contribution of cod-liver oil for the troops.

In view of the predominant role played by the United States, the Security Council, on July 7, 1950, decided to establish a "Unified Command" under the leadership of the United States and to authorize this command to use the United Nations flag. On the following day, President Truman designated General MacArthur as supreme commander of the United Nations forces. The general, however, also retained his title of commander in chief of the United States forces in the Far East. MacArthur viewed his

---

[38] *United Nations Bulletin*, 15 July and 1 August 1950, pp. 50–53, 95, 99.

[39] Leland M. Goodrich, *Korea: A Study of U.S. Policy in the United Nations* (New York: Council on Foreign Relations, 1956), p. 117.

connection with the United Nations as nominal and continued to receive his instructions directly from the president. On August 1, when Yakov Malik, the Soviet representative, returned to the Security Council and assumed the presidency of that body, the council went into eclipse. On September 6, the Soviet Union cast its first veto on the Korean problem and thus removed any further possibility of using the Security Council to direct the UN action in Korea.

When the UN General Assembly met in mid-September, it was confronted with a dramatic change in the military situation in Korea. On September 15, General MacArthur had executed a daring amphibious landing at Inchŏn which took the North Koreans by complete surprise. Two weeks later, the North Koreans were in full retreat and the United Nations forces, in hot pursuit, had reached the thirty-eighth parallel. The question that now confronted the United States and UN General Assembly was whether the UN forces should cross into North Korea. A desperate crisis had suddenly been resolved and an attractive new possibility had arisen: the invader was on the run and could now be taught a lesson. This possibility, however, raised serious questions of tactics as well as of policy, which had to be quickly resolved. The relationship between the United States and the United Nations had to be clarified, especially the role of the supreme commander, General MacArthur. The possible responses of the two great Communist powers, China and the Soviet Union, to a UN crossing of the parallel had to be weighed. The sudden successes of MacArthur's forces, in short, presented entirely new challenges. But only a few weeks later, these events were to precipitate a massive military intervention by China and—in General MacArthur's words—an "entirely new war."

GENERAL MACARTHUR'S GAMBLE

Two explosive events brought the United Nations forces face to face with China on the battlefields of Korea: first, the crossing of the thirty-eighth parallel in October 1950 and, second, the drive toward the Chinese border at the Yalu River in November 1950. Crucial to both events was the personality of General MacArthur, who was widely acclaimed as, and probably believed himself to be, America's greatest living soldier. The startling success of his Inchŏn landing had made the general's confidence in his own military genius unshakable. President Truman and his secretary of state had full confidence in America's most honored soldier and believed the armed might of the United States to be invincible. Despite all this, the United Nations Unified Command was badly mauled in its first encounter with Chinese troops, and MacArthur suffered the worst defeat in his entire military career. An analysis of the outbreak of this "entirely new war" may help explain this paradox.

As the United Nations forces approached the parallel, the problem of whether to cross it or not presented the Unified Command with an acute dilemma. On the one hand, it was impossible to achieve total defeat of the North Korean invaders if the United Nations forces were not allowed to cross the parallel. It could be argued that the North Korean attack had destroyed whatever sanctity the thirty-eighth parallel had as a boundary and that the "hot pursuit" of the invader was therefore perfectly in order. On the other hand, if the mission of the Unified Command was merely to "repel the armed attack," then it could be argued that the UN forces should not be permitted to cross into territory that was not a recognized part of the Republic of Korea before the North Korean attack occurred. Moreover, there was the important question: Who was to decide whether United Nations forces should cross the parallel, and, if so, for what purpose and within what limits? Finally, there was on record an explicit warning that had been made by Indian Ambassador K. M. Panikkar in Peking: if United Nations forces were to cross the parallel, China would probably enter the war.[40]

In view of these conflicting considerations, there was considerable initial confusion over the matter. President Truman's first response on September 22, 1950 was to let the United Nations make the decision.[41] Less than a week later, however, he apparently changed his mind and instructed Secretary Acheson to declare that the resolutions passed by the Security Council in June and July gave the Unified Command the necessary authority to cross the parallel. This was also the view held by General Mac-

[40] K. M. Panikkar, *In Two Chinas* (London: Allen and Unwin, 1955), p. 110.
[41] *New York Herald Tribune*, 22 September 1950.

Arthur and the Joint Chiefs of Staff. MacArthur, in particular, was of the opinion that the resolution of June 27 gave ample authority to cross the parallel. He felt that he required broad and flexible powers and that the safety of his troops rendered impractical any restrictions placed upon him. This view evidently impressed the president and his top advisers. As it turned out, it was never seriously disputed by most other member states at the United Nations.

When the UN General Assembly met in late September, most delegations were quite willing to follow the leadership of the United States. In view of the fact that the United States had been the first to come to the assistance of South Korea, and had now apparently reversed the scales of battle in favor of the UN forces, this willingness to accept the American lead was considered quite natural. Ambassador Austin set forth the American position in a major speech before the General Assembly on September 30. He argued the case for crossing the parallel in the strongest possible terms:

> The artificial barrier which has divided North and South Korea has no basis for existence either in law or in reason. Neither the United Nations, its Commission on Korea, nor the Republic of Korea recognizes such a line. Now, the North Koreans, by armed attack upon the Republic of Korea, have denied the reality of such a line.[42]

The United States took the lead in drafting an eight power resolution calling for the taking of appropriate steps "to insure conditions of stability throughout Korea" and "the establishment of a unified, independent and democratic Government in the sovereign State of Korea." [43] Apart from the Soviet bloc, there was little opposition, and the final vote on October 7 was forty-seven in favor, five opposed, and seven abstentions.[44] The UN General Assembly had now placed its seal of approval on the twin American objectives of destroying the North Korean forces and of unifying the entire country under the flag of the UN command.

On October 8, General MacArthur, speaking as United Na-

---

[42] United Nations General Assembly, *Official Records*, fifth Session, first Committee, 30 September 1950, p. 39.

[43] Ibid.

[44] The negative votes were cast by Byelorussia, Czechoslovakia, Poland, the Ukraine, and the USSR. Abstaining were Egypt, India, Lebanon, Saudi Arabia, Syria, Yemen, and Yugoslavia.

tions commander in chief, called upon the North Korean army to surrender and to "cooperate fully with the United Nations in establishing a unified, independent, democratic government of Korea." [45] He informed the North Korean authorities that, unless a favorable response was forthcoming immediately, he would "at once proceed to take such military action as may be necessary to enforce the decrees of the United Nations." The ultimatum was drafted personally by MacArthur and the style and phraseology were unmistakably his own.

There is no evidence to suggest that President Truman's position on the question of crossing the thirty-eighth parallel differed from that of the general. The president and his top aides felt that by its aggression North Korea had forfeited any right that it might previously have had to prevent the execution of the UN's decree by force. Neither the fact that the UN General Assembly lacked the legal authority to legislate decrees nor that its recommendation of October 7 had only been partially accepted, deterred the American leadership from declaring its own military objectives as identical with those of the United Nations. And neither the fact that the Soviet Union had advisers with the North Korean army down to the battalion level nor that China had issued a stern warning deterred General MacArthur from crossing the parallel and initiating a rapid advance toward the Chinese border at the Yalu River.

South Korean troops crossed the parallel into the North on October 1 and the first American forces, the United States First Cavalry Division, followed suit on October 7. Ambassador Panikkar issued his warning on October 2, and, on October 10, China's foreign minister, Chou En-lai, announced that "the Chinese people [would] not stand idly by in the war of invasion." These warnings received only passing attention in Washington and Tokyo. The tendency among American government officials was to dismiss them as Chinese bombast.

On October 15, however, President Truman and General MacArthur met on Wake Island. As a result of the increasing frequency of Chinese warnings, the president had become sufficiently concerned to ask the general for a professional assessment about the possibility of Chinese intervention. MacArthur considered this possibility remote:

[45] *New York Times*, 9 October 1950.

Had they interfered in the first or second month, it would have
been decisive. We are no longer fearful of their intervention. We
no longer stand hat in hand. The Chinese have 300,000 men in
Manchuria. Of these, probably not more than 100 to 125,000 are
distributed along the Yalu River. They have no Air Force. Now
that we have bases for our Air Force in Korea, if the Chinese
tried to get down to Pyongyang, there would be the greatest
slaughter.[46]

Four days later, when MacArthur's forces entered P'yŏngyang,
the State Department also came to the conclusion that Chinese
intervention in Korea was "unlikely." In the opinion of one leading authority:

> This assessment was by no means confined to the department over
> which Acheson presided. It was shared alike by the President, the
> Joint Chiefs of Staff, members of the National Security Council,
> General Walter Bedell Smith, Director of Central Intelligence,
> prominent senators, congressmen, and political pundits of all
> hues. If questioned, that amorphous character "the man in the
> street" would have expressed the same opinion.[47]

Nevertheless, at the very time that the American leadership denied the possibility of Chinese intervention, the Chinese Fourth
Field Army crossed the Yalu and penetrated the ragged mountain
terrain of North Korea.

Truman and MacArthur were convinced that China neither
would nor could intervene in Korea and relied on frequent pronouncements of America's nonaggressive intentions to reassure the
Chinese leaders. On November 16, the president declared that the
United States had "never at any time entertained any intention
to carry hostilities into China." [48] He added that, "because of
the long-standing American friendship for the people of China,
the United States [would] take every honorable step to prevent
any extension of the hostilities in the Far East." [49] Thus, American policy makers chose to view the tension between America

---

[46] U.S. Senate, *Military Situation in the Far East*, hearings before the Committee on Armed Services and the Committee on Foreign Relations, 82nd
Congress, 1st session, 1950, p. 3483.

[47] Samuel B. Griffith, *The Chinese People's Liberation Army* (New York:
McGraw-Hill, 1967), p. 124.

[48] *New York Times*, 17 November 1950.

[49] Ibid.

and China as a passing phenomenon and felt that assurances of goodwill toward China would suffice to insulate the Korean conflict from Chinese intervention. Operating upon the assumption of long-standing Sino-American friendship, both Truman and Mac-Arthur were deeply astonished at the rising tone of violence in Chinese statements during the month of October. They simply did not see the intervention coming. That the illusion of a firm Sino-American friendship underlying a Communist veneer persisted in the face of growing evidence to the contrary suggests that the United States was not yet prepared to take the new China seriously. Her statements were not as yet considered credible. So far as Ambassador Panikkar's warning was concerned, neither Truman nor MacArthur took it seriously. Truman viewed it as "a bold attempt to blackmail the United Nations" and later observed in his *Memoirs* that "Mr. Panikkar had in the past played the game of Chinese Communists fairly regularly, so that his statement could not be taken as that of an impartial observer." [50]

On the other side of the Yalu, the Chinese leaders regarded the United States as the heir to Japan's imperialist ambitions in Asia. They became increasingly convinced that only a powerful intervention in Korea would prevent the United States from invading China. As one scholar of Chinese-American relations has noted:

> While Secretary Acheson was talking about the traditional friendship of America, the Chinese Communists were teaching their compatriots that from early nineteenth century onward the United States had consistently followed an aggressive policy toward China which culminated in her support for Chiang Kai-shek in the civil war and her present actions in Korea and Taiwan. The Chinese people were told to treat the United States with scorn because she was a paper tiger and certainly could be defeated.[51]

Truman and MacArthur perceived a China that no longer existed. The conviction that China would not intervene represented an emotional rather than an intellectual conclusion, an ascription to the enemy of intentions compatible with the desires

[50] Truman, op. cit., vol. 2, p. 362.
[51] Tang Tsou, *America's Failure in China*, 1941–1950 (Chicago: University of Chicago Press, 1963), p. 578.

of Washington and Tokyo.[52] This misperception prepared the ground for a military disaster of major proportions.

If the Americans misperceived Chinese intentions by refusing to take them seriously, the Chinese erred in the opposite direction. The world as viewed from Peking presented a picture of implacable American hostility. Not only were American troops marching directly up to the Chinese border at the Yalu River, but the United States was protecting the hated Nationalist regime on Taiwan and was aiding the French against the revolutionaries in Indochina. In addition, the United States was rehabilitating and rearming Japan. With this kind of outlook, it was hardly surprising that the Chinese leaders regarded verbal protestations of goodwill on the part of the United States a mockery.

Most basic to an understanding of MacArthur's drive to the Yalu was his peculiar perception of China's power. Despite the fact that the general characterized China as a nation lusting for expansion, he had a curious contempt for the Chinese soldier. He equated the highly indoctrinated and well-disciplined Communist soldier of 1950 with the demoralized Nationalist soldier of 1948. To be blunt, he did not respect his enemy, and this disrespect was to cost him dearly.

Far from regarding the Chinese as military equals, MacArthur insisted that "the pattern of the Oriental psychology [was] to respect and follow aggressive, resolute and dynamic leadership, to quickly turn on a leadership characterized by timidity or vacillation." [53] This paternalistic and contemptuous view of the military power of the new China led directly to disaster in October and November 1950. The story is worth reviewing in some detail.

On October 26, to the accompaniment of fierce bugle calls, shrill whistles, and blasts on shepherd's horns, the Chinese launched a surprise attack on South Korean and American forces some fifty miles south of the Chinese border. The results were devastating. Several United Nations regiments were virtually decimated. Nevertheless, Major General Charles A. Willoughby, MacArthur's main intelligence officer, still voiced the opinion on the following day that "the auspicious time for Chinese intervention [had] long since passed" and that "there [was] no positive evi-

---

[52] Griffith, op. cit., p. 124.
[53] Douglas MacArthur, Message to Veterans of Foreign Wars, 28 August 1950.

dence that Chinese Communist units, as such, [had] entered Korea." [54] On November 1, the Chinese initiated a massive attack against the United States Third Battalion and virtually tore it apart. Then, after shattering the United States Eighth Cavalry, the Chinese abruptly broke contact and withdrew.

Harry Truman was shocked by the Chinese intervention. He concluded that MacArthur had given him bad advice on Wake Island. His instinct was to cut his losses and contain the war. Fatefully, however, he vacillated and, for a few crucial months, permitted MacArthur to make crucial decisions on the battlefield that were to cost the United States dearly.

MacArthur's reaction to the Chinese intervention reveals the classic mentality of the crusader. His wishes, not the facts, determined policy. On the day of the Chinese disengagement, his estimate of total Chinese strength in Korea was between 40,000 and 60,000 men.[55] In fact, as of October 31, the Chinese had deployed, in utmost secrecy and within short distances of the American forces they were about to strike, almost 200,000 men.[56] Some of these had crossed the Yalu before the Wake Island meeting between Truman and MacArthur.

The Chinese troops had done what MacArthur had deemed impossible. They had moved by night in forced marches, employed local guides and porters, and used the barren and hostile terrain of the North Korean hills to their advantage. Then they launched their assault on MacArthur's unsuspecting army. When the Chinese temporarily withdrew, MacArthur immediately ascribed this turn of events to the heavy casualties the enemy had sustained. The Chinese needed to rest, in MacArthur's view, and, hence, a golden opportunity was at hand for a second and victorious American drive to the Yalu.

In retrospect it is clear that:

> The Chinese withdrawal in early November was designed to encourage the enemy's arrogance; to lure the UN forces deeper into North Korea, where their tenuous supply lines could be interdicted and where units separated from one another by the broken terrain could be isolated and annihilated. This was the nature of

[54] *Military Situation in the Far East*, op. cit., p. 3427.
[55] Griffith, op. cit., p. 134.
[56] Ibid., p. 129.

the deadly trap which P'eng, at his Shenyang headquarters, was setting for the overconfident general in the Dai Ichi Building in Tokyo.[57]

Thus, MacArthur, believing that he was faced with 40,000 instead of 200,000 Chinese soldiers and believing that these soldiers were badly in need of rest after their encounter with the American army, advanced northward again for the "final offensive." The Chinese watched for three weeks and, finally, on November 27, attacked in overwhelming force, turning the American advance into a bloody rout. Thus, a peasant army put to flight a modern Western military force commanded by a world-famous American general. In one bound, China had become a world power, and the image of the Chinese ward, almost half a century in the making, was finally shattered at a cost of tens of thousands of battle casualties on both sides. MacArthur, incredibly enough, did not learn much from the experience. In the words of his aide-de-camp, Major General Courtney Whitney, the general "was greatly saddened as well as angered at this despicably surreptitious attack, a piece of treachery which he regarded as worse even than Pearl Harbor."[58] The stark truth was that MacArthur had blundered into the trap of his own rigidity.

This paternalistic attitude toward Communist China died hard. It remained extremely difficult for MacArthur to admit that the new China was growing in power and was fiercely hostile, and that this attitude was more than a passing phenomenon. Many rationalizations were invoked to explain this disturbing new presence on the world scene. Communism was viewed as somehow "alien" to the "Chinese character." It would pass, leaving the "traditional friendship" between China and America to reassert itself—although the paternalism implicit in this traditional friendship was never admitted.[59] At other times, Chinese hostility to the United States was explained as the result of the evil influence of the Soviet Union:

> On November 27, immediately following Mr. Vyshinsky's statement of charges of aggression against the U.S., the United States

[57] Ibid., p. 134.

[58] Whitney, op. cit., p. 394.

[59] Allen S. Whiting, *China Crosses the Yula* (Stanford: Stanford University Press, 1960), pp. 169–170.

representative in this Committee [one of the United Nations], Ambassador Dulles . . . with a feeling of sadness rather than anger, said one could only conclude that the Soviet Union was trying to destroy the long history of close friendship between China and the United States and to bring the Chinese people to hate and, if possible, to fight the United States.[60]

One of the more bizarre examples of this attempt to maintain old attitudes in the face of bewildering new facts was the brief flurry in the press during December 1950 concerning the possibility of a United Nations military action in China—directed not against the Chinese people, but against the Mao faction, which was presumed to be their oppressor. A headline in The *New York Herald Tribune* proclaimed "Declaration of State of War Against Mao's Faction Urged" and stated in the text: "So far as can be determined now, the action of the UN will not be one of war against China or the Chinese people but against one faction in China, namely the Communists." [61] How this distinction was to be put into effect on the battlefield was never made clear, and apparently the utterly unrealistic nature of the proposal lead to its early death. Nevertheless, the distinction between the Chinese people and their Communist leaders persisted for some time. MacArthur, too, subscribed to it, as did leading State Department officials. On December 29, 1950, in a statement for the Voice of America, Dean Rusk, then assistant secretary of state for Far Eastern affairs, accused the Chinese Communists of having plotted the North Korean assault. The press reported: "As all American officials have done consistently, Mr. Rusk drew a distinction between the Chinese people, for whom the United States has a long tradition of friendliness, and their Communist rulers." [62] By denying that the new government of China had a power base and a measure of popular support, these American leaders tried to maintain intact their old illusions about the historical relationship between the two nations. But that relationship had been a predatory one, and it was precisely this that was never admitted.

Indian Ambassador Panikkar detected this blind spot in the American picture of China. He noted that in the early days of

---

[60] United States Mission to the United Nations, Press Release No. 1129, 2 February 1951.

[61] *New York Herald Tribune*, 6 December 1950.

[62] *New York Herald Tribune*, 30 December 1950.

the Korean War, the Western military attachés in Peking had been utterly confident that Chinese troops could not possibly stand up to the Americans. The American defeat in late November, he noticed, came as a profound shock to them, and their attitude thenceforth was very different.[63] In a good summation of the problem, he stated: "China had become a Great Power and was insisting on being recognized as such. The adjustments which such a recognition requires are not easy, and the conflict in the Far East is the outcome of this contradiction." [64]

The Chinese intervention in the Korean War provides a good illustration of the practical, operational consequences of divergent perceptions in foreign policy decisions. These perceptions are, in effect, definitions of the situation at hand. Once the situation has been defined, certain alternatives are eliminated. One does not conciliate an opponent who is perceived as implacably hostile; hence, the Chinese Communists felt in the end that they had no resort but to intervene in Korea. One does not credit the threats of an opponent whose power one feels to be negligible; hence, the American leaders perceived even specific Chinese warnings as bluff. One does not compromise with an opponent whose ideology is perceived as antithetical to one's own values; hence, the United States and China remained poised on the brink of potentially disastrous conflict, neither one accepting the other's perception of its world role as legitimate. This was the central significance of the "entirely new war" that was to ravage the peninsula for another two and a half years.

THE PRICE OF HUBRIS

The outbreak of the Korean War may be divided into three separate and distinct phases: President Truman's decision to repel the North Korean attack; his and MacArthur's decision to cross the thirty-eighth parallel; and MacArthur's drive to the Yalu River that provoked the Chinese intervention. It appears that the first decision was correct, the second dubious, and the third disastrous.

When President Truman made his decision to commit Amer-

[63] Panikkar, op. cit., p. 117.
[64] Ibid., pp. 177–178.

ican ground forces in Korea, Stalin was still alive and the global Communist movement still intact. China and the Soviet Union had just concluded an alliance. Korea was a test of whether the Communist movement was able to impose itself through direct invasion upon the territory of another political entity, or whether that attack could be stemmed through collective action led by the United States.

The president's early decisions were firm, yet graduated: a full week elapsed between his initial response and the infantry commitment. During that week, his top advisers were fully heard on several occasions and their support remained virtually unanimous throughout. The North Koreans had ample opportunity to stop their invasion and thus avoid a full-scale collision with American power. Instead, they pressed the attack and escalated the ferocity of the initial encounter. Finally, even though the president "jumped the gun" on the United Nations by twenty-four hours, he quite genuinely perceived his action as taken on behalf of the principle of collective security set forth in the United Nations Charter.

Temptation beckoned when the tide of battle turned decisively in favor of the Unified Command. Initially, neither President Truman nor General MacArthur contemplated the seizure of North Korea, but the success of the Inchŏn landing provided the opportunity to turn the tables and to invade the invader. At this critical juncture, the general, now speaking as a "United Nations commander," insisted on forging ahead, and the president gave his permission. The United Nations was treated rather cavalierly, as little more than an instrument of American policy, and although the UN secretary general and most member states accepted their role rather meekly, they had serious inner doubts. A United Nations victory, had it occurred, would clearly have been a victor's peace.

Disaster struck at the Yalu, largely because of the hubris of General MacArthur. The UN commander lacked all respect for the new China and preferred, instead, to base his policies on hopes and fears rather than on realities and facts. *By provoking the Chinese intervention, MacArthur probably prolonged the war by another two and a half years and turned it into one of the bloodiest conflicts in recent history.* Aside from the 34,000 American dead, South Korea suffered over 800,000 casualties, and North

Korea more than 500,000. The Chinese suffered appalling casualties of more than one million men. The war ended indecisively in a draw, with the two Koreas remaining fully armed dictatorships, bitterly hostile to one another. The two truncated states were to menace and confront each other for another generation.

In the Korean War, the victim of aggression was tempted by aggression and succumbed to the temptation. The United Nations became a party to the war and remained identified with one side in the conflict to the end. Since its identity became fully merged with the American cause, it lost the power to be a truly neutral mediator in Korea. This is perhaps the clearest lesson of the outbreak of this war: as the United Nations was captured by one of the parties to the conflict and made into its instrument, all sides suffered in the long run including, in particular, the United Nations itself. No objective entity could now be called upon to act as referee or buffer. Hence, the fighting stopped only through exhaustion, when both sides finally despaired of victory. The hubris of General MacArthur had precipitated a world tragedy.

After China's entry into the war, the latent conflict between Truman and MacArthur erupted into the open. MacArthur repeatedly challenged Truman's role as the nation's spokesman on foreign policy. He made numerous public statements urging Generalissimo Chiang Kai-shek's participation in the war against Communist China. While Truman desperately wanted to keep the war limited and actively sought negotiations with the Chinese and the North Koreans, MacArthur urged the Communists to surrender to him and declared that there was "no substitute for victory." In the most flagrant manner, he challenged a time-honored American constitutional principle: civilian control over the military.

Truman, for once, was slow to act. For several months, after the Chinese intervention, he acquiesced in the general's policies even though they infuriated him. But when, in March 1951, MacArthur virtually demanded China's surrender, Truman had enough. It became clear to him that the difference between him and the general was unbridgeable: The president wanted the war to end while the general wanted it to continue. "I'll show that son of a bitch who's boss. Who does he think he is—God?" Truman exclaimed. General Omar Bradley, chairman of the Joint Chiefs of Staff, agreed. "The wrong war, at the wrong place, at the wrong time, with the wrong enemy," was the way he described MacArthur's strategy toward China. On April 30, 1951, Truman, finally dismissed MacArthur from all his commands—United Nations commander, United States commander in chief, Far East, and supreme commander for the Allied powers in Japan. MacArthur returned to the United States to a hero's welcome after an absence of fourteen years while Truman's popularity reached a new nadir. In some parts of the country, the president was burned in effigy. MacArthur's emotional appeal for victory over the Communist enemy was simply more seductive than Truman's policy of long-term, patient containment. Only the passage of time would vindicate the president.

In its essence, the Truman-MacArthur controversy was a conflict between a pragmatist and a crusader. MacArthur's drive to the Yalu had trapped Truman. Once the president had accepted the general's judgment that the Chinese would not intervene, he had to face the awesome consequence: a limited war with China. But the war never became his personal crusade and never engaged his self-esteem in a contest of courage between himself and the Chinese. His mistake was one of excessive trust in the information he had received. But unlike Woodrow Wilson before him and Lyndon Johnson after him, he never committed himself rigidly to a failing policy. He never froze. His character, unlike MacArthur's, never demanded victory over Communist China. Other alternatives always remained open, including negotiation and peace by compromise. Nonetheless, it took two more years and hundreds of thousands of lives—American, Korean, and Chinese—to bring a fragile peace to Korea. The crusading spirit had taken its terrible toll.

And yet, events could have taken an even more dreadful turn. Supposing that Harry Truman had not been the open-minded pragmatist he was, or that MacArthur had been president. A crusader would probably not have kept the limited war against China limited. The United States would probably have been drawn into a major Asian land war. The Soviet Union, still allied with China in 1950, might have been drawn into the conflict. A nuclear holocaust might have ensued. Truman, however, was never victimized by the crusading passion. No obsession ruled him. Time and distance have vindicated many of his decisions. His mistakes never paralyzed him. He generally grew from them, and acted again and again, based on the accumulating facts of his experience. Korea was no exception to this rule, though the final outcome was far from satisfactory. Two hostile Koreas continued to face each other in an uneasy truce. Yet, had it not been for Harry Truman, things might have been far worse. The nuclear abyss might have then been a very real possibility.

ROLLBACK
AND RESPONSE

The Korean War was the first war fought by the United States that did not end in victory. General Douglas MacArthur's flat assertion that there was "no substitute for victory" had struck a deep responsive chord in the American people. The frustration and impatience with an inconclusive war led to a general attack on the containment policy. Korea became the Achilles heel of the Truman presidency and the dismissal of one general thus led to the election of another. The Republican victory of 1952 signaled the beginning of an evangelical era in American foreign policy. The world was divided into two armed camps: the moral and the immoral; the free and the unfree; the children of light and the children of darkness.

President Dwight D. Eisenhower, one of the heroes of the Second World War, had received a large popular mandate. "I shall go to Korea," the general had pledged during his campaign for the presidency. And, indeed, a truce was signed at P'anmunjŏm in July 1953, only a short distance from the thirty-eighth parallel where the war had broken out three years before. As president, however, Eisenhower played a fairly passive role, especially in the conduct of foreign policy. When Secretary of Defense Charles E. Wilson came to him too often with details, Ike was blunt: "Look here, Charlie, I want *you* to run Defense. We *both* can't run it, and I *won't* run it. I was elected to worry about a lot of things other than the day-to-day operations of a department." [1]

---

[1] Barber, op. cit., p. 163.

His heart attack in September 1955 was triggered, Eisenhower said, when he was repeatedly interrupted on the golf links by unnecessary phone calls from the State Department.[2] He did deal with problems at a high level of policy, but did so reluctantly. He resisted a major American involvement in Indochina, for example, overruling both his vice-president and secretary of state, because he did not want the nation to become bogged down in another Asian land war. And he had to immerse himself more in foreign policy matters after the secretary of state was stricken with cancer in 1956. But, on the whole, Eisenhower was inclined not to be "bothered" and hence his advisers were disinclined to "bother" him. Thus, the less he was bothered, the less he knew, and the less he knew, the more dependent he became on his advisers. Thus, Eisenhower, a man of immense popularity and goodwill, during most of the eight years of his presidency, chose not to steer the ship of state. Instead, he delegated.

The main architect of Dwight D. Eisenhower's foreign policy was John Foster Dulles. The new president more than once referred to Dulles as an Old Testament prophet and, indeed, there were few who did not think of Dulles as a formidable figure. Like Wilson, the son of a Presbyterian minister, Dulles also attended Princeton and then embarked upon an extremely successful law career in the prestigious New York firm of Sullivan and Cromwell. Dulles's face was spare and elegant; his mouth was stern and turned down sharply at the edges. He smiled rarely and habitually adopted a severe, even censorious posture. His hands were usually thrust deep into his trouser pockets with his jacket pushed back like wings from his shoulders. When talking, he had the disconcerting habit of not looking at the person he was addressing but staring at the ceiling instead. He exuded great self-confidence and expounded freely on the virtues of spiritual strength. A devout Christian, he maintained a life-long affiliation with the National Council of Churches and believed deeply that the Communist system was inherently evil and immoral. "Bolshevism," he once said to the West German ambassador, "was a product of the Devil, but God would wear out the Bolsheviks in the long run." [3]

[2] Ibid., p. 159.

[3] Richard Challener, "John Foster Dulles: An Electronic Portrait," Lecture at Princeton University, 9 December 1970.

John Foster Dulles was the member of a remarkable family trio. His brother Allen had been inducted into the intelligence service during World War I, then joined the Office of Strategic Services (OSS) during World War II, and finally took over the direction of America's covert policy as head of the Central Intelligence Agency. His career was only eclipsed in 1961, when he advised John F. Kennedy to go ahead with the ill-fated refugee invasion at the Bay of Pigs in Cuba. Foster's sister, Eleanor, embarked on a scholarly career and established her expertise in international economics and German and Austrian affairs, eventually joining the State Department. Foster assumed the leadership position in the family. He was older than the others and Eleanor and Allen often deferred to his authority. His certainty about the rightness of his opinions and conduct was reinforced by his conviction that he was carrying out God's work in an unhappy and, at times, satanic world. He served in a variety of advisory roles under both Roosevelt and Truman and helped the latter in the fashioning of a peace treaty with Japan in 1951. A faithful Republican throughout, however, his greatest opportunity came only when Eisenhower was elected to the presidency.

Little wonder that a man like Dulles, cast in the mold of the old Puritans, would find the containment policy wanting. A bolder approach would have to be fashioned. In the first place, the Soviet Union would have to be surrounded by an iron ring of alliances that left no loopholes for penetration. Dulles was convinced that the North Korean southward drive across the thirty-eighth parallel in 1950 had been the direct consequence of the Truman administation's implication that Korea lay outside the American defense perimeter. This would not happen again. But second, and equally important, a "liberation program" would have to be adopted for the nations that were the captives of the Soviet Union. Containment was not enough. A policy of rollback, of liberation would be initiated. The clarion call of freedom, Dulles hoped, would bring the walls of communism tumbling down.

Shortly before the Republican convention of 1952, Dulles published an article in *Life* magazine, entitled "A Policy of Boldness." In it, he developed the two tracks of his proposed policy. First, the network of alliances must be impregnable and defended with America's atomic might. The "free world," in his words, "must develop the will and organize the means to retaliate in-

stantly against open aggression by Red armies, so that if it occurred anywhere, we could and would strike back where it hurts
by means of our choosing." In other words, if sufficiently provoked,
the United States would respond massively, with hydrogen bombs,
if necessary. And second, Dulles insisted that indefinite coexistence
with the Soviet Union was unworthy of American objectives. The
Communist threat should be removed completely. "It is ironic and
wrong," he wrote "that we who believe in the boundless power of
human freedom should so long have accepted a static role." The
United States should be able to cut the Soviet Union down to
size. The United States "should make it publicly known that it
wants and expects liberation to occur. The mere statement of
that wish and expectation would change, in an electrifying way,
the mood of the captive peoples. It would probably put heavy new
burdens on the jailers and create new opportunities for liberation."
America's cause was morally just and would triumph in the end.
The children of light would prevail over the children of darkness.

A good case can be made for the proposition that the liberation policy was designed "to roll back the Democrats in the United
States, not the Red Army in Eastern Europe." [4] Certainly, the
country yearned for a more vigorous anti-Communist policy and
an end to Koreatype impasses and ambiguities. Senator Joseph
McCarthy's hold on the American public and his ability to manipulate it were indications of a rising mood of danger and frustration. Rollback and liberation, even if unattainable, made good
therapy for a nation that had not yet accepted the fact that its
power in the world was not unlimited.

McCarthy's power had reached its zenith in the early 1950s.
Many Americans were disillusioned with the postwar world. Half
of Europe had gone Communist. So had China. Why were the
Russians "winning"? Joe McCarthy had a clear-cut answer. The
Russians were "winning" because the American people had been
too trusting. The nation was shot through with secret Commu-
nists in high places, eager to sell their country out to Moscow.
And these traitors must be hunted out if America were to survive.
A large portion of the population thought McCarthy was right.
A minority believed him to be a liar and a wanton destroyer of
reputations, but they were afraid to say so.

[4] John Spanier, *American Foreign Policy Since World War II*, 7th ed. (New
York: Praeger, 1977), p. 103.

John Foster Dulles, a pillar of the Church, believer in Christian charity, and a man of impeccable morals, was known to dislike the demagogic senator from Wisconsin. Nonetheless, his attitude toward him can only be described as craven. He assembled the staff of the State Department and demanded of them "positive loyalty." He fired several leading diplomats and Foreign Service officers—in particular John Paton Davies, John Service, and John Carter Vincent—who had predicted the rise of Mao Tse-tung in China. McCarthy had charged that Davies and Vincent were secret agents of the Communists. Even though their dossiers showed clearly that they were loyal Americans, Dulles dismissed them, not as McCarthy had charged, for "treachery and deceit," but for "stupidity and incompetence." They had dared to forecast that Chiang Kai-shek would lose his hold on China and that the Communists would drive him out. The messengers who brought bad news, even though correct, had to be removed. Similarly, Dulles permitted George Kennan, the author of the containment policy, to retire from the State Department without even a letter of appreciation. And· he refused to ride in the same car with Charles Bohlen when that solid Foreign Service officer came under McCarthy's scrutiny during the confirmation hearings over his appointment as ambassador to Moscow. Thus, a number of distinguished careers were blighted and destroyed because of the active hostility or lack of support of the secretary of state. All in all, it was a melancholy performance by a man who purported to believe in the Christian virtues.

Consistent with his purpose to quarantine the Devil, Dulles now set about to ring the Sino-Soviet bloc with a "frontier" of alliances. The Democrats, through NATO in 1949, had already drawn a defense line in Europe, from Norway to Turkey. It now remained to extend that line to Asia and to the Middle East. Thus, in June 1953, the Korean War was concluded after three years of fighting, near the thirty-eighth parallel, almost exactly where it had begun. Shortly afterward, the United States signed a mutual security pact with South Korea, designed as a deterrent against another attack from the North.

The Southeast Asian Treaty Organization (SEATO), which Dulles intended to be an Asian NATO, had its origins in the French debacle in Indochina. France had been fighting a war there against Ho Chi Minh's guerrillas since 1946. Dulles, convinced that China would intervene on the side of Ho against France,

similar to the manner in which it had intervened on the side of
North Korea against the United States, extended massive military assistance to France. By 1954, the United States was paying
over one-half of the cost of the Indochina war. Despite this massive infusion of aid, however, France's position worsened and,
finally, at the fortress of Dien Bien Phu, the French made their
last stand. The commander of the French forces in Indochina informed President Eisenhower that unless the United States intervened with combat troops, Indochina would be lost. Secretary
Dulles and Vice-President Richard Nixon recommended military
intervention but both were overruled by Eisenhower.

The Geneva conference of mid-1954 marked the exit of France
from Indochina, and the formation of SEATO, a few weeks later,
marked the beginning of American involvement. Geneva set up
three independent sovereign states: Laos, Cambodia, and Vietnam. The accords on Vietnam provided for a "provisional military demarcation line" at the seventeenth parallel. The unification
of Vietnam was to be brought about through a general election
two years hence.

The United States never signed the Geneva Accords. Dulles
perceived them as a well-laid Communist trap to engulf all of
Vietnam. Eisenhower agreed. As he put it in 1954: "Had elections
been held as of the time of the fighting, possibly 80 percent of the
population would have voted for the Communist Ho Chi Minh
as their leader rather than Chief of State Bao Dai." [5]

During the course of the Geneva conference an interesting
event took place. Chou En-lai, quite by accident, ran into John
Foster Dulles in one of the corridors of Geneva's Palais des Nations. The Chinese statesman stretched out his hand to Dulles in a
gesture of reconciliation, but the American put his hands behind
his back and walked away. A good Puritan would have no commerce with the Devil. It is tempting to speculate about the reper-
cussions of this episode. What if Dulles had responded? Might
the Vietnam War have been avoided? We shall never know. But
one is forced to wonder.

Instead, Dulles's answer to Geneva was the creation of
SEATO, which linked the United States with Britain, France,

[5] Dwight D. Eisenhower, *Mandate for Change, 1953–1956* (New York:
Doubleday, 1963), p. 372.

Australia, New Zealand, Thailand, Pakistan, and the Philippines. The eight member states designated Cambodia, Laos, and South Vietnam to be under SEATO's protection. Thus, SEATO came into being to offset the effects of the Geneva Accords. The United States had stepped into France's shoes in Indochina. The East-West cold war had superseded a colonial war. SEATO, however, never attained the strength of NATO nor was it a genuine multilateral alliance. Its essence was the unilateral commitment of the United States.

In late 1954, Dulles signed a defense treaty with the Chiang Kai-shek government on the island of Formosa. The generalissimo had fled there with almost two million soldiers in 1949 and regarded the Mao Tse-tung regime as a clique of bandits. Dulles, too, viewed the Peking government as anathema and regarded the Chiang Kai-shek regime as the government of "Free China." The Chinese Nationalist leader promised, however, not to attack the mainland without United States consent. In 1955, the situation became tense when the Chinese Communists shelled two offshore islands, Quemoy and Matsu. Dulles gave Chiang his assurance that the United States would defend the islands and the Seventh Fleet was ordered to patrol the Formosa straits. Thereafter, each side in the China conflict kept what it had and refrained from invading the other.

Thus, by 1955, Dulles had closed the Asian ring: at the thirty-eighth parallel in Korea, at the seventeenth parallel in Indochina, at the line drawn by SEATO, and in the Formosa straits. Later that year, he completed the line around the Sino-Soviet periphery by prevailing upon Britain to join with Turkey, Iraq, Iran, and Pakistan in the creation of a treaty organization. The Baghdad Pact as the treaty came to be called, extended the NATO line from Turkey to India. Within a little over a decade, the United States had changed from a "go it alone" policy to an alliance system of "going it with forty-two others." Dulles's critics referred to this policy as "pactomania." Harry Truman had begun this new collector's approach to alliances, but Dulles had clearly become its leading architect. He constantly appealed to neutral countries in the Third World to join this system of alliances. There was, to him, no room for neutrality in a struggle between Good and Evil. More than once, he called neutral nations that refused to join immoral.

All was not well, however, in the most important bulwark: NATO. Six Western European countries—France, Italy, West Germany, and the Benelux countries—were striving to form a European defense community. Dulles actively supported the idea. The EDC would have a unified command, common uniforms, and common pay scales for the soldiers. If constituted, such a European army would remove the traditional animosity between Germany and France: would make the necessity of German rearmament more palatable to other NATO members by subjecting West Germany's military forces to international control; and finally, it was hoped, would strengthen NATO by providing it with a truly supranational nucleus. The battle for ratification in the six parliaments raged from 1950 to 1954. Five had ratified. But on August 30, 1954, the French parliament rejected the proposed treaty, essentially because most Frenchmen still feared Germany more than they feared the Soviet Union. "They raped us three times in two generations," one parliamentarian exclaimed, "We are not going to marry them now." Dulles was furious. In early 1955, in an "agonizing reappraisal," he decided to admit West Germany to NATO as a sovereign state. To him, the German threat had been superseded by that posed by the Soviet Union. Britain and France were most unhappy with this decision and NATO came under considerable strain.

What about the rollback of Soviet power and liberation behind the Iron Curtain? Here the record is a melancholy one. In 1953, three months after the death of Stalin, the people of East Berlin revolted against their Soviet masters. Dulles expressed his support for the courageous East Berliners and had food packages sent to them. The revolt collapsed. In October 1956, there was an uprising in Poland and again, Dulles expressed his abhorrence for Soviet despotism, but did little more. And most tragically, when the Hungarians succeeded in throwing off the Soviet yoke for a few days in October 1956, and appealed for American help over Radio Budapest, Dulles publicly praised their heroism but simultaneously assured the Soviet Union that the United States was not about to intervene. Shortly afterward, Nikita Krushchev sent Soviet tanks to Budapest and crushed the uprising. The liberation policy suddenly looked like a gigantic bluff. When the Soviet Union called Dulles's hand, the emptiness of "liberation" was shockingly revealed. What had happened? Why did the clarion call to freedom expire in such a pathetic whimper?

The answer was quite simple. Dulles had combined his liberation policy with his "massive retaliation" threat. It was one thing to make such a threat, but it was quite another for an opponent to believe it. The Great Deterrent condemned the United States to an all-or-nothing strategy. It was useless against Soviet moves that did not justify an all-out war. To drop atom bombs on Moscow over an uprising in Hungary would have been disproportionate, to say the least. Hence, Dulles was suspended between Armageddon and paralysis. It was impossible to combine maximum horror with maximum credibility. The Soviet leaders simply did not believe that the United States would risk a nuclear war over Hungary or Poland. And they were right. Thus, "rollback" became containment once again and the liberation policy was bankrupt.

Shortly after the Hungarian fiasco, a young Harvard professor correctly perceived Dulles's dilemma: "If the Soviet bloc can present its challenges in less than all-out form, it may gain a crucial advantage. Every move on its part will then pose the appalling dilemma of whether we are willing to commit suicide to prevent encroachments, which do not, each in itself, seem to threaten our existence directly but which may be steps on the road to our destruction." [6] The young professor was Henry Kissinger.

John Foster Dulles's gravest challenge, however, came from a most unexpected quarter. In October 1956, America's two closest allies launched a major military attack against Egypt without warning the United States. For years, the American secretary of state had assembled allies against the Communists. And now, two NATO members, Britain and France, were apparently behaving as badly as the Soviet Union. Dulles's unique response to this world crisis had a decisive impact upon the future constellation of world politics. It demonstrated once again, how a single individual can change the course of history. If some other man had been the secretary of state in 1956, the results would have been quite different.

The Suez drama was played out in three stages. The first was Dulles's renege of a pledge to Egypt to finance the Aswan High Dam; the second was the Egyptian president's decision to nationalize the Suez Canal, followed by an intensive but futile search by Secretary Dulles for a compromise solution; in the third,

[6] Henry Kissinger, *Nuclear Weapons and Foreign Policy* (New York: Harper, 1957), p. 16.

Britain, France, and Israel made war on Egypt, and the United States, under Dulles's leadership, forced them to terminate their action. Egypt, with Soviet support, remained master of the Suez Canal. After sketching in the background, we shall trace the high points of this incredible story in which the personality of John Foster Dulles played such a decisive role.

4

EVANGELISM
AS FOREIGN POLICY
John Foster Dulles and
the Suez Crisis

Historical tragedies do not arise only from encounters in which right clashes with wrong. They also occur when right clashes with right. This is the heart of the conflict between Israel and the Arab states in Palestine. A large number of Jews, responding to the horror of Hitler's systematic policy of extermination, attempted to save themselves by creating a state of their own. They established it in a land that had been occupied by Arabs for centuries, at the precise moment when the Arab peoples were emerging from the crucible of Western colonialism and were rediscovering their own national destinies, Thus, Jewish nationalism clashed head-on with Arab nationalism in Palestine.

The Zionist movement was actually founded in 1897 by Theodor Herzl, an Austrian journalist, with the publication of a book entitled *The Jewish State* in which he urged the settlement of Jewish agriculturists and artisans in Palestine. These pioneers, Herzl hoped, would realize an ancient Jewish dream—the reestablishment of a Jewish homeland in the Promised Land and the gathering together of the Jewish people from the Diaspora of 2,000 years. Responding to Herzl's vision and reacting to anti-Semitic pogroms in Russia and Poland, 60,000 Jews emigrated to Palestine between 1881 and 1914. The land used for the Jewish settlements was purchased from absentee Arab landlords by wealthy philanthropists like Baron de Rothschild of Paris or through funds collected by the Zionists abroad. By 1914, almost 100,000 acres of Palestinian land had been purchased by the Jews.

In 1917, Chaim Weizmann, a scientist of world renown and a fervent Zionist, persuaded the British foreign minister, Lord Arthur James Balfour, to issue a proclamation that would convert Herzl's dream into a British pledge:

> His Majesty's Government view with favour the establishment in Palestine of a national home for the Jewish people, and will use their best endeavours to facilitate the achievement of this object, it being clearly understood that nothing shall be done which may prejudice the civil and religious rights of existing non-Jewish communities in Palestine, or the rights and political status enjoyed by Jews in any other country.

In 1922, Britain was given a League of Nations mandate over Palestine. In effect, this meant that Britain received the substance of sovereign control over Palestine. The league was entitled to a supervisory role, which it never in fact exercised. Palestine, therefore, between 1922 and 1948, was a thinly disguised British colony.

The Palestinian Arabs, understandably enough, objected to the Balfour Declaration and became increasingly uneasy about the large influx of Jewish immigrants. During the 1930s, when Hitler's persecution of European Jews was gathering increasing momentum, Jewish immigration soared dramatically. By 1937, the Jews constituted almost one-third of the total population of Palestine. Between 1928 and 1937, their number had risen from 150,000 to 400,000. As the Zionist movement looked toward Palestine as the last refuge from the impending Nazi holocaust, Arab alarm grew accordingly. It was no longer a question of land purchased by individual settlers but the threat of an alien state in a land that had been inhabited by Arabs for over one thousand years. The British, caught in a vise between their pledge to the Jews on the one hand, and to Arab oil and strategic interests on the other, tried to temporize, but finally placated the Arabs by imposing a ceiling on Jewish immigration. The Jews, in their plight, tried to run the British blockade. In most cases, the British intercepted the immigrant vessels and shipped the passengers to internment camps. In one particularly tragic case, the British sent the helpless Jews back to Germany. As one survivor put it: "The Germans killed us, and the British don't let us live." [1]

[1] John Neary, "The Bloody Dawn of Israel," *Life*, 15 May 1973, p. 28.

Despite the British blockade, tens of thousands of Jewish immigrants landed in Palestine illegallly. The Arabs became increasingly more restive, and bitter fighting erupted. The British, caught in the lines of fire, were unable to restore the peace. In 1947, in total frustration, Britain announced her intention to relinquish the mandate over Palestine and decided to place the entire problem before the forum of the United Nations.

A few months later, a newly constituted United Nations Special Committee on Palestine (UNSCOP) visited the area and examined the alternatives. After a highly charged debate, the committee finally recommended the partition of Palestine, with its population of 1.2 million Arabs and 570,000 Jews, into two states —one Arab and one Jewish—with Jerusalem held as trustee of the UN. The Jewish state would include 55 percent of the land and a 58 percent Jewish population; the Arab state, 45 percent of the land and a 99 percent Arab population. This partition plan was eagerly welcomed by the Jews and denounced with equal fervor by the Arabs.

On November 29, 1947, the partition resolution was adopted in the UN General Assembly by a vote of thirty-three in favor, thirteen against, and ten abstentions. The Zionists were ecstatic, but the Arabs vowed not to recognize the UN decision.

At 4 P.M. on May 14, 1948, two hours before the termination of the British mandate, the Zionist leader, David Ben-Gurion, announced the birth of Israel. A short time after Ben-Gurion's proclamation, Warren Austin, on the personal instruction of President Truman, announced that the United States had recognized the new state of Israel. Shortly thereafter, the Soviet delegate followed suit.

At dawn on May 15, Israel was simultaneously invaded by the Egyptian army from the south, the Transjordanian Arab Legion from the east, and the forces of Syria and Lebanon from the north.

At the end of several months of fierce fighting, interspersed by periods of truce, Israel was left in possession of the whole of Galilee, a section of central Palestine connecting the coastal area with Jerusalem, and the whole of the Negev. Jerusalem became a divided city. The entire area controlled by Israel in 1949 was somewhat larger than the area that had been allotted to the Zionists in the partition resolution of 1947. Thus, the Arab invasion had played into the hands of the Jews. Almost one million Arabs

were rendered homeless by the conflict and entered Syria, Trans-
jordan, and the Egyptian-controlled Gaza Strip as refugees. From
their midst would rise the fedayeen and the Palestinian resistance
fighters who would hold Israel responsible for the deprivation of
their homeland. Thus, the bloody birth of Israel set the stage for
a mortal conflict between two nationalisms—one Arab, the other
Jewish—both equally desperate and equally determined to secure
what to each was holy ground.

Time did not appease feelings after the conclusion of the
armistice agreements of 1949. On the Arab side, the plight of
almost 1 million refugees constituted, by their very existence, a
constant reminder of the alien Zionist presence. No matter how
defensive or conciliatory Israel's policy would be, this massive dis-
placement would make the Jewish state into a standing provocation in the eyes of the entire Arab world. The Jews, of course,
were fearful of allowing the refugees to return to their former
homes. How could 700,000 Jews risk the return of nearly 1 million Arabs to their land without also risking the destruction of the
Jewish state? And yet, how could they refuse it without inflicting
on innocent people the very injustice that they themselves suffered in the Diaspora? Thus, the Jews took back a few, com-
pensated some, but most continued to linger in refugee camps
in Jordan, Lebanon, Syria, and Egyptian-controlled Gaza. At the
same time, large numbers of Jews were driven out of Iraq, Yemen,
Egypt, and Morocco.

During the early 1950s, Palestinian Arab fedayeen from the
refugee population mounted raids on Israeli territory that steadily
increased in ferocity and frequency. The Israelis, in turn, engaged
in massive and powerful reprisals. Thus, despite the military armistice, a state of belligerency continued to exist.

In 1952, Gamal Abdel Nasser, who had distinguished himself
in the Palestine war, became the leader of Egypt and was soon
the unrivaled champion of Arab nationalism. He instituted a
blockade on Israeli shipping through the Suez Canal and, in 1953,
extended this blockade to include all goods being shipped to Israel. This left the Israelis with only one port, at Elat, at the head
of the Gulf of Aqaba in the Straits of Tiran. In late 1953, Nasser
began to restrict Israeli commerce through the straits by making
its ships subject to inspection by Egyptian coastguards. In 1955,
he broadened the blockade and included a ban on overflights by

Israeli aircraft. In Israel, Prime Minister Ben-Gurion, who considered the port of Elat vital to Israel's survival, wanted to strike at Egypt immediately but was restrained by his colleagues. Relations between Egypt and Israel had reached a boiling point.

At this juncture, the Arab-Israeli conflict blended into a broader confrontation between Arab nationalism and the remnants of Anglo-French colonialism in the Arab world. Two huge engineering structures, one long in existence and the other about to be constructed, brought this confrontation to a head: the Suez Canal and the High Dam at Aswan. President Nasser viewed the former as a leftover from colonial times and the latter as a modern pyramid, to be built as a symbol of resurgent Arab nationalism.

The Aswan High Dam was a vast conception, designed to store and distribute the waters of the Nile so that Egypt's fertile and habitable land areas could be greatly enlarged. In the dam, Egyptians saw the hope of their deliverance from grinding poverty. At Nasser's request, feasibility studies had been undertaken by the World Bank in 1953 and, a year later, Eugene R. Black, the bank's American president, reported to President Eisenhower that the project was technically sound and that its successful completion was Egypt's highest economic and social priority. By December 1955, despite Israel's objections, the World Bank, with the approval of the United States and Britain made an offer to Nasser to finance the dam. The offer was a pledge of Anglo-American cash grants and World Bank loans that were made contingent on these grants. About three-quarters of the burden was to be borne by the United States.

Nasser perceived the Aswan High Dam project as an absolute necessity. It was to be a shining symbol for the attainment of economic prosperity, military strength, and national dignity. He had advertised it throughout Egypt with a slogan—seventeen times larger than the greatest pyramid. But he was irked by some of the World Bank's loan conditions, that, in his opinion, infringed upon Egypt's sovereignty. Black visited Cairo in January 1956, to convince the Egyptian president that the bank's terms were standard loan conditions, but Nasser remained unconvinced. He told Black that he wanted to think over the entire package and refused to close the deal.

Actually, Nasser had plans to play the United States against the Soviet Union. In September 1955, while the dam project was

under active consideration by the World Bank, Nasser had concluded an arms deal with Communist Czechoslovakia. Dulles
though irritated, still decided to support the dam project. But he
sent an assistant secretary to Cairo to speak to Nasser. The Egyptian president responded with a tirade against Israel and accused
the United States of having established the Jewish state, thus
forcing Egypt to purchase arms from Russia in self-defense. When
Dulles did not respond, Nasser became bolder. By the time of
Eugene Black's visit to Cairo, Nasser was deep in negotiations
with the Soviet Union about the Aswan Dam. The Russians, he
said, would make a better offer and build an even bigger dam. In
March 1956, he announced that Egypt might barter 45,000 tons
of cotton for 10,000 tons of Soviet steel. When Dulles expressed
his dismay, Nasser retorted that Egypt was a sovereign neutral
country and had the right to trade with anyone it wished. In
April 1956, Nasser hurled down the gauntlet. "I have in my
pocket," he declared triumphantly, "a Soviet offer to help finance
the Aswan Dam, and I will consider accepting it if there is any
breakdown in negotiating with Washington." On May 15, for good
measure, Nasser recognized the People's Republic of China.

In June, President Eisenhower, speaking from notes prepared
by Secretary Dulles, attacked the Egyptian actions. "Neutral
doesn't mean neutral as between right and wrong, or decency and
indecency," he declared.[2] In July, the French ambassador to Washington, Couve de Murville, pleaded with Dulles not to withdraw
the Aswan loan. The most likely consequence of an American
renege, in the ambassador's opinion, would be the seizure of the
Suez Canal. Dulles and the State Department officials laughed
off the French ambassador's warning. The Suez Canal was an international waterway under a long-standing treaty, they declared.
Nasser would never dare to touch it.

On July 19, 1956, Egypt's ambassador to Washington, Ahmed
Hussein, paid a call on Dulles. Hussein was not an idolator of
Nasser and was inclined toward the American perspective in the
struggle for influence and power in the Middle East. As the two
men began to talk about the loan, Dulles mentioned the difficulties he was having with the Egyptian president. Hussein, becoming agitated, leaned forward and blurted out: "Don't please say

[2] Herman Finer, *Dulles over Suez* (Chicago: Quadrangle, 1964), p. 42.

you are going to withdraw the offer, because we have the Russian offer to finance the Dam right here in my pocket." Dulles retorted immediately, and angrily: "Well, as you have the money already, you don't need any from us! My offer is withdrawn!" [3] These words precipitated a fateful sequence of events.

Why did Dulles rescind the American offer? The official reasons presented later by the State Department were logical enough. Some senators and congressmen had opposed the project; the Egyptian economy was basically unsound; the repayment of the loans was jeopardized by Egypt's commitments to Czechoslovakia for arms; and Nasser's effort to "play both sides against the middle" had pushed the concept of neutrality too far. Yet, Dulles, just before the meeting with Ambassador Hussein, had talked about a postponement of the project, not an outright cancellation. Two high officials of the State Department, who were present at the meeting, were perplexed. One of them, Robert Murphy, a troubleshooter of excellent reputation, believed that it was the ultimatum tone in Hussein's message that pushed Dulles over the brink, and made it impossible for him to say, "let us wait, and talk it over again later.'"

The key to Dulles's renege was Dulles's character. The lawyer in him had become annoyed at being "played for a sucker" by the Soviet Union. More important, the moralist in him smarted from the personal affront when Nasser seemed to prefer the blandishments of Communism to an honest Western offer. At this point, Nasser's neutrality ceased to be neutrality. In the battle between decency and evil, he had been beguiled by evil. "Who is not with me is against me!" And perhaps most important, Nasser had recognized the incarnation of all evil, Communist China. Egypt was the first Arab country to recognize Peking, thus dealing Dulles's policy of liberation a very serious blow. It was too much. A good Calvinist would not be blackmailed by the Devil. He had refused to shake the hand of Chou En-lai in Geneva. He would not make a bargain with his disciple now. A few days later, Vice-President Nixon observed how deeply Dulles felt about the matter. "Blackmail, blackmail!" Dulles muttered indignantly. "Blackmailed by Nasser! Not me!" [4] But there was a serious prob-

[3] Ibid., p. 48.
[4] Ibid., p. 52.

lem with Dulles's policy reversal. The price would not be paid by the United States; it would be paid by the two nations who, thus far, were innocent bystanders in the Dulles-Nasser confrontation: Britain and France. One week after the American renege, Nasser did what Dulles said he would not do: he nationalized the Suez Canal.

DULLES PLAYS FOR TIME

On July 24, 1956, Nasser gave a highly emotional speech in Cairo. He seemed particularly incensed at Dulles's assertion that Egypt's economy was deemed to be unsound. In his rage, he declared that the United States "should drop dead of fury, but [it would] never be able to dictate to Egypt." Two days later, he officially seized the Canal. Russia had offered to build the dam, he announced, but he did not want Russian help either. Egypt would build the dam with the profits from the canal. "This money is ours and this Canal belongs to Egypt." Nasser shouted, "We dug the Canal with our lives, our skills, our bones and our blood." [5] Nationalization, in Nasser's view, was merely a declaration of independence from imperialism.

Dulles heard the news in Lima, Peru, and was caught totally off guard. Yet, he stayed in Peru for another two days, before flying home to Washington. He had not yet grasped the fact that a world crisis was fast breaking. The responses of the British and French leaders to the canal seizure were about to become crucial.

In Britain, Anthony Eden was prime minister. On the night of July 26, as fate would have it, he was giving a dinner for King Faisal of Iraq and his premier, Nuri Said. When a messenger came in with the news, Eden was unable to conceal his rage. Nuri Said, in an effort to relieve the tension, pointed to a bust of Benjamin Disraeli in the hall of No. 10 Downing Street and said. "That's the old Jew who got you into all this trouble." [6] Eden did not smile and quickly got rid of his Iraqi dinner guests.

---

[5] Kenneth Love, *Suez: The Twice Fought War* (New York: McGraw-Hill, 1960), p. 189.

[6] Leonard Mosley, *Dulles* (New York: Dial Press, 1978), p. 405. (Benjamin Disraeli, twice British prime minister, had bought a large block of Suez Canal shares in 1875, thus giving Britain, together with France, a controlling interest in the canal.)

Anthony Eden was in no condition to absorb shocks of this kind, either politically or physically. His memories of Hitler at Munich were still fresh and he now compared Nasser's action to those of the German dictator in the 1930s. In the words of one thoughtful student of British policy at the time, the prime minister "saw Egypt through a forest of Flanders poppies and gleaming jackboots." [7] Physically, he was in a poor way. He had been operated on for trouble in the bile duct and the operation had gone badly. His temper, never known to have been calm, was now choleric and he was subject to fits of ungovernable rage. He perceived Nasser as a tinpot Hitler who would have to be removed before he set the Middle East on fire.

Guy Mollet, the premier of France, shared this perception. He had been an anti-Nazi resistance chief at Arras during World War II and now "saw Nasser as Hitler more plainly than anyone." [8] The two men became so obsessed with Nasser's actions that "Lady Eden is believed to have complained that the Suez Canal was running through her drawing room." [9]

There was, of course, good reason for consternation in Britain and France. The International Convention of Constantinople of 1888 had provided that "the Suez Maritime Canal shall always be free and open, in time of war and in time of peace, to every vessel of commerce or of war without distinction of flag." Thus, the two Western powers considered Nasser's action as a violation of their legal rights. Moreover, to Britain, control of the canal symbolized her status as an empire and as a world power. To the French, who blamed Egypt for supporting the Algerian rebellion against France, seizure of the canal served as a kind of last straw. For both, the issue at stake was not merely safeguarding the economic rights of their shareholders in the Suez Canal Company; far more important was their emotional reaction to the seemingly insolent and Hitlerlike nationalism represented by the Egyptian leader.

To Nasser, on the other hand, the Suez Canal had become the symbol of a shameful colonial past. Its architect, Ferdinand de Lesseps, had become an Egyptian folk ogre. Under his brutal direction, as Nasser saw it, more than 100,000 Egyptian workers

---

[7] Hugh Thomas, *Suez* (New York: Harper and Row, 1966), p. 163.
[8] Ibid.
[9] Ibid.

had died to build a canal that was to belong not to them or their country but to a foreign company that profited for its own enrichment and never for Egypt's benefit. "Instead of the Canal being dug for Egypt," Nasser declaimed, "Egypt became the property of the Canal and the Canal Company became a state within a state. But now the days of alien exploitation [were] over; the Canal and its revenues [would] belong entirely to Egypt. We shall build the High Dam and we shall gain our usurped rights." [10]

These sharply divergent perceptions set the stage for a violent encounter. During the weeks that followed Nasser's action, the conflict broadened. Eden and Mollet privately sounded out American reactions to the situation. They were partially reassured by the fact that Secretary of State Dulles also appeared outraged by Egypt's action. In their conversations with Dulles, the British and French leaders again compared Nasser's action to Hitler's behavior at Munich and stated in the strongest terms that this type of Western appeasement must not be allowed to occur again. Secretary Dulles replied that "force was the last method to be tried, but the United States did not exclude the use of force if all other methods failed." [11] From this statement, Eden and Mollet inferred that the United States would, at best, present a united front with Britain and France in a show of force against Nasser and, at worst, remain benevolently neutral.

During the summer months, Dulles desperately tried to work out a compromise. He found himself in a very tight diplomatic box. Nasser had torn up an international treaty and Dulles, the lawyer, was eager to make the Egyptian president disgorge what he had swallowed. The moralist in Dulles was sympathetic to the Anglo-French predicament especially since that predicament had been triggered by American policy. On the other hand, there was a presidential election in the offing and the president had won on a platform of "peace and prosperity." Eisenhower himself was categorically opposed to the use of force over the Suez Canal, even as a last resort. By hinting that the United States did not rule out force if all other methods failed, the secretary of state

---

[10] Nutting, *Nasser* (New York: Dutton, 1972), p. 145.

[11] Anthony Eden, *Full Circle*, quoted by Herbert Feis in *Foreign Affairs*, July 1960, p. 600.

had already gone beyond the wishes of his president. And then, of course, there was the Soviet enigma. What would Nikita Khrushchev do if a shooting war broke out in the Middle East?

Dulles's first compromise proposal was the creation of an "international authority" to operate a waterway, and ensure freedom of transit under the 1888 convention. The British and French were sympathetic to the idea, but Nasser flatly rejected it as an effort to undo his nationalization move. Eden immediately dispatched a cable to Eisenhower in which he asserted that "Nasser's course [was] unpleasantly familiar," and that "the parallel with Mussolini [was] close." "The removal of Nasser and the installation in Egypt of a regime less hostile to the West," Eden concluded, ranked "very high" among Britain's objectives.[12] Dulles's second idea was the establishment of a Suez Canal user's association. Under this scheme, the canal users would band together, employ their own pilots, transit the canal, pay tolls to the association, and pass on to Egypt what they considered a fair share. When Eden heard of the idea, he asked: "Is he serious?" Nasser publicly replied by suggesting a "Port of London users' association" that would operate at will in that harbor and pay the British what it thought was a fair share of the port charges.[13] The scheme failed, of course. It embodied the staggering assumption that somehow the problem could be resolved on a purely technical level, bypassing the political questions of sovereignty and jurisdiction.

By now it was September and Eden and Mollet were chafing with impatience. Both men had begun to doubt Dulles's intellectual integrity. His moves seemed tactical to them, designed to stall and play for time. Finally, on September 12, in a press conference, Dulles declared that "American ships, if opposed, would *not*, repeat *not* 'shoot' their way through the Canal: They would go round the Cape." [14] This statement was the last straw. In the eyes of Eden and Mollet, John Foster Dulles had now become a liar.

The truth was that Dulles was unable to escape from the di-

---

[12] Love, op. cit., p. 394.

[13] Ibid., p. 429.

[14] Ibid., p. 428.

lemma he had helped create through the Aswan Dam renege. His compromise proposals were legalistic subterfuges that appealed to Anglo-French sentiment but were patently unacceptable to Nasser. The maneuvers were designed to keep Eden and Mollet off balance, to postpone a showdown, and buy time for Eisenhower's reelection. In essence, Dulles played the role of lawyer to a president engaged in an adversary proceeding with allies who were getting out of hand. In the face of these imperatives at home, the moralist was silent. By October, Eden and Mollet recognized that they could no longer count on Dulles.

Eden and Mollet enjoyed considerable popular support at home for their beliefs. "I told Foster as plainly as I could that he could not afford to lose this game," wrote Harold Macmillan. "It was a question not of honor only but survival." [15] This was the reaction of a man who had stood bravely against the perilous drift of 1938. A large number of members of the British House of Commons echoed Macmillan's sentiments. There was a tragic inability to transcend Munich, a fatal tendency to equate Nasser with Hitler, the Middle East with Europe, and 1956 with 1938. Behind this reaction lay a sense of impending doom. A series of erosions and defeats had driven home the truth to many Englishmen that Britain's strength was ebbing. Suez seemed the final insult. The average Englishman shared this anxiety and foreboding. "If Eden's fevered policies had not struck a responsive chord in the hearts of half his countrymen,'" wrote one observer, "'they would have been like a fuse without a bomb." [16] Mollet felt very much the same. The former resistance fighter described Nasser as a Middle Eastern Hitler. Nasser's book, *Philosophy of Revolution*, in Mollet's view, should more properly have been called "Mein Kampf." All French political parties except the Communists supported a severe riposte against Nasser. The French people too, like those of Britain, were living through the decline of their empire. The Indochina war had been lost at Dien Bien Phu and a rebellion in Algeria, supported by Nasser, was gathering momentum. Suez seemed like the *coup de grace*. And so, Eden and Mollet gave up on Dulles and prepared for military action.

[15] Harold Macmillan, *Riding the Storm: 1956–1959* (New York: Harper and Row, 1971), p. 106.
[16] Love, op. cit., p. 419.

THE MORALIST CONDEMNS HIS ALLIES

Eden and Mollet hoped to mount a lightning attack against Egypt, occupy the canal, depose Nasser, and then negotiate with his successor from a position of strength. In the course of these preparations, highly secret meetings took place with Israeli leaders for the purpose of coordinating the attack. Prime Minister Ben-Gurion and his chief of staff, General Moshe Dayan, were intent on seizing Gaza, the main base of terrorist activities, and Sharm-el-Sheik on the Tiran Straits, from where the Egyptians maintained their blockade of the Gulf of Aqaba against ships bound for the port of Elat. Mollet pledged that if the Israelis would thrust into Sinai, French forces would join them, and Israel could seize Sinai and end the Egyptian blockade. Ben-Gurion hesitated; he feared that Egyptian bombers might attack Tel Aviv while Israeli forces were advancing into Sinai. But when Eden pledged to use British air power to prevent Egyptian air attacks on Israel, Ben-Gurion agreed to move to Sinai.

The final plans worked out among the three prime ministers were the following: Israel was to launch her attack on October 29. As soon as Dayan's troops began their advance into Sinai, Britain and France were to issue an ultimatum to Israel and Egypt, requiring them to cease fire, to withdraw their forces ten miles on either side of the canal, and to "accept the temporary occupation by Anglo-French forces of key positions at Port Said, Ismailia and Suez." [17] When Israel had agreed to these terms and Egypt had rejected them, British bombers were to destroy the Egyptian air force and disrupt Egypt's communications and military capabilities in preparation for an Anglo-French invasion by paratroops from Cyprus and sea-borne forces from Malta. Then, when these forces had occupied the canal from Port Said to Suez, a further attack was contemplated, aimed at the occupation of Cairo, if necessary, in order to depose Nasser.

On the afternoon of October 29, Israel's army launched its four-pronged advance against Egypt. Two thrusts were aimed at the canal while the third and fourth were to seal off the Gaza Strip and to seize Sharm-el-Sheik. On the following day, while

[17] Nutting, op. cit., p. 163.

Israeli forces were advancing rapidly across the Sinai Peninsula, Britain and France issued their prearranged ultimatum, which, in effect, told the Egyptians to retreat and the Israelis to advance.

Eden and Mollet were no longer worried about Dulles. When it came to the crunch, they believed, Eisenhower was in charge of the United States and Eisenhower would not let them down. After all, he was an old friend and comrade from the Second World War. Once France and Britain took action, Ike would "lie doggo" and let them get on with it, and that was all they needed. It was the costliest miscalculation the French and British leaders ever made.

When the Israelis struck against Egypt at Sinai on October 29, they hid their real plans. Their first official communiqué declared that they merely intended to liquidate guerrilla bases in the Sinai. Dulles, upon hearing the news, angrily decided that Israel would have to be stopped at once. Otherwise, the temptation for Eden and Mollet to follow suit would be too great. Eisenhower agreed emphatically. "All right, Foster," he ordered, "You tell 'em that, goddamn it, we're going to apply sanctions, we're going to the United Nations, we're going to do everything so we can stop this thing." [18] As yet, the two Americans had no knowledge of the collusion between Britain, France, and Israel. When on October 30, Britain and France issued their ultimatum, Dulles and Eisenhower suddenly understood what had occurred.

The two leaders now exploded with a terrible anger. All close witnesses testify to this. One State Department official, a man of even temper, not given to exaggeration, reported that Dulles was "close to apoplexy." [19] "How could people do this to *me?*" he shouted, "why put me on a spot just when election day is due? They are shoving us, showing contempt for us, they have *betrayed* us! It's criminal that Britain, France and Israel should involve us without our permission or concurrence. Of course, they think, no doubt, that if they get into trouble, the United States will bail them out!" [20] Eisenhower was equally incensed and the White House resounded with barracks language that probably had

[18] Ibid., p. 503.
[19] Finer, op. cit., p. 370.
[20] Ibid., p. 371.
[21] Love, op. cit., p. 561.

not been heard since the days of General Grant. The catalyst of the Anglo-French conspiratorial resort to force had the effect of fusing the positions of the two men. Before the event, the president had flatly opposed the use of force as a means of settling the canal dispute while Dulles obliquely defended its legitimacy as a last resort. Now, both men took the Anglo-French action as a personal affront, a sinister breach of trust.

There was yet another reason for Dulles's and Eisenhower's fury. On October 30, the same day the Anglo-French ultimatum was issued, a continent away, the Hungarian uprising against the Soviet Union seemed to be succeeding. Khrushchev had made a momentous offer to Imre Nagy, the leader of the freedom fighters. He was prepared to negotiate the full withdrawal of Red Army units from Hungary and establish a new basis of Soviet relationships throughout Eastern Europe: noninterference in each other's internal affairs. For a breathless interlude, it appeared that a new modus vivendi between the Soviet Union and its satellites might be achieved. Allen Dulles called it "a miracle." But if the United States now acquiesced in the Anglo-French aggression, it would lose all moral authority. It could not apply one moral standard vis-à-vis the Soviet Union and another vis-à-vis its allies. It would have to stand on principle. "It is nothing less than tragic," Dulles said, "that at this very time when we are on the point of winning an immense and long-hoped-for victory over Soviet colonialism in Eastern Europe, we should be forced to choose between following in the footsteps of Anglo-French colonialism in Asia and Africa, or splitting our course away from their course." [22] In the afternoon of October 30, Dulles met with Hervé Alphand, the French ambassador. In a tone that was a mixture of grief, rebuke, and insult Dulles accused the ambassador: "This is the darkest hour in the history of the Western alliance. It might even be the end of the alliance itself. The actions and intervention of France and Britain is just the same as the behavior of the Soviet Union in Budapest." [23] He would take the matter to the United Nations.

Dulles's man at the United Nations was Henry Cabot Lodge. Lodge took orders from Dulles and carried them out faithfully.

[22] Ibid.
[23] Finer, op. cit., p. 6.

Moreover, he was highly sensitive to the anticolonialist stand of the Afro-Asian bloc in the United Nations. To a scion of an old Bostonian family, 1776 was living history: Britain and France were colonial nations and Suez had certain aspects of the Boston Tea Party. At any rate, Lodge prosecuted Dulles's case at the United Nations with extraordinary vigor and enthusiasm. Israel, demanded Lodge before a packed Security Council, would have to withdraw its armed forces immediately. Britain and France vetoed the resolution. This was the first veto Britain had ever cast. The Soviet Union now competed with the United States in its zeal to crush the British and French. It proposed a similar resolution that again was vetoed. When Dulles heard the news, his fury gave way to mental anguish. Suddenly, the United States had found a most unwelcome ally: the Soviet Union. The moral crusader was in league now with the Devil.

Things were not going well on the battlefield for the British and French. By October 31, Nasser had realized that an Anglo-French invasion was coming. He extricated his army from Sinai and withdrew it to the canal. As soon as the British began to bomb Egyptian territory, Nasser ordered that several large vessels in the canal be sunk, thus totally blocking the waterway. The Israelis had succeeded in their objectives, but the Anglo-French operation was bogging down. As one critical British analyst summed up the operation later: "The spectacle of over one hundred thousand men setting off for a war which lasted barely a day and then returning has few parallels in the long gallery of military imbecility." [24] To add to Dulles's anguish, the Soviet premier, Nikolai Bulganin, in a news conference in Moscow, warned of the possibility of a third world war and declared that Soviet "volunteers" were ready to aid the Egyptian forces. He proposed that the United States and the Soviet Union restore the peace through a joint show of force. This suggestion was rejected as "unthinkable" by President Eisenhower. The United States was eager to see the Anglo-French action ended, but it was equally eager to prevent the establishment of a Soviet presence in the Middle East. Dulles was described by one observer as "ashen gray, heavy-lidded, strained, shaking his head in dazed disbelief

24 Thomas, op. cit., p. 164.

at the news . . . of British bombers over Cairo." [25] Eisenhower called Eden on the telephone and reduced the British prime minister to tears.[26] Eden's policy was facing bitter opposition from the Labour Party and the friendship of his World War II ally seemed to have turned into a bitter prosecuting enmity.

In the evening of October 31, Eisenhower delivered a speech in Philadelphia. He declared that the United States could not subscribe to one law for the weak and another for the strong, that there could only be one law or there would be no peace. On the following day, Dulles addressed the United Nations General Assembly. The speech was a sermon, an appeal to principle. In it he described the military attack as "a grave error." Failure to act strongly would condemn the United Nations to impotence. The United States was accordingly impelled to act against three nations with whom it had ties, because its disagreement with their actions involved principles that far transcended the immediate issue.[27] The moral crusader in Dulles was now in full command. Abstract principle was enthroned above traditional alliance ties. The United Nations was deemed more important than the North Atlantic Treaty. After a long and bitter debate, the United States resolution—essentially the same as the one vetoed in the Security Council—was adopted by a vote of sixty-five to five. Only Australia and New Zealand joined Britain, France, and Israel in opposition. After the vote, Dulles told associates: "If that had been my very last act on earth, it would have been exactly as I would have liked it for my epitaph." [28] On the following day, Dulles collapsed and was taken to the hospital. An operation revealed cancer.

The rest of the melancholy tale is quickly told. On November 4, Soviet tanks entered Budapest and bloodily crushed the Hungarian uprising. The Soviet leadership sent a series of ominously worded messages to Britain, France, and Israel threatening missile attacks. Eisenhower continued to exert pressure on

[25] Emmet John Hughes, *The Ordeal of Power* (New York: Atheneum, 1963), p. 220.

[26] Finer, op. cit., p. 386.

[27] Ibid., pp. 394–396.

[28] Townsend Hoopes, *The Devil and John Foster Dulles* (Boston: Atlantic-Little, Brown, 1975), p. 379.

Britain and France. A run on the British pound developed and the United States secretary of the treasury, George Humphrey, operating on Eisenhower's orders, informed Eden that financial help would be forthcoming only if Britain promised an immediate cease-fire. Besieged from all sides, Eden gave way on November 5 and Mollet followed suit shortly thereafter. Israel tried to hang onto Sinai, but finally American pressure prevailed there, too. Dag Hammarskjöld, secretary general of the United Nations was successful in dispatching to the Middle East a specially constituted peace force, the United Nations Emergency Force (UNEF). Israel agreed to evacuate most of the territories it had captured from Egypt and, beginning on November 15, the UNEF soldiers replaced the Israeli troops. Only an explicit American guarantee, however, that Israel's right to free and innocent passage in the Gulf of Aqaba would not be infringed upon, persuaded the Israelis to evacuate the last fruits of their Sinai campaign, the Gaza Strip and the east coast of the Sinai Peninsula down to the Straits of Tiran. In March 1957, Israel finally gave up all the territories it had captured.

John Foster Dulles, resting in Walter Reed Hospital, provided an unsettling ending to this turbulent drama. On November 7, after the Suez cease-fire was in effect, Selwyn Lloyd, Britain's foreign secretary, came to visit Dulles at the hospital. The American secretary of state, in slippers, came slowly forward, shook hands with Lloyd, and immediately asked: "Well, once you started, why didn't you go through with it and get Nasser down?" Lloyd was somewhat startled. Recovering, he said, "Foster, why didn't you give us a wink?" Dulles answered, "Oh! I couldn't do anything like that!" [29]

AFTERMATH: MORALITY AND POWER

When the Suez crisis was over, the world's power configuration had definitely altered. Of all the roles in the drama, that of the United States was undoubtedly the most problematical. Confronted in the most acute way possible with the dilemma of whether to support the two colonial powers or Egypt, Dulles was

[29] Ibid., p. 381.

bound to lose either way. His actual decision to side with Egypt inevitably alienated Britain and France and put the most severe strains on the NATO alliance. Anthony Eden and Guy Mollet were compelled to resign, and throughout Britain as well as France a growing body of "neutralist" sentiment became articulate. Indeed, in the view of a number of observers, for example, former Secretary of State Dean Acheson, Dulles's policy in the crisis came close to losing the United States its two most trusted allies and thus exposing Western Europe to the domination of communism. On the other hand, if Dulles had sided with Britain and France against Egypt, its risks would have been no less heavy. The new nations of Africa, Asia, and the Middle East would have quickly concluded that when the chips were down, the United States was at heart no less a colonial power than its Western European allies. In disillusionment, the new nationalism would almost certainly have veered sharply away from the United States toward the Soviet Union.

The criticism of the American stand came essentially to this point: the United States had chosen to behave like a collective security power, not like an ally. In the Middle Eastern situation, the United Nations had prevailed over NATO. Yet the American rejection as "unthinkable" of a Soviet proposal for joint superpower intervention in the Middle East suggests strongly that Dulles's position was not determined by the abstract considerations of the collective security ideal. There was, first, the sense of outrage that the president and secretary of state both felt because the British and French had not bothered to consult their NATO ally on a matter as important as military action in the Middle East at a time when a national election was imminent in the United States. Second, from a purely military standpoint, the Anglo-French punitive expedition seemed to be foundering and thus could not be presented to the General Assembly as a *fait accompli.* The United States, by supporting the Anglo-French venture or even by taking a neutral view of it, would have risked the ill will of a large majority of the UN membership and, in addition, might have had to look on helplessly while the military action failed or bogged down. Moreover, such an American response might have persuaded many neutralists that the United States, by countenancing aggression in the Middle East, differed little from the Soviet Union, which was practicing aggression by crushing a rebellion in Hungary with military force. Most important, Dulles feared the possibility of Soviet intervention in the Middle East through "volunteers" and the risk of sparking a major war through direct superpower confrontation in the contested area.

All this does not exclude the possibility that some of the reasons motivating Dulles were of a genuinely moral nature. As stated by him, the United States acted as it did because it insisted on the principle that the same standard of international law and morality should apply to all nations, friends and foes alike. Yet even this seemingly unassailable moral reason rested upon ambiguities. It could be argued, for example, that a "moral" action might under certain circumstances eventuate in "immoral" consequences. Thus the "moral" behavior of the United States in the Suez crisis ran the risk of leading to the disintegration of NATO and the "immoral" result of opening Western Europe to Soviet domination. Conversely, if the United States had decided upon the "immoral" step of supporting the British and French military expedition against Egypt, the outcome might have been the quite "moral" one of restoring the legal economic rights of the Western powers and of reestablishing the Suez Canal as an international waterway. The point here is *not* that the United States acted either morally or immorally. It is, rather, that among other things, the Suez affair demonstrated how subtle and indeterminate the relationship between ethics and power in international relations can be. The most "moral" intentions may lead to highly "immoral" consequences, whereas on other occasions and in different circumstances the very reverse may be true.

The crucial difference between interpersonal and international relations is not that the former permit moral behavior, whereas the latter do not. It resides, rather, in the fact that personal behavior is usually judged by an ethic of *intention* while that of the statesman is essentially one of *consequence*. Hans J. Morgenthau cites an interesting example that illustrates this point:

> Neville Chamberlain's policies of appeasement were, as far as we can judge, inspired by good motives; he was probably less motivated by considerations of personal power than were many other British prime ministers, and he sought to preserve peace and to assure the happiness of all concerned. Yet his policies helped to make the Second World War inevitable, and to bring untold miseries to millions of men. Sir Winston Churchill's motives, on

the other hand, have been much less universal in scope and much more narrowly directed toward personal and national power, yet the foreign policies that sprang from these inferior motives were certainly superior in moral and political quality to those pursued by his predecessor.[30]

The Suez crisis poignantly illustrates the multiple facets of this problem. Dulles's decision to support Egypt and the Soviet Union against Britain and France was justified in terms of "a single standard of international morality." This was clearly an ethic of intention. The British and French, on the other hand, justified their military expedition in terms of its ultimate consequence—the reassertion of their legal rights in the Suez Canal. This difference in interpretation of what constituted "morality" led to a great deal of bitterness and confusion.

The Soviet Union's role in the Suez crisis was much simpler. From its point of view, the only unusual aspect was its strange alliance with the United States in the United Nations. In order to dissociate itself from this somewhat unwelcome association, the Soviet Union interpreted the action of the United States not as being helpful to Arab nationalism but, rather, as a nefarious scheme to replace British and French imperialism with American imperialism. In contrast, it pointed to itself as the only true champion of the new nationalist cause. Its threat of rocket retaliation against Britain and France was designed to underline how firm its commitment to the new nationalism in fact was. From the Soviet Union's point of view, indeed, the Suez crisis constituted a great windfall in its struggle with the United States: the British and French appeared to be digging their own graves in the Middle East and the United States seemed to be doing its best to help them. Thus, by appealing to the cause of Arab nationalism, the Soviet Union saw its opportunity to eject all Western influence from the Middle East and gain a foothold of its own. The fact that Israel was allied with the two colonial powers also played into Soviet hands. Typically, therefore, the Soviet Union showed itself ready to use every facet of this colonial struggle to advance its own cause in the East-West battle. And, from the melee, communism emerged with a clear-cut gain.

[30] Hans Morgenthau, *Politics Among Nations,* 3rd ed. (New York: Knopf, 1960), p. 6.

The main losers in the Suez affair were clearly the two colonial powers, Britain and France. In humiliation, they had to watch Nasser snatch a political victory from a military defeat. Abandoned by their closest and oldest ally, they had to admit that they could no longer act like great powers and that, in the last analysis, their initiative in international politics depended upon the decisions of the United States. The new nationalism had inflicted a painful defeat upon them and the very issue that they had set out to rectify by force of arms—the internationalization of the Suez Canal—now seemed beyond redemption. For all practical purposes, the Suez crisis terminated Anglo-French authority in the Middle East. Suez had become another Dien Bien Phu.

The greatest victory in the Suez crisis was won by Arab nationalism. Nasser was now clearly master of the Suez Canal. The two great superpowers had both supported him. The prestige of the Egyptian leader reached its zenith immediately after the Suez affair. Not only did Nasser triumph in the showdown with Western colonialism, but his other great foe, Israel, had also been compelled to withdraw as a result of American pressure. Only Israel emerged relatively unchanged from the turmoil of the Suez affair. To be sure, it had demonstrated its military superiority over the competing nationalism of Nasser, yet it was prevented from capitalizing on its advantage by strong United States pressure to withdraw. In the end, nearly all the territories it had occupied had to be given up.

One question remains about the Suez crisis that cannot be answered with certitude but that nevertheless ought to be raised. It is quite conceivable that the events in Suez determined the course of another political struggle—a great distance from Suez—that of the Hungarian revolutionaries against the Soviet Union. The simultaneity of the two upheavals may have been more than accidental. The first stage of the Hungarian revolution was completed when Imre Nagy assumed complete control of Hungary and announced on November 1, 1956, that Hungary would be "free, independent, democratic, and neutral." Soviet forces were withdrawing from Hungary and agreement seemed to be near between the Soviet Union and the new Hungarian government. On the same day, however, the British and French mounted their invasion of Egypt, which reached its climax on November 3. On that day Nagy was informed that Soviet forces, in battle formation, were steadily advancing on the capital. On the following day, Soviet armored units had broken through the defenses of Budapest and the Hungarian revolution was drowned in blood.

Is it possible that the Soviet Union, in addition to the other advantages that it derived from the Suez crisis, decided to use the Anglo-French invasion of Egypt as a pretext for deflecting attention from events in Hungary? Or, to put it in other words, would the Soviet Union have decided to let Hungary escape from communism into a position of international neutrality if the Suez crisis had not occurred? Should we ask ourselves the somewhat ironical question whether, because of the actions of Britain and France, the West itself was responsible for the failure of the Hungarian revolution? And did Dulles, therefore, by triggering the Suez crisis through his Aswan Dam renege, bury his own liberation policy?

This brings us back full circle to the foreign policy of John Foster Dulles. What was his share of the responsibility for the Suez tragedy?

First, Dulles did not vigorously protest to Nasser against the arms deal with Czechoslovakia. He made the Aswan loan offer nonetheless and hence, his sudden subsequent renege seemed brusque and insulting. It gave Nasser an excuse to seize the canal in hot blood. The victims were Britain and France.

The canal seized, Dulles had no policy to make Nasser "disgorge." He was less than candid with his allies about the use of force. His legalistic schemes merely incensed Nasser and drove Eden and Mollet to despair. Finally, he lost all credibility with both sides in the deepening conflict. When war broke out, he permitted his personal outrage and indignation to govern the foreign policy of the United States. Dulles now became a moralist who prosecuted criminals before the bar of global justice. He did not recognize his own role in having triggered off the crisis nor did he temper justice with a grain of mercy. Yet, one wonders, if he might have "winked" at his two allies if their military operation had been more successful? Or if developments in Hungary had taken a different turn? But when events unfolded the way they did, the crusader's temptation to teach a moral lesson was probably irresistible. No doubt, his counterplayers were most difficult. Nasser had begun to behave like a fanatic, and Eden and Mollet perceived him through the lenses of their experience with Hitler.

But in the end, Dulles wound up on the side of the initial aggressor. There may be truth in the old aphorism that "no people do so much harm as those who go about doing good."

The British ambassador to the United States, Sir Oliver Franks, expressed an eloquent judgment of John Foster Dulles:

> Three or four centuries ago, when Reformation and Counter-Reformation divided Europe into armed camps, in an age of wars of religion, it was not so rare to encounter men of the type of Dulles. Like them, he came to unshakeable convictions of a religious and theological order. Like them, he saw the world as an arena in which the forces of good and evil were continuously at war.[31]

But Dulles was also a wily and amoral tactician. He was a curious cross between a Christian moralist and a shrewd and ruthless lawyer. The rigidity of his moralism and legalism also defined the limits of his constructive statesmanship. Although he avoided actual war, his strident approach to nearly every crisis weakened the trust and support of his allies and, during the Suez war, led to the almost total diplomatic isolation of the United States. He almost succeeded in wrecking NATO, but he reached no accommodation with the Soviet Union. He lacked the courage, both with allies and with adversaries, to build upon the elements of possible reconciliation. And, in historical perspective, it is this lack of a larger vision that will probably deny him a place among the greatest American statesmen.

Finally, there is the decisive impact of Dulles's personality. Three statesmen are on record as saying that they would have acted differently. Dean Acheson declared that he would not have prosecuted America's two closest allies. Sir Winston Churchill wrote French Prime Minister Mollet: "I would have gone on!"[32] and Charles de Gaulle said at the time that he would have completed the military action despite American opposition.[33] There is no reason to doubt these men. Their credibility is well established. Different choices would have created different problems. But one wonders whether the consequences would have been so convulsive and so far-reaching.

[31] Quoted in Hoopes, op. cit., p. 491.
[32] Finer, op. cit., p. 422.
[33] Ibid., pp. 422–423.

At least three alternatives existed during the crisis over Suez. A policymaker might have sided with America's allies, France and Britain, as Dean Acheson probably would have done. He might have abstained from the Anglo-French-Egyptian conflict altogether and sought refuge in abstention and neutrality. Or, he could, as John Foster Dulles in fact did, censure his allies and side with Egypt and the Soviet Union in the name of principle and abstract justice. Nothing in our case material suggests that these three alternatives did not exist. But the actual choice, for better or for worse, was determined by Dulles's moralist crusading personality. The lawyer in him tried to temporize but, in the end, the moralist in him compelled him to turn on the closest friends of the United States and prosecute them like criminals in the United Nations. And, as he himself declared, it was his proudest day, a fitting epitaph to his career. The other two alternatives, which certainly were feasible, were inconceivable to him. One wonders how the North Atlantic Treaty and the situation in the Middle East would have evolved had Britain and France not been humiliated and had Egypt's Nasser not been permitted to snatch a spectacular victory from the jaws of sure defeat. With John Foster Dulles in command, force failed, but justice did not triumph.

NEW FRONTIERS

Dwight D. Eisenhower's second term as president was a period of increasing Soviet pressure on the United States. The Suez crisis had left NATO in serious disarray and Nikita Khrushchev decided to seize the diplomatic offensive. In 1958, he announced that, at the end of six months, he intended to end the four-power occupation of Berlin and would hand control of East Berlin and the routes leading into West Berlin to the East Germans. The implication was clear: if the East Germans then interfered with Western traffic, the West would have to employ force to break any blockade. And Khrushchev declared that any such Western attempt would meet Soviet resistance. It seemed like 1948 all over again.

Hoping to lower tensions, Eisenhower issued an invitation to Khrushchev to visit the United States in September 1959. The personal meeting of the two leaders did result in Khrushchev's withdrawal of his threat to take unilateral action in Berlin in return for American willingness to negotiate on the problems of Berlin and Germany at a four-power summit meeting at a later date. For Eisenhower, this meant another postponement of the day on which he would have to decide the painful question of whether Berlin was worth the risk of a nuclear war. The European NATO allies were deeply divided over Eisenhower's response. Konrad Adenauer, the West German chancellor, and President de Gaulle of France voiced increasing suspicions of the United States resolution to defend Western Europe. America's apparent willingness to discuss Berlin with the Russians seemed to the French and German leaders to show little American courage or conviction. The British, for their part, denounced Adenauer's "rigidity." Adenauer, in turn accused the British of "appeasement." Franco-British relations cooled considerably. The Treaty of Rome, launching the European Common Market in 1958, did not include Great Britain. To France, West Germany, Italy, and the Benelux countries, the Common Market was not only an effort to integrate the economies of Western Europe. It was also an attempt to make Western Europe stronger and more independent of the United States.

In May 1960, shortly before the scheduled summit conference was to take place in Paris, the Russians shot down an American U-2 "spy plane" thirteen hundred miles inside Soviet territory. Eisenhower reacted to this event rather clumsily. When Khrushchev initially announced only the shooting down of the U-2, the administration responded that the plane had been engaged in meteorological observations and had probably flown off course. When Khrushchev then revealed the real mission of the flight, the administration reversed itself. Eisenhower admitted that the U-2 pilot had been taking aerial photographs of the Soviet Union. Moreover, he claimed that such flights had been dispatched to Russia for several years and that they would continue, since they were essential for the prevention of a Soviet surprise attack. Thus, the Eisenhower administration was caught not only red-handed in an act of espionage, but it blithely announced that such espionage could continue.

Needless to say, Khrushchev was forced to respond. Silence on his part would have implied that he had surrendered to the United States the right to violate Soviet air space. He could hardly have survived such an admission. Thus, he launched a blistering attack on Eisenhower and demanded a personal apology. Eisenhower's promise that no more reconnaissance missions would be undertaken during his term of office did not satisfy Khrushchev. The Soviet leader suggested that the summit conference be postponed for half a year. He also bluntly told the American president that he would not be welcome if he came to the Soviet Union to return the Soviet premier's visit to the United States. In short, Khrushchev said that he wanted nothing more to do with Eisenhower.

During the next few months, Soviet-American relations deteriorated further. Fidel Castro moved Cuba into the Communist orbit and Nikita Khrushchev declared the Monroe Doctrine "dead." In the summer of 1960, chaos overtook the newly independent Congo in Africa. United Nations Secretary General Dag Hammarskjöld succeeded in dispatching a UN peace force of twenty thousand men to the fledgling country, preventing its decline into anarchy. But Nikita Khrushchev suspected Hammarskjöld's motives and accused him of being a "lackey of Western imperialism." In September 1960, the Soviet leader appeared at the United Nations in New York and shocked the entire world when he took off his shoe and thumped it on his desk, demanding the ouster of the secretary general. The move was defeated, but the bizarre incident only served to underline the rising tensions. By January 1961, when John F. Kennedy took over the presidency of the United States, Soviet-American relations had reached a new nadir.

The American presidency is a peculiarly personal institution. The presidency of John F. Kennedy was intensely personal. Kennedy inspired passions that were larger than life. Loyalties blazed with a fierce intensity. His character, style, and habits recast the temper of the government. And when he died, "the people of the world grieved as if they had terribly lost their own leader, friend, and brother." [1] What were the roots of this charisma?

John Kennedy's father, Joseph, was a millionaire who became ambassador to England and his mother Rose was the daughter of the mayor of Boston. Young Jack, the second of nine children, had no material wants, but was a sickly child and ill much of the time. Joe Kennedy, Sr. pressed his children hard to compete, never to be satisfied with anything but first place. The point was not just to try; the point was to win. Despite a bad back and the greater strength of his older brother Joe, young Jack competed. Even though the atmosphere in the Kennedy family was always go, move, fight, and win, Jack's ego strength was never impaired. He sensed that his father cared deeply and never humiliated his children. Beneath the toughness, there was love. Rose Kennedy, like her husband, a devout Catholic, was a sensible and devoted

[1] Arthur M. Schlesinger, Jr., *A Thousand Days* (Boston: Houghton Mifflin Company, 1965), p. 1031.

mother. With nine children in the family, each soon had to fend for himself. Rose, however, exuded a sense of stability and order and thus provided the conditions for growth even though she did not channel its direction.

In the spring of 1939, while a junior at Harvard, Kennedy went on a tour of Europe on the eve of the Second World War. He returned to the United States after the German assault on Poland in September and then drew upon his experiences to write an honors thesis in political science entitled "Appeasement at Munich." With the help of his father, Kennedy published a revised version of the thesis in 1940 under the title *Why England Slept.* The "lessons of Munich" were to reverberate throughout the rest of Kennedy's life.

During the war, Kennedy managed to join the navy despite his bad back and wound up as commanding officer of a patrol torpedo boat in the Pacific. In August 1943, a Japanese destroyer rammed his PT-109 and sliced the little ship in half. Kennedy swam to a small island more than three miles away, pulling a seriously wounded man along with him, and saving his life. Young Kennedy had become a genuine war hero.

And yet tragedy haunted him. His older brother Joe was killed in the war as was his sister's husband. Despite his Catholicism, Kennedy developed a profoundly skeptical bent. "Life is unfair," he once said simply. The poignancy of men dying around him haunted him. After Joe's death, his father wanted Jack to go into politics. Jack complied, ran for Congress and won. His manner was quiet, factual, direct, and increasingly confident as he gathered experience. As senator, his "star quality" and "mystique" became evident. His youth and personal grace, his self-deprecating wit, his call for excellence, his thirst for action, all these, resonated with the American people, especially the young. And in 1960, John F. Kennedy, at forty-three, was elected as the youngest president in the history of the United States.

The foreign policy of John F. Kennedy continues as a subject of debate. "We shall pay any price, bear any burden . . . to assure the survival and the success of liberty," the young president had said at his Inaugural. Loyalists have pointed to this passage as proof of Kennedy's respect for liberty and human rights. Critics have regarded it as cold war rhetoric. Neither side has had the final word. He had had so little time. It was as if Lincoln had been killed after the Gettysburg Address or Truman had died before the Marshall Plan.[2] The New Frontier lasted but a thousand days.

Kennedy brought a young and exuberant team with him to Washington. Whereas most of Eisenhower's appointees had been lawyers or businessmen, Kennedy's appointees tended to have backgrounds in government or academic life. Like the young president, they aspired to a world of new ideas as well as to the world of power. The Peace Corps was one result of this new intellectual vitality. Many of Kennedy's men had fought in the war, and some, like the president himself, were war heroes. This made for toughness, a mistrust of evangelism, and, above all, a driving pragmatism, a determination to get things done. The president's exhortation, "Let us begin," was no idle rhetoric.

A few weeks after his inauguration, however, Kennedy committed a major blunder. During the last year of the Eisenhower administration, the Central Intelligence Agency under the leadership of Allen Dulles, John Foster's brother, had conceived a plan to overthrow Premier Fidel Castro's government in Cuba. A band of some fourteen hundred Cuban exiles—most of them disillusioned former Castro associates—were to land in Cuba and secure a beachhead. The CIA believed that, once the exiles had gained such a foothold, the Cuban population and even units of Castro's army would welcome the invaders as liberators. Kennedy inherited the plan and considered it at several cabinet meetings. All of his top advisers, with the notable exceptions of Senator J. William Fulbright and special assistant Arthur Schlesinger, Jr., endorsed the project. Kennedy, after overcoming serious misgivings, authorized the landing of the refugee commandoes in the Bay of Pigs area in Cuba. He made it clear, however, that if the Cubans failed, the United States would not bail them out by sending American marines in after them. The exiles would then have to become guerrilla fighters in the mountains.

The Bay of Pigs operation turned out to be an appalling failure. Everything went wrong, almost from the start. A ship carrying most of the ammunition for the refugees was sunk. Castro did not panic, but responded with cool effectiveness. His air force and militia quickly pinned the refugees down on the beaches and

[2] Ibid., p. 1030.

took them prisoner. There were no defections from Castro's armed forces, nor was there a popular uprising in Cuba. The refugees never had a chance. Kennedy, after considerable agony, decided not to involve the United States militarily through air cover or ground operations.

The CIA had been wrong. The experts and generals also had been wrong. Kennedy, however, took the blame upon himself. "How could I have been so stupid?" he asked himself again and again.[3] His anguish was deepened by the knowledge that those who admired him all over the world were asking the same question. It was an expensive lesson. "Success has a hundred fathers, but failure is an orphan," he commented dryly. From now on, he would rely less on "experts" and more on his own judgment. He regained his balance easily. When asked whether American prestige had suffered as a result of his decision not to get the United States involved more deeply, Kennedy retorted: "What's prestige? Is it the shadow of power or the substance of power? We are going to work on the substance of power. No doubt we will be kicked in the can for the next couple of weeks, but that won't affect the main business." [4]

Two months later, Kennedy journeyed to Vienna for a meeting with the Soviet leader, Nikita Khrushchev. The meeting was abrasive and once again centered on the issue of Berlin. Khrushchev complained that a rearmed West Germany had become predominant in NATO since her admission in 1955, and had now become a threat to the Soviet Union. Again he threatened that he would sign a treaty with East Germany that would make American access rights to West Berlin subject to East German control. Kennedy rejected this ultimatum and explained that the presence of the United States in the former German capital was based on contractual rights. "I want peace," Khrushchev declared, "but, if you want war, that is your problem." "It is you, and not I, who wants to force a change," Kennedy retorted. Khrushchev declared once again that his decision was irrevocable. "It will be a cold winter," Kennedy said before the two men parted.[5]

[3] Theodore C. Sorensen, *Kennedy* (New York: Harper and Row, 1965), p. 309.

[4] Schlesinger, op. cit., p. 276.

[5] Ibid., p. 374.

By July 1961, the crisis over Berlin had heated up. "If Khrushchev wants to rub my nose in the dirt," said Kennedy, "it's all over. We cannot and will not permit the Communists to drive us out of Berlin, either gradually or by force." [6] The crisis had its most spectacular effect in East Germany itself. Thousands of East Germans were voting with their feet against their Communist regime by fleeing to West Berlin. During July alone, more than thirty thousand escaped. If this exodus went on unchecked, all of East Germany would be depopulated.

On August 13, 1961, East German troops and police began the construction of a wall that sealed off the East German border crossing into West Berlin. Kennedy sent Vice-President Lyndon Johnson to Berlin and ordered a battle group of fifteen hundred men to move from West Germany to West Berlin. He did not, however, decide to bulldoze down the wall since this would have necessitated an invasion of the eastern sector of Berlin and the risk of nuclear war. Moreover, the French and British governments, whose support he would have needed, were not enthusiastic. The allies perceived the wall as an attempt to stop the refugee exodus from East Germany, rather than as an offensive move against the West. Shortly afterward, the crisis faded away, but a year later, when Kennedy visited the Berlin Wall, he was sufficiently moved to declare that he, too, was a Berliner.[7]

In his Asian policy, John F. Kennedy deepened the American involvement in Vietnam considerably. By the time of his death, the United States had greatly increased the number of military advisers in Vietnam, napalm and other antipersonnel weapons had been authorized for limited use against the enemy, and the United States had become identified with the highly unpopular regime of President Diem.

Kennedy felt impelled to demonstrate his toughness in the international arena, especially after the Bay of Pigs disaster and the Berlin crisis, yet he was deeply skeptical about the possibility of a decisive American victory in Vietnam. In a revealing moment, he exclaimed: "In the last analysis, it is *their* war; it is they who must win it or lose it." He was pressed relentlessly by the military to commit combat troops to Vietnam, but refused to do so to

[6] Ibid., p. 391.
[7] "Ich bin ein Berliner," stated in Berlin, 25 June 1962.

the end. Yet, under his leadership, the United States entered a crucial period of transition, from a marginal commitment to a fateful and direct involvement. The reason for this tragedy was that most of the men around the president, including his secretary of defense and the chairman of the Joint Chiefs of Staff, perceived Vietnam essentially as a military rather than as a political problem. In their view, greater quantities of more sophisticated weapons would guarantee victory in a relatively short period of time. Shortly before his death, his doubts prevailed, but by then it was too late. Close to 17,000 Americans were serving as advisers in Vietnam at the time of his assassination.

In April 1961, in order to boost President Diem's morale, Kennedy decided to ask Vice-President Johnson to visit Vietnam on his Asian tour. Johnson was favorably impressed with Diem. He hailed him publicly as "the Winston Churchill of Southeast Asia." When asked by a reporter whether he really believed that about Diem, Johnson answered: "Shit, man, he's the only boy we got out there." [8] Thus, Johnson committed the president more deeply to Vietnam and, in addition, committed himself personally to the war.

The most crucial single event that escalated the American commitment during the Kennedy administration was the Rostow-Taylor report. In October 1961, the president decided to send two of his own special representatives to Vietnam for an on-site fact-finding trip. He chose Walt Rostow and Maxwell Taylor because of the interest these two men had displayed in Kennedy's own favorite approach to the Vietnam problem: limited anti-guerrilla warfare.

The report came as a profound shock to Kennedy. Rostow and Taylor recommended the introduction of 8,000 American combat troops into Vietnam and stated flatly that without such a commitment, Vietnam could not be saved. So far as fighting conditions for the proposed American combat troops were concerned, Taylor and Rostow declared that they found South Vietnam "not an excessively difficult or unpleasant place to operate." They thought it comparable to Korea where American troops had learned to fight efficiently and well.

Kennedy's own misgivings about this report were echoed by

[8] David Halberstam, *The Best and the Brightest* (New York: Random House, 1972), p. 135.

George Ball, undersecretary of state for economic affairs. He had observed the French disaster in Indochina and noted the parallels. He warned the president that even a small combat commitment of 8,000 men would change the nature of the commitment and the future of the war. Within five years, he warned, the commitment would be escalated to 300,000 men. Kennedy, who had his own doubts about the Taylor-Rostow recommendations, nevertheless expressed his belief in the capacity of rational men to control irrational commitments. He was reported to have laughed at Ball's warning and to have said: "George, you are crazier than hell." [9]

In a conversation with Arthur Schlesinger, Jr., the president expressed his own reservations very clearly:

> They want a force of American troops. They say it is necessary in order to restore confidence and maintain morale. But it will be just like Berlin. The troops will march in, the bands will play, the crowds will cheer, and in four days everyone will have forgotten. Then we will be told we have to send in more troops. It's like taking a drink. The effect wears off and you have to take another.[10]

Finally, the president compromised. Instead of 8,000 combat troops, he authorized 17,000 military advisers and support units. In making this crucial decision, he made a future withdrawal from Vietnam more difficult. Yet, by doing less than he was called upon to do, Kennedy was under the illusion that he was holding the line rather than taking the United States deeper into the war.

Thus, President Kennedy—essentially a man of reason—became seduced by that particularly American form of hubris that blithely assumed that technology, computerlike efficiency, production, air power, and above all, competent American management, could bring down an army of guerrillas who were quite prepared to die for their cause.

In the spring of 1963, however, Kennedy apparently had a change of heart. He told Senator Mike Mansfield that he intended to withdraw all American forces after the 1964 election. It seemed that the senator's arguments had persuaded him that this was the only possible course. "But I can't do it until 1965, after I am reelected," he declared.

[9] Ibid., p. 174.
[10] Schlesinger, op. cit., p. 371.

In 1965, I'll be damned everywhere as a Communist appeaser. But I don't care. If I tried to pull out completely now, we would have another Joe McCarthy red scare on our hands, but I can do it after I'm reelected. So we had better be damned sure that I *am* reelected.[11]

That fall, before he went to Texas, Kennedy issued an order for the withdrawal of one thousand American troops from South Vietnam by the end of the year, despite strong objections from some of his advisors. On October 2, 1963, he convened the National Security Council to hear the reports of Secretary of Defense Robert McNamara and General Maxwell Taylor, who had just returned from Saigon. Kennedy asked McNamara to make a public announcement after the meeting that one thousand men were being withdrawn immediately and that the United States would probably withdraw all American forces by the end of 1965. "And tell them that means all the helicopter pilots too," Kennedy added.[12] A few days before Dallas, Kenneth O'Donnell and Dave Powers asked Kennedy how he could withdraw from South Vietnam and still maintain American prestige in Southeast Asia. "Easy," Kennedy reported, "put a government in there that will ask us to leave." [13]

Whether Kennedy would have carried through on this intention if reelected, we shall never know. But it is not likely that, under his leadership, Vietnam would have been transformed from a relatively small infection into a virulent and raging cancer.

President Kennedy's gravest foreign policy ordeal occurred in October 1962, when Nikita Khrushchev shipped offensive missiles to Cuba. Few episodes illuminate so poignantly the decisive role of an individual personality as those thirteen days in October 1962 when John F. Kennedy held the fate of the world in his hands. Our case study will trace the Cuban missile crisis day by day and highlight the relationship between Kennedy and Khrushchev. We shall witness how two men looked down into the abyss and drew back, just in time, from nuclear catastrophe.

[11] James D. Barber, op. cit., p. 337.
[12] Ibid.
[13] Kenneth O'Donnell, "LBJ and the Kennedys," *Look*, 7 August 1970, pp. 51–52.

5

THE BRUSH WITH
NUCLEAR HOLOCAUST

*Kennedy and Khrushchev and
the Cuban Missile Crisis of 1962*

ANATOMY OF A CRISIS

President John F. Kennedy, reviewing the thirteen days of the Cuban missile crisis of 1962, estimated that the probability of disaster at the crucial point in the confrontation had been "between one out of three and even." [1] In the light of this estimate, mankind's escape from the nuclear abyss seems awesome. A slight shift of the pendulum might have doomed more human lives to sudden extinction than ever before in history. Previous calamities, whether of human or natural origin, would have been dwarfed by comparison. The fact that two mortal men should have held such terrible power demands that we study the event with every tool at our command in order to prevent its recurrence. Mankind might not be so fortunate a second time.

A great deal has been written about the missile crisis, particularly in the United States. Virtually every member of the small group of men who participated in the deliberations of those crucial thirteen days has expressed his thoughts in print. Numerous writers on both sides of the Atlantic have subjected the event to careful scrutiny. Few analyses exist, however, that focus on the role that personalities played in the interaction of the Soviet and American leadership and how these personalities affected the decision-making process. The interplay of personalities will form the focus of this chapter.

[1] John F. Kennedy, quoted in Theodore Sorensen, op. cit., p. 705.

The missile crisis was the climax to rising tensions between the superpowers during 1961. The Soviet Union's action in testing nuclear weapons of unprecedented explosive force had triggered off a major debate over fallout shelters in the United States; the erection of the Berlin Wall had made the tension almost palpable; and the memory of the abortive American-sponsored invasion of Cuba was still fresh. But as yet there had been no direct confrontation.

In mid-October 1962, hard evidence that the Soviet Union was secretly building offensive missile bases in Cuba with headlong speed had been gathered by United States intelligence services. High-altitude photographs had disclosed a medium-range ballistic missile site near San Cristóbal and one near San Diego de los Baños. Tanker trucks, power and instrument installations, missile guidance stations, and erector launchers were clearly visible. And pictures of cylindrical shapes on incoming Soviet freighters confirmed the worst.

The American leadership, which had had evidence of the missile sites by October 15, now weighed its decision silently. For one week the president and his closest associates constituted themselves as an executive committee of the National Security Council and pondered the alternatives. The deliberations were intense, but no word leaked out to the public. The president continued his preparations for the forthcoming political campaign, and as late as October 18, met with Soviet Foreign Secretary Andrei Gromyko, who professed ignorance of the offensive nature of the missile sites in Cuba.

Inside the White House and Pentagon, the War Council considered the alternatives along a kind of "escalation ladder." Six possible responses developed in ascending order of severity: (1) do nothing; (2) submit an American appeal to the United Nations Security Council; (3) make a secret approach to Castro; (4) conduct a naval blockade of Cuba; (5) conduct a "surgical air strike" to eliminate the bases; and (6) launch an invasion of Cuba. The War Council eliminated the first three alternatives as ineffective and the last as unwarranted. The discussion centered around alternatives (4) and (5). The problem confronting the American planners was the classic one of deterrence strategy: how to combine both capability and credibility so that the Soviet leader would be checked by the actual and potential display of American power. Too little power could be interpreted as surrender, too much power as a bluff. Only controlled and flexible use of power at every step would make deterrence effective in the mind of the opponent.

An immediate invasion of Cuba was ruled out because it might have provoked the war that deterrence was designed to prevent. An air strike at the missile bases was also rejected, since Soviet personnel would be killed at the sites and such an action would have been difficult to justify by the nation that had made Pearl Harbor a symbol of infamy. A quarantine seemed to hold out the best hope for a solution. It would entail the requisite show of strength by throwing a naval ring around Cuba, especially if it was coupled with a demand that the Soviet Union dismantle its bases there. Yet it offered the Soviet Union a way out: Khrushchev could avoid a direct confrontation by ordering his ships to change their course. Furthermore, a quarantine would entail no violence, at least not immediately. Thus, on the evening of October 22, 1962, President Kennedy announced the American decision to impose a quarantine and added that "any nuclear missile launched from Cuba against any nation in the Western Hemisphere" would be regarded "as an attack by the Soviet Union on the United States requiring a full retaliatory response on the Soviet Union." [2] The issue was now squarely joined between the superpowers in the most dramatic military confrontation of the cold war. It was clear to participants and onlookers alike that Castro's Cuba was only a pawn. The United States had announced a check to the king.

The announcement was accompanied by an unprecedented peacetime mobilization of military power in the United States. The Polaris submarine fleet armed with nuclear missiles was moved within striking range of the Soviet Union, and for the first time Strategic Air Command (SAC) bombers were dispersed to civilian airfields. Half of the SAC force was on airborne alert. If necessary, the United States was ready to deliver an equivalent of 30 billion tons of TNT upon the Soviet Union. An atmosphere of impending showdown also pervaded the Soviet Union, where all military leaves were cancelled. The next seven days took the world to the brink of war.

On October 23, Secretary of State Dean Rusk obtained the unanimous report of the Organization of American States

---

[2] *Department of State Bulletin*, 47, 12 November 1962, pp. 715–720.

(OAS) for the quarantine. The NATO allies came to the support of the United States, though with misgivings, and not without reminding the United States of its behavior during the Suez crisis. The United Nations Security Council met in the afternoon: the United States demanded the immediate withdrawal of the offensive weapons under international inspection; the Soviet Union condemned the blockade as piracy and asked for its immediate termination. Neither resolution was voted on and the Security Council presented a spectacle of complete helplessness. October 24, United Nations Day, took the world a step closer to the brink. Acting Secretary General U Thant advanced a plan for a two week cooling-off period to explore the issues. Khrushchev accepted the proposal, but Kennedy rejected it on the grounds that the issue of removing the missiles was not negotiable. An appeal by Khrushchev to the British pacifist leader Bertrand Russell to use his influence to effect a general lowering of temperatures was also rejected as irrelevant by the United States. On October 25, Ambassador Adlai Stevenson challenged Soviet Ambassador Valerian Zorin in the United Nations to admit the existence of the missiles, stating that he was prepared to wait for his answer "until hell freezes over." Toward evening, the Russian tanker *Bucharest* approached the blockade zone, and the American destroyer U.S.S. *Gearing* steamed to meet it. Since the Russian vessel carried no contraband it was allowed to proceed. Khrushchev claimed that the ship had not stopped; the United States claimed that the captain had acknowledged inspection. Neither side had backed down.

On October 26, it was learned that several Soviet ships bound for Cuba were changing their course. But, on the other hand, continued photo scrutiny of the missile bases indicated a speed-up in their construction since the announcement of the quarantine. The American offensive had to gather speed before the sites were ready and the missiles operational. President Kennedy spoke of possible "further measures" and did not rule out an air strike at the bases. He also pointed out the numerous possibilities for accidental war if the Soviet Union would not comply. That evening a letter from Premier Khrushchev arrived that looked like a conditional surrender. In it, the premier indicated his willingness to withdraw the missiles, provided Cuba was guaranteed against invasion. This seemed like a fair offer.

On the morning of the following day, however, the White

House received a second letter from the Soviet leader that was much tougher in tone and more demanding in content. This time a deal was suggested: the United States was to dismantle its missile bases in Turkey, and the Soviet Union would withdraw its missiles from Cuba.

The War Council now had to make a crucial decision. Superficially, the Soviet proposal seemed reasonable. It expressed a widespread feeling among neutralists that both sides should compromise and sacrifice something. It was generally approved in the United Nations, and several distinguished Western commentators, such as Walter Lippmann, supported it. Nevertheless, the War Council turned down the proposal. First, President Kennedy felt that the first Soviet letter reflected more clearly than the second the Soviet leader's real feelings. And second, to bargain away NATO bases under pressure would be to undermine the entire alliance and engender a Munich psychology. Each time the Soviet Union would gain a strategic advantage in the cold war, it might offer to give it up in exchange for an existing NATO base, until the alliance would be totally dismantled. Thus, by turning down the barter offer, the United States in effect presented the Soviet Union with an ultimatum: remove the bases or further measures would be taken. The brink had been reached.

On Sunday morning, October 28, the confrontation came to an end. Kennedy's gamble on the first Soviet letter had paid off. The Soviet leader reiterated his offer of withdrawing the missiles in return for an American "no-invasion" pledge. The American president accepted immediately and welcomed Khrushchev's "constructive contribution to peace." Other differences were settled in short order. Castro refused to admit on-site inspection by the United Nations to survey the dismantling of the bases, but the United States decided to forgo such inspection and continued to rely upon its own aerial surveillance. The missile sites were completely stripped within a few weeks and outgoing Soviet ships laden with shrouded shapes, which everyone took to be missiles, brought the crisis to an end. The world had gone to the brink of nuclear hell and come back.

The basic thesis of this case study is threefold: first, the proposition that, before the crisis entered its acute phase on October 15, the leadership of each superpower had lost hold of the reality of the other. Thus, President Kennedy was convinced that the Soviet Union would never attempt to place offensive missiles in Cuba; and Premier Khrushchev was convinced that he could do so and that the United States would take no forceful action. In other words, both leaders permitted their desires to control their perceptions: Kennedy perceived the Soviet leader as prudent, rational, and respectful of the status quo, and Khrushchev perceived the American president as weak, irresolute, and lacking in determination.

Second, and equally important, both leaders managed to gain a much clearer and more realistic perception of each other during the heat of the thirteen days. Thus, Kennedy learned that Khrushchev, though far from irrational, was still capable of taking dangerous risks and of holding invalid assumptions of America's vital interest; Khrushchev learned that Kennedy, though apparently lacking resolve in the Berlin Wall and Bay of Pigs episodes a year earlier, was nevertheless capable of taking a forceful and determined stand in Cuba in October 1962.

Third, and most important, both leaders corrected their perceptions to conform more closely to reality and based their policy decisions on this more realistic appraisal. This ability on both sides may well have saved humanity from nuclear destruction.

The evidence indicates that neither President Kennedy nor his top aides were prepared for the possibility of Soviet offensive missiles in Cuba. Robert Kennedy described the reaction of the group of men assembled by the president on October 15, shortly after the missiles were discovered: "The dominant feeling at the meeting was stunned surprise. No one had expected or anticipated that the Russians would deploy surface-to-surface ballistic missiles in Cuba." [3] The president, in Theodore Sorensen's words, "had not expected the Soviets to attempt so reckless and risky an action in a place like Cuba." [4]

Prior to October, the president and his advisers were thus predisposed to disregard clues that otherwise might have been examined much more closely. During September, for example, numerous Soviet ships on their way to Cuba were noticed to be riding "high in the water." These ships were later identified as those that had carried the offensive missiles, but at the time intelligence sources largely dismissed them as innocuous lumber ships.

---

[3] Robert F. Kennedy, *Thirteen Days* (New York: Norton, 1969), p. 24.

[4] Sorensen, op. cit., p. 673.

A large increase in Soviet personnel in Cuba was detected as early as August, and a U-2 flight over Cuba on August 29 revealed evidence of the construction of surface-to-air missile (SAM) sites. At the same time, however, Soviet Ambassador Anatoly Dobrynin assured both Robert Kennedy and Ted Sorensen that Soviet intentions in Cuba were peaceful. He apparently succeeded in dispelling any doubts that might have lingered in the minds of the two men or the president.

President Kennedy's perception of Premier Khrushchev before the crisis as a rational statesman too prudent to risk anything so dangerous as a direct threat to the security of the Western Hemisphere thus led directly to a policy of nonaction with regard to Cuba. If the president or his advisers had perceived the Soviet leader differently, surveillance of the Soviet vessels and of the island would probably have been much more thorough. The clues that were ignored would have led to far more careful analysis, and, in all probability, the missile bases would have been detected earlier. Thus, the "selective inattention" that characterized the American leadership led to the discovery of the missiles only when it was almost too late. "Psycho-logic," the tendency to ignore or explain away evidence that conflicts with needs and wishes, was also at work. Not only did Kennedy perceive Khrushchev as prudent and rational, but he also desired a détente with the Soviet Union. To admit the possibility of Khrushchev's plan to place offensive missiles in Cuba would have jarred the American president's mental picture most severely.

On the Soviet side, some speculative reconstruction is necessary. The critical determinants of Khrushchev's perception of Kennedy as weak probably were three events that had taken place during the first year of the Kennedy administration: the Bay of Pigs invasion, the Vienna conference, and the Berlin Wall. In all cases, Kennedy did not perform according to Khrushchev's criteria of firmness and strength. In April 1961, Kennedy initiated an invasion of Cuba, but then failed to complete it and allowed more than one thousand Cuban refugees to be taken prisoner by Castro. Khrushchev no doubt studied the events of the Bay of Pigs. He would have understood it if Kennedy had left Castro alone or if he had completely destroyed him. But when Kennedy was rash enough to strike at Cuba but not bold enough to finish the job, Khrushchev probably decided that he was dealing with an inexperienced young man who could be intimidated and blackmailed. Khrushchev's decision to place offensive missiles in Cuba was the final gamble of this assumption. In Vienna, in June 1961, while Kennedy talked of the dangers of miscalculation that led to war, Khrushchev threatened him with a separate Soviet peace treaty with East Germany. And when, in August 1961, Khrushchev built his wall between East and West Berlin, Kennedy did nothing to remove it.

Khrushchev did not announce publicly that he saw Kennedy as weak, but there are strong indications that this was so. In September 1962, the Soviet premier had a meeting with Robert Frost who was visiting the Soviet Union. The aged American poet reported Khrushchev as saying that democracies were "too liberal to fight." [5] In the course of a conversation with the American businessman William Knox on October 24, 1962, Khrushchev reportedly said about Kennedy: "How can I deal with a man who is younger than my son?" [6] An immature man, almost a boy in the Soviet premier's eyes, might not stand up under the pressure of a powerful and determined adversary. Henry Pachter, in his analysis of the missile crisis, stated that "Kennedy seemed open to blackmail. Ever since the confrontation in Vienna, Khrushchev professed to doubt that Americans would stand up in a test of will power." [7] And Edward Crankshaw, in his biography of Khrushchev, wrote that "Kennedy's fumbling at the Bay of Pigs affair and his acceptance of the Berlin Wall suggested that he might be the President most amenable to such a lesson." [8]

In addition to perceiving Kennedy as weak, Khrushchev also perceived Cuba to be of less than vital importance to the United States. Roger Hilsman has suggested that "American attitudes toward Latin America, particularly Cuba, derive from an intimate history, which the Soviets seem not to have fully understood." [9] Another observer described the Soviet premier's perception of the American interest in Cuba in the following terms:

[5] Cited in Arthur M. Schlesinger, Jr., op. cit., p. 281.
[6] Cited in Elie Abel, *The Missile Crisis* (New York: Bantam Books, 1966), p. 133.
[7] Henry M. Pachter, *Collision Course* (New York: Praeger, 1963), p. 25.
[8] Edward Crankshaw, *Khrushchev* (New York: Viking, 1966), p. 281.
[9] Roger Hilsman, *To Move a Nation* (New York: Doubleday, 1967), p. 182.

He [Khrushchev] ridiculed the Monroe Doctrine, perhaps the most revered political text in American diplomatic history. Historically, the Monroe Doctrine has encompassed vital national interests. Yet Khrushchev claimed it to be totally outmoded and irrelevant to the current era of international politics.[10]

In 1961, Khrushchev had seen Kennedy act with greater firmness with regard to Berlin than with regard to Cuba. Kennedy might go to war over Berlin, but not over Cuba. With the missiles installed in Cuba, greater pressure could be placed on Berlin. The place to strike first, then, was Cuba.

On balance, it is most doubtful whether Khrushchev would have placed offensive missiles in Cuba had he not perceived Kennedy as weak and Cuba as relatively unimportant to the United States.

It should be pointed out here that Khrushchev, like his American counterplayer, seemed also to have been the victim of "psycho-logic." He saw what he wanted to see and minimized discordant evidence, thus arriving at the clear picture that allowed him to act. Kennedy may have talked about miscalculation and the need for conciliation at Vienna, but he did nothing to accede to Khrushchev's demands. He may have let the wall go up in Berlin, but he gave no indication of giving up Western interests in the city itself. And even though the Bay of Pigs may have been a fiasco, the American president made numerous policy pronouncements underlining the continuing special concern of the United States for Cuba and the nation's determination to oppose any further Soviet initiatives in the Western Hemisphere.

In sum, then, before the crisis entered its acute phase both leaders saw what they wanted to see. In Kennedy's case, this led to inaction, in Khrushchev's to swift and determined action.

KENNEDY RESPONDS TO KHRUSHCHEV

The thirteen days of the missle crisis can be divided into two distinct phases: the first, or secret phase, which began with the discovery of the missiles on October 14, and ended with President

---

[10] Joseph G. Whelan, "Khrushchev and the Balance of World Powers," *The Review of Politics*, April 1961, p. 149.

Kennedy's speech on October 22; and the second, or public phase, which came to an end on October 28.

On the American side, President Kennedy made three crucial decisions during the first phase and three more during the second. Each of these decisions flowed directly from his image of himself or of his opponent. Kennedy's perception of Khrushchev had changed significantly since the discovery of the missiles. While Kennedy still perceived the Soviet leader as a rational man who would not risk a nuclear war once convinced of the American determination to get the missiles out of Cuba, he now saw another dimension in the Soviet leader's personality: volatility and the capacity for dangerous, even reckless, action. This dual perception was responsible for the fine sense of balance that dominated Kennedy's subsequent decisions, his sensitively calibrated crisis management, and his adroit use of power, without erring in applying too much or too little. Let us examine the three decisions President Kennedy made during the secret phase of the crisis.

First, the president decided to seek advice from a group of men with different political outlooks. The most prominent members of this executive committee were the president, Robert Kennedy, Vice-President Lyndon Johnson, Secretary of State Dean Rusk, Secretary of Defense Robert McNamara, Chairman of the Joint Chiefs Maxwell Taylor, CIA Director John McCone, UN Ambassador Adlai Stevenson, and special assistants McGeorge Bundy and Theodore Sorensen. Others participated in some of the deliberations, notably Dean Acheson, George Ball, Douglas Dillon, and Arthur Schlesinger, Jr.

Kennedy had learned from the Bay of Pigs disaster about the danger of one-sided, uncontested viewpoints guiding the decision-making process in foreign policy. On that occasion, most of the new president's advisers had perceived a Cuba ripe for an anti-Castro uprising that could be sparked by a handful of Cuban refugees. Almost everyone close to the President had seen what he wanted to see, not what the reality actually was. Kennedy had also learned from Barbara Tuchman's *The Guns of August* how miscalculations can lead to war. In order to minimize this possibility he wanted to avail himself of the widest possible range of opinion to assist him in reaching a decision. As he said to his brother, "I am not going to follow a course which would allow anyone to write a comparable book about this time, *The Missiles of October*." [11] And in order "not to be dragged along in the wake of events, but to control them," Kennedy was determined to keep the committee deliberations secret. "If our deliberations had been publicized, if we had had to make a decision in twenty-four hours," Robert Kennedy wrote after the conclusion of the crisis, "I believe the course that we ultimately would have taken would have been quite different and filled with far greater risks." [12] In essence, the president's decision to be seriously responsive to a group of advisers with a wide variety of viewpoints and to encourage frank and uninhibited discussion in that small group, removed from all publicity, was a decision to reject "psycho-logic," to make sure that opinions with which the president might be out of phase emotionally would nevertheless be weighed on their objective merits. Most important, perhaps, the decision to assemble the executive committee was the alternative to an immediate military strike; Kennedy rejected the latter because he perceived Khrushchev as not only a dangerous but also a "rational, intelligent man, who, if given sufficient time and shown our determination, would alter his position." [13] In short, the president's perception of the Soviet leader provided guidance not only for what to do but, perhaps more important, for what not to do.

The naval blockade of Cuba was by far the most important decision the president took during the secret phase of the crisis. An analysis of the discussion of the six alternatives reveals significant linkages between the perceptions held by the participants and the decisions that were actually made. Kennedy ruled out nonaction from the very beginning, even though he realized that the emplacement of Soviet missiles in Cuba would not have substantially altered the strategic balance in fact. But he was convinced that the balance would have been substantially altered in *appearance*; and in matters of national will and world leadership, as the president was to say later, "such appearances contribute to reality." [14] "If we did nothing, we would be dead," [15] Schlesinger

[11] John F. Kennedy, quoted by Robert Kennedy, op. cit., p. 127.

[12] Ibid., p. 111.

[13] Ibid., p. 126.

[14] John F. Kennedy, quoted in Sorensen, op. cit., p. 678.

[15] John F. Kennedy, quoted in Schlesinger, op. cit., p. 811.

quotes him as saying, and "the worst course would be to do nothing," he said to Sorensen.[16] Douglas Dillon, commenting on the first meeting of the committee, observed that "the first reaction of the President, with the others in full agreement, was that we simply could not accept the fact of Soviet missiles in Cuba, trained on the United States." [17] Defense Secretary McNamara, who argued at first that "a missile was a missile," regardless from where it was fired, soon changed his mind, apparently persuaded by the president's distinction between reality and appearances.

To bring the crisis to the United Nations was dismissed as a dilatory tactic and to make a secret *démarche* to Castro was seen as futile. The first three levels of response were thus considered to be too weak, even though no one on the executive committee seriously argued that the missiles posed an objective military threat. The president, in the last analysis, "was concerned less about the missiles' military implications than with their effect on the global balance of power." [18] Given this definition of the situation, there was little alternative but to initiate a forceful remedy.

Perception of self and of the adversary also played a crucial role in the discussion of the higher levels of escalation. An invasion of Cuba was rejected almost immediately since Kennedy did not wish to make it appear that his primary aim was the overthrow of Castro. The possibility of an air strike against the missile bases, however, was considered most seriously and for several days was deemed to be the only real alternative to the naval blockade. Several committee members argued that an air strike was the quickest and safest way to eliminate the missiles. A blockade, they argued, might well be irrelevant since the missiles were already on the island. Robert Kennedy, however, found such a course to be incompatible with his perception of the American heritage. "Sunday morning surprise attacks on small nations are simply not in the American tradition," he said, adding: "My brother is not going to be the Tojo of the 1960s." [19] Schlesinger suggests that most of the members of the committee turned away from the air strike

---

[16] John F. Kennedy, quoted in Sorensen, op. cit., p. 694.

[17] Douglas Dillon, quoted in Abel, op. cit., p. 35.

[18] Sorensen, op. cit., p. 683.

[19] Robert Kennedy, quoted in Abel, op. cit., p. 51, and Schlesinger, op. cit., p. 807.

route as a result of Robert Kennedy's statement.[20] The president displayed a keen sense of empathy with his Soviet counterplayer. "They cannot permit us to kill a lot of Russians and then do nothing," [21] he said, adding: "It isn't the first step that concerns me but both sides escalating to the fourth and fifth steps." [22] Reflecting on the crisis in a speech at American University, in the summer of 1963, he put it most succinctly: "Nuclear powers must avert those confrontations which bring an adversary to a choice of either a humiliating retreat or a nuclear war." [23] An air strike would have done that, a blockade did not. In his book on the missile crisis, Robert Kennedy stressed his brother's empathy with Khrushchev's position:

> Always he asked himself: Can we be sure that Khrushchev understands what we feel to be our vital national interests? Has the Soviet Union had sufficient time to react soberly to a particular step we have taken? All actions were judged against that standard.[24]

The evidence suggests that, in the last analysis, Robert Kennedy's argument against a "Pearl Harbor in reverse" and John Kennedy's empathy with and multifaceted perception of Khrushchev led away from the physical violence of an air strike to the more limited and nonviolent course of the quarantine. Specifically, the placement of Soviet missiles in Cuba was perceived as a challenge to the American will. A low-level response would have made America *appear* weak, even though little would have actually changed. An air strike, on the other hand, would have made America appear immoral. Thus, the course that was the most compatible with the executive committee's perceptions of the United States was the quarantine.

The third decision during the secret phase of the crisis involved Kennedy's perception of his adversary's intention. Khrushchev, in Kennedy's view, was intent on presenting the United States with a *fait accompli* when the missiles were in place. In the president's words: "They thought they had us either way. If we

[20] Schlesinger, op. cit., p. 807.

[21] John F. Kennedy, quoted in Robert Kennedy, op. cit., p. 36.

[22] Ibid., p. 98.

[23] John F. Kennedy, quoted in Abel, op. cit., p. 193.

[24] Kennedy, op. cit., p. 125.

did nothing, we would be dead. If we reacted, they hoped to put us in an exposed position .with regard to Berlin, Turkey, or the UN." [25] Hence, Kennedy decided to keep the committee deliberations secret and to announce the quarantine decision to friend and foe alike in a surprise speech, thus presenting Khrushchev with his own *fait accompli.*

The quarantine speech of October 22 ushered in the public, or direct, phase of the crisis. During the next six days, President Kennedy made three more crucial decisions, each based on his perception of himself and of Premier Khrushchev. After obtaining the unanimous support of the Organization of American States for the quarantine on October 23, he drew the blockade line on the morning of October 24. The first two decisions pertained to the enforcement of that line.

On October 24, Acting Secretary General of the United Nations U Thant sent identical letters to Kennedy and Khrushchev urging suspension of both the blockade and further arms shipments to Cuba for two weeks. While Khrushchev accepted U Thant's suggestions almost immediately, Kennedy decided to put off a reply until the following day. To accept the suggestions, would, in Kennedy's view, have relieved the diplomatic and military pressure on Khrushchev that the quarantine had set in motion, and that was precisely what the president did not want to do. Kennedy wanted to impress on Khrushchev his determination to stand fast. Thus, he decided to refuse negotiations until Khrushchev showed some willingness to dismantle the missile bases. Once again, Kennedy acted on his perception of Khrushchev as a rational man, who if shown determination without violence and given sufficient time, would alter his position. Accordingly, on October 25, the president rejected U Thant's proposal in the following words: "The existing threat was created by the secret introduction of offensive weapons into Cuba, and the answer lies in the removal of such weapons." [26]

The second decision concerned the first actual encounter between Soviet and American ships on the high seas. "The greatest danger of war as we saw it then," Assistant Defense Secretary Paul Nitze recalls, "was that we would sink a Russian ship trying to run

---

[25] John F. Kennedy, quoted in Schlesinger, op. cit., p. 811.
[26] John F. Kennedy, quoted by Abel, op. cit., p. 148.

the blockade. If that happened, it seemed highly doubtful that Khrushchev would hold still without further action." [27] In the afternoon of October 25, several Soviet ships approached the quarantine line, with the tanker *Bucharest* in the lead. Even though the ship was thought to carry only oil, which was on the contraband list, "there were those on the ExCom," Robert Kennedy recalls in his memoir, "who felt strongly that the *Bucharest* should be stopped and boarded so that Khrushchev would make no mistake of our intent and will." [28] The president, however, permitted the ship to pass through the blockade line with only a signal from an American destroyer. This move clearly was based on Kennedy's perception of Khrushchev as a man who, if pushed too hard, might initiate violence. In the president's words, "We don't want to push him to a precipitous action—give him time to consider. I don't want to push him into a corner from which he cannot escape." [29]

The most crucial decision that Kennedy made, however, involved the two fateful letters sent to him by Khrushchev on October 26 and October 27. When, on October 26, Kennedy received Khrushchev's first letter hinting at his willingness to remove the missiles in exchange for a pledge from the American president not to invade Cuba, the president and his advisers were inclined to respond favorably. Only Dean Acheson, who felt that Khrushchev when writing the letter must have been "either tight or scared," thought that "so long as the President had the thumbscrew on Khrushchev, he should give it another turn every day." [30] On October 27, however, just as the president was about to draft an affirmative reply, the second letter arrived in which the Soviet leader raised the price for the removal of the missiles. In this letter, which was released simultaneously to all the news media, Khrushchev asserted that if Kennedy wanted him to remove the Soviet missiles from Cuba, he would have to remove the American missile base in Turkey. On the same morning, there occurred the only casualty of the missile crisis: Major Rudolf Anderson, Jr., a U-2 pilot, was shot down by Soviet surface-to-air mis-

---

[27] Paul Nitze, quoted in ibid., p. 134.
[28] Kennedy, op. cit., p. 73.
[29] John F. Kennedy, quoted by Robert Kennedy, op. cit., p. 76.
[30] Dean Acheson, quoted in Abel, op. cit., p. 162.

siles over Cuba. Under this pressure, the consensus against an air strike in the executive committee almost broke down. In Sorensen's words: "Our little group seated around the Cabinet table . . . felt nuclear war to be closer on that day than at any time in the nuclear age." [31] Schlesinger reports that:

> We had no choice, it was argued, but a military response, and our tactical analysis had already shown that strikes at the bases would be of little use without strikes at the airfields, and strikes at the airfields of little use without further supporting action, so once the process began, it would hardly stop short of invasion.[32]

Nevertheless, Kennedy refused to bomb the bases. He still believed that a determined, but nonviolent, posture by the United States would persuade Khrushchev to retreat, and that an air strike might well push the Soviet leader over the thermonuclear brink.

Most difficult of all, of course, was the specific problem of responding to Khrushchev's two contradictory messages. "No one knew which letter superseded the other; no one knew whether Khrushchev was still in power." [33] Robert Kennedy made the suggestion that the president should respond to the first letter. After all, it had arrived first and probably indicated more accurately than the second the Soviet leader's real perception of the crisis. The president, apparently reluctant to bargain away the Turkish bases under Soviet pressure and fearful of threatening the unity of NATO, agreed to gamble on the first letter, thus rejecting the Cuba-Turkey exchange proposal. This decision was so crucial that it deserves careful analysis.

Robert Kennedy wrote the following account of his brother's rejection of the Cuba-Turkey deal:

> He obviously did not wish to order the withdrawal of the missiles from Turkey under threat of the Soviet Union. On the other hand, he did not want to involve the United States and mankind in a catastrophic war over missile sites in Turkey that were antiquated and useless.[34]

The fact remains, nevertheless, that President Kennedy risked precisely such a catastrophic war. The rejection of the Cuba-

[31] Sorensen, op. cit., p. 714.
[32] Schlesinger, op. cit., p. 827.
[33] Ibid., p. 829.
[34] Kennedy, op. cit., p. 95.

Turkey swap was in effect an ultimatum to Khrushchev. Kennedy let Khrushchev know that, unless he dismantled the bases within the next day or two, military action would follow. "The expectation was a military confrontation by Tuesday and possibly tomorrow," [35] the president's brother said of that Saturday. And the president said on Saturday night, "Now it can go either way." [36]

To argue, as Sorenson does, that "the President had no intention of destroying the Alliance by backing down" [37] seems superficial. The evidence suggests that the answer must be sought at a deeper level and that Kennedy's perception of himself and of the United States played a crucial role in the decision. "We cannot tell anyone to keep out of our hemisphere," young Jack Kennedy had written twenty-two years earlier in *Why England Slept*, "unless our armaments and the people behind these armaments are prepared to back up the command, even to the ultimate point of going to war." In his speech of October 22, 1962, he had said, "One path we shall never choose, and that is the path of surrender and submission," adding, with specific reference to the missiles, "It is difficult to settle or even discuss the problem in an atmosphere of intimidation."

It seems that President Kennedy, in his eagerness to impress his determination upon Khrushchev, may have confused weakness with compromise. In his desire not to appear weak, he apparently never fully distinguished between the danger of the missiles remaining in Cuba and the danger resulting from a removal of the missiles through compromise. Certainly the latter danger was much smaller, but the president seems to have perceived both as equally unacceptable challenges to the American will. A deeply ingrained reaction against the "Munich syndrome" and the determination not to appear weak—stemming perhaps from his encounter with Khrushchev in Vienna—made him risk nuclear war over missile bases in Turkey, which, by his own admission, were obsolete and useless and which, by his own order, should have been dismantled two months earlier. Thus, after twelve days of almost incredible balance and restraint, he risked nuclear Armageddon on the thirteenth day over what appeared to be a side issue. Fortunately for humanity, his luck held and he won the gamble. But

[35] Ibid., p. 109.
[36] John F. Kennedy, quoted by Abel, op. cit., p. 179.
[37] Sorensen, op. cit., p. 714.

by turning down the barter deal, Kennedy relinquished the ultimate choice between peace and war to Nikita Khrushchev.

We have seen that Khrushchev probably perceived Kennedy as
lacking in determination and that this perception was probably
responsible for his conviction that Soviet missiles could be placed
into Cuba without eliciting a forceful American response. In the
course of the public phase of the crisis, however, Khrushchev gradually learned to perceive the American president differently and this
changed perception led directly to the decision to withdraw the
missiles. Naturally, since there is hardly any access to the Soviet
decision-making process, this analysis must be based largely on
circumstantial evidence, but even the bits and pieces that can be
assembled add up to an impressive case.

Khrushchev's perception of Kennedy as weak seems to have
been so firmly embedded that the Soviet leader pursued his course
without hesitation, and despite some telltale signs in September
and early October that Kennedy might not be soft, to further
Soviet initiatives in Cuba. When, on September 4, Kennedy publicly warned the Soviet Union that if Cuba were ever to become
an offensive missile base, the United States would take action to
protect itself, Khrushchev responded with a tough public statement: "Today one cannot attack Cuba and expect the aggressor
to go unpunished for the attack. If such an attack is made, it will
be the start of the unleashing of war." [38] Khrushchev probably regarded Kennedy's warning as political oratory and felt that a
threat of war would be sufficient to deter the United States from
responding forcefully. Because of this perception, the Soviet leader
was unable to see that Kennedy was "drawing a line, and making it
extremely unlikely that he would back down if that line was
crossed." [39] Even when Kennedy activated the reserves, Khrushchev seemed to remain unaffected. Arnold Horelick suggests some
other reasons that might have prompted Khrushchev to continue

[38] Nikita Khrushchev, cited in *Digest of the Soviet Press*, 19 October 1962,
    p. 14.
[39] Wohlstetter, op. cit., p 701.

the missile program. These reasons included the expectation that the United States would respond with diplomatic action, namely, that Kennedy would consult with his NATO allies and be persuaded to adopt a nonviolent approach and that the OAS would probably oppose any military action by the United States.[40] These expectations were all based on the assumption of a fictitious Kennedy, one that Khrushchev needed in order to implement his missile program.

The first decision that confronted the Soviet leader during the public phase of the crisis was how to respond to Kennedy's quarantine speech of October 22. It seems that the Soviet leadership was as stunned by the American response as the executive committee had been when it first learned of the Soviet move on October 15. There was no immediate reaction from the Kremlin. Dean Rusk said to George Ball on the morning after the speech, "We have won a considerable victory. You and I are still alive." [41] Neither in Berlin nor anywhere else did a Soviet move materialize. A front-page editorial in *Pravda* on October 24 condemned the United States for a "crude form of blackmail that is bringing down catastrophe upon all mankind" but concluded by declaring that "in the situation that has arisen, a special responsibility falls on the United Nations." [42] This reaction suggested that the Soviet leadership had been thrown off guard by the blockade and now adopted a policy of "wait and see." Though Khrushchev was probably confused by the American move, his precrisis perception of Kennedy had yet to be shaken. After all, Kennedy had thus far only called for a blockade. He had not yet proved his determination to enforce it.

The blockade line was drawn on October 24. Khrushchev now had to make the crucial decision of what to do about it. In the morning of that day, the Soviet leader issued a stern warning: "If the United States Government carries out the program of piratical actions outlined by it, we shall have to resort to means of defense against the aggressors to defend our rights." [43] In the afternoon, he summoned to the Kremlin the American busi-

---

[40] Arnold L. Horelick, "The Cuban Missile Crisis: An Analysis of Soviet Calculations and Behavior," *World Politics*, April 1964, p. 381.

[41] Dean Rusk, quoted in Abel, op. cit., p. 110.

[42] Cited in *Digest of the Soviet Press*, 12 November 1962, p. 4.

[43] Nikita Khrushchev, quoted in Abel, op. cit., p. 126.

nessman William Knox who happened to be in Moscow on behalf of Westinghouse International. Elie Abel renders a vivid account of this meeting, which deserves to be quoted in full:

> Knox arrived fifteen minutes late to find Khrushchev in a state of near-exhaustion. He looked like a man who had not slept all night. For three hours he treated Knox to a succession of threats, complaints and peasant jokes. It was true, he said, the Soviet Union had missiles and attack planes in Cuba; moreover he would use them if need be.
>
> He wanted the President and the American people to know, Khrushchev added, that if the United States Navy tried to stop Soviet ships at sea, his submarines would start sinking American ships. And that would mean a third world war. Khrushchev complained that he could not understand Kennedy. Eisenhower had been troublesome enough, but Eisenhower was a man of his own generation. "How can I deal with a man who is younger than my son?" he asked the astonished Westinghouse man. Then, extending a stubby index finger across the table in Knox's direction, he talked of weapons, offensive and defensive. "If I point a pistol at you like this in order to attack you," Khrushchev said, "the pistol is an offensive weapon. But if I am to keep you from shooting me, it is defensive, no?" [44]

This exchange suggests that Khrushchev's perception of Kennedy was shaken by October 24, but not yet undermined. This ambivalence was reflected in Soviet policy decisions on that day. Khrushchev issued orders to some of his ships to change course. The ship that was ordered to test the blockade was a freighter that carried no contraband. On the other hand, Khrushchev ordered a speed-up in the construction of the missile sites. His ready acceptance of U Thant's proposal for a cooling-off period suggests that such a period would have given him the necessary time to render the missiles fully operational.

Khrushchev probably changed his perception of Kennedy sometime during Thursday, October 25. Kennedy's rejection of U Thant's proposal, his insistence that the missiles be removed, his warning that "further action will be justified should these offensive military preparations continue," and the continuing massive arms build-up in the United States probably persuaded Khrush-

[44] Ibid., pp. 132–133.

chev that Kennedy was not bluffing. What Khrushchev now began to perceive was that Kennedy was determined to get the missiles out of Cuba, that he was planning to bomb Cuba if necessary to attain this objective, and that such an attack could precipitate a nuclear war. The note of desperation that permeated his personal letter to Kennedy suggests this sudden recognition. He wrote:

> Mr. President, we and you ought not now to pull on the ends of the rope in which you have tied the knot of war, because the more we pull, the tighter the knot will be tied. . . . Only lunatics or suicides who themselves want to perish and destroy the whole world before they did, could do this.[45]

The preception of acute danger was reinforced by the strategic realities of the situation. Khrushchev had known that the American military machine was exceedingly powerful. But so long as he felt that Kennedy was unwilling to use that power, he had felt relatively safe. As soon as this assumption became questionable, however, the terrible consequences became obvious. If war came, Khrushchev had the choice of either being overwhelmed in a limited air or naval engagement in the Caribbean or of having his country devastated by a nuclear attack. Neither alternative was acceptable. Hence, Khrushchev's new perception of Kennedy as having "tied the knot of war" and willing to commit "suicide," if necessary, to get the missiles out of Cuba probably led him to write his personal letter to the American president.

There has been considerable speculation about the sequence of the two Khrushchev letters. The actual timing of the notes and the reasons for their contradictory content may never be fully known. Michael Tatu suggests that the Cuba-Turkey letter was prompted by the reaction of other Presidium members that Khrushchev had backed down too quickly. He advances the hypothesis that the Cuba-Turkey swap proposal constituted a middle approach between the offer contained in Khrushchev's personal letter and the demands of Soviet hard-liners who insisted on an American withdrawal from all foreign bases.[46] Henry Pachter, in his *Collision Course*, suggests that the second letter, proposing the Cuba-Turkey exchange, had actually been drafted and sent

[45] Nikita Khrushchev, quoted in ibid., p. 152.
[46] Michael Tatu, *Power in the Kremlin* (New York: Viking, 1969), p. 263.

first, but through the regular diplomatic channels of the foreign ministry. The personal letter, Pachter contends, was actually written and sent later, but directly by Khrushchev without clearance with the foreign ministry. Hence it overtook the other more formal and demanding communication.[47] The evidence seems to support Pachter's thesis. The Cuba-Turkey letter mentions Kennedy's rejection of U Thant's proposal but does not make reference to the military arms build-up. This seems to suggest that the slow letter, proceeding through channels, had been overtaken by events. Khrushchev's new perception of Kennedy, now reinforced by the ominous events of October 26, probably prompted him to write the personal letter indicating his desire to avoid a showdown and his willingness to remove the missiles in exchange for a pledge from President Kennedy not to invade Cuba. When Kennedy did indeed respond to the personal letter rather than to the barter proposal, Khrushchev did not press the matter; he had become convinced that Kennedy would bomb Cuba if he did. In a revealing speech before the Supreme Soviet on December 12, 1962, Khrushchev related how the crisis appeared to him on that day. "Immediate action was necessary," he said "to prevent the attack on Cuba and to preserve peace." [48] He added that "In these circumstances, if one or the other side had failed to show restraint, failed to do all that was necessary to prevent the outbreak of war, an explosion would have followed with irreparable consequences." [49] He also gave the Supreme Soviet a detailed and vivid account of the military preparations that President Kennedy had made:

> Several paratrooper, infantry, and armored divisions, numbering some 100,000 men were allocated for the attack on Cuba. In addition, 183 warships with 85,000 sailors on board were moved toward the shores of Cuba. Several thousand war planes were to cover the landing in Cuba. About 20 percent of the U.S. Strategic Air Command planes, carrying atomic and hydrogen bombs, were kept aloft around the clock.[50]

[47] Pachter, op. cit., p. 68.

[48] Nikita Khrushchev, cited in *Digest of the Soviet Press*, 16 January 1963, p. 5.

[49] Ibid.

[50] Ibid.

Hence, when Kennedy pledged not to invade Cuba, Khrushchev was ready to withdraw the missiles and thus to terminate the crisis. "We are interested that there should be no war in the world," he wrote Kennedy on October 28.[51] He now firmly believed that Kennedy had been ready to risk war over the missiles in Cuba and perhaps even over obsolete missiles in Turkey.

A word should be said about Khrushchev's self-image during the crisis. First, it was possible for Khrushchev to withdraw the missiles without severe damage to his self-esteem. In December, he told the Supreme Soviet: "Our purpose was only the defense of Cuba." [52] With a pledge from Kennedy not to invade Cuba, Khrushchev could claim that he terminated the crisis with the main Soviet objective accomplished. Second, Marxism-Leninism does not equate retreat with the stigma of defeat. Lenin's concept of "one step backward, two steps forward" could be made to apply to the Cuba encounter. Indeed, anything other than withdrawal might have seemed like reckless adventurism under the circumstances, a shortcoming that Lenin had once condemned as an "infantile disorder."

With all this said, however, the fact remains that retreat for Khrushchev was probably not easy. It takes an honest man to admit that his perception of an adversary might have been wrong all along. It takes a flexible and resourceful man to change his policy upon such recognition. And it takes a courageous man not to place the preservation of his ego before the preservation of the peace.

AFTERMATH

President Kennedy's and Premier Khrushchev's personal perceptions of themselves and of each other deeply influenced the course of the Cuban missile crisis. Both saw what they wanted to see before the crisis. As a result, Kennedy lowered his guard in Cuba and Khrushchev shipped his missiles.

Kennedy viewed the missiles basically as a challenge to the

---

[51] Nikita Khrushchev, quoted in Kennedy, op. cit., p. 210.

[52] Nikita Khrushchev, cited in *Digest of Soviet Press*, 16 January, 1963, p. 5.

American will. They had to be removed, not because they made America weak, but because they made her *appear* weak. And in order to get them out, Kennedy went to the brink of war. Khrushchev was able to withdraw the missiles with his ego and self-esteem substantially intact. Had he not been able to do so, had he been forced to *appear* weak, nuclear disaster might well have been the consequence.

Each leader showed empathy with the other's perception of the crisis. Robert Kennedy wrote that:

> The final lesson of the Cuban missile crisis is the importance of placing ourselves in the other country's shoes. During the crisis, President Kennedy spent more time trying to determine the effect of a particular course of action on Khrushchev or the Russians than on any other phase of what he was doing.[53]

Khrushchev's ultimate recognition of Kennedy's determination and his flexibility at the brink showed similar empathy and self-restraint.

There is one final sense in which these personal perceptions were perhaps decisive. Neither leader could say to the other, "Do as I say or I shall kill you," but each was reduced to saying, "Do as I say or I shall kill us both." Force, in the crude physical sense, was no longer a predictable instrument of national policy. Each superpower could have annihilated the other, but by so doing, would have destroyed itself. To put it crassly: since everybody was somebody, nobody was anybody. Since physical force on each side was equally devastating and thus virtually cancelled out, subjective perceptions and appearances of power loomed particularly large. Psychology thus superseded hardware, and a state of mind became decisive. *The missile crisis was in its essence a nuclear war, but one that was fought in the minds of two men and their perceptions of themselves and each other.* Fortunately for all of us, these were men with political wisdom, moral courage, and a gift for empathy. They grasped not only with their minds but also felt deeply in their hearts both the burden and the terror of the human condition in the nuclear age.

The world was fortunate that Kennedy and Khrushchev were in power then. What if Stalin had still controlled the Soviet

---

[53] Kennedy, op. cit., p. 124.

Union? And what if Lyndon Johnson had been president? Or Richard Nixon? "Iffy questions," Franklin Roosevelt might have said. Note quite. We *do* have some clues for what these men might have done had they been in Kennedy's shoes. Lyndon Johnson, for example, was against the quarantine decision. "I never knew what he was for but he was against it," Robert Kennedy wrote.[54] And Richard Nixon thought that Kennedy had "enabled the United States to pull defeat out of the jaws of victory." [55] Moreover, "the 10 or 12 people who had participated in all these discussions," Robert Kennedy wrote in November 1963, "were bright and energetic people. . . . And if any one of half a dozen of them were President, the world would have been very likely plunged in a catastrophic war." [56]

The case of John F. Kennedy in the Cuban missile crisis shows us the pragmatic leader at his best. Here, *all* the possible alternatives were *in fact* exhaustively discussed and the quarantine decision was reached only after the most careful analysis of all the other options. Kennedy not only based his decision on the facts, but also had the imagination and the courage to place himself into the shoes of his Soviet adversary. A lesser man might have neglected that dimension. A moment's thought will show us how crucial Kennedy's personality was in this encounter. Would a Lyndon Johnson have explored all the alternatives equally objectively? Or would he have been compelled to bomb the Cuban missile bases in order to demonstrate to Khrushchev that LBJ could not be pushed around?

We shall never know what might have been. But we do know this: the American who was killed by an assassin's bullet and the Russian who was made into an "unperson" by his successors displayed that sterling form of courage that Ernest Hemingway had once called "grace under pressure." But for that courage, there might have been no history.

[54] Arthur M. Schlesinger, Jr., *Robert Kennedy and His Times* (Boston: Houghton Mifflin Co., 1978), p. 525.

[55] Ibid., p. 531.

[56] Ibid., p. 525.

THE TWILIGHT
OF BIPOLARITY

The Cuban missile crisis of 1962 marked a turning point in Soviet-American relations. Both superpowers had gone to the edge of the abyss and turned back just in time. The narrow escape from atomic holocaust had left its mark on the Soviet and American leaderships alike. Both sides understood the risks of nuclear diplomacy in a bipolar world. One side's gain was now the other's loss. There was little, if any, maneuverability left. Direct confrontations might easily lead to atomic catastrophe. Hence, it was no accident that the bipolar world gradually began to loosen. Three developments occurred. First, competition *within* the two camps became almost as important as competition *between* them. Second, the battleground between East and West began to shift to the frontiers of the two great empires; the new nations of the Third World became the "swing vote" in the East-West struggle. And finally, as Asia increasingly became the object of the contest, China loomed ever larger as a threatening adversary, second only to the Soviet Union. Americans, after all, had fought Chinese on the battlefields of Korea. They had not fought Russians. This was the world that was taking shape when Lyndon Johnson was thrust into the presidency of the United States.

In Western Europe, the American leadership of NATO came under increasing challenge. This process of reappraisal confronted the United States with renewed dilemmas of power and responsibility. While some of the NATO nations, such as Britain and France, had succeeded in joining the "nuclear club," the latter through a *force de frappe*, others counted on the United States to supply them with technical knowledge and materials with which to develop independent atomic arsenals. Yet for the United States to grant this request entailed serious responsibilities. It meant the dispersion of atomic power to many countries, with unforeseeable consequences. Although under the terms of the Atlantic Pact all partners were equal, in the American view some were "less equal than others"—that is, less dependable. If the United States were to give atomic weapons to West Germany, a democracy, would she be duty-bound to grant them also to Portugal, a dictatorship? In any case, the dissemination of atomic weapons throughout NATO might increase the mathematical chances of a war through inadvertence. This fact had to be weighed against the opposing claim that independent atomic arsenals for each member nation would strengthen the alliance as a whole. Furthermore, if the United States were to vest nuclear power in its NATO allies, could it refuse similar requests from SEATO, and if so, on what grounds? But if the United States refused to furnish any atomic weapons to its allies, would the Soviet Union believe the American claim that it would protect a European ally even at the risk of exposing the United States to Soviet atomic attack? For example, if the Soviet Union were to threaten the "liberation" of West Berlin and were to warn the United States of atomic retaliation if Washington interfered, would the United States then honor its obligations to its West German partner in NATO? Or would the Soviet Union only take seriously a threat from the country that it intended to attack, in this case West Germany itself? Many observers were convinced that the Soviet Union would find only those threats of nuclear reprisal credible that came from the nation whose own survival was at stake. Hence the most serious dilemma that the United States now faced was how to respond to a Soviet attack that was limited to a particular member of NATO. The uncertainties and ambiguities of alliance strategy in the nuclear age created an extreme ambivalence between the United States and its partners, a kind of love-hate relationship, a "dialectic of dependence and counterdependence," a constant process of asking "who needs whom most and who will defend whom?" As long as the United States was safe from Soviet atomic attack, she tended to doubt the readiness of her NATO partners to fulfill their obligations in a war that would involve the two superpowers. Would France "come through" if the Soviet Union were to launch an attack upon the

United States and threaten France with complete destruction unless she remained neutral? But even while the United States still possessed an atomic monopoly, some of her NATO allies feared the opposite, namely that the United States would not "come through" in case of a Soviet attack on a NATO country that was not considered vital to America's defense. With mutual deterrence a fact of life between East and West, the mutual suspicions between the United States and her NATO partners grew apace. Would the United States stand by the defense of France if this might mean the destruction of her own national substance? President Charles de Gaulle believed that no American president would do this. Moreover, he was determined to resist any "Anglo-Saxon" influence in the affairs of Western Europe. In March 1966, the French president, in a dramatic move, announced his intention to withdraw French units progressively from the NATO command. He declared that the American deterrent was at best "indeterminate," and that American military involvements in other parts of the world might drag France into an undesired war. The United States deplored the French move and President Johnson found it "difficult to believe that France [would] long remain withdrawn from the common affairs and responsibilities of the Atlantic." However, in March 1967, NATO headquarters were shifted from Paris to Brussels. The disengagement of France from NATO was now a physical reality.

France was not the only NATO trouble spot. Britain, ever since the Suez crisis, was menaced by threats to the ever vulnerable pound sterling; her ambivalence toward the European Common Market, that had been launched by West Germany, France, Italy, and the Benelux countries in 1959, created further fissures. West Germany was torn between de Gaulle's appeal for greater European self-reliance and dependence on its protector, the United States; Greece and Turkey were quarreling over Cyprus; and Belgium, Holland, Italy, and Luxembourg were eager to get on with the work of economic integration that was the objective of the Common Market. No NATO country remained a docile follower of the United States. Even Canada was beset by a separatist challenge in the province of Québec. An American effort to create a multilateral force of ships with integrated NATO crews (MLF) was rejected by the Europeans because the United States insisted on retaining a veto over the use of nuclear weapons. By the mid-1960s, the United States was presiding over a very troubled partnership. The euphoria of the Kennedy years was gone. Doubt and suspicion had replaced the earlier trust in America's leadership. NATO was in serious disarrary.

The Soviet Union's troubles were even more severe. In 1964, Nikita Khrushchev was ousted as a "harebrained schemer" and replaced by Party Chairman Leonid Brezhnev. Khrushchev was held responsible for mismanagement of Soviet agriculture and the fiasco of the missile crisis. Moreover, during the 1960s, the Sino-Soviet conflict worsened and communism's expansionary momentum shifted from Moscow to Peking. Indeed, while China made gains against the West, the Soviet leadership had to expend its energies in maintaining control over what it had gained earlier.

Chinese disenchantment with Soviet leadership reached a new high when the latter withdrew all its technicians from China, thus postponing temporarily China's entrance into the atomic club. In 1962, two dramatic events brought the conflict into the open: the Cuban missile crisis and China's border war with India. In the former, China attacked the Soviets for backing down before a paper tiger while Premier Khrushchev pointed out that the American tiger happened to be equipped with nuclear teeth. In the latter, the Soviet Union gave neither aid nor encouragement to the Chinese, but used its influence to bring about a rapid and peaceful settlement. The outcome of these two simultaneous crises favored the Chinese: while Russia had to back down from the most serious East-West confrontation in a decade, China was achieving a major diplomatic and military victory. She did not return the Himalaya border regions that she had occupied during the war with India.

By the time Lyndon Johnson assumed the American presidency, the differences between the two major Communist nations began more and more to take on the coloration of a major power conflict between two great national states. Ideology began to decrease in importance as competitive nationalism began to increase. Serious border disputes broke out along the Sino-Soviet frontier over contested territory in Sinkiang, Mongolia, and the Ussuri River. Communist parties throughout the world were deeply split over the issues raised by the dispute. China no longer recognized the ideological leadership of the Soviet Union and accused Khrushchev of plotting with Washington for Russo-American world domination. In 1964, just as Khrushchev was becoming an "unperson" in Russia, the Chinese exploded their first atomic device. Thus, while a serious succession crisis shook the Soviet government, China was crashing the gates of the exclusive nuclear club.

In Eastern Europe, too, the Soviet Union had its problems. For almost two decades, Czechoslovakia had been an apparently tranquil nation in the Soviet orbit. In January 1968, Alexander Dubček, a reform-minded liberal, was appointed first secretary of the Communist Party of Czechoslovakia. During the spring of 1968, the Dubček regime lifted press censorship and promised full civil rights to the Czech people. In order to reassure the Soviet Union, Dubček reiterated that Czechoslovakia would remain Communist and a faithful member of the Warsaw Pact.

Leonid Brezhnev, the general secretary of the Soviet Communist Party, was not convinced. On August 20, Soviet troops crossed the Czechoslovak border in a surprise move and occupied the country. The invasion came as a profound shock to most of the world and virtually split the Communist movement down the middle. Rumania and Yugoslavia as well as China opposed the Soviet move, as did most of the Communist parties in Western Europe. The Soviet Union, however, insisted that its troops remain in Czechoslovakia until the situation was "normalized," that is, until in its eyes, the threat of counterrevolution had disappeared.

Thus, even though the bipolar system had begun to loosen, spheres of influence continued to exist. Each superpower still risked intervention by force of arms when faced with the possible loss of a nation that it considered vital to its national interest. The United States sent marines into the Dominican Republic in 1965 to prevent "another Castro" from coming to power and the Soviet Union invaded Czechoslovakia in 1968 to prevent the detachment of that nation from the Soviet orbit. But increasingly, during the 1960s, the major arena of the East-West competition moved from direct confrontations to the "frontier" areas of the Third World.

During the 1950s and 1960s, a new nationalism swept through Asia, Africa, and the Middle East. The colonial empires of Britain, France, Portugal, Belgium, and Holland were dismembered and new sovereign states rose, phoenixlike, from their ashes. Ghana led the procession when it gained its independence from Britain in 1957. Thereafter, the birth of a new nation became virtually a monthly event. More nations were born in the short span of twenty years than throughout the entire history of the nation-state system. The membership of the United Nations doubled and then almost tripled. Most of these new nations feared western colonialism more than they feared communism. Most were nonwhite and had bitter memories of racial discrimination. And most were "uncommitted," or "nonaligned" in the struggle between the Soviet Union and the United States. John Foster Dulles had been impatient with these "neutralist" nations and had called them "immoral." John F. Kennedy was less judgmental but no less concerned about their ultimate allegiance. But it was Lyndon Johnson who subordinated everything else to the struggle over a remote Third World country called Vietnam. During the five years of his presidency, Johnson sent more than half a million American combat troops to Asia. The result was the longest and most divisive war in American history since the Civil War. How did this happen? What kind of man was Johnson?

Lyndon Johnson was one of the most complex and most tragic figures in recent American history. His rise from obscurity in Texas is a Horatio Alger story. But his decline and fall is an American tragedy.

As a young boy, Johnson was very close to his grandfather. The old man liked to talk about the old days of the frontier. Fantasy mingled with memory, lifting ordinary events to the level of heroic legend. Extravagant claims were made for the courage and daring of the cowboy: the tall, strong he-man, ready for action in any situation. After his grandfather's death, young Lyndon began to idolize his father. But Sam Johnson had very definite ideas about manliness. He taught Lyndon how to hunt animals and, once, when the boy had thrown up after killing a rabbit, his father called him a coward. Later, as president, Johnson forced people around him to submit to *his* tests of manhood. Visitors to the LBJ ranch were handed rifles and expected to shoot an antelope or deer in Johnson's presence. From the boy's fear of being tested came the man's determination to *give*, rather than take the tests. Courage had become synonymous with machismo.

Very early, Johnson developed a strong tendency to manipulate those around him. When a student at San Marcos State Teachers College, he managed to work for the college president, because the powerful man's favor would have a multiplier effect with the faculty and student body. His mother, however, had taught him that power had value only when used to benefit people. Whether it was the student manipulating the college president or the president of the United States promising houses and jobs for the American people, Johnson always associated the delivery of "good works" with the attainment of power and position.

Lyndon Johnson always believed that America was the best of all possible worlds. This assumption of superiority imposed a moral obligation to share the American way with the world. He felt a sense of outrage at the slightest criticism of America. Lack of faith in the United States or its heroes was tantamount to treason. The problem was with the critic, not the country.

Johnson's manipulativeness soon made him into a consummate political animal. Politics became his passion. Every human contact had a purpose. He wanted to be liked by everyone he met, but defined friendship in terms of a willingness to accommodate to his ends. Relationships with other men were perceived by him in terms of domination or submission. Only with his wife, Lady Bird, did Johnson attain a deep and lasting human bond. Otherwise, he was a profoundly lonely man.

In his political campaigns, for the Congress and later for the Senate, Johnson was completely single-minded. He poured his massive energy into every political meeting. There emanated from him a torrential, tireless flow of labor and activity that no other candidate could match. He would visit every village, walk countless streets, and shake hands with everyone he met. Winning was essential to his emotional survival. Defeat was an unbearable humiliation.

When Lyndon Johnson became president of the United States, his political personality was clearly defined, immovable, and fixed. He was eager to be generous with those who acknowledged his mastery. Those who provoked him, he would fight relentlessly. Like a sheriff in a Western town, he would bring criminals to justice. And above all, he would manipulate so that those he would dominate would also learn to love him. In his virtues and his flaws, Lyndon Johnson was an American original.

The personality of Lyndon Johnson played an absolutely crucial role in the unfolding of the Vietnam tragedy. Here was a man of colossal pride and ego who perceived Vietnam through the lenses of the Second World War, saw Mao Tse-tung as Adolf Hitler, and himself as a Western sheriff in a confrontation with

Ho Chi Minh, Red China's puppet. A man who knew nothing about Asian history now led the country into a major Asian war. A man who had spent most of his adult life in the Congress now deceived the nation's representatives and expanded the war by stealth. A man who had promised that "no American boys would fight the wars of Asian boys" now became responsible for a national catastrophe.

Lyndon Johnson thought of the United States as the "policeman of the world." Hence, any challenge, even at the most remote frontiers of the empire, would have to be met with force. Such remote frontiers were particularly vulnerable since they tested the credibility and will of the imperial center. Any hole in the dike would have to be filled without hesitation. No incursion by the enemy, however small, could be ignored. Thus, Vietnam, a small peasant country, suddenly became crucial to the security of the United States. American troops would have to emulate the ancient Roman legions and march out into the "provinces." And at the center of the empire stood the president, sending "his boys" into battle, dispatching "his planes," deciding Godlike, which Vietnamese cities should be bombed and which be spared, overwhelming "his" experts and advisers, and finally destroying the country that he had meant to save.

When George Ball had warned John F. Kennedy that some day 300,000 American troops might wind up in Vietnam, Kennedy had laughed and retorted that Ball was "crazier than hell." Kennedy had believed that the Vietnamese, in the end, would have to win or lose their own war. Johnson, on the other hand, almost single-handedly, Americanized the war. The bullet that had struck down John F. Kennedy and brought Johnson to the presidency, echoed down into the 1960s with a terrible ferocity. At war's end, 56,000 Americans had died in Indochina.

And yet, Lyndon Johnson was no monster. He also planned to build a "Great Society" in the United States. He wanted hospitals and schools and an end to poverty. There is little doubt that he was sincere in these endeavors. But not even Franklin Roosevelt, his idol, had waged the New Deal and the Second World War simultaneously. He had made a choice. Johnson did not, could not, choose. He wanted greatness in *both* peace and war. In the end, his presidency was a catastrophic failure: he destroyed both Vietnam and himself.

6

THE AMERICAN EMPIRE

Lyndon Johnson and Vietnam

Lyndon Johnson's personality had a decisive impact on the course of the Vietnam war. To be fair to Johnson, we must admit that he inherited a world view, shared by most Americans in 1964, that Vietnam would have to be defended. It is entirely possible that Truman or Dulles might have reached similar decisions in the early stages of the war, including the bombings of North and South Vietnam. Dulles had in fact been prepared to commit ground troops to Indochina in 1954. But there were some aspects of Johnson's handling of the war that bore the unmistakable stamp of his own extraordinary personality. The first of these was the degree of deception employed by Johnson vis-à-vis the American people around election time in 1964. Briefly stated, Johnson ran against Barry Goldwater on the pledge that he would not expand the war. In fact, in his campaign literature, Johnson specifically linked Goldwater to an escalation in Vietnam. At that very time, however, he asked the Congress for a virtual blank check over Vietnam policy. The Congress readily obliged with the Tonkin Gulf resolution, passed in response to an incident that never happened, except in the president's imagination. Lyndon Johnson misled Congress and the people, and through subterfuge was able to obtain congressional authorization for a war that he had decided on months before while he was promising the voters peace. The sequence of these events is worth examining.

During his campaign for reelection in 1964, Johnson tried to keep Vietnam out of the public view as much as possible. When later asked why, he answered: "If you have a mother-in-law with only one eye and she has it in the center of the forehead, you don't keep her in the living room." [1] As far as the voters were concerned, Johnson had disposed of the bothersome mother-in-law completely. As 1964 moved toward election day, he emphasized more and more the contrast between himself and his opponent, Senator Barry Goldwater, on the issue of Vietnam. Five examples will show this progression.

On August 16, Johnson declared: "Some others are eager to enlarge the conflict. They call upon us to supply American boys to do the job that Asian boys should do." [2] Two weeks later, his accusations became more specific: "I have had advice to load our planes with bombs and to drop them on certain areas that I think would enlarge the war." [3] On September 25, for the first time, he took a clear stand against escalation: "We don't want our American boys to do the fighting for Asian boys." [4] And again, on October 21: "We seek no wider war." [5] On October 27, one week before the election, Johnson stated categorically, in a speech in Pittsburgh: "There can be and will be, as long as I am President, peace for all Americans." [6] He won the election by a landslide. Yet, all throughout 1964, the Joint Chiefs of Staff urged Johnson to increase the Vietnam commitment in order to win the war more quickly. As early as January 1964, they had addressed the following memorandum to the president: "The United States must be prepared to put aside many of the self-imposed restrictions which now limit our efforts, and to undertake bolder actions which may embody greater risks." [7] Specifically, the Joint Chiefs were of the opinion that aerial bombing would bring North Vietnam to its knees. Policy-planning chief Walt Rostow, in support of this recommendation, stated that "Ho Chi Minh has an industrial

[1] Halberstam, op. cit., p. 424.
[2] New York Times, 17 August 1964.
[3] Ibid., 30 August 1964.
[4] Ibid., 26 September 1964.
[5] Ibid., 22 October, 1964.
[6] Ibid., 28 October 1964.
[7] Halberstam, op. cit., p. 350.

complex to protect; he is no longer a guerrilla fighter with nothing to lose." [8]

In the meantime, Robert Johnson, Rostow's deputy, undertook a careful study of the probable effects of bombing. The study concluded that the bombing would not work and predicted, prophetically, that it would imprison the American government. Economic growth was not a major Hanoi objective, the study said, challenging one of Rostow's favorite theses; rather, it was the unfinished business of throwing the foreigners out of the country. Hanoi had two formidable pillars of strength: the nationalist component of unity and the Communist component of control, which made for an organized, unified, modern state. Bombing would not affect such a regime. On the contrary, it might even strengthen it.

This remarkable study was ignored. Rostow, who was totally committed to bombing, never brought it to the president's attention. More and more, as 1964 drew to a close, the president's advisers, both civilian and military, moved toward a consensus on the bombing policy. Robert McNamara, McGeorge Bundy, Maxwell Taylor, and Dean Rusk—all of them perceived a chain of aggression emanating from China that urged on North Vietnam. Ho Chi Minh, in turn, was reported to be the source of the Vietcong aggression in the South. Thus, bombing would stop aggression at the source—in the North—and would convince China of American determination. No more dominoes would be permitted to fall to communism. In a revealing memorandum to McNamara, John McNaughton, former Harvard law professor and assistant secretary of defense in 1964, set forth American goals in South Vietnam in terms of the following priorities:

> 70 percent—To avoid a humiliating U.S. defeat
> 20 percent—To keep South Vietnamese territory from Chinese hands
> 10 percent—To permit the people of South Vietnam to enjoy a better, freer way of life.[9]

Thus, the official reason that was given to the American people for the intervention in Vietnam with air power and ground troops made up only one-tenth of the real reason.

Lyndon Johnson was in essential agreement with his ad-

---

[8] *The Pentagon Papers, op. cit.*, p. 249.
[9] Ibid., p. 263.

visers. Vietnam would have to be defended. If the Americans "turned tail" and got out, it would be Hitler all over again. As Johnson declared:

> Everything I knew about history told me that if I got out of Vietnam and let Ho Chi Minh run through the streets of Saigon, then I'd be doing exactly what Chamberlain did in World War II. I'd be giving a big fat reward to aggression. . . . And so would begin World War III.[10]

Thus, Lyndon Johnson faced a dilemma: He was convinced that he would have to escalate the war in order to win, but his political instincts told him that such a course would jeopardize his re-election. Johnson's solution was to fashion himself an instrument whereby he could escalate by stealth. This instrument was the Tonkin Gulf resolution.

In the first days of August 1964, an American destroyer escorting South Vietnamese ships was approached by three North Vietnamese torpedo boats. The American skipper later said he fired the first shot, and then sank two of the PT boats. On August 4, the president went on television to talk about a second "unprovoked attack" on the destroyers *Maddox* and *C. Turner Joy*. "These acts of violence," Johnson warned, "must be met not only by alert defense, but with positive reply. That reply is being given as I speak to you." On that day American bombers destroyed twenty-five North Vietnamese PT boats and blew up the oil depot at Vinh in North Vietnam. Defense Secretary Robert McNamara reported to the president that, at Vinh, "the smoke was observed rising to 14,000 feet." Johnson was overheard to say to a reporter: "I didn't just screw Ho Chi Minh; I cut his pecker off." [11]

The North Vietnamese provocation, as was revealed much later, never really occurred. The North Vietnamese vessels were later dismissed by a *Maddox* officer as "nothing more than a flock of geese on radar screens." [12] The *Maddox*'s captain told reporters: "Evaluating everything that was going on, I was becoming less and less convinced that somebody was there." [13] And a Mad-

---

[10] Doris Kearns, *Lyndon Johnson and the American Dream* (New York: Signet, 1977), pp. 264–265.

[11] Halberstam, op. cit., p. 414.

[12] Anthony Austin, *The President's War* (Philadelphia: Lippincott, 1971), *passim*.

[13] Ibid.

dox lieutenant confessed: "I had nothing to shoot at. . . . We didn't have any targets." [14] "Hell," Johnson said later, "For all I know, our Navy was shooting at whales out there." [15]

Nonetheless, this fictitious episode in Tonkin Gulf became the pretext for the passage of one of the most momentous congressional resolutions in modern American history. On August 4, 1964, Lyndon Johnson called upon Congress "to approve and support the determination of the President, as Commander-in-Chief, to take all necessary measures to repel any armed attack against the forces of the United States and to prevent further aggression." Furthermore, the president asked the Congress for authority "to take all necessary measures, including the use of armed force, to assist any member or protocol state of SEATO requesting assistance in defense of its freedom." [16] In a political master stroke, Johnson asked his old friend, Senator J. William Fulbright, to serve as floor manager in the Senate for the Tonkin Gulf resolution.

As chairman of the Senate's Committee on Foreign Relations, Fulbright enjoyed considerable power and prestige. He feared Barry Goldwater and believed that Johnson would always consult him about the war. Thus, while he was aware of the dangers of the wording of the resolution, he was willing to take the risk. Besides, he did not seek the stigma of opposing the president on an issue of patriotism. Only two senators asked unfriendly questions during the discussion on the Senate floor: Ernest Gruening and Wayne Morse. Both men believed that the resolution was so open-ended that it gave the president the power to take the nation into war without a congressional declaration. Nonetheless, on August 7, the Senate approved the resolution by a vote of eighty-eight to two. Senator Morse, explaining his negative vote, declared:

> I believe that history will record that we have made a great mistake in subverting the Constitution of the United States . . . by means of this resolution. We are in effect giving the President . . . warmaking powers in the absence of a declaration of war. I believe that to be a historic mistake.[17]

---

[14] Ibid.

[15] Halberstam, op. cit., p. 414.

[16] U. S. Foreign Relations Committee, Senate, *Vietnam: Policy and Prospects 1970.* Hearings, 90th Congress, 2nd session, 1970.

[17] Quoted in Halberstam, op. cit., p. 419.

He was right, of course. Johnson had it both ways. Congress gave him a blank check without really declaring war. Both Gruening and Morse lost their next elections, largely because of their opposition to Lyndon Johnson. In 1966, Fulbright was to remember Tonkin Gulf with deep regret and bitterness. Like so many people, he had been used by Lyndon Johnson. And when American combat troops were committed to Vietnam and the debate over the war intensified, lawmakers began to ask who had given the president authority for such drastic measures. *You* did, Lyndon Johnson was pleased to be able to reply.

What is the explanation for this incredible duplicity? The answer must be found in Johnson's second major goal: The Great Society.

Johnson deeply admired FDR. He went back past Kennedy's New Frontier all the way to the New Deal. He was determined to get legislation through the Congress that would dwarf even Roosevelt's initiatives. The Great Society, he hoped, would spell an end to poverty and squalor in America. But the war, too, had to be fought. And, fatefully, he did not believe that he would have to make a choice. As Johnson confessed:

> I was determined to keep the war from shattering that dream, which meant I simply had no choice but to keep my foreign policy in the wings. I knew the Congress as well as I know Lady Bird, and I knew that the day it exploded into a major debate on the war, that day would be the beginning of the end of the Great Society. . . . I was determined to be a leader of peace. . . . I wanted both, I believed in both. . . . After all, our country was built by pioneers who had a rifle in one hand to kill their enemies and an ax in the other to build their homes and provide for their families.[18]

A full-scale public commitment to Vietnam would have forced Johnson to make choices and accept limits. This he was not prepared to do. Instead, he hoped that he could conduct a major war in virtual secrecy while simultaneously summoning the American people toward the Great Society. He did not feel it necessary to make full disclosure. In the Senate, Johnson had been able to keep his dealings with one group a secret from the next. He had developed manipulation into a fine art form. Now, as presi-

[18] Kearns, op. cit., p. 296.

dent, he would manipulate the American people for their own good. As a result, they would be able to "pull off" both the war in Vietnam and the Great Society at home. Specifically, he would conceal the costs of the war so that he might receive the Great Society appropriations before the truth came out. In short, he would accomplish the impossible.

In 1970, two years after he left office, Lyndon Johnson appeared to have some insight into his own folly. "If I left the woman I really loved, the Great Society," he said, "in order to get involved with that bitch of a war on the other side of the world, then I would lose everything at home. All my programs. All my hopes and all my dreams. . . ." [19]

But these words were spoken after the catastrophe. In late 1964, Lyndon Johnson was at the zenith of his power. He had received a massive mandate from the people and was now president in his own right. The tragic flaws in his character, so fateful for his conduct of the war, were yet to be revealed.

JOHNSON'S PERSONAL WAR

Not only did Lyndon Johnson perceive Vietnam through the lenses of World War II, but he also perceived it as a personal challenge, a threat to his manhood and virility. The dangers of appeasement were clear enough to him. "If we quit in Vietnam," he said, "tomorrow we'll be fighting in Hawaii and next week we'll be fighting in San Francisco." [20] But the challenge was sexual as well. "If you let a bully come into your front yard one day," he explained, "the next day he'll be up on your porch and the day after he'll rape your wife in your own bed." [21] It was this intensely *personal* challenge that made Johnson's conduct of the war unique. He saw himself, Western-style, locked in a shoot-out with Ho Chi Minh. No American war had ever been fought in such a personal way by an American president before.

Johnson's initial commitment to the war was already perceived in personal terms. "*I* am not going to lose Vietnam," he declared in 1964, "*I* am not going to be the President who saw

[19] Ibid., p. 263.
[20] James D. Baker, op. cit., p. 54.
[21] Kearns, op. cit., p. 270.

Southeast Asia go the way China went." [22] By 1965, Johnson was speaking of "my Security Council," "my State Department," "my troops." It was *his* war, *his* struggle; when the Vietcong attacked, they attacked *him*. On one occasion, a young soldier, escorting him to an army helicopter, said: "This is your helicopter, sir." "They are *all* my helicopters, son," Johnson replied.

On February 7, 1965, the Vietcong attacked the American advisers' barracks at Pleiku. Nine Americans were killed and sixty were wounded. Johnson responded immediately by authorizing air strikes against four targets in North Vietnam. "I've had enough of this," he said. "This is just like the Alamo; someone damn well needs to go to their aid; well, by God, I'm going to Vietnam's aid." [23] Discussing his decision with the National Security Council, he said: "We have kept our guns over the mantel and our shells in the cupboard for a long time now. And what was the result? They are killing our men while they sleep in the night." "The Vietcong," he continued, "actually thought that pressure on an American President would be so great that he'd pull out of Vietnam. They don't know the President of the United States. He's not pulling out!" Johnson failed to point out that the American troops were on Vietnamese territory, having been sent to help the South Vietnamese fight the Communists for the right to rule that territory. Instead, in Johnson's mind, Pleiku was like the Alamo.

On the following day, Johnson received a unanimous recommendation for the sustained bombing of North Vietnam. The six signatories were Secretary of State Dean Rusk, Secretary of Defense Robert NcNamara, Special Assistant McGeorge Bundy, and Generals Maxwell Taylor, William Westmoreland, and Earle Wheeler. "The international prestige of the United States and a substantial part of our influence are directly at risk in Vietnam," the report stated. A policy of "sustained reprisal" was therefore indicated. Undersecretary of State George Ball disagreed. South Vietnam was not vital to America's national security, he declared. If we did nothing, its collapse would not be serious. If escalation was tried and failed, however—and he believed that failure was quite likely—then the consequences would be profoundly serious. France had almost collapsed under the weight of her failure in

[22] Barber, op. cit., p. 51.
[23] Ibid., pp. 51–52.

Vietnam. An old Eisenhower aide, Emmett John Hughes, asked Bundy what he would do if the North Vietnamese retaliated by matching the American air escalation with their own ground escalation. "We can't assume what we don't believe," Bundy replied.[24]

A few words should be said here about Johnson's relationships with his advisers. He was not, as some scholars have argued, the prisoner of a bureaucratic structure that deceived him into escalation.[25] His circle of advisers was extremely small and he overwhelmed almost all of them with the sheer force of his personality. They sensed what he wanted to hear and gave it to him. In an atmosphere where access to the president was the coin of the realm, nothing less would do. Johnson wanted men around him he could trust. "How loyal is that man?" he asked a White House staffer about an applicant for a high-level position in 1965. "Well, he seems quite loyal, Mr. President," the staffer said. "I don't want loyalty. I want *loyalty*. I want him to kiss my ass in Macy's window at high noon and tell me it smells like roses," Johnson shouted. "I want his pecker in my pocket." [26] Dean Rusk was *his* secretary of state, Bundy and McNamara were *his* intellectuals, and Taylor, Westmoreland, and Wheeler were *his* generals.

Typically, when a Vietnam decision was to be made, Johnson would bring together a small group and achieve a consensus by polling each man in turn. In *The Lost Crusade*, Chester Cooper tells how he used to feel when one of Johnson's polling sequences got under way in the National Security Council:

> During the process I would frequently fall into a Walter Mitty-like fantasy: When my turn came, I would rise to my feet slowly, look around the room and then directly at the President, and say very quietly and emphatically, "Mr. President, gentlemen, I most definitely do *not* agree." But I was removed from my trance when I heard the President's voice saying, "Mr. Cooper, do you agree?" And out would come a "Yes, Mr. President, I agree." [27]

If Johnson had wanted different advice, or a wider range of opinion, he could have changed his group of advisers. He could

[24] Halberstam, op. cit., p. 528.

[25] Lee Leslie Gelb, "Vietnam: Some Hypotheses About Why and How," paper delivered at meeting of the American Political Science Association, September 1970.

[26] Halberstam, op. cit., p. 434.

[27] Chester Cooper, *The Lost Crusade* (New York: Dodd, Mead, 1970), p. 223.

have dismissed Dean Rusk and made George Ball secretary of state. He could have replaced McNamara and Bundy. He did not. He did not have advisers to seek advice, but to elicit emotional support for his personal beliefs. And his advisers were indeed supportive. McNamara considered victory through air bombardment as technologically feasible. Bundy made it intellectually respectable; and Rusk thought of it as historically necessary. Johnson was not above humiliating his advisers. He would make Bundy deliver papers to him while in an open-door bathroom. "Mac, I can't hear you," he would shout, "Mac, get closer, Mac, get in here!" [28] Once, when he was berating George Ball and Robert McNamara, Dean Acheson stopped him with these words: "Mr. President, you don't pay these men enough to talk to them that way—even with a federal pay raise." And when Walt Rostow moved into his inner circle of advisers, he exclaimed triumphantly: "I'm getting Walt Rostow as *my* intellectual. He's not Bundy's intellectual. He's not Galbraith's intellectual. He's not Schlesinger's intellectual. He's going to be *my* goddamn intellectual and I'm going to have him by the short hairs." [29]

Lyndon Johnson was not led by these men. In the most fundamental sense, he led and even dominated them. It must be remembered that the members of the White House staff possessed no independent constituencies of their own and were completely dependent upon the president. He alone had the power to appoint, promote, or fire them. Compelled to explain their actions to no one but the man at the top, the president's advisers tended to become mirrors of their chief. In George Reedy's words: "No White House assistant could stay in the President's graces for any considerable period without renouncing his own ego." [30] With increasing dependence came increasing submission, even sycophancy. In some cases, the dynamics resemble a folie à deux, a psychological phenomenon in which strong, overbearing personalities are able to make others accept their own delusional systems. In the words of Doris Kearns: "The White House machinery became the President's psyche writ large, transmitting his wishes

[28] Halberstam, op. cit., pp. 517–518.

[29] Ibid., p. 627.

[30] George Reedy, *The Twilight of the Presidency* (New York: World, 1970), p. 18.

throughout the Executive Office with a terrifying force." [31] Even strong personalities like Bundy and McNamara were not exempt. Weak men were humiliated mercilessly. Johnson was in the habit of putting up his feet on Jack Valenti's lap, using it as a stool in front of visiting dignitaries.[32] Nonetheless, Valenti declared in a public speech that he slept "each night a little better, a little more confidently because Lyndon Johnson [was his] President." When the speech was widely ridiculed, Valenti was surprised. "What did they expect me to do?" he asked, "denounce the President?" [33] Lyndon Johnson ruled the White House like a monarch with his advisers as his court.

This is how, in early 1965, the bombing campaign or "Operation Rolling Thunder," as it was referred to in *The Pentagon Papers,* got under way. In Johnson's view, the bombing was a form of bargaining without words, seduction rather than rape. As he put it, "I saw our bombs as my political resources for negotiating a peace. On the one hand, our planes and our bombs could be used as carrots for the South, strengthening the morale of the South Vietnamese. . . . On the other hand, our bombs could be used as sticks against the North, pressuring North Vietnam to stop its aggression against the South." [34]

When the bombing failed to improve the situation, Johnson responded by enlarging the size of both sticks and carrots. He approved more targets for more intensive bombing raids, but he also offered a new inducement: a billion dollar project for the social and economic betterment of both Vietnams. If only North Vietnam would "leave its neighbors alone," he said, he was prepared to "turn the Mekong into a Tennessee Valley." [35] Johnson now promised the reconstruction of the country even as his orders brought mounting destruction. The bombs were meant to destroy the Ho Chi Minh trail, which was the major infiltration route leading from North to South Vietnam. But the bombs also destroyed the forests that were vital to the organic layer of the soil; the defoliants did not distinguish between jungles and crops;

---

[31] Kearns, op. cit., p. 275.
[32] Halberstam, op. cit., p. 437.
[33] Ibid.
[34] Kearns, op. cit., p. 277.
[35] Ibid., p. 279.

and forced migration from the countryside to the cities tore peasants from villages where they had lived for generations. "We will
help the Vietnamese to stabilize the economy," he promised, "to
increase the production of goods, to spread the light of education
and stamp out disease." [36] All this destruction, in short, was
necessary for the salvation of the Vietnamese.

As 1965 wore on, it became clear that the bombing program
was useless. Ho Chi Minh did exactly what McGeorge Bundy
had been unwilling to assume: he matched every American bombing escalation with a ground escalation of his own. As Johnson
escalated the bombing program, he got into the habit of approving every target personally. Tracing his fingers across a map of
Vietnam, he would point to various potential targets—railroad
bridges, army barracks, oil-storage depots, airfields, factories—demanding to know the costs and benefits of attacking each one.
"How many tons of bombs will it take to destroy this?" he would
ask while waving a photograph of a railroad bridge.[37] He feared
that if he went beyond a certain point, he would trigger a secret
treaty that the North Vietnamese had signed with the Soviet Union or with China. "I never knew," he said, "as I sat there in the
afternoon approving targets one, two, three, whether one of these
three might just be the one to set off the provisions of those
secret treaties. In the dark of night, I would lay (sic) awake
picturing my boys flying around North Vietnam, asking myself an
endless series of questions. What if one of those targets you
picked today triggers off Russia or China?" [38] "I couldn't stand it
anymore," he confided to Doris Kearns, "I jumped out of bed, put
on my robe, took my flashlight, and went into the Situation
Room." [39] There he would receive reports about completed missions. A giant map on the wall indicated which strikes had destroyed what targets. Actually, much of the time, the bombers,
flying over hundreds of villages and hamlets, were unable to separate enemies from innocents, or soldiers from civilians. Often, a
large area was saturated with bombs to compensate for the difficulties of accurate aim. Usually, entire villages were thus de-

[36] Ibid., p. 280.
[37] Ibid., p. 282.
[38] Ibid., p. 283.
[39] Ibid.

stroyed, just to make sure that the target was also hit. It was like weeding a garden with a bulldozer. Gradually, large sections of North and South Vietnam were so pockmarked with craters that they began to resemble a moonscape.

The introduction of American troops took place in a succession of easy incremental steps. In March 1965, General Westmoreland, the commander of U.S. forces in Vietnam, requested a few troops to protect the air base near Da Nang from which American air strikes were launched. Johnson promptly approved the request and on March 10, two Marine battalions—fifteen hundred men—landed in Vietnam. A few weeks later, Westmoreland submitted a second request for more troops. Johnson approved this request too, in order to "protect his boys," the same "boys" who were originally there to protect the airfield. By April, more than 50,000 American soldiers were in Vietnam. Missions expanded as numbers increased. The original mission of the troops was simply to protect air bases. In April, American troops were permitted active participation in combat if a nearby Vietnamese unit was in serious trouble. By May, permission had been granted to commit American troops to full-scale combat.

As the number of American troops reached 50,000, some senators became a trifle uneasy. They were quickly reassured by Vice-President Hubert Humphrey who said: "There are people at State and the Pentagon who want to send three-hundred thousand men out there. But the President will never get sucked into anything like that." [40] In May, the troop figure was revised to more than 50,000. George Ball was appalled, but could not reverse the trend. He was virtually alone in his resistance. In July, five months after the initiation of the bombing, McNamara, Bundy, Rusk, Taylor, and Westmoreland presented the president with three options: one, cut losses and withdraw; two, continue fighting at current levels; three, substantially expand the military pressure. The memo revealed a preference for the third option. Johnson, not surprisingly, chose option three and authorized the raising of troop levels to 200,000 men. Thus, without consulting the Congress, he crossed the Rubicon and turned Vietnam into a major American war.

In the words of one thoughtful observer, Johnson made this

[40] Halberstam, op. cit., p. 572.

decision as a response "to a personal challenge from Ho. If Ho wanted a challenge, a test of wills, then he had come to the right man. Lyndon Johnson of Texas would not be pushed around. . . . He was a man to stand tall when the pressure was there. To be counted. He would show Ho his mettle, show the toughness of this country." [41]

There was, of course, the troublesome question of paying the bill. The president's advisers recommended that Johnson ask the Congress for higher taxes to pay for the war, issue a presidential declaration of a "state of emergency," put the economy on a war-time footing, and order the mobilization of 235,000 reservists. Johnson rejected this course of action. Going to Congress meant admitting that the country was involved in a major war that would demand major sacrifices. This would imperil his plans for the Great Society. Johnson therefore decided to tell Congress and the public no more than was absolutely necessary. He would request an additional appropriation of only $1.8 billion, thus de-ferring the full revelation of the war's mounting costs until the following year. He would announce only that 50,000 new troops were to be sent immediately and would extend enlistments and increase draft calls rather than mobilize the reserves. In short, Johnson now clearly opted for a full-scale, though covert, war in Asia. This course of concealment and deception was decided by the president alone. It was difficult to imagine another president, even in the same situation, making the same choice. [42] Clark Clif-ford, who sat in on the meetings as a friend of the president and as a member of the intelligence advisory board, sounded an om-inous warning. "I see catastrophe ahead for my country," he de-clared. [43] "We have learned from Hitler at Munich that success only feeds the appetite for aggression," the president responded. "We did not choose to be the guardians at the gate, but there is no one else." [44]

The die was cast and General Westmoreland now began to occupy center stage. Whatever "Westy" requested, Johnson ap-

[41] Ibid., p. 500.
[42] Kearns, op. cit., p. 298.
[43] Halberstam, op. cit., p. 597.
[44] Ibid., p. 600.

proved. The general had estimated that "only" 300,000 troops would be needed by the end of 1966. He quickly revised that figure to 400,000, however, and projected a probable figure of close to 600,000 men by the end of 1967. It turned out that he had hoped that North Vietnam would not commit major reinforcements if the United States upped the ante. This hope proved to be illusory. Ho Chi Minh matched each American escalation with one of his own. Thus, it was North Vietnam, not the United States that controlled the rate of the war. It could escalate or de-escalate the tempo by deciding how many of its own men to send into battle at a given time. When Harrison Salisbury of the *New York Times* visited Hanoi in December 1966, he was told by a North Vietnamese leader: "And how long do you Americans want to fight? One year? Two years? Three years? Five years? Ten years? Twenty years? We will be glad to accommodate you." [45] Thus, the war raged on, but despite massive infusions of new combat troops, the American position steadily deteriorated. Even though South Vietnamese or American troops would capture a village during the day, the Vietcong usually came back at night and did as well as before. A reporter asked McNamara whether Vietnam did not resemble a bottomless pit. "Every pit has its bottom," McNamara answered.[46]

As 1966 and 1967 wore on and the troop level gradually reached 500,000 men, failure began to take its toll. One by one, the intellectuals departed. In 1966, McGeorge Bundy left and was replaced by Walt Rostow who was an enthusiastic supporter of the war and a fervent believer in an eventual American victory. In 1967, McNamara became increasingly ambivalent and recommended a bombing halt. The president refused to give in. "A bombing halt," he would say, "I'll tell you what happens when there is a bombing halt: I halt and then Ho Chi Minh shoves his trucks right up my ass. That's your bombing halt." [47] A few months before he left the Defense Department, McNamara authorized a comprehensive study of all materials pertaining to Vietnam, going back to the 1940s. When he read the first few chapters

---

[45] Ibid., p. 665.
[46] Ibid., p. 616.
[47] Ibid., p. 624.

of these "Pentagon Papers," he told a friend that "they could hang people for what's in there." [48] His successor was Clark Clifford who, two years before, had predicted catastrophe for the United States in Indochina.

The White House now began to resemble a fortress under siege. Johnson's gigantic ego, pride, and machismo made it impossible for him to admit that he had made a colossal mistake. If he ever evinced doubts, if he ever admitted the truth even to himself, it would become reality. Hence, he fought the truth and sought comfort in charts and statistics that predicted victory. He simply could not lose and thus had to plunge onward. Gradually, critics became enemies and enemies became traitors. Anybody who voiced doubts about the war soon lost access to the president. By late 1967, only Rostow and Valenti enjoyed Johnson's complete trust. Valenti was a total sycophant and Rostow was, according to an aide, "like Rasputin to a tsar under siege." [49]

A word should be said at this juncture about peace negotiations. After all, Johnson had claimed that the main purpose of the bombing of North Vietnam was to force its leaders to the negotiating table. Actually, a carefully documented case has been made that the president's behavior showed a "somber, recurring pattern of political exploration cut short by American military escalation." [50] In other words, Johnson repeatedly responded to possibilities of negotiations by raising the level of killing in Vietnam. In 1964, General de Gaulle called for a new meeting of the Geneva Conference that had led to an Indochina agreement in 1954. Johnson categorically rejected this proposal. Between 1964 and 1967, United Nations Secretary General U Thant made at least *two dozen* efforts to get the Americans together with the North Vietnamese for talks. On one such occasion, in February 1965, a meeting was actually arranged in Rangoon, Burma, but Johnson cancelled at the last minute since he was worried that "any rumors of such a meeting might topple the Saigon government." [51] U Thant, at a press conference submitted the following sad report:

48 Ibid., p. 633.
49 Ibid., p. 628.
50 Barber, op. cit., p. 39.
51 Ibid., p. 40.

I am sure that the great American people, if only they knew the true facts . . . will agree with me that further bloodshed is unnecessary. The political and diplomatic methods of discussions and negotiations alone can create conditions which will enable the United States to withdraw gracefully from that part of the world. As you know, in times of war and of hostilities, the first casualty is truth.[52]

As casualties mounted, Senator J. William Fulbright began hearings on the war in Vietnam. Johnson broke with his old friend and became increasingly incensed at Senator Robert F. Kennedy who, too, had turned against the war. In April 1967, he brought General Westmoreland home to speak before the Congress. At that point, Westmoreland had 470,000 American troops and was asking for an increase that would bring the total to 680,000 men by June 1968. And even with this increase, there was no end in sight. Instead, the United States had dropped more than seven million tons of bombs on Indochina. This was equal to three hundred of the atomic bombs that fell on Japan in 1945. The bombs had left twenty million craters. America, too, was in anguish over the war. The president had lost respect in the eyes of an entire generation, universities were disrupted, careers were blighted, and the economy was bloated with war inflation. More and more metal caskets bearing the remains of dead Americans came back from Indochina. And still, Johnson would not yield. He began to resort to violent name calling. Lunches and dinners were dominated by complaints about the "traitors." He saw conspiracies everywhere. By late 1967, the barriers separating irrational thought from delusion were fast crumbling. Members of the White House staff were frightened by what seemed to them signs of paranoia. Besides, Vietnam was devouring the president's popular support. As casualties began to hit American homes everywhere, opposition to the war mounted steadily. When Johnson had begun his presidency in 1963, eight out of ten Americans—as measured by the Gallup poll's question—"Do you approve or disapprove of the way the President is handling his job?"—approved of his actions. By the end of 1964, his level of support had dropped to seven out of ten. By 1965, it was down to six out of ten; by 1966, to five out of ten, and by 1967, to four out of ten. In other words, with each year in office Johnson lost one supporter in ten.[53] Nonetheless, he stuck to his illusions. The folie à deux continued. For the New Year's Eve party at the American embassy in Saigon in 1967, the invitations read: "Come see the light at the end of the tunnel."

Finally, after three years of persisting in the same disastrous policy, Lyndon Johnson decided on March 31, 1968, both to de-escalate the air war and to withdraw from politics. Three events occurred that, at long last, changed the president's mind: the "Tet" offensive, the presidential primaries, and the influence of the new defense secretary, Clark Clifford.

The "Tet" offensive, which began in late January 1968, at the time of the Vietnamese New Year, completely destroyed Johnson's and Westmoreland's credibility. In the past, the Vietcong and North Vietnamese had always fought a guerrilla war in the jungles, striking quickly and slipping back into the night. In the "Tet" offensive, they deliberately changed that strategy and fought in cities. This meant that millions of Americans watching television now became witness to the enemy's toughness, resilience, and failure to collapse according to American timetables. In the space of six weeks, between late January and early March of 1968, the percentage of Americans who approved of Johnson's handling of the war dropped from 40 to 26 percent. Even as General Giap launched his offensive in Vietnam, Senator Eugene McCarthy of Minnesota campaigned in New Hampshire. To Johnson's consternation, McCarthy won 42 percent of the vote and pushed Robert Kennedy into the race for the presidency. What crumbled in Saigon now crumbled in Washington and New Hampshire. Nonetheless, Johnson remained obstinate. As late as March 16, 1968, he told his staff:

> Let's get one thing clear! I'm telling you now I am not going to stop the bombing. Now I don't want to hear any more about it. . . . I've heard every argument. I'm not going to stop it. . . . Now, is there anybody here who doesn't understand that? [54]

By now most of the intellectuals had turned against the war. Daniel Ellsberg who had been in the Marine Corps and had done

[53] These figures are taken from the "Gallup Opinion Index," December 1968.
[54] Barber, op. cit., p. 41.

some early planning on the war under John McNaughton in the Defense Department, symbolized this conversion. As Ellsberg gradually turned against the war, an old friend asked him: "Are you the Dan Ellsberg I used to know in college?" "I haven't been for a long time, but I am again," Ellsberg was reported to have replied.[55]

Defense Secretary Clark Clifford was not a man whom Johnson could dismiss as a "lightweight intellectual." When McGeorge Bundy had left, Johnson ascribed his quitting to his greater loyalty to the dead John Kennedy. When Robert McNamara left, Johnson blamed the decision on McNamara's friendship with Robert Kennedy. But none of these motives could explain Clifford's shift. He was neither dissenter nor turncoat but an emissary from the corporate world of financial interest and political power. When Clifford patiently explained that businessmen and opinion leaders across the nation felt that the United States was sinking deeper and deeper into a hopeless bog, Lyndon Johnson was shaken. He knew now that he was losing the support of the rich and powerful, the barons of his realm. The herald had finally arrived and the walls were crumbling.

Nonetheless, Johnson struggled with himself literally to the last minute. As he put it in *The Vantage Point:* "When did I make the decisions that I announced the evening of March 31, 1968? The answer is: 9:01 P.M. on March 31, 1968." [56] And he added a typical personal, proprietory note: "I have 525,000 men whose very lives depend on what I do, and I must not be worried about primaries. I must be working full time for those men out there. . . ." And so, there was to be no light at the end of the tunnel for Lyndon Johnson. Vietnam had made the man elected by one of the largest landslides in American history into a one-term president. The cycle had been completed. His massive ego had locked him into an increasingly rigid posture: calculated deceit became self-deception; self-deception became delusion; but finally, there was a limit even to Johnson's insulation and reality came back into play. Faced with a precipitous drop in public standing and the loss of support from key interest group leaders,

[55] Halberstam, op. cit., p. 652.

[56] Lyndon B. Johnson, *The Vantage Point* (New York: Holt, Rinehart and Winston, 1971), p. 424.

he finally accepted the fact that the situation had moved beyond his control. He now had no choice but to withdraw. Perhaps his withdrawal might enable him to exercise a measure of control over another constituency: that of history.

After his retirement from politics, Lyndon Johnson spent much more time on his cattle ranch in Stonewall, Texas, than on his memoirs or in public arenas. Old habits could not be easily abandoned. Perhaps the most poignant, even terrifying, part of Doris Kearns's brilliant portrait is Johnson's life on his ranch. He ran the ranch exactly the way he had run the Vietnam war. Control that had once spanned the world was now reduced to a pitiful domain. For hours every day, Johnson would drive around the fields checking up on his men, finding tasks undone, spotting problems, talking with field hands about the cattle or the tractors. At morning meetings, he would deliver his instructions to the hands with the same tone of voice and with the same urgency that he had communicated at early morning staff meetings at the White House. "I want each of you to make a solemn pledge," he said to the hands, "that you will not go to bed tonight until you are sure that every steer has everything he needs." [57] When the rains failed to come, he announced that he hadn't slept all night and ordered that special pumps be shipped to him by air. "I kept thinking about those pump parts and about the rain and about my fields. And I couldn't stand it. I must have those parts before the end of the day. I simply must. If I don't, everything's going to fall apart. Everything." [58] And when the pumps arrived on time, Johnson was triumphant. "Now for the first time, I've got reasonable confidence I'm not going to fail," he said, "We *will* have two hundred head of cattle, well fed and ready to sell by October. It's going to work. Thank God. I feel better tonight than I can remember feeling in a long time." [59] All the skills, all the tools shaped over decades of public life, were now directed at four or five field hands. Work on the ranch consumed what was left of Lyndon Johnson's energies. On January 22, 1973, he died there, alone.

[57] Kearns, op. cit., p. 376.
[58] Ibid., p. 377.
[59] Ibid., p. 379.

THE PRICE OF IGNORANCE

It is unlikely that history will show that Lyndon Johnson was an intentionally evil man who deceived his people for an evil cause and led them into war in Indochina. The villain was not malevolence or evil. True, there was a great deal of deceit, but there was also the president's total ignorance of Asia in general and of Vietnam in particular. By his own admission, Johnson had not read more than six books since his days in a state teachers' college in Texas. The only book he remembered reading carefully was Barbara Ward's *The Rich Nations and The Poor Nations*. His advisers, brilliant intellectuals though they were, were almost equally ignorant about Asian affairs. Rusk, Bundy, Taylor, Rostow, and Westmoreland had no real Asian expertise. These were successful men, but their vision was limited to American and European experiences. Their historical analogies to Vietnam were drawn from Munich and the Second World War. Incredible though it may seem, neither the president of the United States nor the handful of men with whom he was in daily touch understood the facts that were confronting them. They simply superimposed their own misperceptions on Asian realities.

In Johnson's view, aggression had to be stopped "at the source" and the "source" was communism in North Vietnam and China. The fact that communism had broken up into numerous diverse political and ideological fragments seemed to have been lost upon him. He never understood that this was a revolutionary war in which the other side held title to the revolution because of the colonial war that had just ended. After all, the United States had replaced France, the old colonial power. Revolution and antirevolution were the real issues, rather than communism and anti-communism. For the other side, the war was being fought to drive out the foreigners, who now happened to be Americans. That is why the North Vietnamese and the Vietcong were willing to fight to the death and the South Vietnamese were not. That is why McNamara's statistics were valueless; they overlooked the fact that even if the ratio was ten-to-one in favor of South Vietnam, it had no meaning because the one man was willing to fight and die and the ten were not.

Johnson and his men should have known, even from their experiences in the Second World War, that bombing tends to unite a people and stiffen its resistance. The fire bombings of Dresden and of Hamburg did not break the German will nor did the saturation bombings of Japan force the Japanese into surrender. Only the atom bomb did and even Johnson shrank from the use of that ultimate weapon. Thus, there was the paradox of a great power of 200 million people fighting a limited war against a small peasant country of 17 million people fighting a total war. The small peasant country, however, had the nationalist element of unity and the communist element of control. Its people were lean and tough and believed in their mission to rid the country of the foreign intruders. On the other side, a leader had sneaked his country into a major war twelve thousand miles away from home. The purposes of the war were murky, victory seemed more and more elusive, a free press became increasingly critical, and opposition to the war was mounting steadily. It was not likely that such a country could emerge victorious in an attrition war.

And then there was Ho Chi Minh. Lyndon Johnson had never met that kind of man before. The president used all the time-honored American political techniques. When force did not work, he tried manipulation. But neither bombs nor dollars would tempt Ho Chi Minh. Johnson, unable to understand an adversary who was unwilling to bargain, used the only instrument of compulsion he had left: military force. And given his character and the depth of his ignorance, Johnson dropped yet more bombs and sent yet more men to their deaths. He always believed that the Americans were in Vietnam for selfless and idealistic reasons. This myth of false innocence now permitted the United States to wreak destruction on an enormous scale in Indochina, all in the name of kindliness and helpfulness. Gradually, the means became so horrible that it became increasingly difficult to justify the ends. The war finally became a lost crusade.

Ho Chi Minh, the man, was very different from Lyndon Johnson's image of Ho as Mao Tse-tung's puppet. True, the North Vietnamese leader was an old Bolshevik who had been one of the founders of the French Communist Party in 1920. But he was a more senior member of the communist world than Mao and a unique figure in his own right. He was as much a Vietnamese nationalist as he was a Communist. David Halberstam described him as "part Gandhi, part Lenin, all Vietnamese." [60] After his victory over the French at Dien Bien Phu in 1954, Ho not only enjoyed the veneration of his people but was also treated with a special respect throughout the Third World. Mao Tse-tung had simply defeated other Chinese, but Ho Chi Minh had defeated a powerful Western nation.

Ho Chi Minh's most distinctive quality, however, was his incorruptibility. In a country where the population had seen leaders reach a certain plateau and then become more Western and less Vietnamese, corrupted by money and power, Ho Chi Minh remained a Vietnamese Everyman. The higher he rose, the less he sought the trappings of authority. He shunned monuments, marshal's uniforms, and general's stars, always preferring his simple tunic. The "black pajamas," which Lyndon Johnson mocked, became his source of strength, for they symbolized his closeness to the peasants. This capacity to walk humbly among his own people was the secret of his success. He was never separated from the people by police motorcades and foreign advisers. He was *both* obeyed and loved. *Time* magazine referred to him once as a "goat-bearded agitator who learned his trade in Moscow." It was this very contempt from the West, however, that made Ho so effective. For he remained a Vietnamese, a peasant like his ancestors, and therefore the only leader who had the title to the revolution: to drive the French and then the Americans, from Vietnam. Even as a Communist, he was unusual. The Communist Party of Vietnam survived the Stalin years without the slightest touch of purge. The leadership of Ho Chi Minh was such that even Stalin decided not to interfere. Ho even had a sense of humor. In 1945, after the defeat of Japan, he had dinner with an old American friend, Robert Isaacs. "Come on, you will have dinner with the President of the Republic," Ho announced to his guest. They went through a corridor and two young Viet Minh guards snapped to attention and, their revolvers showing, followed Ho to his car. Ho laughed. "How funny life is!" he exclaimed. "When I was in prison, I was let out for fifteen minutes in the morning and fifteen minutes in the evening for exercise. And while I took my exercise in the yard, there were always two armed guards

[60] David Halberstam, *Ho* (New York: Random House, 1971), p. 12.

standing right over me with their guns. Now I'm President of the
Vietnam Republic, and whenever I leave this place, there are two
armed guards right over me with their guns." [61] In his fundamental human qualities, Ho Chi Minh was the very opposite of
Lyndon Johnson.

Johnson used the strategy of the strong against the weak with
Ho Chi Minh. He believed that he could bend the enemy to his
will so that the North Vietnamese could avoid pain, death, and
material destruction. It was a plausible strategy for someone who
was rich, loved life, and feared pain. But Johnson confronted the
strategy of the weak. The weak defied the American president by
their readiness to struggle, suffer, and die on a scale that seemed
beyond the bounds of reason. Prisoner interrogations repeatedly
revealed this phenomenon. When asked what would happen if
more and more Americans would come and bigger and bigger
bombs were dropped, the answer very often was a fatalistic and
unimpassioned: "Then we will all die." Such defiance forced
Lyndon Johnson to confront the necessity of carrying out the
threat of ultimate escalation: to bomb North Vietnam into the
stone age. In short, to commit genocide. At that point, Johnson
hesitated, remembering Hitler and Hiroshima. And ultimately, the
only answer was withdrawal. Withdrawal meant losing but massive escalation would also have meant losing, because the United
States would have lost its soul and would have torn itself apart
completely. Thus, Ho Chi Minh's strategy of the weak prevailed
over the strategy of the strong. Ho had less and less to lose by
fighting on while his American opponent had more and more to
lose. Time was always on the side of Ho Chi Minh.

Perhaps the overarching truth about Lyndon Johnson and
the men who advised him was that they never had the kind of
experience in tragedy of which the stuff of empathy is made.
These were rich men of the West, their vision limited to that experience. None of them knew, until it was too late, that states,
like men, could die. None of them knew that intelligence alone,
without wisdom and an empathy for suffering, was only emptiness.

In historical perspective, the great unanswered question over
Vietnam will probably be: Which would have been less costly,

---

[61] Ibid., p. 83.

an earlier Communist victory or the agony of this war? One cannot help but wonder what might have been if Lyndon Johnson had never bombed Vietnam or sent a single soldier there. Vietnam might indeed have gone Communist much earlier. It would, however, probably have been a form of communism of the Titoist variety—with a strong dose of nationalism and a fierce tradition of independence vis-à-vis both Moscow and Peking. The United States could have lived with that, it seems. Certainly, the delay was hardly worth the sacrifice of so many thousands of lives, American and Vietnamese.

Lyndon Johnson was overwhelmingly American in his attitudes toward Asia. He believed with millions of Americans that the United States had "lost China," as if China had ever been America's to lose. He believed, as John Foster Dulles had believed before him, that China was the embodiment of evil and aggression in the world, and that North Vietnam was China's puppet. Not having studied Asian history, he never understood that it was the West that had carved up China more than a century before and that Mao Tse-tung was not *only* a Communist, but also the first modern Chinese leader who had driven the Westerners from China. He did not know that whenever a Western nation had come to Asia, it had done so violently, and, that, in the process, Asian leaders had learned this fateful lesson from the West. Neither China nor Japan had used force as a major vehicle of its foreign policy before the West had come. But after a century of Western tutelage, there finally rose a Chinese leader who preached that power grew out of the barrel of a gun. And a century after Commodore Perry's ships "opened" Japan with cannon blasts, Japanese planes bombed Pearl Harbor. In larger historical perspective then, it is a very open question who victimized whom in the relations between the United States and Asia.

Finally, there is the question of Lyndon Johnson's personal role in the disaster of Vietnam. The record of the Johnson presidency in Vietnam is a story of self-delusion, deceit, and misperception on a scale so vast that it turned into a national catastrophe. Despite relentless bombing raids on both North and South Vietnam and the introduction of more than half a million American troops, the enemy was not defeated. Instead, Johnson's ego, stubbornness, and pride destroyed his presidency and divided his people in a spiritual civil war. And once again, as in the Bay of

Pigs fiasco, the "experts" were completely wrong. But while John Kennedy was able to admit that he had made a colossal blunder, Johnson was emotionally unable to admit any error or misjudgment. Therein, perhaps is the heart of the catastrophe. Like a desperate gambler, hoping to recoup his losses, Johnson raised the stakes again, again, and yet again. But the stakes were not just money, they were human lives.

Lyndon Johnson is one of the clearest and most tragic examples of a leader who was prevented by his personality from seeing other possibilities that clearly were available. While it is true that Johnson inherited a world view that Vietnam must be defended, there is abundant evidence for the claim that he could have kept that defense at a modest and relatively low-key level. But the compulsions of his enormous and yet fragile ego made him deceive the Congress, escalate the war by stealth, and finally turn Vietnam into one of the most terrible and self-destructive conflicts in American history. Until ruination and defeat stared him in the face, he was simply unwilling—and later unable—to consider a whole range of alternatives that continued to be open. What if Kennedy had lived and made Vietnam policy instead of this crusader run amuck? If Kennedy's statements of intent before his death are to be believed, the United States would have withdrawn, or at worst, limited its involvement without committing combat troops. In Johnson's case, for three long years, between 1965 and 1967, the personal impact of one man was totally decisive. In those years, Lyndon Johnson's power to send men to war was probably greater than Leonid Brezhnev's in the Soviet Union. And yet it was in vain that combatants and civilians had suffered, the land was devastated, and the dead had died.

Interchapter

BEYOND VIETNAM

During the final phase of Lyndon Johnson's presidency, the United States did not have a foreign policy. With over half a million combat troops fighting in Vietnam, it only had a Vietnam policy. In almost every other part of the globe, American initiative was virtually paralyzed. The self-destructive enterprise in Indochina had absorbed most of the nation's resources and energy.

There was little movement in the relations with the Soviet Union and China. In 1967, Lyndon Johnson met with Soviet Premier Aleksei Kosygin at a "summit" in Glassboro, New Jersey, but Vietnam prevented any progress on substantive issues, such as arms control. China policy also remained frozen. The United States continued to ignore the mainland government of Mao Tse-tung and insisted that the Chiang Kai-shek regime on Taiwan constituted the legitimate government of China. In Western Europe, European leaders became increasingly concerned with the American predicament in Vietnam and seriously questioned the United States commitment to the North Atlantic Treaty. Not only did President de Gaulle remove France from NATO in 1966, but the following year, West German Chancellor Willy Brandt, in a new move toward "Ostpolitik," began to explore the possibilities of rapprochement with the Soviet Union. Britain, too, veered away from the United States and seriously weighed membership in the European Common Market. In the Middle East, in June 1967, a third war broke out between Israel and her Arab neighbors after Egypt's president Nasser had instituted a blockade of the Gulf of Aqaba. Within six days, Israel quadrupled her size by conquering five territories from three Arab countries: the Sinai Peninsula and the Gaza Strip from Egypt; the Golan Heights from Syria; and the West Bank of the Jordan and East Jerusalem from Jordan. Lyndon Johnson made no effort to break the dangerous and icy impasse that characterized relations between Israel and the Arab world in the wake of the Six-Day War of 1967. Nor were there any new departures in American relations with Southern Africa or the Third World.

Almost everywhere, there was increasing revulsion and disillusionment with America's Vietnam policy. In the United States, too, anguish and opposition mounted. Sensitive men and women, watching the daily carnage of history's first televised war, recoiled in increasing horror. In 1967, Senator J. William Fulbright, now repenting his earlier support of Lyndon Johnson, attacked America's self-appointed role as world policeman as evidence of a new "arrogance of power." Not only was the nation's Vietnam policy disastrous, the senator asserted, but its wanton exercise of military power was corrupting America's moral substance. Fulbright's trenchant critique found a deep responsive chord in American popular opinion.

Little wonder then, that Richard Nixon, the newly elected president in 1968, and his national security adviser, Henry Kissinger, had an absolute priority: how to spring the United States from a lethal trap in which the country had become ensnared.

Richard Nixon and Henry Kissinger, though very different men by temperament, were both survivors and had reached power after long and arduous struggles. Nixon was the political man incarnate. He had been a congressman and senator during the late 1940s and early 1950s; from 1953 to 1960, he had served as vice-president under Dwight D. Eisenhower; in 1960, he was narrowly defeated by John F. Kennedy and two years later he lost a bid for the governorship of California. In 1964, he backed Barry Goldwater, who lost badly to Lyndon Johnson. Just when commentators were writing Nixon's political obituary, the experienced tactician saw his opportunity. In 1968, he ran against Hubert Humphrey who had never completely disassociated himself from Lyndon Johnson's Vietnam policy. Nixon pledged to bring the American troops home from Vietnam, and he won the presidency by a narrow margin.

Henry Kissinger was a Jewish refugee from Germany, who had come to the United States in 1938, at the age of fifteen. After working in a bristle factory and attending night school in New York, he joined the United States Army and served in the occupation forces of his former homeland. In 1946, he was admitted as an undergraduate to Harvard where he performed brilliantly. In 1950, he began his graduate studies and earned his Ph. D. degree four years later. In 1957, Kissinger received national acclaim for a book that he had written while at the Council on Foreign Relations. *Nuclear Weapons and Foreign Policy*, a treatise on limited nuclear war, was debated nationally. It also attracted the favorable attention of Vice-President Richard Nixon.

On numerous occasions, during the 1960s, Henry Kissinger expressed his disagreement with official policy. When John F. Kennedy committed 17,000 military advisers to South Vietnam, Kissinger stated that he did not think that the United States could accomplish with 17,000 advisers what France had failed to do with 200,000 combat troops. When Kissinger returned from his first visit to Vietnam in 1965, he believed that the military escalation then underway was not only imprudent but absurd. When the American commitment reached a figure of 500,000 men, Kissinger thought of Indochina as a national disaster.

Thus was the stage set in 1969 for a partnership between the politician and the intellectual. Nixon was impressed with Kissinger's depth and imagination. He also believed, as did Kissinger, that new initiatives toward China and the Soviet Union were long overdue. Besides, he had written that "lawyers in politics need non-lawyers around them to keep them from being too legalistic, too unimaginative." In Kissinger, Nixon found such a non-lawyer who also had evolved a general philosophy that the new president found congenial to his own. For Kissinger, in turn, the appointment in 1969 to the post of assistant to the president for national security affairs, afforded him the chance, for the first time in his life, to test his conceptual theories in the world of power.

Henry Kissinger has written history as a scholar and made history as a statesman. His diplomacy was deeply rooted in the insights of the young doctoral student at Harvard of a quarter century before. It was, in fact, a virtual transplant from the world of thought into the world of power. Hence, if we are to understand the statesman, we must first understand the philosopher-historian.

Kissinger's favorite book in his early student days at Harvard was Oswald Spengler's *The Decline of the West*. The deep strain of pessimism that permeated every page of Spengler's classic struck a responsive chord in Kissinger. It was reflected in a concluding passage of his undergraduate honors thesis where he observed that "life involves suffering and transitoriness," and that "the generation of Buchenwald and the Siberian labor-camps [could] not talk with the same optimism as its fathers."

Kissinger regarded history as the memory of states. As the knowledge of a person's past gives us some clues about his future, history provides us with clues about a nation's future. It never repeats itself exactly. If it can teach us anything at all, it teaches through analogy, not through identity. Like the Oracle at Delphi, a particular historical event may be open to several interpretations. The supreme challenge of the statesman is to make the correct analogy. In this undertaking, he may be given only a single opportunity, for he is his own subject. In effect, he performs the experiment upon himself and his own nation. He may not have a second chance.

Kissinger's choice of a subject for his doctoral dissertation was deeply influenced by these considerations. He stated these reasons in his preface with perfect clarity:

> The success of physical science depends on the selection of one crucial experiment; that of political science in the field of international affairs, on the selection of the crucial period. I have chosen for my topic the period between 1812 and 1822, partly, I am frank to say, because its problems seem to me analogous to those of our own day.

Thus, Kissinger's interest in the diplomacy of the early nineteenth century was not academic in the usual sense. He wanted to know how these statesmen in the distant past had managed to erect such a durable structure of peace; and he wanted to find out whether their insights could be transplanted into the modern world. For most students pursuing a Ph. D. degree, the dissertation is viewed as a gateway into the academic world. This was only partially true of Henry Kissinger. He hoped that the knowledge he would derive from his research would prepare him for action on a larger stage. The title of his doctoral dissertation was *A World Restored*. In it, he explored how Austria, England, Russia, and Prussia restored the peace of Europe after Napoleon's defeat in 1815. His later diplomacy was deeply rooted in the intellectual insights of this dissertation.

Henry Kissinger differed from most American statesmen in the sense that his policies were based on doctrine and deliberate design rather than on the more day-to-day approach that has often characterized the conduct of American diplomacy. This doctrine, which rested on three main pillars, emerged very clearly in *A World Restored*. First, to be secure, a peace must be based on a negotiated settlement, with all sides in equilibrium, rather than on a victor's peace. Everybody is a little bit unhappy, but no one is completely unhappy. Thus, no one will try to overthrow the settlement through yet another war, and the relative insecurity of each guarantees the relative security of all. Second, a victorious power, in order to have peace, will not attempt to annihilate the vanquished but will co-opt it into the established order by giving it something of its own substance. Thus, the victor decontaminates the defeated of his revolutionary ardor and transforms him subtly from a "have-not" into a "have" nation. Third, in the absence of a globally controlled system, the best guarantor of peace is balance and, hence, a balancer is essential. This balancer will seldom ask the question, "Who is right and who is wrong?" but rather, "Who is weak and who is strong?" He will throw his weight on the weaker side whenever an imbalance occurs and by so doing restore the equilibrium and maintain the peace. Hence, peace, to Henry Kissinger, was a bonus of a successful balance policy.

Kissinger's policy was, in fact, a transplantation process of these three concepts into the modern world. The first principle was embodied in Kissinger's arms control policy vis-à-vis the Soviet Union. The United States was no longer to strive for nuclear superiority; it would do better to settle for parity and equilibrium. Such a course would safeguard the security of the United States more effectively. By slowing down the arms race, Kissinger hoped to achieve a modern peace without victory or defeat. The second principle was also applied to Russia. The Soviet government received gigantic credits from the United States and, unlike Nikita Khrushchev who in 1959 talked about "burying" capitalism, Leonid Brezhnev began to be engaged in "borrowing" from capitalism. Kissinger's hope was that, subtly and over time, a community of economic interests would be established between the capitalist and communist worlds. The third principle was illustrated by Kissinger's trip to China in 1971, which created a triangle between the Soviet Union, China, and America. In this triangle, Kissinger attempted to place the United States into the role of the balancer, where it would be wooed by both China and the Soviet Union.

Unlike John Foster Dulles, who divided the world into "good" and "evil" states and tended to judge those in the middle as "immoral," Henry Kissinger perceived the international arena as infinitely more complex. In his view, the statesman could seldom choose between right and wrong. Most of the time, he had to choose between one right and another right or one wrong and a greater wrong. And there was no escape from choice itself for, as Albert Camus had reminded us, "not to chose [was] also a choice." Nor could one wait until all the facts were in, because, by then, foreign policy had become history.

Henry Kissinger thus believed that, in creating a design for world order, realism was preferable to idealism. The great American moralists, in his judgment, were failures. In the end, Woodrow Wilson proved ineffectual and John Foster Dulles turned foreign policy into a crusade that led straight into the Indochina quagmire. Kissinger never made peace or justice the objective of his policy, nor was he particularly interested in "making the world safe for democracy." He merely wished to make the world safer and more stable. This was a lesser goal, one that offered no illusions but that also brought fewer disappointments. It also was a goal not quite in the mainstream of American history. But, then, Kissinger was a European in America, and his thought was rooted firmly in the European philosophical tradition.

When Kissinger entered Harvard as an undergraduate, in 1946, another Jewish refugee, almost a generation older, had just published his first book in the United States. Hans J. Morgenthau's *Scientific Man Versus Power Politics* contains a paragraph that made a deep impression on the young man who had just returned from the war:

> We have no choice between power and the common good. To act successfully, that is, according to the rules of the political art, is political wisdom. To know with despair that the political act is inevitably evil, and to act nevertheless, is moral courage. To choose among several expedient actions the least evil one is moral judgment. In the combination of political wisdom, moral courage and moral judgment, man reconciles his political nature with his moral destiny. That this conciliation is nothing more than a

modus vivendi, uneasy, precarious, and even paradoxical, can disappoint only those who prefer to gloss over and to distort the tragic contradictions of human existence with the soothing logic of a specious concord.[1]

What, then, in the light of this sophisticated theory, is the explanation for Kissinger's failures in Vietnam and Cambodia? The answer is *not* that Nixon's hardline views prevailed over the more liberal outlook of his adviser for national security affairs. The explanation rather, must be found in Kissinger's overall philosophy of foreign policy. For the sake of its global commitments and for the morale of its allies, America would have to depart from Indochina in such a way that it would not appear to have abandoned an ally to whom it had committed 500,000 troops. American credibility was now at stake. And since a stable equilibrium with Russia would depend upon America's steadfast honoring of its commitments, an abrupt or precipitous withdrawal was no longer possible. A "peace with honor" would now have to be sought, or at the very least, a "decent interval" between America's departure and a victory for communism in Vietnam. Thus, though Kissinger despised the war, his larger conceptual design for a stable world order deepened the entrapment and prevented him from acting on his earlier instincts. His global vision now dictated a harder line on Vietnam, but the harder line on Vietnam made the attainment of his global objectives that much more difficult. This was the paradox of Kissinger's approach to the Indochina war and its tragedy as well.

Thus, the quest for stability and order that was so basic to Nixon's and Kissinger's grand design made them seek a "peace with honor." In the search for such a peace, the war was widened and the trap tightened even more. Cambodia, a neutral nation, was drawn into the conflict in 1970. North Vietnam's harbors were mined and its major cities bombed to rubble in 1972. And still, there was no end in sight. Finally, in January 1973, peace seemed to be "at hand." A peace settlement was signed in Paris. American combat troops were to be withdrawn; North Vietnam was to be Communist and South Vietnam was to be "free." It seemed like Geneva 1954, all over again.

[1] Hans J. Morgenthau, *Scientific Man versus Power Politics* (Chicago: University of Chicago Press, 1952), p. 202.

But the war never really stopped after the American withdrawal. Casualty figures never decreased, either for Saigon or for North Vietnam. The "decent interval" lasted two years, and then the dam broke. In the spring of 1975, the Communist insurgents in Cambodia, the Khmer Rouge, marched upon the capital, Phnom Penh, and forced Marshal Lon Nol, Cambodia's American-supported president, to flee the country. At the same time, the South Vietnamese army lost what remained of its fighting spirit and collapsed entirely. In a matter of weeks, almost all of South Vietnam fell to the Communists. In the United States, a test of wills took place between Gerald Ford and Kissinger, both of whom favored continued military assistance to Cambodia and South Vietnam, and the Congress, which refused to cooperate. In a last, futile effort to extract close to one billion dollars in military aid for South Vietnam from a reluctant Congress, Kissinger declared on March 26: "The United States cannot pursue a policy of selective reliability. We cannot abandon friends in one part of the world without jeopardizing the security of friends everywhere." But, by then, the American people had simply become tired of the war and had reconciled themselves to a Communist victory in Indochina. Finally, the United States was left with the elementary human responsibility of rescuing terror-stricken refugees fleeing from the advancing North Vietnamese armies. In April, Saigon surrendered to the Communists and was renamed Ho Chi Minh City.

Thus, all of Kissinger's efforts to bring peace with honor to Indochina had come to naught. For one brief moment, in early 1973 at Paris, he hoped that a genuine compromise, patterned after the model of an earlier age, had at long last been attained. He believed that the right admixture of diplomacy and force had finally yielded a negotiated settlement without victory or defeat.

But there was one terrible flaw in Kissinger's approach. He regarded his meetings with the North Vietnamese as negotiations between two states that would ultimately have to strike a bargain. But North Vietnam was never interested in a bargain. It regarded the Americans as invaders who used the Saigon regime as their puppet. Death was not too high a price to pay in order to rid the country of such intruders. Kissinger did not want another Munich; but neither did Hanoi. And its determination to outlast the United States guaranteed its final victory.

Yet, though Vietnam always haunted Kissinger, it did not paralyze him. In October 1973, two weeks after he had been sworn in as secretary of state, the fourth Arab-Israeli war broke out. Syria and Egypt had begun a massive ground assault against the Jewish state on Yom Kippur, the holiest day in the Jewish calendar.

Kissinger's role in the October war, once again, was based on his conceptual design. It can neither be described as pro-Israeli nor pro-Arab. In its essence, it was pro-equilibrium.

Before the war erupted, Kissinger perceived Israel as the stronger side and thus warned the Jewish leaders "not to pre-empt." But when he turned out to have been mistaken and Syria and Egypt launched their coordinated surprise attack, Kissinger switched sides and provided American military aid to Israel in order to restore the military balance. And when the Israelis, with this American assistance gained the upper hand, Kissinger switched sides again and insisted on the rescue of 100,000 trapped Egyptian soldiers. When a cease-fire was finally proclaimed by the United Nations, both sides were exhausted and roughly even —exactly what Kissinger had wanted. It had always been his firm belief that only a war without victory or defeat could contain the seeds of peace.

As Kissinger surveyed the ravages of the October war, he conceived his plan for peace in the Middle East. He decided to subdivide the problem into manageable segments instead of addressing it in its totality. He would approach it step by step, beginning with the least forbidding obstacle and then, after having built a basis of trust between the rivals, he would try to negotiate the more formidable hurdles. Once Egypt had entered negotiations with Israel, Saudi Arabia might be persuaded to lift her oil embargo and, if luck held, it might even be conceivable to think about a compromise between Israel and Syria. Such was Kissinger's train of thought. The peace-making process would be like a steeple chase, with each successive hurdle higher and more treacherous. But at least, Kissinger believed, the step-by-step approach would yield some limited successes and should not be a total failure.

The objective that Kissinger had in mind, of course, was equilibrium. Israel would have to withdraw from some of the conquered territories, but within the context of her national security. The diplomatic reemergence of the Arabs would be encouraged, but within a context of realism and responsibility. An effort would be made to woo the Arabs away from the Soviet Union. They would come to the United States because, in Kissinger's judgment, "they could get weapons from the Russians, but territory only from the United States." Thus, by delivering some real estate to the Arabs, Soviet power in the Middle East would be diminished and American influence strengthened. To achieve this objective, however, pressure would have to be applied on Israel. She would have to be encouraged to trade territory for security. And if Kissinger's reasoning was wrong, he would have to protect Israel by always being generous with arms.

Kissinger's step-by-step approach to peace was not greeted with general acclaim. The Soviet Union was highly critical and pushed for a general peace conference to be held in Geneva. There was also criticism in the United States. Numerous Middle East experts asserted that Kissinger's approach was that of a doctor who planned to stitch up only part of a wound while permitting a raging infection to continue unattended.[2]

Kissinger was undaunted by these attacks. He believed that the aftermath of an inconclusive war was the best time for a concentrated peace effort. Shortly after the last shot had been fired, he decided to commit his skill, energy, and reputation to a highly personal diplomatic peace offensive in the Middle East. During the next few months, he would visit virtually every Arab capital, shuttle between Aswan and Jerusalem, and later between Damascus and Jerusalem. The president of Egypt, Anwar Sadat, would call him "brother"; King Faisal of the Saudis would welcome him even though he was a Jew; King Hussein of Jordan would pilot him in the royal helicopter; even President Assad of Syria would learn to like him; and the former Israeli prime minister, Golda Meir, would have endless conversations with him in her kitchen. The end result of this extraordinary diplomatic tour de force was the Sinai agreement between Israel and Egypt, reached in September 1975.

The Sinai agreement bore the typical imprimatur of a Kissinger settlement. Neither side was happy with it but neither side was able to produce a better alternative that was acceptable to both. The Israelis promised to return two mountain passes and

[2] See, for example, George W. Ball, *Diplomacy for a Crowded World: An American Foreign Policy* (Boston: Atlantic—Little, Brown), 1976, *passim.*

two oil fields. In exchange, they received pledges from Sadat to the effect that Egypt would refrain from the threat or use of force against the Jewish state. A United Nations buffer force of five thousand men was placed between the hostile armies. Kissinger also offered to provide two hundred American civilian technicians who would be stationed in the Sinai *between* the contending parties. They would serve as a kind of early warning system in case either side planned an attack upon the other, and they would report to both Israel and Egypt. Israel, which did not trust the UN buffer force, found the pledge of a small, symbolic American presence reassuring. In addition, Kissinger pledged that he would recommend an American aid commitment of $2.3 billion to Israel. This aid package, too, was attractive to the Israelis who still retained over 85 percent of Sinai and the entire Gaza Strip. Sadat, on the other hand, received his coveted mountain passes and oil fields plus an American commitment for $700 million needed for the impoverished Egyptian economy. The two hundred Americans were welcome too, since their presence only underlined Sadat's growing independence from the Soviet Union. Thus, Egypt gained some territorial allowances and Israel received political concessions. What could not be bridged between the parties directly was bridged by American commitments.

On the whole, Kissinger was pleased with the Sinai agreement. It was, after all, the first accord between Israel and an Arab nation that was not the immediate consequence of war. He knew that it was far from a genuine peace treaty, but he was convinced that his step-by-step approach was still the best way to proceed. And this had to be done through compromise. Kissinger's entire life as an historian and statesman had convinced him that victories and defeats merely led to other wars. Only a settlement without victory or defeat could create stability. And without stability and balance, peace could not be born at all.

Henry Kissinger, in his approach to foreign policy was thus, above all, a *conceptualizer*. He had borrowed a theory from the nineteenth century and applied it to the problems of the twentieth. We shall now examine this remarkable fusion between scholarship and statesmanship in Kissinger's two most historic policy initiatives: the new openings to the Soviet Union and China.

7

KISSINGER AND NIXON

The Search for a Stable World Order

THE SOVIET UNION AND THE LIMITATION OF STRATEGIC ARMS

For Henry Kissinger, America's relationship with Russia was absolutely basic to any policy that sought stability. Détente would depend, at least to some extent, on the ability of the United States to convert the Soviet Union from a "revolutionary" power with unlimited ambition to a "legitimate" state with more circumspect objectives. A legitimate state, in Kissinger's view, could still remain a dictatorship vis-à-vis its own people. This was not his main concern. What mattered enormously to him was adjusting the *external* goals of Soviet Russia to the overall imperatives of a stable world order. If he succeeded in this task, all else, he hoped, would fall into place. Of Kissinger's numerous pronouncements on détente with Soviet Russia, the following statement, made in April 1974, conveyed this central message with the greatest clarity:

> Détente is not rooted in agreement on values; it becomes above all necessary because each side recognizes that the other is a potential adversary in a nuclear war. To us, détente is a process of managing relations with a potentially hostile country in order to preserve peace while maintaining our vital interests. In a nuclear age, this is in itself an objective not without moral validity—it may indeed be the most profound moral imperative of all.[1]

[1] Henry Kissinger, "The Process of Détente," *American Foreign Policy*, 3rd ed. (New York: Norton, 1977), pp. 141–176.

Without stability, no peace was possible. Without the Soviet Union's participation in this quest, there could be no stability and there might not be any survival. These were the twin premises on which Kissinger set out to build détente with Soviet Russia.

When Henry Kissinger assumed office in 1969, nearly a quarter of a century had elapsed since the end of World War II. This twenty-four-year span had witnessed the most relentless arms race in the history of man. By 1969, the money devoted each year by the Soviet Union and the United States to military expenditures amounted to nearly three times what all the world's governments were spending on health and nearly twice what they spent on education. The record of disarmament negotiations was one of total failure. Despite endless conferences, both bilateral and multilateral, not a single weapon, either conventional or nuclear, had been scrapped as a result of a Soviet-American agreement. Mutual mistrust simply was too profound.

By the 1960s, the frustrations over disarmament had led some thinkers to approach the problem in a somewhat different way: in terms of arms *control* rather than disarmament. While the disarmer was primarily concerned with the actual scrapping of existing weapons, the arms controller was more interested in stabilizing the climate in which these weapons existed and in preventing additional arms build-ups. The emphasis here was less on hardware and more on psychology. The hope was that progress on disarmament-related issues might build confidence and ultimately lead to actual disarmament agreements. The partial Nuclear Test Ban Treaty of 1963 and the Nuclear Nonproliferation Treaty of 1968 were examples of this approach. The former prohibited nuclear testing in the atmosphere and the latter tried to prevent nuclear states from giving nuclear materials for war purposes to nonnuclear states. The only breakthroughs between the superpowers had taken place in arms control rather than disarmament.

Kissinger, too, was impressed by the arms control approach. Its emphasis on stability appealed to him. But there was a more fundamental reason for his preference. He had always shunned the technical, formula approach to problems that he considered basically political in nature. He simply did not believe that nations went to war because they had arms; rather, he felt, they had arms because they deemed it necessary to fight. Hence, he was convinced that efforts at disarmament were bound to fail unless they were preceded by more fundamental, political accommodation. The way to begin, in his view, was not to seek the magic disarmament formula but to concentrate instead on the acceptance, and possible settlement, of political differences.

To put it somewhat differently, Kissinger believed that the problem of disarmament was not disarmament at all, but rather forging détente between the Soviet Union and the United States. Moreover, it was his conviction that even the more modest search for arms control could not take place in a political vacuum; it would first be necessary to narrow the distances between American and Soviet positions in other areas, as well. This linkage approach was absolutely basic to his conception of détente. Every problem between the United States and the Soviet Union was linked with every other problem; progress on one would affect progress on all. Kissinger was determined to move on as broad a front as possible. Détente, like peace, was seen by him as indivisible.

To Kissinger, the linkage concept was a good test of Soviet sincerity on détente. If the Soviet Union was now willing to engage in the "give and take" of diplomatic barter, which linkage diplomacy implied, then this would indeed be evidence that Soviet Russia had at last accepted the legitimacy of the existing international order and abandoned its goal of global conquest.

Richard Nixon, by Inauguration Day, was a respectful student of Kissinger's philosophy. He had read most of Kissinger's books and had even scanned, at Kissinger's request, Spengler's *Decline of the West*. The linkage concept appealed to the president.

Kissinger's overall philosophical approach to the limitation of strategic arms was consistent with his quest for a stable world order. He had never believed that American nuclear superiority over the Soviet Union would be helpful. In his judgment, a rough equilibrium in nuclear arsenals was most desirable. Superiority would be destabilizing and exact parity might be impossible to attain because of the differences in American and Soviet weapons systems. The term he preferred was "sufficiency." Nixon, who in earlier years, had been an ardent advocate of American superiority, now echoed Kissinger's opinion. "I think *sufficiency* is a better term," the president declared shortly after he took office, "than either *superiority* or *parity*."

The American and Soviet negotiators both knew from the

start that it would probably be hopeless to aim for actual physical disarmament. There was simply not enough trust or good faith between the superpowers to justify such an ambitious goal. Thus, Kissinger's more modest objective of stabilizing the existing balance of terror was preferred by both sides as more realistically feasible. Kissinger assumed, and the Russians agreed, that the balance would have to be stabilized with each side retaining invulnerable retaliatory power. This meant that neither side— even if it struck first—could destroy the other's ability to strike back. The logic of Kissinger's position was the somewhat Machiavellian assumption that the safety of weapons would increase the safety of people. If each side knew that no blow, however massive, could destroy the other's capacity to return the blow, stability would prevail. Mutual deterrence, therefore, rested on the awareness by each side of the other's retaliatory—or second-strike capacity. The common recognition of this basic premise became the point of departure for the SALT negotiations.

The talks focused on weapons that approached the outer limits of the human propensity for self-destruction. Both sides had offensive weapons of such stupendous destructive power that, in comparison, the Hiroshima bomb virtually paled into insignificance. These intercontinental ballistic missiles (ICBMs) could be launched from a base on land or sea and guided with a fair degree of accuracy to an enemy target an entire continent away. As if this were not enough, the United States had developed a new technology whereby each missile was able to release individual warheads at varying times and angles. Thus, each individual missile could be assigned multiple targets. For a while, this multiple independent reentry vehicle (MIRV) was regarded as the ultimate weapon, against which no defense was possible. It seemed like the Hydra-headed monster of Greek mythology had come back in modern form to haunt mankind.

By 1969, however, both the Soviet Union and the United States were experimenting with a possible defense against the MIRV—an antiballistic missile (ABM), which would function like a bullet aimed to shoot down another bullet. Each side believed that the perfection of an ABM system would give it a decisive edge in the power balance, since it could then risk a first strike against the enemy without having to fear the consequences of retaliation. Needless to say, the cost of an effective ABM system was prohibitive, and its dependability was considered far from certain. Nevertheless, by 1969, both superpowers were already spending billions of dollars on the research and development of the ABM.

When the SALT talks opened in the fall of 1969, the Soviet Union had ICBMs with bigger "throw-weight," or as Pentagon jargon put it, "more bang for a buck." The American ICBMs, however, were purported to have greater accuracy. Besides, the United States had "MIRV'd" a considerable number of its ICBMs and was also working on the ABM. The Soviet Union was striving feverishly to catch up with the United States in MIRV technology.

Kissinger perceived MIRV and ABM as two sides of a single coin, each justifying the existence of the other. He believed that, if the nuclear balance were truly to be stabilized, the talks would have to be addressed simultaneously to both offensive and defensive missiles. Agreement on one but not the other was unacceptable to him.

Kissinger's approach to SALT was quite imaginative. Rather than tie himself down to a specific proposal or even to a number of proposals, he was prepared to accept, as a basis for negotiations, any proposal put forward by the Russians, *provided* it would ultimately yield a balance that was roughly even. It did not matter to him whether an agreement would permit a hundred or a thousand missile launchers; his goal was symmetry. Nor did he care whether an ABM would be limited to the defense of only a single city of ten; equilibrium was what counted. This emphasis on flexibility saved much valuable time, since it avoided bickering over specific proposals advanced by one side or the other. Kissinger's flexibility, however, never extended to the principle of equilibrium itself. He believed that any nuclear imbalance would be a threat to the stable world order that he was pursuing. "Flexibility," as he had written long before, was "a virtue only in the purposeful."

Despite Kissinger's profound knowledge of the subject and extraordinary negotiating skill, the initial phase of the SALT process of achieving equilibrium was a long and arduous one. SALT I, as it was later designated, went through eight stages and lasted almost three years. John Newhouse, in *Cold Dawn*, his authoritative study of SALT, described the process as "probably the most fascinating episodic negotiation since the Congress of Vienna."

Kissinger was clearly in command of the negotiating process, though he delegated many of its technical aspects to a group of specialists headed by Gerard C. Smith, an official with extensive experience in the field of arms control. At crucial moments, when deadlock threatened, Kissinger would move the negotiations forward, usually by persuading the president to make numerical concessions without impairing the objective overall balance. For example, he permitted the Russians to keep a larger number of missile launchers because he knew that the United States had more individual warheads.

Finally, on May 26, 1972, in Moscow, Nixon and Brezhnev signed two historic arms control documents, which signified the end of the first phase of SALT. On that day the United States and the Soviet Union renounced the defense of most of their territory and people against the other's nuclear weapons. This was the historic essence of SALT I. The agreement was signed even though ten days before Nixon had decided to mine the harbor of Haiphong. The Soviet leadership apparently considered SALT to be more important than its alliance with North Vietnam.

The first document was an ABM treaty of unlimited duration, which placed limits on the growth of Soviet and American strategic nuclear arsenals. The treaty established a ceiling of 200 launchers for each side's defensive missile system and committed both sides to refrain from building nationwide antimissile defenses. Each country was limited to two ABM sites, one for the national capital and the other to protect one field of ICBMs. Each site would consist of 100 ABMs. The United States already had a protected ICBM field in North Dakota and thus, under the terms of the treaty, could add an ABM site around Washington, D.C. The Soviet Union already had an ABM site for the defense of Moscow and thus was permitted to add an ABM site to protect an ICBM field. At the time of the agreement, the Soviet Union had a total of 2,328 missiles: 1,618 land-based ICBMs and 710 on submarines. The United States had a total of 1,710 missiles: 1,054 land-based ICBMs and 656 on submarines.

The second document was an interim agreement limiting ICBMs to those under construction or deployed at the time of the signing of the agreement. Kissinger and Soviet Foreign Minister Andrei Gromyko had held a number of nocturnal meetings in order to define what was meant by "under construction." They finally managed to agree that a missile was deemed to be "under construction" after its parts had been riveted to the hull. This meant the retention of 1,618 ICBMs for the Soviet Union and 1,054 for the United States. The agreement also froze at existing levels the construction of submarine-launched ICBM missiles on all submarines—656 for the United States and 710 for the Soviet Union. However, each side could build additional submarine missiles if an equal number of older land-based ICBMs or submarine-based missile launchers were dismantled. This "trade-in" provision had been a major stumbling block because the Soviet and American nuclear arsenals were so asymmetrical. How many old missiles were worth one new missile? Once again, Kissinger recommended a numerical concession to Nixon, and this finally broke the deadlock.

SALT I placed no limitations whatever on the qualitative improvement of offensive or defensive missiles; nor did it impose ceilings on the number of warheads that could be carried by offensive missiles or on the number of strategic bombers permitted to each side. Modernization of missiles, including the emplacement of new missiles in new silos, was permitted. Both sides pledged "not to interfere with the national technical means of verification of the other party," and each side retained the right to withdraw from either agreement if it felt that its supreme national interest was in jeopardy.

SALT I thus managed to freeze a rough balance into the nuclear arsenals of the two superpowers. There remained "missile gaps," of course, in specific weapons. The United States, for example, retained the lead in MIRV technology, while the Soviet Union possessed a larger quantity of missile launchers. Nevertheless, the overall effect was the achievement of a rough equilibrium—Kissinger's main objective, in the first place.

Kissinger's skill and flexibility were indispensable qualities in bringing SALT I to a successful conclusion. But fortunately for him, he could be flexible without endangering his goal of overall stability. The higher degree of accuracy of the American missiles and the generally more advanced development of American MIRV technology made it possible to concede an advantage in overall missile numbers to the Russians. It is most unlikely that the Soviet Union would have agreed to SALT I without this numerical advantage. They pursued it with single-minded tenacity. It provided an illusion of superiority for the hard-line members of the Soviet Politbureau who had challenged Brezhnev's commitment to détente with the United States.

The heavy-handed approach of the Soviet leaders stood in striking contrast to Kissinger's flexibility and nimble sense of humor. Brezhnev told Nixon and Kissinger repeatedly that "the terrible things" the Western press had said about him simply were not true. He had shaved down his bushy eyebrows for the Moscow summit and wanted to be reassured by Kissinger that he did not look brutal. He also seemed to be quite eager to be accepted as a fellow Westerner. "For a European mind like mine," he said to Kissinger, "the Chinese are impossible to understand." An amusing exchange took place between Kissinger and Soviet President Nikolai Podgorny at the Moscow airport after SALT I had been signed. A Soviet plane that was to take Nixon and Kissinger to Kiev simply would not start. Kissinger, eager to ease Podgorny's embarrassment, asked the Soviet president if he had ever heard of the "Law of the Wickedness of Objects." "No," Podgorny answered, looking puzzled. "Well," Kissinger explained, "if you drop a piece of buttered bread on a new carpet, the chances of its falling with the buttered side down are in direct relationship to the cost of the carpet." Podgorny's face looked vacant; he did not get the joke. Kissinger decided he would provide another example of his "law." "If you drop a coin on the floor," he said, "the chances of it rolling away from you rather than toward you, are in direct relationship to the value of the coin." Podgorny still looked blank. Finally, he said: "Whenever I drop coins, they roll toward me," Kissinger who had had C students before briskly changed the subject. On one occasion, however, during one of the all-night meetings between Kissinger and Gromyko, the Soviet foreign minister stole a march on Kissinger. Teasing Gromyko, Kissinger wanted to know whether he should speak closer to an apple or to an orange in a bowl of fruit, implying that one of them probably contained a miniature microphone. Gromyko, glancing at the ceiling, indicated a sculpture of a buxom woman. He painted to one of her breasts. "I believe it is in there," he said.

Kissinger was ecstatic about the success of SALT I. He

thought of it as a great historic step toward a saner world. To his delight, less than a week after the Moscow summit had ended, the United States, together with the Soviet Union, Britain, and France, signed the final protocol of an agreement on the status of Berlin. In addition, the final instruments of a peace treaty between West Germany and the Soviet Union were exchanged. It seemed that the German problem, for so long at the center of the cold war, had finally yielded to a rational solution.

Détente was sinking roots at last. In the summer of 1973, the two Germanies were admitted as separate sovereign states to the United Nations. In June 1973, a second Nixon-Brezhnev summit was arranged by Kissinger, this time in Washington. On that occasion the two leaders agreed to continue negotiations on the limitation of strategic offensive arms. They also reached an accord on the avoidance of nuclear conflict with each other or with a third nation, pledging restraint on the use of force or the threat of force and agreeing to consult with one another if potentially dangerous situations should arise. Nixon visited Moscow once more in July 1974, only one month before his resignation, but by then his position had been eroded too much by Watergate to permit any further substantive progress.

SALT I had placed no restrictions of any kind on the qualitative improvement of missiles. During 1973, the Soviet Union made rapid strides in the evolution of MIRV technology, and threatened to catch up with the United States. As a result, Kissinger began to feel that it was a matter of great urgency for the United States to reach a second SALT accord with the Soviet Union that would include offensive weapons. He and Secretary of Defense James R. Schlesinger, however, developed profound differences over the most effective way in which this all-important negotiation should be approached.

Schlesinger favored either a dramatic mutual reduction in offensive missiles, or, if the Russians did not agree, an all-out arms race. Kissinger maintained that the Soviets would not agree to drastic cutbacks since they were still behind the United States. Hence, the Schlesinger proposal would result in an unchecked arms race.

Kissinger thus argued for an agreement that would establish an equilibrium at high force levels, to be followed by step-by-step reductions over a period of time. The Joint Chiefs of Staff agreed with Kissinger since high force levels would permit them to complete their missile modernization programs. They also contended that Schlesinger's alternative of an all-out arms race was not politically feasible since Congress would be reluctant to appropriate the necessary funds.

When President Gerald Ford met with Leonid Brezhnev on the Soviet Pacific coast in Vladivostok in October 1974, in order to discuss the possibilities of a SALT II agreement on offensive missiles, he was accompanied by Secretary of State Kissinger as his main adviser. Once again, the bargaining was tough. Kissinger, after a marathon negotiating session with the Soviet leader, got Brezhnev to drop his demand for numerical superiority. In exchange, Kissinger agreed to a higher ceiling for all kinds of missiles for both countries. This overall ceiling was set at 2,400 missiles for each side with 1,320 of these permitted to be MIRV'd. No restrictions were set on further qualitative improvements such as missile flight tests to increase accuracy or on the development of land-mobile and air-mobile intercontinental ballistic missiles. Nor were any restrictions placed on the development of cruise missiles launched from submarines.

Ford and Brezhnev did not sign a final accord, but reached agreement only in principle. Kissinger, however, expressed the hope that SALT II, once signed, would "put a cap on the arms race" for the ten years "between 1975 and 1985." "In terms of permament achievements," Kissinger said in December 1974, "I would rank the outline for SALT II near the top."

Actually, Vladivostok was a rather modest achievement. The "cap" on the arms race did not signify a reduction of existing weapons stockpiles, but merely a quantitative limitation on the development of further weapons. The United States would have fairly good assurances of the maximum number of Soviet missiles over the next decade. On the crucial matter of verification, however, a major asymmetry prevailed. Since the United States was an open society with weapons systems subject to constant public scrutiny from their research and development phase to their actual deployment, the Soviet Union could have a high degree of confidence in American compliance with any limitation agreement. This was, of course, not equally true of American faith in Soviet honesty. The verification problem was now particularly crucial since it was important to know, under the Vladivostok accord, whether a missile was MIRV'd or not.

The verification issue began to haunt Kissinger in 1975 and

placed in serious question further progress toward SALT II. Admiral Elmo R. Zumwalt, retired chief of naval operations, declared in December 1975 that the Soviet Union had committed "gross violations" of the SALT I accord of 1972 and that Kissinger had not properly informed President Ford. He charged that the Soviets were constructing launch silos for additional missiles and thus were surreptitiously upgrading their ABM defensive potential. He also accused the Soviets of converting "light" ABM missiles into "heavy" ones and thus violating the spirit of SALT I. Kissinger heatedly denied the charges and was supported in his defense by the Central Intelligence Agency. By this time, however, the ire of the Soviets was aroused. *Pravda* not only denied any violations of the 1972 accord, but in turn voiced serious doubts about the American compliance. It now blamed the United States for the delay in reaching a final SALT II agreement, which Brezhnev had hoped would be sealed by the time the 25th Communist Party Congress was to convene in February 1976.

Progress toward SALT II was also stalled over two new weapons that the United States and the Soviet Union wanted to add to their respective arsenals. The Pentagon had developed a "cruise missile," which was a long-range, jet-propelled, extremely accurate, guided nuclear bomb that could be launched from a bomber, a ship, or a submarine. Pentagon spokesmen declared that since the cruise missile traveled through the atmosphere, it should not be included in the SALT II ceiling of 2,400 ICBMs that traveled through space. The Soviet Union insisted that the "cruise missile" be included in the ceiling. At the same time, the Soviets had developed a new "Backfire" bomber, which, they declared, should be excluded from SALT II because of its limited range. The Pentagon, insisting that air-to-air refueling could enable it to reach the United States and return, demanded its inclusion in the ceiling.

Kissinger, convinced that "ninety percent of SALT II had been completed" and that an agreement was essential in order to maintain the momentum of détente, clashed more and more with Schlesinger. The defense secretary, in turn, accused Kissinger of making disadvantageous agreements with the Soviets in order to preserve a dubious illusion of détente. While Ford's dismissal of Schlesinger in late 1975 left Kissinger in primary control of foreign policy, the position of assistant for national security affairs was taken away from him. Thus, by early 1976, the future of SALT II was very much in doubt. The allegations of cheating by the Soviet Union, the dispute over the inclusion of newly developed weapons in the overall ceiling, and a deepening suspicion of Soviet behavior in Angola and in the Middle East made Kissinger's position on SALT II extremely vulnerable. It seemed that despite the breakthrough on SALT I, the safety of the superpowers still depended, first and foremost, on their capacity for mutually assured destruction. SALT had made a dent into the balance of terror, but it was little more than a beginning.

Kissinger's conception of détente was a synthesis of all that he had learned from his study of nineteenth century history. *Si vis pacem, para bellum*—"If you wish peace, prepare for war," was the credo that had been emblazoned on the ministry of war of imperial Austria. Kissinger's insight lay in his ability to translate that motto into a setting of the nuclear age. The old Roman maxim no longer quite sufficed; a whole network of linkages and agreements had to be created in order to gain leverage over the Soviet Union. But this too, was not at all that different from what the nineteenth century diplomats had done. They, too, had attempted to exercise control over the revolutionary power through manipulations and alliances. But in their time, no mistake was irretrievable. No outcome was completely fatal. There was no sense of ultimate catastrophe. This was the basic difference that haunted the conscience of Henry Kissinger. It was the reason why he believed with absolute conviction that there was no meaningful alternative to détente.

The credo of the cold war years had been updated since the times of imperial Austria. For the generation of the cold war, the appropriate motto might have been *Si vis vitam, para mortem* —"If you wish to live, prepare for death." For Henry Kissinger, this simply was not good enough.

THE OPENING OF CHINA

Kissinger was Nixon's teacher on how to build détente with the Soviet Union. In contemplating an American opening to China, however, both men reached similar conclusions at approximately the same time. Nixon, in October 1967, had written in *Foreign*

Affairs, that "any American policy must come urgently to grips with the reality of China. There is no place on this small planet for a billion of its potentially most able people to live in angry isolation." [2] He also was the first to see the possibility of leveraging the widening rift between China and the Soviet Union to the advantage of the United States. One week after Inauguration Day, Nixon sent a memo to his new assistant for national security affairs asking him to explore discreetly the possibility of rapprochement with China. Kissinger promised to do so, though he believed that it might take some time to build a bridge to China.

When Mao Tse-tung had taken control of China in 1949, there were few objective quarrels between him and the United States that might not have been resolved through a policy of compromise. There was no defense treaty with Chiang Kai-shek, there were no American ships in the Taiwan straits, there was no Korean conflict yet, and the Indochina war was years away. But Americans and Chinese had memories of one another that prevented compromise. More than a century of tragic history made reconciliation difficult. The Chinese remembered America's policy of the "Open Door" as a pretext for plunder and exploitation. They had never opened the door, they thought, but rather the Americans had smashed it in. Americans in turn, believed that they had played the role of China's benevolent guardian, and now China had been lost, as if China had been America's to lose. Both nations thus felt utterly betrayed and regarded one another as deadly enemies. It would take more than twenty years of hate, two bitter wars on Asian soil, and suffering on a horrendous scale, before China and America were to make fact, not fear, the basis of their policy.

In March 1969, shooting broke out along the Ussuri River near the Chinese-Soviet border. Tensions over disputed territory that had been escalating for some time, finally erupted into open conflict. The "fraternal unity" of the two colossi of the Communist world now lay shattered in ruins.

Kissinger's view of China was affected fundamentally by these events. He now believed that China's fear of Russia might be greater than her fear of the United States, and that China, there-

---

[2] Richard Nixon, "Asia After Vietnam," *Foreign Affairs*, October 1967. Also see *RN: The Memoirs of Richard Nixon* (New York: Grosset and Dunlap, 1978), p. 235.

fore, might respond to an American gesture of reconciliation. It was not until 1967 that Kissinger had considered such an opening a realistic possibility. But now that he was sure, he quickly made it a centerpiece of his entire policy. Rapprochement with China would give the United States enormous leverage over the Soviet Union. So long as the hostility between China and the Soviet Union prevailed, Kissinger could thrust the United States into the position of the balancer. America, in short, would then be wooed by both the leading powers of the communist world. The possibilities of this new constellation suddenly seemed limitless.

Kissinger informed Yahya Khan, the president of Pakistan, of his new interest in China. During the next few months, Yahya Khan served as Kissinger's confidential courier to Peking. The Pakistani president was received by Mao in November 1970. Kissinger received unsigned notes from Peking at periodic intervals, all handwritten on white paper with blue lines, and each more cordial than the preceding one. In March 1971, another unsigned handwritten note was delivered to Kissinger by Pakistan's ambassador. The note extended an invitation for an "American envoy" to come to Peking. Two names were mentioned in the note: one was William Rogers, the secretary of state, the other was Kissinger.

There was never any question in Nixon's mind that it would be Kissinger who would go to China.

Kissinger left Washington on July 1, allegedly on a round-the-world trip. Yahya Khan, who was privy to his plans, helped him camouflage the real purpose of his global tour. When Kissinger arrived in Islāmābād, the Pakistani capital, it was announced that he had come down with a slight case of intestinal flu and would have to rest for a few days in a mountain resort near the capital. Actually, Kissinger was in excellent health. Shortly after 3 A.M. on July 9, a Pakistani International Airlines jet took off from Islāmābād's airport for China. Kissinger was on board, scheduled to arrive in Peking at noon.

One day in 1976—almost five years after Kissinger's first meeting with Chou En-lai—the author asked him about those two days in July 1971, that had changed so dramatically the world's power constellation.

"I had no idea what the Chinese were like," Kissinger admitted frankly. He had taken a "briefing book" with him to China, which he brought with him to his first meeting with the

Chinese leader. "Put your book away," said Chou En-lai, "and let us talk."

Kissinger spent more than twenty hours of his two-day visit in conversations with Chou En-lai. The experience had a profound and lasting effect on him. The two men discovered very quickly that, despite the gulf of time and culture that separated them, they were very much alike. Both had powerful intellects, with a penchant for philosophy and history. They engaged in a wide-ranging discussion of Sino-American relations without attempting to place blame on either side for the two decades of estrangement and hostility. Both men shared an elitist disdain for bureaucracy and mediocrity though they recognized the importance of pragmatic adjustments to reality. Both men had had their share of domestic opposition. During the Cultural Revolution in 1966, Chou En-lai's residence had been besieged by 100,000 Red Guards who had accused him of being a "cosmopolitan traitor." Chou had debated with the students for forty-eight hours before the throng had finally dispersed. Kissinger had his own memories of debates with students and professors during the Cambodian invasion of a year before. Finally, both men had survived adversity and achieved great power. Chou En-lai had been a member of the Long March, which had decimated the Chinese Communists to a remnant of 10,000 men seeking refuge in the dank caves of Yenan in the 1930s. Kissinger's own refugee background and meteoric rise from obscurity to power gave him a measure of empathy for the Chinese leader. Thus, Kissinger and Chou En-lai developed a genuine respect for one another that became the basis for a real friendship. Insofar as two world leaders separated by light-years of culture and tradition can become friends, Kissinger and Chou En-lai formed such a bond. As Kissinger told the Senate at the confirmation hearings on his appointment as secretary of state in September 1973: "I have been accused of perhaps excessive admiration for Prime Minister Chou En-lai, and it is true that I have very high regard for him." When the older man succumbed after a long illness in January 1976, Kissinger felt a keen sense of loss. "There is turmoil under the heavens," Chou En-lai had said to him in 1971. "And we have the opportunity to end it." Certainly the first encounter began the process of reconciliation. Fact gradually began to replace fear as the major basis of America's China policy.

Only a single specific agreement was reached between Kissinger and Chou during the first visit. Chou extended an invitation to Nixon to visit China in early 1972. Beyond that, the two negotiators reached a meeting of minds in one important area that had caused Sino-American tensions in the past. They agreed in principle that Taiwan should be considered as a part of China and that the political future of the island should be settled peacefully by the Chinese themselves. The precise circumstances of such a future settlement were left purposely ambiguous. Kissinger, who knew when to be precise, but also when to be ambiguous, proposed that no specific plan be adopted for Taiwan except that the process of change be a peaceful one. Chou En-lai agreed to this vague formulation and expressed his admiration for Kissinger by saying, only half in jest, that his American visitor had a "Chinese mind."

In November 1971, Nixon announced that he would visit China for a week, beginning on February 21, 1972.[3] He also stated that, in his view, "the ultimate relationship of Taiwan to the People's Republic of China would have to be settled by direct negotiations between the two parties concerned." Chiang Kai-shek, in his exile on Taiwan, now felt utterly betrayed by Kissinger and Nixon. The Peking leadership, on the other hand, prepared to welcome the American president. Kissinger hoped that now, at last, he might have the opportunity to meet the aging, legendary leader of China's 800 million people, Chairman Mao Tse-tung.

The Soviet leadership was, of course, alarmed. Kissinger had a soothing word for Brezhnev immediately upon his return from his first trip to Peking. "Nothing that has been done in our relations with the People's Republic of China," he declared on July 16, "is in any way directed against any other countries, and especially not against the Soviet Union." The Russians were not convinced. They were expecting Nixon in the Soviet capital in May 1972. Nixon decided to echo Kissinger's reassuring note. "Neither trip is being taken," he asserted, "at the expense of any other nation."

When Kissinger and Nixon arrived in Peking on schedule on

[3] For Nixon's own description of his trip to China, see his *Memoirs*, pp. 544–580.

February 21, Chou En-lai was on hand to greet the two Americans. He and Kissinger were friends by now and were pleased that they had done their work so well. Another similarity the two men shared was their loyalty to their respective leaders. Chou, despite his superior intellect, saw himself as a subservient follower of Mao Tse-tung. And Kissinger, during the crisis of Cambodia, had been a loyal supporter of the president.

To Kissinger's surprise and delight, he and Nixon were invited to meet Mao immediately after their arrival. The two men spent an hour with Mao and Chou, and once again, as on the occasion of Kissinger's first visit, the subjects were philosophy and history.

What impression did Kissinger have of Mao Tse-tung? After all if ever there was a "revolutionary," the chairman certainly was such a man. He had helped to organize the Chinese Communist party half a century before his encounter with Henry Kissinger. He had led the Long March in the 1930s and taken the remnants of the Red Army to a sanctuary more than six thousand miles away. He had led his forces against Chiang Kai-shek, the Japanese, and finally against the Americans in Korea. In 1966, at the age of seventy-four, fearful lest China might emulate the ossified bureaucracy of Soviet Russia, Mao, always the adventurer, had set out to rejuvenate the revolution. What did the author of *A World Restored* think of this authentic twentieth-century revolutionary?

Again, Kissinger admitted that he had been wrong. His description of Mao Tse-tung bordered on awe. "Wherever he sat or stood," Kissinger said, "there was the center of the room. Even though his voice was weak with age and each word was a struggle, he was quite lucid and in absolute command. Chou En-lai fell silent in his presence." Kissinger saw Mao as a modern visionary, a heroic figure, but also a man who could be co-opted into a stable international order. "Here was a statesman," Kissinger said, "who combined revolutionary ardor with a sense of pragmatism, a man who had a vision for his people, but who had remained in touch with the practical realities as well." It was clear that both Mao and Chou appealed enormously to Kissinger's own romanticism, and resonated with his admiration for the solitary figure in adversity. In 1971 and 1972, Kissinger developed a genuine fondness for one Chinese Communist leader and a profound admiration for the other.

The next few days in Peking were devoted to serious delibera-tions. On the American side, Nixon and Kissinger were the main negotiators on matters of principle, such as Taiwan and Indochina. Their two opponents were Chou En-lai and Chiao Kuan-hua, a deputy foreign minister. Parallel negotiations were being held between Secretary William Rogers and China's Foreign Minister Chi Peng-fei on questions of travel, tourism, and trade. The eve-nings were taken up with banquets, table-tennis exhibitions, and a performance of *Red Detachment of Women,* hosted by Mao Tse-tung's wife, Chiang Ching. The theme of the ballet was the victory of a young peasant girl over Chiang Kai-shek's troops. Nixon found the performance "excellent theater and superb act-ing." Kissinger and Chiao worked late into the night in an effort to put together a joint communiqué.

Both sides wanted a positive statement about the visit. Nixon had made the occasion into a television spectacular and needed a successful outcome for the voters at home. The Chinese wanted to justify Nixon's presence to their people and also to impress the Russians with proof of tangible Chinese-American cooperation. Yet it became increasingly obvious as the talks progressed, that it would not be possible to draft a joint statement to which both sides would be able to subscribe. Some of the differences, espe-cially on the problems of Taiwan and Indochina, could not be simply papered over by a document of studied ambiguity.

Kissinger and Chou came up with an idea that broke the deadlock. Both sides would agree to write separate sections into the communiqué, one expressing the American view of a particu-lar problem and the other setting forth the Chinese position. This technique enabled the negotiators to focus honestly on differ-ences rather than cover them up with diplomatic double-talk. On two occasions, Kissinger and Chiao worked until dawn in order to formulate a communiqué that would set forth the differences between the two nations without making them appear to be un-bridgeable. In four areas—Indochina, Korea, Japan, and India-Pakistan—the difficulties were manageable. On the matter of Tai-wan, however, the two positions were so far apart that even the technique of drafting separate statements ran into virtually in-superable difficulties.

On Indochina, the United States declared its long-range goal of self-determination for the Indochinese people, while the Chi-nese affirmed their support for the Provisional Revolutionary Government; on Korea, Nixon underlined his support for South Korea, while Chou supported North Korea; on Japan, the United States affirmed its alliance with that nation, while the Chinese declared their opposition to a revival of Japanese militarism; and on the Indo-Pakistani war, the United States evenhandedly supported the cease-fire, while the Chinese declared their firm support for Pakistan. In essence, the four statements were little more than agreements to disagree.

Kissinger spent most of his negotiating time and skill on the problem of Taiwan. The Chinese pressed him hard to concede Peking's sovereignty over the island. Implicit in their position was the demand that the United States must abrogate its defense treaty with Chiang Kai-shek, since, the Chinese argued, a province could not legitimately maintain a pact with a foreign country. Kissinger, in turn, refused to scrap the Taiwan treaty and insisted that Peking renounce the use of force against the island. Both sides realized that full-fledged diplomatic relations between their two countries would have to be postponed until some mutually acceptable formula could be agreed upon.

Finally, on February 26, Kissinger and Chiao reached agreement on two paragraphs that set forth the two opposing positions with a minimum of rhetoric. In the American paragraph, Kissinger acknowledged that there was "but one China and that Taiwan [was] a part of China," but insisted on "a peaceful settlement of the Taiwan question by the Chinese themselves." He also pledged "the ultimate withdrawal of all U.S. forces and military installations from Taiwan," and a gradual reduction of American forces "as the tension in the area diminish[ed]." The implication was that the United States would gradually withdraw as the Vietnam war drew to a close, but would pull out completely only after Peking had renounced force as a way of "liberating" Taiwan. The Chinese paragraph asserted that "the Taiwan question was the crucial question obstructing the normalization of relations between China and the United States," and reasserted the position that the island was a Chinese province. It also implied, however, that Taiwan's ultimate absorption into China would not take place by force. This was about as far as the two sides were able to move toward a compromise.

These were the major problem areas that Kissinger and Nixon covered in a communiqué issued in Shanghai the day before they

departed from Chinese soil. Neither side was very happy with the
Taiwan statement, but both agreed that a solution by force
was to be ruled out. Thus, this delicate issue was neatly transformed from a problem to be solved immediately into a process to
be managed over a period of time.

In addition, Rogers and Chi Peng-fei had worked out some
initial agreements on travel, tourism, and trade. It was also agreed
that a "senior U.S. representative" would be stationed in Peking.
At the final banquet, Nixon proclaimed that his visit to China had
been "a week that [had] changed the world." Kissinger's euphoria
was almost greater. "What we are doing now with China is so
great, so historic," he stated at a news conference, "that the word
'Vietnam' will be only a footnote when it is written in history."

Kissinger and Nixon returned to Washington to heroes' wel-
comes. In Moscow, the reaction was one of sullen anger and suspicion. In Tokyo, the Sato government collapsed, and on Taiwan,
Chiang Kai-shek declared that the United States could no longer
be trusted as an ally. One thing was clear to all, however: the
bipolar world was clearly over. A triangular constellation now
loomed on the horizon.

Nixon and Kissinger had every intention of broadening and
deepening the new understanding with China. In March 1972,
the Chinese table-tennis team visited the United States, and in
April the first American businessmen were invited to visit the
Canton spring trade fair. Then, however, the blossoming relationship was temporarily halted because of the Haiphong mining of
May 1972, and the "Christmas bombing" in December. On February 15, 1973, however, less than a month after the Paris accords
on Indochina, Kissinger once again visited Peking. Eager to pursue
the further normalization of United States-China relations, but
frustrated in this quest by the American defense treaty with Taiwan, Kissinger and Chairman Mao settled on a compromise. The
United States and China agreed to open liaison offices in Washington and Peking. In addition, each nation made another concession to the other. In exchange for China's release of two
captured American pilots and review of the sentence of John
Downey, a CIA agent held prisoner in China since the Korean
War, the United States agreed to negotiate the settlement of
American claims against China and the release of Chinese assets
"blocked" in the United States since Korea. In March 1973, David

Bruce was appointed to head the United States liaison office in
Peking and Huang Chen, China's former ambassador to France,
was named to fill the Washington post. The liaison offices were
formally opened in May 1973. In practical terms, they fulfilled
most of the functions of regular embassies, without, however,
stumbling over the divisive issue of Taiwan. Kissinger was greatly
pleased with this compromise solution.

In late 1973, however, a "mini-cultural revolution" in China
slowed down the process of rapprochement. The ancient sage
Confucius came under severe attack for his "bourgeois" philosophy. The music of Beethoven and Schubert was compared unfavor-
ably to *The White-haired Girl*, a Chinese opera that had put
Kissinger to sleep during his previous visit. Richard Bach's *Jona-
than Livingston Seagull* was denounced for its "reactionary" tendencies, and Michelangelo Antonioni was attacked as a "decadent"
filmmaker. Both Huang Chen and David Bruce went home for
about a month before taking up their posts again. The "mini-
cultural revolution," however, was far milder both in scope and
content than the upheaval of 1966. It apparently was an expression of bitter disagreements between those forces in the Chinese
Politbureau led by Madame Mao, who considered the United
States as the principal threat to China, and those of Premier
Chou En-lai, who perceived the Soviet Union as the greater danger.
Both groups agreed on the philosopher Confucius and on Defense
Minister Lin Piao—both "unpersons" and dead—as convenient
symbols for the reactionary enemy.

Kissinger steadily encouraged intellectual exchange and trade,
but the Taiwan problem kept these contacts at a fairly modest
level. On the issue of academic exchange, for example, China retained virtually exclusive power to decide who would visit, for how
long, to see what and to meet whom, and under what circumstances. In fact, the Chinese restrictions on American contacts
were more severe than those imposed by the Soviet Union.

The trade pattern followed an erratic course. Two-way China-
American trade approached the $1 billion mark in 1974. During
that year, the United States became China's second most important trading partner. In 1975, however, the figure was slashed in
half and the Chinese abruptly cancelled a large order for American wheat and corn. Taiwan's trade with the United States in
1975 was almost ten times as large and Hong Kong's was four

times as large. The evidence suggests that the Taiwan issue inhibited a more rapid expansion of commercial contacts. Financing problems, the American refusal to grant China most-favored-nations status, and the lack of a formal trade agreement could all be traced back to the absence of full diplomatic relations. Thus, Kissinger's "liaison office" solution did not resolve the Taiwan problem, but merely circumvented it. By 1975, rapprochement between China and America had reached a fairly stable plateau. There was little, if any, forward movement. Even a trip to Peking by Kissinger and Ford in the fall of 1975 did not restore the old momentum.

In February 1976, exactly four years after his first visit as president, Richard Nixon again went to China, this time in the role of tourist. The Chinese government had extended the invitation to the former president apparently as a signal to Ford and Kissinger that the United States was paying too much attention to détente with the Soviet Union and not enough to China. Chairman Mao hoped that the meaning of an invitation to the architect of the American opening to China would not be lost on his successor. Kissinger, who denied any part in the plans for Nixon's China visit, nevertheless decided to "debrief" his former chief who had not only been entertained by Chairman Mao personally but also by Chou En-lai's successor, Hua Kuo-feng.

By 1976, a chill wind was blowing out of China in Kissinger's direction. While he was not an "unperson" in Peking, Chou En-lai's successors regarded him with growing mistrust and ambivalence. They felt that he had overplayed the Soviet card and that the time had come perhaps to turn the tables on the United States. They sensed that Kissinger's triangular policy was vulnerable. In politics as well as love, triangles were inherently unstable. There was no guarantee that the United States would always remain the "lady."

What had brought Henry Kissinger to Peking for the first time in 1971 and what brought him back seven more times by the end of 1976 was, first and foremost, the possibility of using this odd Sino-American coupling as leverage on the Soviet Union. Kissinger made sure that he would hold the best position in the triangle, as the only point with lines to the other two. He was careful to keep the United States in a position of equidistance between the two communist powers. Yet, his triangular policy was based on one fundamental assumption that was absolutely essential for its success: the permanent hostility between China and the Soviet Union. His thinking on this crucial subject is therefore vital to any examination of his foreign policy.

Kissinger, the historian, was quick to point out that the decade of the 1950s was the only period in the entire history of Chinese-Russian relations in which the two nations were closely allied. This ten-year aberration from a century-long pattern of nationalist tension and territorial competition, was in essence, a response to a common enemy that, temporarily, was perceived as the greater threat: the United States. As this threat receded in the wake of détente, the historical animosities between China and Russia resurfaced and the relationship reverted to its fundamental hostility. The end of the Indochina war removed the major policy issue on which the two nations had found themselves in agreement in the past.

Kissinger believed that it was idle to speculate about the relative importance of traditional nationalism and communist ideology in the Sino-Soviet constellation. The crucial point to be made was that both forces were destabilizing elements in the picture.

On the question of traditional nationalism, Kissinger emphasized that China considered Russia to be the last Western state that still occupied, without consent, territories that China regarded as her own. The fact that Russia showed little if any inclination to accede to these irredentist claims continued to maintain tension at a high level.

As for sharing a common ideology, Kissinger believed that communism had long since ceased to be a unifying factor. On the contrary, the strident claims made by each leadership in aspiring to the role of exclusive torchbearer of Marxism-Leninism widened the gulf even further. It was unlikely, in Kissinger's view, that these powerful forces making for tension and discord were easily reversible.

Kissinger believed that both China and the Soviet Union had a fairly accurate perception of each other's military power. It was for this reason that a major war between them was certainly not inevitable, or even very likely. The Chinese were aware that they were no match for the vastly superior Soviet military apparatus, and the Soviets seemed to have learned sufficiently from history, including recent American history, the possible calamitous consequences of a major land war in Asia.

Kissinger had predicted the most likely pattern of future Sino-Soviet relations to be a kind of cold war. He did not believe that the succession to Mao in China or to Brezhnev in the Soviet Union was likely to affect this pattern in any fundamental way. The subjective impact of new leadership personalities might, of course, result in temporary rapprochment, but it was most unlikely, in Kissinger's opinion, that any single individual could decisively reverse a long-established negative historical encounter, only briefly interrupted for a decade by the perception of a common enemy.

Hence, while rapprochement with the United States was likely to come under periodic attack in China, Kissinger was confident that the long-run trend was for the continuation of such a policy. This trend was the result of objective changes in the global power constellation. America's withdrawal from Vietnam, the Soviet presence on the Chinese border, and the American decision to balance its relations with China and the Soviet Union but to remain equidistant from them both, were primarily responsible for this great turning. Yet it was also true that both China and America had been fortunate to have as leaders men of the caliber of Henry Kissinger and Chou En-lai, both equipped with realistic perceptions of themselves and of each other, a rare knowledge of history, and an even rarer gift for empathy. This personal dimension had no doubt accelerated the movement away from fantasy and fiction toward rapprochement and reality. Kissinger and Chou En-lai had recognized the objective conditions necessary for a turn-for-the-better in the relations between China and America. They had seized the crucial moment at one of history's great junctions and helped to make it happen. By this recognition and determined action, Chou En-lai and Kissinger made their claim to historic statesmanship.

THE KISSINGER LEGACY

A great deal has been written about Henry Kissinger's personal diplomacy. His insistence on conducting important negotiations personally and his habit of establishing close relationships with adversary leaders are well-known characteristics of his statecraft. His low opinion of the bureaucracy has also been widely commented upon. This penchant for the solo performance has been variously attributed to Kissinger's "enormous ego," his "obsessive secrecy," or to his "elemental need for power and glory." [4]

There is another interpretation. In order for Kissinger to succeed in his most historic diplomatic initiatives, he *had* to establish personal dominance over the bureaucracy. To establish such control moreover, he had to act decisively, often secretly, and, at times, alone.

Kissinger had never had much patience with bureaucracy. When a professor at Harvard, he had reserved his most acid comments for university administrators. His tolerance for bureaucracy in government was not much greater. After having studied the American "foreign policy-making apparatus," he had come to the conclusion that it was a kind of feudal network of competing agencies and interests, in which there was a "powerful tendency to think that a compromise among administrative proposals [was] the same thing as a policy." The bureaucratic model for making a decision, in Kissinger's opinion was a policy proposal with three choices: the present policy bracketed by two absurd alternatives.

Kissinger had been a consultant to both the Kennedy and Johnson administrations. While he never said so publicly, he had been deeply disappointed. So much had been promised, so much less had been attempted, and, in his judgment, so little had been done. He had had the opportunity to observe government decision making from a fairly close perspective. What impressed him most was that the foreign policy bureaucracy had a way of smothering initiative by advocating a path of least resistance. The lawyers, businessmen, and former academics who ran the hierarchy generally seemed to place a premium on safety and acceptance rather than on creativity and vision. The result was that any innovative statesmanship tended to expire in the feudal fiefs of the bureaucracy or come to grief on the rocks of organizational inertia.

There was ample basis for Kissinger's impatience. SALT might have been initiated at the Glassboro summit in 1967, between Lyndon Johnson and the Soviet leaders, but there had been no decisive leadership. Nor had there been a clear-cut stand on the possible limitation of strategic arms. Instead, there were endless arguments among the Joint Chiefs of Staff, the Pentagon, the State Department, and academic experts in the field of arms con-

---

[4] George W. Ball, op. cit., *passim*.

trol. Similarly, the Arab-Israeli war of 1967 had presented opportunities for American diplomacy and mediation, but there had
been no one with a plan, let alone the courage to place himself
between competing claims. Instead, there emerged from the bowels
of the bureaucracy countless position papers by learned academic
experts. There was no agreement on an overall strategy for mediation in the Middle East, only an almost fatalistic sense of hope-
lessness and drift.

This was the reason why Kissinger decided, immediately after
January 20, 1969, to establish personal control over the bureaucracy. Those whom he could not dominate, he would manipulate.
And those whom he could not manipulate, he would try to bypass.
He embarked on this course of action as a result of a rational
decision. He simply feared that *unless* he dominated, bypassed, or
manipulated, nothing would get done. He, too, would ultimately
be submerged in a long twilight struggle of modern feudal baronies.
This he was simply not prepared to accept.

In his position as assistant for national security affairs, Kissinger came to dominate the bureaucracy as no other figure before
him had done, and as no other is likely to do for a very long time
to come. He promptly established his control through the establishment of a few small committees, each of which he personally
chaired. There were a number of interdepartmental groups: a review group, a verification panel for SALT, a Vietnam special
studies group, the Washington Special Actions Group for Crisis
Control, and the Forty Committee, which dealt with covert intelligence operations.

It was out of these committees that Kissinger forged the
great initiatives that have assured his place in history: SALT I
in 1969, the opening to China after his secret trip to Peking in
1971, and the diplomatic mediation in the Middle East after the
October war in 1973. It is true, of course, that some of the more
dubious decisions also had their genesis in this small elitist
structure, particularly in the Forty Committee. The "destabiliza-
tion" of the Allende government in Chile in 1971, alleged payments to Italian neo-Fascists in 1972, and the denouement in Indochina are some of the more disturbing examples. Only history
can provide the necessary distance for a balanced assessment of
these various initiatives. But what can already be asserted with a
fair amount of certainty is that Kissinger was right in his as-

sumption that, in order to put into effect a coherent global policy, he would have to concentrate as much power in his hands as possible.

Kissinger's pursuit of power had a very clear-cut purpose. During two decades of reflection he had evolved a theory of global order that, in his judgment, would bring the world a few steps closer to stability and peace. Nothing was more important to him in 1969 than the chance to test that theory. He believed with the most absolute conviction that he was the one best qualified. On one occasion, in 1968, when Nelson Rockefeller's speech writers had made some changes in a Kissinger position paper, the author exclaimed furiously: "If Rockefeller buys a Picasso, he doesn't hire four housepainters to improve on it." In Kissinger's own view, this was not an arrogant statement. It was merely the reflection of an enormous, though quite genuine, intellectual self-confidence. He believed, quite matter of factly, that he was the Picasso of modern American foreign policy.

The drawing up of any balance sheet on the centerpiece of Kissinger's foreign policy—détente with the Soviet Union—must remain a highly personal business on which thoughtful people may have widely differing opinions. Any such analysis must enter in the realm of competing values, since in creating that centerpiece, choices had to be made and a price had to be paid. Hence, it is only fair that, as we enter this discussion, the author should reveal the basis of his judgment and share his values and prejudices with the reader.

It seems that Henry Kissinger was right when he declared that the overriding reason for détente with Russia was the avoidance of a nuclear catastrophe. It also appears that if such a world cataclysm has become less likely, this is in no small measure to be credited to Kissinger. This is not to deny that the American relationship with Russia leaves a great deal to be desired. But there is no question that the danger of nuclear war has substantially receded. It no longer intrudes into our daily lives the way it did when Kissinger was a professor. Mothers then worried about radioactive waste and strontium-90 in their children's milk and John F. Kennedy almost went to nuclear war with Khrushchev over missiles in Cuba. Today, we argue with the Soviet Union about strategic arms control, trade, and human rights, but we no longer live in daily terror of a nuclear exchange. The fearful scenarios that were conjured up in Herman Kahn's *Thinking About the Unthinkable* today read almost like horrible anachronisms. In addition to the elements of luck and timing, it was also Kissinger's design and courage that made détente possible at all.

Clearly, the price that Kissinger has paid on behalf of the United States has been enormous. But, to be fair, we must ask ourselves whether the alternatives would have yielded better results. In strategic arms control, Kissinger's accusers have blamed him for his acceptance in SALT I of Soviet superiority in missile numbers. They have also been suspicious of his lack of interest in alleged evidence that the Soviet Union had violated the spirit and perhaps even the letter of SALT I. Critics have also taken umbrage at his reported willingness—during the SALT II negotiations—to exclude the Soviet Backfire bomber from an overall ceiling while including the American cruise missile.

But the critics, in my judgment, have never given a convincing answer to Kissinger's own questions: "What in God's name," he asked in 1974, "is strategic superiority? What is the significance of it, politically, militarily, operationally, at these levels of numbers? What do you do with it?" Kissinger simply did not believe that a marginal "overkill" capacity on either side could be translated into a meaningful strategic or political advantage. It does not appear that there is conclusive evidence that such a translation can in fact be made.

The great paradox of Kissinger's conception of détente is in his relative tolerance vis-à-vis the Soviet Union, still the fountainhead of communism, and his combativeness toward local Communist movements in peripheral areas. How can Kissinger proclaim détente with the Soviet Union, the supporter of Communist causes everywhere, and yet fight communism to the death in Indochina, warn Western European heads of state against coalition governments with Communists, and demand action against the Communists in Angola?

The key to this riddle is to be found in Kissinger's primary commitment to stability. In the central relationship between the superpowers, there can be no decisive change in the power balance, short of nuclear war. The balance could be changed dramatically, however, if a minor nation shifted its allegiance from one side to the other and thus added appreciably to the strength of one of the two main contenders. The direct jockeying for mutual advantage between Russia and the United States was not likely to affect the global balance. But Communist advances elsewhere could, at least cumulatively, affect the balance of power in the world: hence, Kissinger's concern with stemming Communist advances in peripheral areas.

This logic, however, runs into serious difficulties. It may stand up in an area such as Angola where thousands of Cuban troops were imported to do battle for the Communist cause. In such a case, there was at least good circumstantial evidence for direct Soviet-sponsored intervention. But there was little, if any, evidence that the Soviet Union was very active in helping the Communists in Portugal, Italy, France, or Chile. The growth of the Italian Communist movement in Italy under Enrico Berlinguer might be attributable more to that Italian's "historic compromise" with democratic socialism than to subversion by the Soviet Union. Yet, Kissinger accused the Portuguese foreign minister of being a "Kerensky," quarantined Portugal from NATO, had secret payments made to a neo-Facist Italian general, and helped in the overthrow of the Allende government in Chile. In such cases, a good argument can be made that, by his indiscriminate opposition to all local forms of communism, Kissinger might force breakaway groups back into Moscow's arms and thus bring about the very developments he was so eager to prevent.

On a deeper level, Hans Morgenthau has made the most telling criticism:

> Since the causes and effects of instability persist, a policy committed to stability and identifying instability with communism is compelled by the logic of its interpretation of reality to suppress in the name of anticommunism all manifestations of popular discontent and stifle the aspirations for reform. Thus, in an essentially unstable world, tyranny becomes the last resort of a policy committed to stability as its ultimate standard.[5]

This is how, in Morgenthau's opinion, Kissinger, despite his extraordinary brilliance, often failed. He tended to place his great gifts at the service of lost causes, and thus, in the name of preserving stability and order, aligned the United States on the wrong side of the great historic issues.

[5] Hans J. Morgenthau, "The Kissinger Legacy," *Encounter*, November 1974, p. 57.

Morgenthau may be a little harsh in such a judgment. What if the Italian Communists recounced their "historic compromise," made common cause with Moscow, and other European countries followed suit? The result could well be a catastrophe for the United States. Morgenthau, as critic, does not have to make that awesome choice. But can a statesman dare to take such risks at a moment when he must base his decisions on conjecture rather than on facts? Here the scholar, it appears, owes the statesman a measure of empathy and tolerance.

There may be a psychological interpretation of Kissinger's paradoxical approach to communism. It may be found in his profound suspicion of the revolutionary as the greatest threat to a stable world order. In theory, it made little difference to him whether a revolutionary was "red" or "white." But in practice, he always feared the "red" revolutionary infinitely more. It is not that he approved of a Greek or Chilean junta, but he simply did not believe that it posed the kind of threat to international stability as that presented by an Allende, a Castro, or a Ho Chi Minh. These were the types of leaders, rather than a Brezhnev or a Mao Tse-tung, who were most likely to upset the global balance. They still retained that messianic revolutionary quality that had a vast potential for dislocation and contagion. In relation to the Soviet Union and China, one could afford to take some chances without risk to equilibrium. But when it came to the smaller revolutionaries, Kissinger believed that the warmaker still made the most effective peacemaker.

The opening of China was probably Kissinger's most uncontaminated triumph in his tenure as a statesman. It was also his greatest diplomatic adventure. Once he perceived the depth of the rift between China and the Soviet Union, he became convinced that rapprochement with China might make the Soviet Union more receptive to a genuine détente. In short, China, in his view, had become the key to Russia. In addition to establishing this triangular linkage, Kissinger's secret trip to Peking in 1971 had made him the first messenger of reconciliation. Furthermore to discover that beyond the Himalayas, there were men who elicited his admiration and respect only added to his elation. One of the few times that Kissinger happily admitted that he had been wrong was an occasion when he discussed his change of heart about Mao Tse-tung and Chou En-lai. In 1966, during the Cultural Revolution, he had perceived the Chinese leaders as the two most dangerous men on earth. Five years later, he had come to regard them as rational statesmen who pursued China's national interest in a manner not altogether inconsistent with the rules of international stability. But then it was Henry Kissinger who had once said about himself that while he had a first-rate mind, he had third-rate intuition about people. In the case of China, fortunately, the reality turned out to be more pleasant than the fantasy.

 .   Perhaps the most haunting questions about Kissinger's foreign policy are of a philosophical nature. What is the role of ethics in Kissinger's world of stability and power? What is the relationship between personal and political morality? What room does Kissinger's pursuit of a stable world order leave for justice? What should be our criterion for judging his success—his intentions or the consequences of his actions? In short, what must concern us is the problem of statesmanship and moral choice.

As the German philosopher Immanuel Kant might have put it, Kissinger made the pursuit of a stable world order the categorical imperative of his foreign policy. If, in the process, the human element had to be sacrificed at times on the altar of stability or of a larger strategic vision, so be it, since without stability, peace could not be born at all and justice, too, would be extinguished. He felt that in a tragic world, a stateman was not able to choose between good and evil, but only among different forms of evil. Indeed, whatever decision he made, *some* evil consequences were bound to flow from it. All that a realistic statesman could do in such a world was to choose the lesser evil.[6]

Was Kissinger's conceptual approach to foreign policy closer to the crusading or the pragmatic mode? It appears that Kissinger was a pragmatist who explosed possibilities, but *only* those that fitted into his conceptual design. Thus, the initiative to open China and the pursuit of détente with the Soviet Union stemmed from Kissinger's personal conviction that his design for a stable global order was the best hope for world peace. The key to this design was balance. Whenever the conditions for balance *objectively* existed, as in the relations between Russia and America,

---

[6] For a more detailed discussion of these dilemmas, see the author's *Henry Kissinger: The Anguish of Power* (New York: Norton, 1976), *passim.*

China and America, and the Arab states and Israel, Kissinger pushed his opportunities with remarkable success. But he would also try to squeeze the facts into his conceptual design even when they did not fit. At such times, he came close to being a crusader. Thus, he believed that a fifty-fifty compromise between North and South Vietnam would achieve a balance that would be acceptable to all when, in fact, the North Vietnamese were determined to throw out *all* Americans. A mind more open to the unique historical experience of the Indochinese people might not have superimposed a nineteenth-century intellectual design on a twentieth-century Asian reality. Thus, when doctrine coincided with reality, Kissinger was successful. But when, as in Vietnam, the reality principle was abandoned, failure was the consequence.

Finally, there does remain the question: What was Nixon's share and what was Kissinger's between 1969 and August 1974? There is little doubt that, until Nixon became mired down in Watergate in 1973, he took a leading role in foreign policy. He and Kissinger reached similar conclusions on fundamentals, such as the openings to Russia and China, though for somewhat different reasons. Kissinger thought primarily in terms of global strategy while Nixon was more concerned with political support at home. For example, both men agreed that a rapprochement with China was overdue, but Kissinger saw the move primarily as leverage over the Soviet Union while Nixon already had an eye on the 1972 election. Watergate, of course, had a decisive impact on Kissinger's career. During the early years, Kissinger's relationship with Nixon had resembled that of Acheson to Truman. At the end, however, the secretary of state had completely eclipsed the president. *During the last year of Richard Nixon's presidency and the two years of Gerald Ford's, Henry Kissinger became virtually the sole architect of American foreign policy.*

Timing thus plays a crucial role in an individual's power over policy. Henry Kissinger, with all his brilliance, could not have opened China in 1950 or 1960; the country simply was not ready yet for reconciliation with the United States. In 1970, it *was* ready, and Kissinger grasped the opportunity. A crusading moralist, such as John Foster Dulles, might have let the moment pass. It took the right man at the right time to seize the day and change direction. Luck, too, may be crucial. Without Watergate, would Kissinger have enjoyed such a free hand? Would he have been allowed to bypass the bureaucracy so completely if Nixon had survived as president? Would he have become a solo performer on the stage of history? These, of course, are unanswerable questions. But they point up the difficulty, perhaps the impossibility, of any "scientific" analysis of foreign policy. Thucydides, the great historian of ancient Athens, had realized this long ago when he had elevated fortune to the rank of goddess.

THE POSTIMPERIAL PRESIDENCY

The "imperial" presidencies of Lyndon Johnson and Richard Nixon had taken a terrible toll on the American people. Vietnam was the longest American war and Watergate the gravest internal upheaval since the Civil War. During the time of Gerald Ford's "accidental" presidency, Congress awoke from its long torpor. During 1975 and 1976, it placed severe restrictions on Henry Kissinger's freedom to maneuver in virtually every single area of foreign policy, from Turkey to Angola. His autocratic temperament, highly personal style, and persistent secrecy made him a natural target. He now had to pay the price exacted by a resurgent Congress in the postimperial presidency.

The former governor of Georgia, who was elected president of the United States in November 1976, sensed and articulated this new mood. He had referred to Henry Kissinger as the "Lone Ranger" and, in an interview with *Playboy* magazine, declared that both Lyndon Johnson and Richard Nixon had lied to the American people. He, on the other hand, had promised in hundreds of campaign speeches a "government as good and as honest and as decent and as competent and as compassionate and as filled with love as the American people." [1] "Trust me, I will never lie to you," Jimmy Carter had said over and over again to the American electorate. And the people trusted the outsider from the South and elected him over Gerald Ford by a narrow margin.

[1] James Wooten, *Dasher* (New York: Summit Books, 1978), p. 355.

Who was this man who, two short years before he became president, had been so obscure that reporters had sarcastically referred to him as "Jimmy who?"

Jimmy Carter grew up in a family of "characters" in the small town of Plains in Georgia. His father Earl was a successful business-man who made his son work hard at a very early age. Young Jimmy had to get up with the rest of the workers at 4 A.M. and do his share in field plowing, cotton mopping, peanut stacking, and chicken tending. He had to call his father "sir" and the older man was not above using a peach switch over his son's bottom to enforce discipline or express displeasure. Yet, after the whipping was over, Earl took back his son, fully and freely. He was no Reverend Wilson, tormenting young "Tommy" into near-retarda-tion. Love was unconditional.

Jimmy's mother, "Miss Lillian," was a nurturing presence. A craggy-faced, warm, no-nonsense farm woman, she had lived essentially for other people's needs. Yet, she had a fierce streak of independence, a passion for decency and justice and a highly developed sense of humor. When pressed in 1976 for childhood anecdotes about her son, she declared that Jimmy had "the dumb-est boyhood of anybody I've ever seen." [2] When Jimmy first told his mother that he was going to run for president, her question was "president of what?" Lillian Carter hated racism. Where did Jimmy's liberalism on race come from? "Yes, he got that from me," his mother said, "I've always been like that. My father was never a racist, and I grew up trying to be compassionate and kind to everyone . . . I've stood alone in Plains; Jimmy and I have stood alone." [3] "I am much more like my mother than my father," Jimmy Carter said in 1976.[4] There were three younger children: Billy, who developed into a joke-loving, beer-drinking owner of a gas station; Gloria, who liked fast motorcycles; and Ruth who played an important part in Jimmy's later decision to be "born again." In 1946, at the age of twenty-two, Jimmy married the "girl next door." The union with Rosalynn became not only a close-knit marriage but a formidable team in the political campaigns to come.

[2] Martin Schram, *Running for President: A Journal of the Carter Campaign* (New York: Pocket Books, 1976), p. 47.

[3] Barber, op. cit., p. 515.

[4] Schram, op. cit., p. 51.

All the members of the Carter family, despite their individuality, loved Jimmy. And they *were* individuals. As brother Billy, the family's *enfant terrible,* put it:

> I got a mamma who joined the Peace Corps and went to India when she was sixty-eight. I got one sister who's a holy roller preacher. I got another sister who wears a helmet and rides a motorcycle. And I got a brother who thinks he's going to be President. So that makes me the only sane person in the family.[5]

But they were all there for Jimmy when he needed them. He received encouragement and love from all and early developed a strong sense of self-esteem. Life for Jimmy Carter, unlike for Woodrow Wilson, became an adventure, not a dismal duty based on guilt.

The major key to Jimmy Carter's political personality, however, is his religion. His father had taken him to church on Sundays and his mother, too, attended services regularly in a little Baptist church in Plains. Jimmy taught Sunday school at eighteen and when he got homesick as a freshman at Annapolis, he went to chapel and prayed. Back in Plains, he taught Sunday school again and spoke in neighboring communities on "Christian witnessing." His favorite theologian was Reinhold Niebuhr. It was not until 1966, however, the year he ran for governor of Georgia and lost to Lester Maddox, that Jimmy Carter made evangelical Christianity the central tenet of his life.

Sitting in the Plains Baptist Church, he heard the preacher demand to know, "If you were arrested for being a Christian, would there be enough evidence to convict you?" The thought occurred to Carter that he had made only 140 "visits for God" but 300,000 "visits for himself" in his political campaigns. He was a "pharisee," not a committed Christian. After talking to his sister Ruth, he expanded his personal service to the church and engaged in missionary life. Yet, he did not give up politics. Quite the contrary. In 1970, he became governor of Georgia after an intensive campaign. In the middle of the campaign, however, he excused himself for a week to work at a mission in an Atlanta slum. Jimmy Carter now served *both* Christ and his political ambition. He never saw an inconsistency between his two callings. His aspiration was to be God's man in a secular world.

5 Ibid., p. 135.

Jimmy Carter's most important secular mentor was Admiral Hyman Rickover. When the admiral had asked young Carter about his class standing at Annapolis, Jimmy had answered: "Fifty-ninth in a class of 820. "Did you do your best?" Rickover asked. "No, sir. I didn't always do my best," Carter responded. "Why not?" Rickover wanted to know. Carter had no answer.

"Rickover," Jimmy Carter said later "demanded from me a standard of performance and a depth of commitment that I had never realized before that I could achieve. And I think second to my own father, Admiral Rickover had more effect on my life than any other man." Jimmy Carter's autobiography was entitled *Why Not the Best?* And as candidate for president in 1976, he declared, "I want to be tested in the most severe way." [6]

Thus, Carter's political personality was marked, first of all, by self-esteem, provided by a nurturing and loving home. His religion was evangelical, but not rigid like Wilson's. More like Niebuhr, he saw a new world dawning through a transforming Presence but held back by an old one still in darkness, with justice yet to be established. Racism had no place in such a better world. He voted against segregation in his Baptist church in Plains and hung a portrait of Dr. Martin Luther King in the state capitol in Atlanta, Georgia. His religion was at the center of his life. It was a deeply personal commitment. But unlike that of Woodrow Wilson, it was never a fixed and immutable conclusion. It always remained a search, perhaps at times naïve, but always authentic and sincere. And his conviction that he was God's soldier lent his campaign a particular intensity. He was inspired by his ideal, Jesus Christ, yet conscious of Reinhold Niebuhr's warning that "the sad duty of politics [was] to establish justice in a sinful world." This became the genesis of Carter's concern for human rights in foreign policy. At worst, this world view resembled that of Don Quixote flailing his sword at windmills; but, at best, it energized a faith that held that nothing was impossible.

Needless to say, Carter's personality was totally different from that of Henry Kissinger. Obviously, given these differences, the former secretary's virtuoso diplomatic style was not the only thing that irritated the new president. There were more funda-

[6] Transcript of Bill Moyers interview with Jimmy Carter, 6 May 1976, on *USA: People and Politics*, produced for PBS by Wallace Westfeldt, p. 6.

mental substantive objections. In Carter's view, Kissinger had spent far too much time and energy on the adversary relationships of the United States, specifically those with the Soviet Union and China. Détente with the two leading communist powers had been the centerpiece of Kissinger's foreign policy. But, in the meantime, the old and trusted allies of the United States, the NATO countries and Japan, had been left to languish. Kissinger had haggled with Communist dictators while the world's democracies were becoming an endangered species. During Kissinger's tenure in office, communism had made headway in Western Europe. One out of every three Italians and one out of every four Frenchmen voted Communist in the mid-1970s. While these "Eurocommunists" had broken with the Soviet Union and were pursuing their "own roads to socialism," they were not particularly friendly to the United States. Greece and Turkey were still feuding over Cyprus. And even though Britain had joined the Common Market in 1973, together with Ireland and Denmark, and the Europe of the Six had become the Europe of the Nine, Western Europe was still in danger. The Proclamation of "The Year of Europe" had yielded few tangible results. Latin America and Japan had been virtually ignored. And the Third World touched only the suburbs of Henry Kissinger's consciousness. The author of *The Troubled Partnership* had not heeded his own warnings. Instead, he had simply taken his friends for granted.

These criticisms of Kissinger, were, of course, not unique to Jimmy Carter. They were widely shared throughout the Western world. In 1973, David Rockefeller, the chairman of the Chase Manhattan Bank, had organized the Trilateral Commission, a gathering of citizens of prominence and stature from Japan, North America, and Western Europe. Its specific purpose was to coordinate the foreign policies of these Western countries and to prevent a further deterioration in their relationships with the United States. In a time when democracy was on the defensive in the world—there were no more than about two dozen working democracies left—the West would have to rally. In short, the United States should be concerned a little less with its adversaries and a great deal more with its traditional friends.

Jimmy Carter had been deeply impressed with some of the people he had met in the Trilateral Commission. Zbigniew Brzezinski, its executive director, a Soviet expert and a professor at

Columbia University, briefed Carter on the major issues of foreign policy. The president later appointed him as his adviser on national security affairs. Carter also met Cyrus Vance in the commission, and later made him his secretary of state. Vance was a lawyer by profession and had participated in the Vietnam peace negotiations. His style was low-key, methodical, and unemotional, the very opposite of the flamboyant Kissinger. The commission's membership was an impressive list of leading lights on both sides of the Atlantic and Pacific. It was a "splendid learning opportunity" for a governor from Georgia with little experience in world politics.

Following up on his intention to pay more attention to allies, Carter later proposed the "rationalization" of NATO. In 1978, the members of the alliance were prodded toward closer cooperation, and a more sensitive American leadership was promised them. A new NATO logistics command was created, a great deal of modern American equipment was stocked on the European continent, and an integrated air-defense system was set up. Anti-tank weapons were doubled, electronic warfare countermeasures were instituted, and improvements were made in reserve forces and mobilization systems. A decision on the production and deployment of the neutron bomb, however—an effective nuclear device against Soviet tanks—was deferred by the president.

There was yet another even stronger, objection Carter had to Kissinger than indifference to allies. The former secretary of state had been too indifferent to human rights. He had not been sufficiently concerned with the internal indecencies of governments *unless* these indecencies destabilized the Soviet-American balance. So long as a nation did not export its unattractive features and thereby tilt the balance in favor of the Soviet Union, Kissinger did not seem overly perturbed. He did not back black majority rule in Africa because it was ethically right and just; he finally backed it very late and then only for strategic reasons, after Angola had gone Communist. He did not criticize Franco's Spain or Salazar's Portugal. After all, these two right-wing dictators did not export their ideologies. But he was very much concerned about Castro, as well as Ho Chi Minh and intervened in Chile against Allende because he believed that left-wing leaders were prone to export revolution and thus become potential destabilizers of the global balance.

Carter found Kissinger's approach somewhat foreign to the

American tradition. Americans, he believed, needed a measure of idealism in their foreign policy. The United States was different from other countries. It had once been a moral beacon light to others. It should be so again, despite Vietnam and despite Watergate. Kissinger had "Europeanized" American foreign policy and made it almost indistinguishable from the chessboard politics of power. What was needed now was an infusion of morality and ethics. In his debates with Gerald Ford, Carter emphasized that the Soviet Union, by signing the Helsinki Accords of 1975, had promised to observe the human rights of its citizens. A new concern with human rights throughout the world would become the centerpiece of Carter's foreign policy. America would once again be "a city on a hill." Like its president, the nation's foreign policy, too, would have to be cleansed and born again.

In March 1977, Carter sent Cyrus Vance to Moscow with new proposals for a strategic arms limitation treaty. The missile numbers agreed upon at Vladivostok in 1974 were too high, in his opinion. There should be real cutbacks in Soviet and American ICBMs and MIRVs. Genuine disarmament should supersede mere arms control. At the same time he made these proposals, however, Carter sent an open letter to a Nobel Prize-winning Soviet dissident, nuclear physicist, Andrei D. Sakharov, in which he declared himself to be in full sympathy with Sakharov's objectives. Not surprisingly, the Soviet leadership replied to Carter's new SALT II proposals with an extremely curt *nyet* and sent Vance home empty-handed. Jimmy Carter had collided with reality. His policy of human rights seemed to be in direct conflict with détente. Almost immediately, he reversed himself, observed a tactful silence on the dissidents, and continued to pursue SALT II. Vance was also sent to China, but Carter at no point criticized Mao Tse-tung's successors for their shortcomings in observing the human rights of their one billion citizens. Instead, in late 1978, to the intense displeasure of the Soviet leadership, Carter formally recognized the People's Republic of China and "derecognized" the Chinese regime on Taiwan. "Playing the China card" might make the Russians more tractable on SALT II, was the president's opinion. Besides, American businessmen were clamoring to sell their products to "one billion customers." On the Chinese side, Teng Hsiao-ping, the new Chinese strong man, had abandoned Mao Tse-tung's revolutionary ideology and set China on a course of industrialization and modernization. America, the former enemy, had suddenly become the model. In his visit to the United States in early 1979, Teng emphasized the need for China and America to stand together against the threat of "Soviet hegemony." And shortly afterward, China invaded pro-Soviet Vietnam in order to administer a bloody nose to the nation that had tried to dismember China's protégé, Cambodia. China and the Soviet Union thus waged a limited war by proxy while the United States observed a scrupulous neutrality. Clearly, Kissinger's triangular policy was still very much in fashion. The new Sino-American friendship was made in Moscow as much as Soviet-American détente had been made in Peking a decade earlier. And the United States was still the "lady in the triangle." In June 1979, in Vienna, Carter and Brezhnev finally signed SALT II. In its final form, the treaty did not differ very much from the earlier draft conceived in Vladivostok in 1974. It underlined the fundamental continuity between Kissinger and Carter in their approaches to America's main adversary.

In his Middle Eastern policy, Carter at first increased the tension between the United States and Israel. Kissinger had always been ambiguous on the crucial question of the return of the Arab territories. Carter was a great deal more precise: almost all of the territories that Israel had conquered in the war of 1967 would be negotiable. Kissinger had managed to duck the explosive issue of the Palestinians. Carter, on the other hand, made it central to a resolution of the conflict and spoke about Palestinian rights and interests. Kissinger had virtually frozen out the Soviet Union from the Middle East arena. Carter invited the Soviet Union to participate in a Geneva conference. In November 1977, Egyptian President Anwar Sadat, in a dramatic peace mission, visited Jerusalem. Thereafter, the "special relationship" between Israel and the United States suffered even greater strains. Carter believed that Israel's Prime Minister Menachem Begin's response to the Sadat peace initiative was not sufficiently generous. After all, the Egyptian president had offered to recognize the Jewish state in exchange for the return of Arab territories. Begin, however, while offering to return Sinai to Egypt, seemed totally unwilling to give up Israeli sovereignty over the occupied West Bank of the Jordan River. All he was willing to grant was "home rule" to the population of the West Bank. Basing his claims on the Old Testament, Begin declared that Israel had not occupied any lands, but had merely "liberated" the ancient Jewish territories of Sumeria and Judea. Carter, on the other hand, insisted that the new Jewish settlements on the West Bank were illegal and an obstacle to peace. In May 1978, the American president announced the sale of jet aircraft to Israel, Egypt, and Saudi Arabia. The Senate, after an intense and often acrimonious debate, approved the controversial sale by a vote of fifty-four to forty-four. The vote was a clear signal that the United States henceforth would help not only Israel, but also moderate Arab states in order to prevent incursions by the Soviet Union. The American people, it appeared, were still willing to support Israel but no longer Israel's military conquests. In Kissinger's time, Israel had been the "good guy" and Sadat had been the warmaker; now, it appeared, Sadat was the "good guy" and Begin was prepared to risk another war.

In September 1978, President Carter, in a desperate attempt to resuscitate the stalled peace talks between Begin and Sadat, invited the two leaders to a "summit" at Camp David. After two weeks of intense and secret deliberations, two important agreements were finally hammered out. First, Begin and Sadat agreed on a "Framework for Peace Between Egypt and Israel," which provided for the phased withdrawal of Israeli forces from Sinai and the signing of a full-fledged peace treaty. Second, the two leaders agreed on a broader "Framework for Peace in the Middle East," which was designed to permit the progressive resolution of the Palestinian issue and of the West Bank problem over a five-year period. At that very moment, however, the shah of Iran was driven into exile by the fundamentalist Islamic forces of the Ayatollah Khomeini. As Iranian oil exports dried up, the United States became increasingly dependent on Saudi Arabia. The Saudis, realizing their advantage, insisted on a linkage between the separate Egyptian-Israeli peace treaty and progress toward the far more difficult issues of the West Bank, the Palestinians, and the status of Jerusalem. Carter, under the pressure of American energy needs, in turn exerted greater pressure on Israel to be more flexible. For several months, the talks were stalled. Then, at last, in March 1979, Begin and Sadat, after yet another Carter visit to the Middle East, signed a separate peace treaty. All three leaders staked their political futures on a successful outcome. Moreover, the United States had underwritten the agreement with a five billion dollar pledge to the two countries. There is little doubt that the American mediation was absolutely crucial. The president's tenacity and faith had finally borne fruit. After thirty years of war, the Middle East had moved a large step closer toward peace.

Many vexing issues remained unresolved, of course. The Israelis remained in agony over the fate of Jewish settlements in the Sinai and the West Bank. They also worried about the very real possibility of the ultimate creation of a Palestinian state, which they regarded as a dagger pointed at the heart of Israel. On the Arab side, Jordan and Saudi Arabia were dubious about the treaty; Syria and the PLO were bitterly opposed and looked at Sadat as a traitor. Nonetheless, the treaty was a triumph for the president. Very much like Kissinger in 1975, the president had become the "honest broker" between Israel and Egypt. "Open covenants" had yielded to successful personal diplomacy.

In Africa, too, Carter inherited some of Kissinger's old problems. The Soviet Union, by employing Cuban proxy troops, had made considerable inroads into the Horn of Africa as well as in Rhodesia and Angola. Moreover, a pro-Soviet coup had toppled the government of Afghanistan. Carter faced the traditional American dilemma: intervention might lead to an African Vietnam, but doing nothing would give the Soviet Union a blank check. The problem of linkage also reappeared. Should the SALT II negotiations be made contingent upon Soviet behavior in Africa or should they be conducted strictly on their merits? Carter decided to adopt a middle course. He agreed to give material support including cargo planes to antirebel forces in Zaire. He also warned the Soviet Union against the use of Cuban forces in other parts of Africa, but chose not to interrupt the SALT negotiations. Apparently, the two superpowers perceived détente somewhat differently. The Soviet leadership, seemed to believe that the "code of détente" included active competition in peripheral areas. Carter, while not precluding economic and other peaceful forms of competition, was not prepared to tolerate without objections the Soviet use of proxy troops, quite possibly because the United States had no "Cubans" of its own to send abroad.

In its relations with Latin America, the Carter administration won the Senate's approval, in 1978, of two new treaties governing the Panama Canal. Under the old Hay-Bunau-Varilla Treaty of 1903, the United States had the right to exercise sovereign rights "in perpetuity" over the Canal Zone. The new treaties—scrutinized by the Senate word for word and finally approved in both cases by a single vote—arranged for the transfer of the Canal to Panama by the year 2000 and for the waterway's permanent neutrality. The treaties' progress through the Senate was arduous and slow and the outcome was in doubt until the final vote was cast. But in the last analysis, open diplomacy, after years of congressional passivity, proved workable again.

There were two further departures from the Kissinger era. In the first place, the struggles between rich and poor, black and white, producers and consumers, haves and have-nots, had to be addressed. Hence, a "North-South dialogue" was initiated between the industrialized nations and the Third World. And since most of the issues in the dialogue were economic in nature, Carter, unlike Kissinger, paid a great deal of attention to the economic implications of his foreign policy.

Finally, Jimmy Carter, an engineer by trade, had an overriding concern with the energy crisis facing the United States. Americans, he believed, stood at the edge of an awesome watershed: the coming energy transition. For decades, the United States had depended on cheap oil as its major energy resource. But the Arab oil embargo of 1973–74 and the subsequent fivefold increase in the price of oil had rudely reminded Americans of their dependency on imported oil. More fundamentally, it had focused attention on an even more disturbing prospect: a global energy crisis. A CIA report, released by the Carter White House in April 1977, predicted that "in the absence of greatly increased energy conservation, projected world demand for oil will approach productive capacity by 1985." [7] In short, the world would face serious oil shortages before the end of the century.

"Each new inventory of world oil reserves has been more disturbing than the last," President Carter declared in his address to the American people on April 18, 1977. A dramatic shift had occurred in the global supply-and-demand situation. While consumers were in control in the 1960s, the picture had changed in the 1970s, and according to most projections, would continue to change in the same direction during the 1980s. One oil-producing

[7] Central Intelligence Agency. *The International Energy Situation: Outlook to 1985*, April 1977, p. 1.

country after another had approached the limits of its productive capacity, while world consumption had steadily continued to rise. For the world to maintain its current rate of consumption and yet keep its reserves intact, we would have to discover another Kuwait or Iran roughly every three years, or another Texas or Alaska every six months.[8] Clearly, this seemed an unlikely prospect.

Let us look at the inventory a bit more closely. The United States produces approximately 10 percent of the world's known petroleum resources. Regrettably, America's oil is now almost certainly half gone. Most experts agree that the rate of extraction will decline sharply after 1985. The Middle East has roughly 40 percent of the world's oil, of which one-tenth has been used up. Africa has about 10 percent, most of which is still in the ground. Latin America, including Mexico, is believed to have 15 percent, of which one-fifth has been consumed, and Western Europe produces less than 5 percent. The remaining 20 percent is distributed throughout other parts of the world, including China and the Soviet Union. The trilateral nations—the United States, Western Europe, and Japan—face an immediate oil squeeze. Most other areas still have ample oil to meet their immediate requirements. But the oil-short nations encompass most of the world's industrial base and all import huge amounts of oil from the oil-rich regions. Even the Soviet Union is expected to become a net importer of oil by 1985. And China, whose petroleum resources are only one-tenth of those of the USSR, is even more vulnerable. Even if one assumes a relatively peaceful Middle East—a dubious assumption at best—the prospects are bleak. And the Iranian crisis of 1978–1979 showed just how dubious that assumption in fact was. Even though the CIA published a somewhat more optimistic report in 1978, it is still possible that the world will have reached the end of its oil supplies not long after the year 2000. What, then are America's alternatives as we enter the twilight of an era?

Coal has been the world's most plentiful fossil fuel and has been used for at least two thousand years. There is no shortage of coal, yet it is not likely that coal will ever replace petroleum. At best, it will be a transitional source of energy. A conversion to coal as a major energy resource would create formidable environmental problems. Specifically, it would release huge amounts of

[8] *The National Energy Plan*, White House Press Release, 29 April 1977, p. viii.

The Postimperial Presidency   259

carbon dioxide into the atmosphere, which might raise the earth's temperature to a dangerous level. Conversely, some scientists have warned that soot might blanket the Northern Hemisphere, shield the sun, and thus usher in a new ice age. Either way, the climatic consequences of a new coal era might prove catastrophic. Coal's future, therefore, is dubious at best.

The United States long nurtured the hope that nuclear power would reduce its dependence on oil and perhaps even replace it altogether. The dream of replacing oil with atomic energy seems to be fading fast, however. In the first place, nuclear power is not cheap. Research and development as well as capital construction costs are formidable. The hope for "electricity too cheap to meter" has proved to be unfounded. Second, the dangers of converting to a nuclear-powered world are legion. Problems of radiation, radioactive waste, and reactor safety loom large. A serious nuclear accident near Harrisburg, Pennsylvania, in 1979 demonstrated this. Even worse, it is very difficult to divorce the peaceful from the warlike atom. India's explosion of a "peaceful bomb" in 1974 was a compelling example of this danger. President Carter has been concerned about the dangers of nuclear proliferation. In a nuclear world, terrorists and criminals would have far more ready access to nuclear bombs, with potentially disastrous consequences for society. The only hope of "safe" nuclear power is the replacement of fission with fusion. But the commercial uses of the fusion process may still be a quarter century away.

More recently, President Carter, with the support of several leading experts, has turned to the sun for new hope. One scholar, for example, has maintained that, by the year 2000, the sun's inexhaustible energy could provide 40 percent of the global energy budget, by furnishing heat and electricity.[9] Wind and water could also be tapped more efficiently. Solar energy, this advocate declared, would be clean, cheap, safe, and self-sustaining.

While the prospect of a solar-powered world is seductively attractive, it is not likely to be attained in the near future. Perhaps an estimate of 20 rather than 40 percent by the year 2000 is more realistic. The sun, despite its enormous heat, is not very efficient as an energy provider. Solar power involves using a source that has a temperature of 600 degrees celsius to heat water to less

[9] Denis Hayes, *Rays of Hope* (New York: Norton, 1977), p. 155.

than 100 degrees. The almost boundless potential of the sun, while theoretically available to us, simply still eludes us in practical commercial terms on a worldwide basis. Even for our primitive ancestors, the sun was not enough. They invented fire. Solar energy is indeed a hope, but it is a rather distant hope.

It is very likely that the best hope of the United States to get through the transition period without major turbulence may lie in conservation. This is one of the major thrusts of President Carter's energy program. A barrel of oil saved may be as useful as a barrel produced—perhaps even better in some respects. Carter again stressed conservation in a major speech in July 1979 in which he promised to lead the nation more forcefully. It is true that half of the current energy budget is waste. For the next quarter of a century, the United States could meet all its new energy needs simply by improving the efficiency of existing uses. One must bear in mind here a crucial distinction between curtailment and conservation. Curtailment means a cold, dark house; conservation means a well-insulated house with an efficient heating system. Gas-guzzling cars will have to give way to less conspicuous, more energy-efficient modes. Small will truly have to become beautiful. A vigorous conservation program might see the world through the energy transition without becoming hooked on hazardous technologies or unreliable sources of supply.

The search for new sources of energy will be painful and competitive. The United States will have to struggle for its survival. But there is a strangely positive side to this as well. There is bound to be a great deal of international cooperation. The long-term demands for energy are so gigantic and the economic and political linkages among nations are so strong that, as a practical matter, competition may very well give way to cooperation in conservation, research, development, and discovery. The energy transition will not respect national boundaries or sovereignties. There may have to be created an international consortium on energy distribution and conservation. The implications of this challenge for American foreign policy will be enormous.

In broad perspective, therefore, the Carter foreign policy was a blend of old and new ideas. While the approaches to the Soviet Union and China closely resembled Kissinger's, Carter had to confront a generational change in the Soviet Union's leadership. The old men on the Politbureau would have to make room for younger blood. The policies toward the Middle East and Africa also did not depart too much from precedent. There were some major overhauls in the relations with traditional allies in Western Europe, Japan, and Latin America. A new dialogue between "North and South" was initiated. And there was a new and timely focus on the coming energy transition.

But the most distinctive Carter innovation in foreign policy doubtless was his emphasis on human rights. This initiative was Jimmy Carter's own idea and in a very real sense, represented his personal contribution to the American mainstream. It was deeply rooted in his religious conviction. Few doubted the new president's sincerity when he declared before the UN General Assembly that "no member of the United Nations [could] claim that mistreatment of its citizens [was] solely its own business." [10] But the road that leads from good intentions to results is strewn with booby traps and pitfalls. And Carter did not have a roadmap. He had to chart his course as he felt his way along. The results have already covered the entire spectrum, from dismal failures to tentative successes. An analysis of these initiatives will form the substance of our concluding case study.

[10] Speech before the UN General Assembly, 17 March 1977.

8

ETHICS IN A WORLD OF POWER

Jimmy Carter and the Global Human-Rights Campaign

JIMMY CARTER'S HUMAN-RIGHTS OBJECTIVES

"Because we are free," Jimmy Carter said in his 1977 Inaugural, "we can never be indifferent to the fate of freedom elsewhere." A "born-again" Baptist and deeply religious person, the new president had decided to make a concern for human rights the cornerstone of his foreign policy. Actually, such a concern had often characterized American diplomacy. The Declaration of Independence had invoked a universal appeal for "unalienable rights"; Woodrow Wilson had issued a call to make the world "safe for democracy"; and John F. Kennedy had pledged that the United States would "bear any burden, pay any price to assure the survival and the success of liberty." Jimmy Carter had not invented human rights, but he had correctly sensed a new national mood.

The disenchantment with Vietnam, the excesses of the "imperial" presidency, the revulsion with Watergate, the protest movements of the young, the civil-rights movements—all these had helped to set the stage for a new emphasis on international human rights. Carter's personal convictions thus blended most fortuitously with the emotional state of the nation. He sensed that the electorate, ready for reaffirmation in bicentennial rhetoric, would respond well to a foreign policy that would "make Americans feel proud again." The defeat in Vietnam, the disgrace of Watergate, could be erased. Americans would not really have to look inward and face themselves. Instead, they could bury the ghosts of their recent past by looking outward and becoming secular missionaries. Human rights would shape a new and better world. In a psychological sense, therefore, the president asked all Americans to be "born again."

It was not an accident that the president's leading appointees in the human-rights arena had been either activists in the civil-rights movement or opponents of the American involvement in the war in Indochina—or both. For example, the new United Nations ambassador, Andrew Young, had been deeply involved in civil rights but lacked experience in foreign affairs. Perceiving the world in that perspective, he was quick to attach the racism label to a number of foreign countries, including Britain and even Sweden. His outspokenness and lack of diplomatic tact embarrassed the administration but Carter gave his man at the UN a great deal of latitude. The representative to the U.N. Human Rights Commission, Allard Lowenstein, and the assistant secretary of state for human rights and humanitarian affairs, Patricia Derian, had been civil-rights activists as well. A presidential directive soon declared: "It shall be a major objective of U.S. foreign policy to promote human rights throughout the world." On April 30, 1977, Secretary of State Vance defined the scope of the new program in comprehensive and ambitious terms. It was to comprise:

> The right to be free from governmental violations of the integrity of the person. Such violations would include torture, cruel, inhuman or degrading treatment or punishment; and arbitrary arrest or imprisonment, as well as denial of fair public trial and invasion of the home. The right to the fulfillment of such vital needs as food, shelter, health care, and education. The right to enjoy civil and political liberties, such as freedom of thought, religion, assembly, speech and the press, as well as freedom of movement within and outside one's own country and freedom to take part in government.[1]

The policy, therefore, embraced *all* rights proclaimed in the United Nations Universal Declaration of Human Rights. This meant not only political and civil liberties, but economic and so-

---

[1] Quoted in Sandra Vogelgesang, "What Price Principle? U.S. Policy and Human Rights," *Foreign Affairs*, July 1978, p. 821.

cial rights as well. The president also proclaimed that the United States would ratify the Genocide Convention of 1948 and two UN covenants on human rights that had come into force in 1976.

The need certainly was great. Amnesty International, winner of the 1977 Nobel Peace Prize for its work on behalf of "prisoners of conscience" had warned that "serious violations of human rights continue[d] in 119 countries." These violations included torture, death squads, kidnapping, political imprisonment without recourse to legal defense, food, water, or health care, and even genocide.[2]

The basic problem with human rights was not lack of support for the idea. Most Americans applauded it. It was the gap between preaching and principle. Words can be cheap, but deeds are not. The perennial question that plagued any attempted marriage between morality and diplomacy came to the surface once again. What was the price of principle? What would happen to détente, for example, if the United States declared its support for Soviet dissidents? Would American trade interests be undermined if the United States invoked economic sanctions against South Africa? Would Americans pay higher taxes to pay for increased foreign aid so that poor foreigners might attain their economic and social rights? Most human rights initiatives thus had price tags attached to them. These would have to be considered in the light of competing strategic or economic interests. In some instances, the price might be considered much too high; in others it might be paid grudgingly, and with difficulty; and only in a few exceptional cases, the cost was small. Much of the time, moreover, choices tended to be unpleasant ones. If the United States was too selective about the countries it denounced, if for example, it singled out its foes and spared its friends, it risked becoming hypocritical. If it pursued the cause of human rights everywhere, equally, such a course was likely to end in an interventionist crusade. And if the policy was limited to verbal statements only, it might become a luxury cruise without a port of call. All this is not to say that the human-rights policy was totally impossible. But the challenges of calibration were real and often formidable ones. For the student of American foreign policy, the experiment was fascinating since it illuminated, with painful clarity, the pos-

2 Ibid., p. 822.

sibilities and limits of morality in a world of economic interest and power.

The evidence suggests that the human-rights campaign has been an almost total failure vis-à-vis totalitarian societies that insist on nonintervention in their domestic policies. President Carter's impact on the fate of dissidents in Russia, on human-rights abuses in China, and on the abatement of genocidal violence in Cambodia has been virtually nil. In the Soviet case, the human-rights offensive may even have had a retrograde effect. The question must be asked, therefore, whether public pronouncements, often stridently proclaimed, are more effective in securing human rights than quiet diplomacy, tactfully constructed. After all, in human rights, as in other policy pursuits, success is measured more by result than intent. In this respect, the contrast between Henry Kissinger and Jimmy Carter is instructive.

A comprehensive trade agreement which President Nixon had signed with the Soviet Union in October 1972, had ignited a debate in the United States on the entire issue of détente. In the first place, the Soviet grain purchases contributed to a dramatic rise in food prices in the United States, and angry American consumers were complaining bitterly about the "great Russian grain robbery." Second, and more important, the trade agreement of October 1972 had granted the Soviets most-favored nations status. This meant, in effect, the restoration of normal trade relations, which had been suspended at the height of the cold war in 1951.

The trade relations between the United States and the Soviet Union had made Kissinger's approach to détente a subject of intense domestic controversy. Détente was no longer discussed solely by strategists of power politics; it now affected the daily economic lives of millions of Americans. Farmers wanted greater exports to the Soviet Union, which would result in higher prices for their products; consumers hoped for lower food prices and criticized the Soviet grain purchases; and politicians suddenly had to become sensitized to these crosscurrents in American politics. In this debate, Senator Henry Jackson preferred to confront the Soviets bluntly with conditions: concessions on Jewish emigration in return for concessions on trade. Kissinger preferred to deal with the question of Jewish emigration through quiet diplomacy, sometimes on boar hunts with Party Chairman Brezhnev in the woods near the Soviet leader's *dacha*. He pointed out that thirty-five thousand Jews had left the Soviet Union for Israel in 1973, but that the rate of emigration had turned down sharply in 1974 and 1975 because the Soviet Union would not accept such humiliating conditions. In his judgment, it was a serious mistake to try to influence Soviet practice in domestic matters. He thought that it would be far better to try to induce changes in Soviet foreign policy. He did, in fact, attempt to use American grain sales in 1975 as a lever on Soviet foreign policy when he sought Soviet acquiescence to his diplomatic step-by-step initiatives in the Middle East. But he remained convinced that any attempt to change the domestic behavior of the Soviet Union would have a boomerang effect. Linkage, in short, was a concept that was meaningful only in international diplomacy. If misapplied to internal policies, it would set back, rather than advance, the process of détente.

Jimmy Carter's open letter to Soviet dissident leader Andrei Sakharov in 1977, on the other hand, infuriated the Soviet leadership and contributed to Brezhnev's peremptory rejection of the new American SALT II proposals. Almost worse, the president's subsequent reversal and silence on the subject of Soviet dissidents made him appear irresolute and weak. The dissidents' hopes had been raised by the encouraging words in Carter's letter, but when it came to deeds, the American president seemed impotent. It seemed like Dulles in Hungary all over again.

In July 1978, the Soviet leadership decided to teach Jimmy Carter a brutal lesson in *realpolitik*. It brought to trial two leading Jewish dissidents: Anatoly B. Shcharansky who was charged with high treason—the passing of secret information to American intelligence agents—and Alexandr Ginzburg who was tried on the lesser charge of anti-Soviet agitation. Both Shcharansky and Ginzburg belonged to a Moscow group that monitored Soviet observance of the human-rights provisions of the 1975 accords reached by thirty-five nations in Helsinki. The Shcharansky case was a particular affront to President Carter since the president had publicly denied the Soviet espionage charge and had declared that the accused had no connection whatsoever with any American intelligence group. Hence, a conviction was tantamount to calling the president of the United States a liar. Nonetheless, Shcharansky was convicted and sentenced to thirteen years in a Soviet prison camp. Ginzburg received an eight-year term. The situation was further exacerbated by a statement made by UN Ambassador Andrew Young to the effect that "there [were] hundreds, perhaps even thousands of people whom I would call political prisoners" in the United States.[3] After rebukes from both Carter and Vance, Young apologized and called his statement "a mistake."

The trials were a tough expression of resentment over what the Soviet leadership considered unwarranted interference in its internal affairs. From Moscow's point of view, Carter had violated an unwritten code by raising in public human-rights questions that, in the Kissinger years, had usually been discussed in private. The former secretary of state, after all, had advised President Ford not to meet with Alexander Solzhenitsyn. And perhaps, if Carter had not launched his human-rights campaign, the Soviets might have exiled Shcharansky and Ginzburg as they had exiled Solzhenitsyn. As *Pravda* put it, "President Carter [was] like a fisherman caught on his own hook."

There was indeed not much the president could do. Aside from declaring that his "voice would not be stilled," the only concrete action taken by the administration was the cancellation of some computer and oil technology sales intended for the Soviet Union. The SALT negotiations were not broken off, even though numerous senators and congressmen demanded tougher action. Both Carter and Vance agreed to keep the issues separate. Besides, it would have been ironic in the extreme to discontinue SALT. Life, after all, was the most basic human right, and life was the ultimate concern of the arms-limitation talks because the American and Soviet nuclear arsenals were the greatest threat to life in human history. The administration had some hope that cutbacks in trade might affect the Soviet government. As one official said: "We have never had any illusions about preventing the Soviet Union from cracking down on dissidents, but at least we can make them pay for it."[4] Past evidence does not support such optimism.

The conclusion, then, is melancholy and somewhat paradoxi-

---

[3] *New York Times*, 16 July 1978.
[4] *Newsweek*, 17 July 1978, p. 24.

cal. Kissinger, who always chose détente over human rights, greatly increased Jewish emigration from the Soviet Union. As soon as Henry Jackson demanded public linkage of trade with human rights, Jewish emigration declined sharply. Carter, once he had publicly endorsed Sakharov, had painted himself into a corner. And when the Soviet leadership called his hand, it was revealed to be a bluff. Words that could not be backed by deeds had a boomerang effect. Soviet dissidents soon were in worse shape than before. If result, rather than intent, is the criterion of effectiveness in human rights, Kissinger had more success than Carter. The balancer had done better than the evangelist.

The American relationship with China offered an interesting contrast to that with the Soviet Union. Despite the fact that China was one of the most regimented societies in the world and political and civil rights were virtually nonexistent there, the Carter administration had exempted the People's Republic from criticism in the field of human rights. This omission may be explained in part by the strategic value of the new relationship between the United States and China, especially after Carter extended formal recognition. There is another reason, too, however. Carter included *both* political and economic rights in his policy objectives. Very often, particularly in Third World countries, the two may not necessarily go together. A daily bowl of rice may be far more important to a poor peasant than the right of free speech. There was no doubt that China under communism had improved the population's economic and social lot. There was almost no starvation and the level of public health had risen sharply. Modern China had simply stressed economic and social progress at the cost of political freedom. The Carter administration has been uneasy with this formula but sensitive enough not to demand the impossible. Besides, the Chinese leadership would hardly be responsive to a demand for civil liberties. It might easily perceive this as an American attempt to "use" human rights in order to thwart economic development and promulgate a new form of moral imperialism. Hence, the case of China illustrates yet another complication. There is no single standard of human rights to which all societies adhere. If the United States supports only its own brand, the danger of a unilateral crusade would be very great indeed. Thus, in addition to the question "at what cost," one must ask the further question, "whose morality for whom?"

Yet a different challenge was posed by the new Communist government in Cambodia, the Khmer Rouge. Since this regime came to power in 1975, an estimated one million Cambodians were systematically murdered. Cities were emptied and some four million people were forced on long marches into the countryside. Survivors were herded into agricultural communes and all vestiges of previous Cambodian society were eradicated. Money, wages, and commerce were abolished and travel and contact with the outside world were forbidden. The slightest infraction was punishable by torture and death.

The world was slow to awaken to the terror of Cambodia. President Carter addressed himself to the subject only in April 1978, when an international conference convened in Oslo, Norway, in order to look into the Cambodian genocide. The president declared the Cambodian government to be "the worst violators of human rights in the world today." One observer, deploring the slow pace of world reaction to events in Cambodia, perceived a morbid parallel to the international blindness that first met the news of the concentration camps in Nazi Germany.[5] The ruthlessness that these two states employed in the extermination of their enemies was unique in its total disregard for human life. In Nazi Germany, the goal of genocide was racial purity; in Cambodia it was political purity.[6]

On one level, the lateness of Jimmy Carter's response was understandable. There was absolutely nothing the American government could do to affect developments inside Cambodia. The Khmer Rouge regime was totally autarkic and the United States had no leverage whatever, economic or otherwise, over its behavior. On another level, however, the president's tardiness was puzzling, for there were thousands of Cambodians whom he could have helped. Approximately 100,000 Indochinese "boat people" risked death in order to escape from Communist Cambodia and Communist Vietnam.[7] The United States has not been particularly generous to these homeless men and women. A quota of 25,000 was established in 1978 for all Indochinese boat people. Words were cheap, but when Indochinese refugees began to compete for scarce American jobs, the price tag seemed too high. One rabbi,

---

[5] Leo Cherne, "The Terror in Cambodia," *Wall Street Journal*, 10 May 1978.
[6] Ibid.
[7] Vogelgesang, op. cit., p. 827.

recalling comparable disregard for Jews fleeing for Nazi Germany, sensed a new American "epidemic of callousness." [8] Carter's response to the helpless refugees from Indochina mocked his own human-rights policy, which had been intended after all, in part, as an antidote to the American involvement in the Indochina war. True, the president was impotent to affect the basic cause of this inhumanity. And Congress might have resisted *any* form of reengagement in Indochina, even a purely humanitarian one. Yet, it seems that more could have been done to protect the most basic rights of the human flotsam that had escaped from the Cambodian holocaust.

The ending of this story did not lack in irony. In 1978, Vietnam, now a Communist nation backed by the Soviet Union, invaded Cambodia, which was backed by China. Cambodia was virtually dismembered. The inhumanity of the Cambodian Khmer Rouge was thus brought to an end not through moral pressures brought to bear by an outraged humanity, but through the power interests of the Sino-Soviet conflict. Very soon after the American withdrawal from Vietnam the only wars in Asia were those by Communists against other Communists. In 1979, the quota for Indochinese refugees who wished to escape to the United States was raised to 40,000. By then, the total number of Asian refugees had reached the half million mark.

In sum then, vis-à-vis totalitarian dictatorships, the Carter policy of human rights has not been a spectacular success. In the case of Soviet Russia, Carter has played the role of Don Quixote: well-intentioned, but completely ineffectual. The victims of his inexperience were the dissidents who were worse off than before. In the case of China, he wisely recognized these limits and exercised restraint. But the Cambodian case is particularly disturbing. One Cambodian school teacher who had escaped, asked the following question at the Oslo conference: "Can you let these things go on until our race disappears?" [9] So long as nonintervention in the internal affairs of sovereign states remains the code of conduct of the international community, there is little the United States can do. All the more reason, it would seem, to protect the human

---

[8] Ibid.

[9] John Barron and Anthony Paul, "Cambodia: The Killing Goes On," *Reader's Digest*, July 1978, p. 174.

rights of those who survived to tell the story. But once again, the response was slow. Finally, in July 1979, when the number of refugees in Asia had passed the half million mark, the United Nations convened a special conference in Geneva. The Western nations, including the United States, promised to accept a quarter million of these helpless people. But what about the human rights of those who were refused? Are they to drift on boats forever in the interstices of the international community? Is the voyage of the hopeless to replace the voyage of the damned? Anyone concerned with the reality of human rights would have to be moved to sympathetic action.

NEUTRALS: UGANDA AND SOUTH AFRICA

President Idi Amin of Uganda was not far behind the Cambodian Khmer Rouge in the practice of official mass murder. The ferocious brutality and terrible capriciousness of the Ugandan leader made him one of the grossest violators of human rights in modern times. In the eight years he held power, between 1971 and 1979, between 100,000 and 300,000 people were killed by his death squads. Many victims were "guilty of nothing more than catching the eye of the killer—a shopkeeper with coveted goods, a Christian in a Muslim village, a civil servant who questions a command, a judge with foreign friends." [10] Amin's government was so murderous that it invited comparison with Hitler's Germany and Stalin's Russia.

Nonetheless, Uganda escaped formal censure by the United Nations and the Organization of African Unity (OAU). Most African leaders were vociferous in their condemnation of the white racist regime in South Africa but remained silent regarding the brutal black regime in Uganda. There were two reasons for this apparent double standard. First, African leaders refused to speak or act against Amin for fear of violating the OAU's cardinal rule against interference in a member state's internal affairs. They felt that such a process might rebound against themselves. Second, Amin enjoyed a certain popularity throughout Africa because of

[10] Richard H. Ullman, "Human Rights and Economic Power: The United States versus Idi Amin," *Foreign Affairs*, April 1978, p. 529.

his theatrical humiliation of whites. As one observer put it: "The photograph of his bulk, chairborne, being carried into an OAU rally in a Kampala Stadium by a clutch of sweating British businessmen—a modern 'white man's burden,' as Amin himself put it—will not soon be forgotten." [11] On that occasion, Amin received a rousing ovation.

Yet, unlike Cambodia, Uganda was vulnerable to American pressure. Uganda's only significant export was its coffee crop, which earned it $750 million in 1977. One-third of that crop went to the United States, one-fifth to the United Kingdom and the rest to West Germany, France, Italy, Japan, and the Netherlands.

Uganda's coffee was not grown on plantations, but by peasant small holders. The peasants were required to sell their crops to a state marketing board and were paid at a set price in almost worthless Ugandan currency. During his eight years in power, Amin received all of the foreign exchange, which he used to buy weapons and luxury goods for himself his army, and his police. The peasants depended for their livelihood upon subsistence agriculture and participated only marginally in the coffee-cash economy. Thus, there was a direct relationship between foreign purchases of Ugandan coffee and Amin's murderous regime. A boycott of Idi Amin's coffee crop would primarily affect the Ugandan leader and his military clique, while the coffee growers' economic lot would remain largely unaffected. Whether a boycott would misfire and cause Amin to rule with even greater brutality was, of course, an open question. But there was a good chance that the Ugandan dictator would be seriously hurt by effective boycotts and might even fall from power.[12]

The price tag of a Ugandan coffee boycott for the United States was virtually nil. There was probably no situation in the world where the United States's power to affect a human-rights violator was so great and the culprit's power to affect the United States so small. Doing without Ugandan coffee would scarcely cause a ripple in the American coffee market. So painless would a boycott be that on November 29, 1977, the president of the National Coffee Association, representing the entire industry, wrote to Secretary of State Vance stating that the association's members awaited the government's orders. The association's board of direc-

11 Ibid., p. 531.
12 Ibid., p. 533.

tors had agreed unanimously that "the violations of human rights occurring under the Ugandan Government—of President Idi Amin [were] abhorrent and morally repugnant." [13] Perhaps most important, a boycott would punish the Amin government but leave the peasants essentially untouched. In most cases, economic sanctions are blunt instruments and cannot be "fine tuned." Innocent and guilty alike are affected. This would not be the case in Uganda. All things considered, the Amin clique was an ideal test site for human-rights action by the United States.

Nonetheless, the Carter administration waited for over a year before it finally approved an American boycott of Ugandan coffee in October 1978. Douglas J. Bennett, Jr., assistant secretary of state for congressional relations, had stated in September 1977, that he was "not convinced" that a boycott "would be effective in bringing about an improvement in human rights conditions" in Uganda.[14] Bennett's objections, however, were couched in general terms and did not address the Ugandan situation specifically:

> Boycott actions are not consistent with the principles of the General Agreement on Tariffs and Trade (GATT), to which the United States is committed as the basis for international commercial relations. Whenever these principles are set aside, their overall authority as a protection for our own international trade interests is undermined. Therefore, as a general matter, we are extremely reluctant to take actions which contradict these principles.[15]

Put in another way, the Carter administration had opposed any effort to restrain trade for political purposes. Economics and politics belonged on "separate tracks." Within this framework, economic pressure should be used only to counter economic pressures by others. Human-rights violations such as Amin's were in the political realm and would have to be countered by political measures. The only exception to the "separate tracks" rule was an action mandated by an international organization such as the sanctions used by the UN Security Council against Rhodesia. Hence, Carter had passed the initiative for censoring Amin right back to the United Nations.

Carter's long reluctance in the Ugandan case was not lost

13 Ibid., p. 538.
14 Ibid., p. 534.
15 Ibid., p. 534.

upon the Congress. In 1977, Democratic Congressman Don J. Pease of Ohio introduced legislation to bar Ugandan coffee from entering the United States. In the summer of 1978, a resolution to that effect was adopted unanimously by the House of Representatives. Yet, in the absence of executive leadership, the coffee industry did not take concerted action. Instead, it requested the administration "to declare and implement a uniform national policy." Finally, the Carter administration responded and imposed a boycott. An angry Idi Amin declared that he would take retaliatory measures against the three hundred Americans still living in Uganda. In effect, these three hundred men and women now became hostages of the Ugandan dictator.

It would, of course, have been preferable if action against the Amin regime had been taken collectively, either under the aegis of the United Nations or that of the Organization of African Unity. But this was not to be, hence the United States had to act alone. By applying America's economic power, Jimmy Carter challenged a mass murderer's moral right to lead a nation.

In 1979, Idi Amin's barbarous reign finally came to an end. A combination of invading forces from neighboring Tanzania and rebellion from within brought the dictator down. It is impossible to determine the exact contribution of the coffee boycott to Amin's downfall. But there is no doubt that it *did* play a role. And to the degree it did, it was at least a partial vindication of the American human-rights campaign.

If the Ugandan government practiced official murder, the South African government has engaged in the official degradation of its black subjects. Less than 20 percent of the population of South Africa is white, but this minority owns 87 percent of the land, two-thirds of the world's gold, and half of the world's diamonds. Under South Africa's apartheid laws, not one of its twenty million blacks has ever been able to vote for the nation's central government. They have been allowed to vote in the "homelands," or Bantustans, that comprise 13 percent of the country's territory. But in the white 87 percent, the blacks have never been citizens. At best, they have been second-class foreigners.

The economic implications of apartheid have been enormous. Cheap black labor has been one of the major pillars of the South African economy. Wages for whites and blacks reveal enormous gaps. In manufacturing, for example, the average monthly wage for whites in 1976 was $714; for blacks, it was $148.40. In mining, the corresponding figures were $868 and $103.60.[16] These are typical examples of economic exploitation on the basis of race. Abraham Lincoln spoke of "government of the people, by the people, for the people." Apartheid has been government of the blacks, by the whites, for the whites.

Central to the human-rights crisis in South Africa has been the problem of sharing political power. So far, the blacks have only shared what little power the whites have been prepared to yield voluntarily. But the "homelands" solution has never satisfied the blacks. Increasingly, their demand has been for a formula that would represent the wishes of *all* South Africans. Stated differently, the ultimate aspiration of the blacks has been "one man, one vote." On this basic question, the whites have yielded nothing. On the contrary, in October 1977, the South African government embarked on a policy of almost total suppression of internal dissent. Leading moderate newspapers were closed and their editors banned or detained. Steven Biko, the black liberation movement's leader, was placed under arrest and, shortly thereafter, died in prison. Apparently, the ruling African government had decided on an ambitious program to annihilate all organized opposition.

Over the past twenty-five years, United States policy toward South Africa has been a study in ambivalence. On the one hand, Americans have found the apartheid principle morally repugnant. As the civil-rights movement in the United States gathered momentum during the 1960s, criticism of South Africa became more and more vocal. On the other hand, there have been heavy pressures in the opposite direction. South Africa has presented itself to the United States as a bulwark against communism in Africa. Perhaps even more important, American investments in South Africa's gold, chrome, diamonds, and iron ore have been extremely profitable. Investors have included the top fifty American corporations and annual returns have ranged between 15 and 20 percent. The fact that the wellspring of this profitability has been cheap black labor has not acted as much of a deterrent. Hence, moral principle and the profit motive have been in conflict for a quarter of a century. The resolution of this conflict has been simple: American

---

[16] Clyde Ferguson and William R. Cotter, "South Africa: What Is to Be Done," *Foreign Affairs*, January 1978, p. 262.

leaders have paid lip service to the evils of the apartheid system, but American businesses have continued to benefit from its firm grip on the South African economy.

Finally, in 1976, there was a change. Secretary of State Kissinger, in response to the victory of a pro-Communist regime in Angola, placed the United States firmly behind the goal of eventual black majority rule in all of Southern Africa. In no mood to leave the field to the Soviet Union, Kissinger called for the end of apartheid in South Africa, even though he made no suggestions for a timetable. The time had come, however, he declared, for an internal dialogue to begin between the nation's whites and blacks in order to work out a formula for a just sharing of political and economic power.

Jimmy Carter has gone beyond the Kissinger initiative. In early 1977, he asserted that the United States was prepared to take "effective measures" aimed at encouraging the African government to try "internal dialogue" and to stop suppressing its black leaders. The House of Representatives supported the presidential call by a vote of 347 to 54. In the fall of 1977, UN Ambassador Andrew Young led his Western allies in a unanimous vote in the UN Security Council mandating an international arms embargo against South Africa. That same week, however, the three Western powers cast vetoes in the Security Council against the adoption of *full* economic, political, and diplomatic sanctions against the Vorster regime. Why did the United States support one form of sanction but not the other?

The reason for the Carter administration's reluctance to move to trade sanctions becomes clear when one looks at the size of the price tag. Quite obviously, a great deal of American trade with South Africa would be undermined and leading members of the business community would become thoroughly aroused. Even though Andrew Young frequently compared the American South of the 1850s to South Africa today, the analogy is misleading. Blacks in the United States constitute approximately 10 percent of the population. Even in the South, they never constituted more than 40 percent of any one state's population. Hence, the American challenge was always that of a white majority sharing political and economic power with a black minority. In South Africa, the situation is reversed: a white minority is called upon to share power with a black majority. In the event of a "one man, one vote" formula, this black majority would ultimately exercise power *over* the white minority. It may be too much to expect American businesses to push for significant changes in conditions that have made profitable operations possible. And it is probably impossible to ask the South African government to commit what it considers to be political and economic suicide.

There is a further difficulty with American economic sanctions. South Africa's blacks may be hurt as much as the country's ruling whites. In this respect, the situation differs substantially from that in Uganda. The innocent would suffer together with the guilty. The South African government has pointed out to the Carter administration that the severance of economic links would harm the blacks of South Africa even more than the whites. Interestingly enough, however, the blacks seem prepared to take that risk. The nation's black leaders—Albert Luthuli, Nelson Mandela, Robert Sobukive, and Steven Biko—all were unequivocal in this fight.[17] They preferred unemployment to the continuation of the economic links that helped to maintain the system that oppressed them.

On balance, the South African case is one of the most complex challenges to Jimmy Carter's human-rights offensive. Clearly, he must balance the morally desirable with the politically possible. From a purely human-rights perspective, the president would have to urge the whites of South Africa to accept their fellow Africans who are black as fellow citizens in every sense of the word. Clearly, the political and economic obstacles to such a course are probably too great. The African government would "go down first class," fighting for its racist ideology. Conversely, Carter cannot accept South Africa's call to the United States not to interfere in its domestic politics. That would make a mockery of the human-rights campaign. What, then, are the realistic possibilities for action?

Perhaps U.S. businesses might be advised that if they decided to stay in South Africa, they would do so at their own risk. Moreover, U.S. firms remaining in South Africa might be encouraged to establish and maintain fair employment practices. That would include a program to recognize and deal with black labor

---

[17] Donald Woods, "South Africa's Face to the World," *Foreign Affairs*, April 1978, p. 525.

unions. The travel of U.S. tourists to South Africa—now totaling more than fifty thousand a year—might be discouraged. Conversely, these "sticks" might be balanced by "carrots" if real progress toward racial equality were made. South Africa's acceptance of UN supervised elections in Namibia was an encouraging case in point. In 1978, the United States, together with Britain, France, Canada, and West Germany finally prevailed upon South Africa to grant Namibia majority rule and independence. Within South Africa itself, however, most changes remained minor and, in the words of two astute observers, resembled "desegregation of the deck chairs on the Titanic." [18]

Clearly, then, consistency in the pursuit of human rights may not be possible. The stress on human rights must at all times be weighed against other factors. In Cambodia, all that could apparently be done was to save the refugees from the regime's barbarism. In Uganda, a boycott that does not affect the coffee growers and is virtually painless for Americans was finally instituted. In South Africa, the pursuit of human rights clearly bears a formidable price tag. But perhaps one must choose the instruments at one's disposal. The fact that economic leverage can be applied only with difficulty against South Africa, and probably not at all against Cambodia, is no argument for not using it against Uganda. Yet virtue that is costless may hardly be called virtue. To take action against Idi Amin while continuing to conduct business with South Africa would be an affront to the rest of Africa. Jimmy Carter's rhetoric has not liberated him from making hard choices. The human-rights campaign has made these choices even harder.

FRIENDS: UNEVEN JUSTICE

The pursuit of his human-rights policy vis-à-vis adversaries and neutrals such as the Soviet Union and South Africa has confronted President Carter with awesome dilemmas of principle and power. His options have not been much easier in the relations with the United States's friends and allies. Yet, here too, a fairly clear-cut pattern has emerged. Wherever the United States has had an important strategic or economic interest, that interest has tended

[18] Ferguson and Cotton, op. cit., p. 274.

to push human-rights considerations into the background. Only where the power interest has been negligible, have human rights dominated policy.

The first and most obvious case in point has been the American arms trade. As a candidate, Carter had made the issue of America's arms exports peculiarly his own. The United States, in terms of Carter's rhetoric, was to be the world's moral beacon light and breadbasket, not its gunshop. In May 1977, the president announced a new policy of "arms restraint." The spiraling arms traffic by then was worth $20 billion a year, and half of it was American. "Because we dominate the world market to such a degree," Mr. Carter said, "I believe that the United States can and should take the first step" in reducing arms sales.[19] It would then try to persuade other suppliers—the Soviet Union and Western European sellers—to do likewise.

Instead, the president continued to preside over business as usual. America's military sales still account for half of the entire world's. The sales of jet aircraft in 1978 to Israel, Egypt, and Saudi Arabia were cases in point. Sales to Iran, while the shah was in power, were enormous. Yesterday's evangelist became today's purveyor of arms. Needless to say, the Soviet Union, Britain, France, and West Germany did not see fit either to exercise restraint.

The sales to the three Middle Eastern countries were made without attaching any human-rights conditions. Strategic considerations were absolutely paramount. In the case of Iran, the shah released some political prisoners and reportedly placed rugs in some Iranian jails.[20] Only in Latin American countries where U.S. interests were relatively minor were arms sales linked to progress in human rights. Some sales to Argentina, for example, were suspended because of human-rights violations.

Similar problems in other strategic areas were resolved in a similar manner. In early 1978, Carter spent several hours discussing with his top officials whether Vice-President Walter Mondale should go ahead with a planned visit to the Philippines in the wake of the violence and fraud that had surrounded the national

---

[19] Emma Rothschild, "Carter and Arms Sales," *New York Times*, 4 June 1978.

[20] *Wall Street Journal*, 11 May 1978.

election there. Yet, the president was eager to keep two important military bases in the Philippines. In the end, the strategic concern prevailed and Mr. Mondale went as planned. As one official admitted: "We've gotten ourselves in a bad fix: We either appear to be reneging on human rights or pass over important interests." [21]

Similarly, massive American aid to South Korea has continued even though General Park"s regime has frequently punished political dissent with prison. But South Korea has been a strategically vital ally. And despite the continuation of repressive practices in oil-rich Iran, Carter warmly toasted the shah during a 1978 New Year's visit declaring: "The cause of human rights is one that is shared deeply by our people and by the leaders of our two nations." [22]

The case of Iran is particularly instructive. At first, Jimmy Carter criticized the shah and pressed him to institute reforms in human rights. But when it became clear that the shah was a valuable oil supplier, a good customer of American hardware, and a staunch anti-Communist ally, Carter backtracked. On the occasion of his New Year's visit, the president declared: "Your Majesty, your country is an island of stability in a turbulent sea." Less than a year later, Carter had to eat his words: the shah was driven into exile and a government hostile to the United States came to power in Iran. Carter had been caught off guard. There had been a failure of intelligence in both senses of the word: information as well as judgment. The CIA had failed to predict the coming revolution and the United States had been committed to the shah with no links whatever to the opposition. Ironically enough, Carter had been right the first time. Had he remained consistent and pressed for human rights, the new government might have been more friendly when it came to power. As it turned out, Carter's policy of vacillation got him the worst of both worlds. It did not save the shah nor did it save his victims while he ruled Iran. Henry Kissinger, in early 1979, added the final touch: "A foreign policy that makes human rights its cornerstone, invites revolution." Jimmy Carter did not have an answer. Iran, more starkly than any other case, showed up the dilemma of human rights and naked power.

[21] Ibid.
[22] Ibid.

Whenever vital interests have been involved, the president has tended to make his own decisions. The distribution of human-rights rewards and punishments to less important countries has been left to Patricia Derian's office or to that of Warren Christopher, the deputy secretary of state. Once every two or three weeks, committees meet to decide who is deserving and who is not, in terms of human-rights criteria. A typical agenda item included a debate in the spring of 1978 over how the U.S. representative at the World Bank should vote on a proposed loan for grain silos in Argentina. As one reporter described the discussion:

> Was Argentina's recent decision to release names of 3,600 political prisoners and free a few hundred of them sufficient improvement to merit U.S. acknowledgment? If so, should the U.S. vote yes, but make a public statement criticizing Argentina's repressive policies? Or perhaps it would be better to vote no and issue a statement approving the freeing of the prisoners. In the end, the committee decided the U.S. representative should abstain.[23]

In July 1978, the State Department instructed the Import-Export Bank to withhold a $270 million loan from Argentina because the human-rights situation, in the government's opinion, still had not improved sufficiently.[24]

Washington also stopped military aid to Nicaragua, a country of no strategic importance whatsoever to the United States, after the Somoza government had decided to crack down on its critics. "Your policy is so selectively applied," commented a Latin American diplomat, "that we have to assume you care about human rights only where you have no other interests." [25] And a humorous observer added: "Nicaragua's situation may not improve until U.S. cars run on bananas." [26]

It seems that Latin America, where the United States has limited economic and strategic interests, has borne the brunt of the human-rights campaign. When Terence Todman, assistant secretary of state for Latin America, complained that the region was being singled out, he was reassigned as ambassador to Spain.

---

[23] Ibid.
[24] *New York Times*, 21 July 1978.
[25] Ibid.
[26] Vogelgesang, op. cit., p. 827.

But several nations in that region have echoed his complaint and gone on the offensive. In 1978, for example, five South and Central American countries rejected U.S. military aid because Washington had criticized their oppressive policies. "We aren't ever going to be perfectly consistent," Patricia Derian explained, "But our objective is consistent: to improve the observance of human rights everywhere." The goal, in Deputy Secretary Christopher's words, was to develop a "sequential and calibrated" strategy.[27]

To be fair to the administration, there have been some significant achievements. Specifically, since early 1977, thousands of political prisoners were released in such nations as Indonesia, Morocco, Bangladesh, Pakistan, Tanzania, and the Dominican Republic. Bolivia, Peru, and Ecuador promised elections; and El Salvador and Haiti agreed to visits by the Inter-American Commission on Human Rights. The 1978 meeting of the General Assembly of the Organization of American States was shifted from Uruguay, a major violator of human rights, to the United States. By contrast, Henry Kissinger had gone to Santiago for the 1976 meeting of the OAS General Assembly even though the atrocities committed by Chile's military junta had been severely criticized at the time. The UN Human Rights Commission was upgraded, and announced in 1978, that it had established a procedure for dealing with complaints by individuals and nongovernmental organizations in Bolivia, Cambodia, Equatorial Guinea, Malawi, the Republic of Korea, Uganda, Ethiopia, Indonesia, Paraguay, and Uruguay.[28] In July 1978, an inter-American court of human rights came into existence. Finally, the president himself made it a practice, during state visits abroad, to make human rights an important talking point and at times, as in Poland and Brazil, to meet with church or opposition leaders. The Congress, too, has responded with alacrity to the new initiatives. At times it has even been ahead of the administration. The Ugandan coffee boycott vote in the House was a case in point. A mandatory congressional requirement that the State Department publish a study each year that must detail human-rights conditions in all countries receiving American aid, was another.

27 Ibid., p. 836.
28 Ibid., p. 824.

Yet, two serious problems remained even in this area of modest achievement. First, since the president did not wish to embarrass dictators by taking credit for human-rights improvements, he was forced to prove his commitment by pointing to repressive regimes he had punished. As one official put it, "All our trophies tend to be aid programs we've cut, because to reward a bit of success when repression remains is to risk charges that we're winking at abuses." [29] When a number of State Department officials argued that the administration would accomplish more by rewarding improvements than by punishing shortcomings, they were overruled by Patricia Derian. "We aren't the tooth-fairy handing out sugar plums to kids," the former Mississippi civil-rights activist declared, "why should we pass out a treat to nations that treat their citizens as they should?" [30]

The second problem concerned a certain holier-than-thou attitude that has tended to characterize Carter's human-rights bureaucracy. A group of people meeting every few weeks and deciding who was good and who was bad and meting out rewards and punishments smacked somewhat of cultural imperialism. "The rest of the world thinks the collective good is more important than the individual," one official commented, "we, not they, are the aberration". There has been an evangelical flavor to a policy that has advertised American moral concern to the rest of the world. Yet, the inconsistencies and double standard inherent in that policy have often made it appear hypocritical and moralistic, rather than moral. It may be true that Jimmy Carter's pursuit of human rights has created a greater world sensitivity to that vital issue. But it appears that the president's approach could benefit from less judgmentalism and more humility.

The ultimate problem that must be addressed in conclusion seems to be: Can human rights be an export commodity? The record seems to indicate that the answer is largely, but not totally, in the negative. In the case of major adversaries such as the Soviet Union, the pursuit of human rights is probably *impossible*; in the case of a nation like South Africa, a human-rights policy would be *desirable*,

[29] *Wall Street Journal*, op. cit.
[30] Ibid.

but the difficulties of execution are enormous; in some cases such
as Uganda and nations in the Latin American region, human-
rights initiatives seem *possible*.

Jimmy Carter's personal influence was largely that of catalyst.
He recognized an issue that was in cyclical upswing and correctly
gauged the nation's temper and the mood of a resurgent Congress.
But he discovered very quickly that evangelism was not enough.
In his collisions with realpolitik, human rights were almost always
sacrificed. *Only when power interests were minimal or nonexistent, did the pursuit of human rights become the nation's policy.*

Jimmy Carter, in his approach to foreign policy, falls some-
where between the crusader and the pragmatist. His religious conviction, while profound, did not have the rigidity of Wilson's or of
Dulles. His tenacity and perseverance did not lock him into an obsession. Unlike the crusader's zeal, his faith did not become a
dogma. It always remained a quest. And it inspired him in 1979 to
mediate a peace treaty between Israel and Egypt. On the other
hand, his global human-rights campaign was often ineffectual and
even boomeranged when it collided with the realities of power.
And after such collisions, instead of exerting determined leadership,
Carter tended to withdraw in confusion. His decision, in mid-1979,
to shake up his cabinet did not entirely dispel this impression of
indecisiveness. The president's faith thus lacked a practical dimension, and hence, his foreign policy, especially in the human-rights
arena, had some aspects of the amateur. But then, perhaps even
the most sophisticated statesman would be bound to fail if he
based his foreign policy on a cornerstone of human rights. Such
an attempt might always come to grief on the rocks of national
interest and power. Perhaps it cannot be done.

Perhaps the United States itself must remain the most important arena of Americans' concern for human rights. Few nations could have survived assaults of the magnitude of Watergate
and Vietnam without serious damage to the fabric of democracy.
The United States might not be so fortunate again unless its citizens and leaders become more vigilant guardians of human rights.
Protection of the Bill of Rights, concern for due process of law,
equal opportunity to all classes and colors of the citizenry—these
remain the human-rights pursuits for Americans at home. Throughout history, nations have seldom fallen because they were pushed
from the outside. They were usually destroyed through corrosive

forces from *within*. The United States is no exception to this rule. Its greatness will not be measured by its successes or failures in remaking the world in its moral image. It will be measured by the degree to which it lives up to the human-rights convictions of its founding fathers. In that fundamental sense, the past should perhaps become the nation's prologue.

EPILOGUE

The "Might-Have-Beens" of History

Throughout this book, a basic assumption has been made: It makes a difference *who* is there at a given moment. This is particularly true when high threat, surprise, and short decision time combine to form a crisis situation. Under such conditions, a leader's personality—his character and values—may even be decisive. Stated in another way, if the decision maker had been a different person, the course of events might have taken a different turn. This premise raises an important question: What about the "ifs" and "might-have-beens" of history?

It is true that we shall never know the road not taken. History does not reveal its alternatives. "Ifs" and "might-have-beens"' are not scientifically provable. By definition, they must always remain hypothetical. They are based on analogies that, by their very nature, are imprecise comparisons. History never repeats itself exactly.

But it does not follow from these arguments that only non-hypothetical questions are meaningful. The attitude behind such an approach seems to be that what has been has been and we need to know no more. But if we seek understanding from history's vast tapestry, we must pay attention to the "might-have-beens." Some of them may be as relevant to the chances of the future as a recognized mistake is to the successful action that follows it. These "might-have-beens" are not just ghostly echoes, but, in many instances they were *objective possibilities* that were missed. They might have been missed for a variety of reasons but, most of the time, they were missed for want of a *free intelligence*, prepared to explore alternatives. Hence, it is our responsibility not to ignore these "ifs" and "might-have-beens" for they *could have been*.

In this context, our distinction between "crusading" and "pragmatic" personalities becomes most meaningful. The crusader usually blinds himself to policy alternatives while the pragmatic leader will tend to be open to a variety of options. *Hence, the most tragic "ifs" and "might-have-beens" of history tend to apply more to crusaders than to pragmatists.*

One cannot say, of course, with certitude that a greater openness to alternatives would definitely have prevented a specific alternative that did in fact occur. But one *can* say that, in the law of averages, a more open mind would probably have helped.

How can the foreign policy decision maker maximize his understanding? Clearly, he must guard against the mentality of the crusader: the tendency to see what he wants to see and to respond to situations not on the basis of evidence, but on the basis of his needs or wishes; the tendency to rationalize decisions and to surround himself with people who will tell him what he wants to hear rather than what he ought to know; the tendency to personalize an issue and link it to his ego; and above all, the tendency to confuse morality with moralism, to preach and judge rather than to listen and try to understand. In the postatomic era leaders must decontaminate their policies of shopworn slogans that only narrow possibilities. They must be open to new concepts and new facts, not offer up their people's bodies in defense of shadows.

But how can we recognize the crusader *before* he reaches power? Usually, there *are* clues. Woodrow Wilson's rigid posture, for example, in his confrontation with Dean West at Princeton foreshadowed his rigidity vis-à-vis the U.S. Senate on the League of Nations issue. There is a more general rule of thumb, however. The crusader generally finds it impossible to admit a mistake, while the pragmatist can do so without serious injury to his self-esteem. Wilson, Johnson, and Nixon almost never were able to say "I was wrong." Their personalities compelled them to compound defeat until they were destroyed. Kennedy, on the other hand, freely admitted his foolishness after the Bay of Pigs fiasco. His candor endeared him to the American people even more and his popularity reached new highs *after* this admission. These different attitudes toward error are usually visible *long before* a person reaches foreign policy decision-making power. And they are important clues to later attitudes.

We have seen in our cases that the failure of many leading figures in American foreign policy lay in their inability to explore alternatives. Another way of stating this is to say that what these mistakes amounted to was a repeated underestimation of man's power to control his future.

How often have we heard that a particular tragedy in world politics was "inevitable"? Crusaders are particularly fond of making such assertions. In truth, *no* event in the affairs of states has *ever* been inevitable. History does not make history. Men and women make foreign policy decisions. They make them in wisdom and in folly, but they make them nonetheless. Often, after a war or other national calamity, historians look back and speak of fate or inevitability. But such *historical determinism merely becomes a metaphor for the evasion of responsibility.* There is, after all, in our lives, a measure of free will and self-determination.

We must, of course, remember that a statesman's lot is often hard and cruel. When faced with a decision, he cannot postpone it until all the facts are in and historical perspective has illuminated the situation. He must decide and act in the present and cannot but act on incomplete knowledge. Once all the facts are in, foreign policy has become history. In that sense, the statesman's burden is a heavy one and the scholar, who does not have to face this existential imperative, owes him a measure of empathy and tolerance.

The future would look rather bright if the great movers of American foreign policy were pragmatists rather than crusaders. But unfortunately, the moralist mentality is embedded very deeply in America and seems to come in cycles. It is not likely that we have seen the last of the crusaders.

All this is not to say that pragmatists never make mistakes. They often do. But as a general rule, such mistakes are more easily reversible than those of the crusaders. It is also true that a pragmatist may lack an overall blueprint or design for American foreign policy. But this does not mean that the pragmatic mind is unable to conceive a general philosophy. The crucial difference is this: the pragmatist always tests his design against the facts of his experience. If the design does not hold up against the facts, the design will have to change. The crusader, on the other hand, tends to sacrifice unwelcome facts on the altar of a fixed idea. If the facts do not conform to his design, it may be too bad for the facts. A pragmatist may thus be an idealist, but he will be a *practical* idealist. In contrast, the crusader's idealism all too frequently congeals into an obsession.

Finally, where so few apparently decide so much, it is not only essential that such people be intelligent. Intelligence alone, as Vietnam has demonstrated amply, is not enough. Such men and women must have the *wisdom* to explore alternatives and the *courage* to create new ones when the opportunity arises. A leader may lose, of course, even after he has chosen wisely and acted courageously. Folly guarantees failure, but wisdom does not ensure success. But, as our case studies have shown, wisdom and courage will win more often than rigidity or drift. *Wherever we look at the world today, we can see the fateful consequences of yesterday's lost chances.* Hence, we must always be aware of "ifs" and "might-have-beens." The mistakes of past leaders may serve as *our* warnings; their wisdom and their courage as *our* inspiration. In their triumphs, we can rejoice; into their darkness, perhaps we can see and understand.

Annotated Bibliography

Introduction:
YOUNG AMERICA AND THE WORLD

ALMOND, GABRIEL A. *The American People and Foreign Policy.* New York: Praeger, 1960.
The classic analysis of the role of elites and of the "common man" in the formulation and control of American foreign policy.

BAILEY, THOMAS A. *America Faces Russia.* Ithaca, N.Y.: Cornell University Press, 1950.
The best analysis of America's relations with pre-revolutionary Russia.

CLAUDE, INIS L., JR. *Power and International Relations.* New York: Random House, 1962.
A thoughtful and original comparison of the balance-of-power, collective security, and world government approaches to international politics.

FAIRBANK, JOHN K. *The United States and China.* 4th ed. Cambridge: Harvard University Press, 1978.
A definitive account by America's leading China scholar.

FOX, WILLIAM T. R., and MORGENTHAU, HANS J. "National Interest and Moral Principles in Foreign Policy," *American Scholar*, Spring 1949.
A classic debate between the "idealist" and "realist" schools in American foreign policy.

GILBERT, FELIX *To the Farewell Address.* Princeton: Princeton University Press, 1961.
A fine account of the tension between realism and idealism in early American foreign policy.

HARTZ, LOUIS *The Liberal Tradition in America*. New York: Harvest Books, 1955.
A leading American political theorist explores the liberal value system of the American Republic.

HOFSTADTER, RICHARD *The Paranoid Style in American Politics*. New York: Vintage, 1967.
An analysis of the tendency toward "conspiracy theories" in the United States. Particularly good on Senator Joseph McCarthy.

KENNAN, GEORGE F. *American Diplomacy, 1900–1950*. New York: Mentor Books, 1952.
A trenchant indictment of the "moralist-legalist" approach to foreign policy by a leading American diplomat and elder statesman.

LEFEVER, ERNEST W. *Ethics and United States Foreign Policy*. New York: Meridian Books, 1957.
A balanced exposition on the roles of ethics and power politics in American foreign policy.

LIPPMANN, WALTER *Public Opinion*. New York: Macmillan, 1947.
A classic study on the subject.

MAHAN, ALFRED T. *The Influence of Sea Power Upon History, 1660–1783*. Boston: Little, Brown, 1898.
An American geopolitician of the late nineteenth century argues for the decisive importance of sea power.

MORGENTHAU, HANS J. *Politics Among Nations: The Struggle For Power and Peace*. 5th ed., rev. New York: Knopf, 1978.
The classic work of the "power politics" school in international relations. Shows little patience with "moralism" and "legalism" in the conduct of foreign policy.

NEUMANN, ROBERT G. "Toward a More Effective Executive—Legislative Relationship in the Conduct of America's Foreign Affairs," *CSIS Monograph*. Washington, D.C., Center for Strategic and International Studies, Georgetown University, 1977.
To improve the relationship, the author advocates not institutional change but changes in attitudes.

OSGOOD, ROBERT E. *Ideals and Self-Interest in America's Foreign Relations*. Chicago: University of Chicago Press, 1953.
A "national interest" interpretation of American foreign policy.

SPYKMAN, NICHOLAS J. *America's Strategy in World Politics*. New York: Harcourt, Brace, 1942.
One of the earliest defenses of realpolitik in American foreign policy.

STOESSINGER, JOHN G. *Nations in Darkness: China, Russia and America*. 3rd ed. New York: Random House, 1978.
A study of the impact of misperceptions on the foreign policies of the United States, Russia and China in the nineteenth and twentieth centuries.

TANNENBAUM, FRANK *The American Tradition in Foreign Policy.* Oklahoma City: University of Oklahoma Press, 1955.
A vigorous polemic against the realpolitik and balance of power approaches to foreign policy.

WOLFERS, ARNOLD, and MARTIN, LAWRENCE W., eds. *The Anglo-American Tradition in Foreign Affairs.* New Haven: Yale University Press, 1956.
A scholarly comparison of British and American foreign policy styles.

Chapter 1
WOODROW WILSON: CRUSADER FOR A BETTER WORLD

BAKER, RAY STANNARD, and DODD, WILLIAM E., eds. *The Public Papers of Woodrow Wilson,* 6 vols. New York: Harcourt, Brace, 1925–27.
An indispensable source for an understanding of Wilson's perception of his own role, the United States, and the world.

BARBER, JAMES D. *The Presidential Character.* 2nd ed. Englewood Cliffs, N.J.: Prentice-Hall, 1977.
Contains perceptive insights into Wilson's character formation.

BUEHRIG, EDWARD H. *Woodrow Wilson and the Balance of Power.* Bloomington: University of Indiana Press, 1955.
A sound analysis of Wilson's futile efforts to eliminate the balance of power system.

CURRY, ROY WATSON *Woodrow Wilson and Far Eastern Policy, 1913–1921.* New Haven: Yale University Press, 1957.
Ranges from Wilson's attitude toward Japanese demands on China to the American intervention in Siberia.

FILENE, PETER G. *Americans and the Soviet Experiment, 1917–1933.* Cambridge: Harvard University Press, 1967.
Brilliantly explores and recreates early American attitudes toward the Soviet Union.

FOLEY, HAMILTON *Woodrow Wilson's Case for the League of Nations.* Princeton: Princeton University Press, 1923.
A moving plea by a Wilson admirer.

GELFAND, LAWRENCE E. *The Inquiry: American Preparations For Peace, 1917–1919.* New Haven: Yale University Press, 1963.
Wilson's policy toward Germany after America's entry into the war.

GEORGE, ALEXANDER L., and GEORGE, JULIETTE L. *Woodrow Wilson and Colonel House: A Personality Study.* New York: John Day, 1956.
An extraordinarily perceptive psychohistorical account of the Wilson-House relationship.

GRISWOLD, A. WHITNEY *The Far Eastern Policy of the United States.*
New York: Harcourt, Brace, 1938.
A classic study, suggesting that American policy toward Asia has
swung like a pendulum from intense involvement to complete
indifference.

HOUSE, EDWARD M., and SEYMOUR, CHARLES, eds. *What Really Happened at Paris: The Story of the Paris Peace Conference, 1918–1919.* New York: Harcourt, Brace, 1921.
An intimate and tragic portrait of Wilson's role as peacemaker in
Paris, by his aide and closest friend.

KENNAN, GEORGE F. *Russia Leaves the War.* Princeton: Princeton University Press, 1956.
A superb study of Lenin's decision to conclude a separate peace
with Germany at Brest-Litovsk.

KENNAN, GEORGE F. *The Decision to Intervene.* Princeton: Princeton University Press, 1958.
A definitive account of Wilson's decision to participate in the
Siberian intervention against the Bolsheviks.

LINK, ARTHUR S. *Wilson the Diplomatist.* Baltimore: Johns Hopkins
University Press, 1957.
A profound and sensitive assessment by a leading Wilson scholar.

LINK, ARTHUR S. *Wilson: The Struggle for Neutrality, 1914–1915.*
Princeton: Princeton University Press, 1960.
A definitive account of that crucial period.

MAYER, ARNO J. *Politics and Diplomacy of Peacemaking: Containment
and Counterrevolution at Versailles, 1918–1919.* New York:
Knopf, 1967.
A provocative analysis of the political constellations in Europe on
the eve of the Versailles Conference.

PIPES, RICHARD *The Formation of the Soviet Union.* Cambridge: Harvard University Press, 1954.
A fine analysis of the tensions between Communist ideology and
nationalist tradition in the early Soviet Union.

SMITH, GENE *The Shattered Dream.* New York: Morrow, 1970.
A moving, at times, shattering, account of Wilson's losing battle
for the League of Nations.

WALWORTH, ARTHUR *Woodrow Wilson.* New York: Norton, 1978.
A reissue of a superb and comprehensive biography of Wilson the
man and statesman.

WHITE, JOHN A. *The Siberian Intervention.* Princeton: Princeton University Press, 1950.
One of the best accounts of this abortive expedition.

WILSON, WOODROW *Constitutional Government in the United States.*
New York: Macmillan, 1908.
Wilson, the political scientist, on American government and
politics.

Interchapter: THE WORLD BETWEEN TWO WARS

ARON, RAYMOND *The Century of Total War.* Boston: Beacon, 1954.
A leading French social scientist reflects on the nature of war in
the twentieth century.

BARROS, JAMES *The Corfu Incident of 1923: Mussolini and the League
of Nations.* Princeton: Princeton University Press, 1965.
Shows the beginnings of Fascist diplomacy in the 1920s.

CARR, E. H. *The Twenty Years' Crisis, 1919–1939.* New York: Harper,
1939.
Probably the most clear-sighted analysis of the interwar period
by a contemporary British observer.

CHURCHILL, WINSTON S. *The Gathering Storm.* Boston: Houghton
Mifflin, 1948.
Brilliantly summarizes the failures of diplomacy during the 1930s.

CRAIG, GORDON *The Politics of the Russian Army.* New York: Oxford
University Press, 1955.
A first-rate analysis of the destructive impact of the German
military establishment on the Weimar Republic.

CRAIG, GORDON, and GILBERT, FELIX, eds. *The Diplomats, 1919–1939.*
Princeton: Princeton University Press, 1953.
A comprehensive treatment of foreign affairs during the interwar
years.

DEUTSCHER, ISAAC *Stalin: A Political Biography.* New York: Oxford
University Press, 1949.
A detailed and comprehensive biography of Stalin by a Trotsky
sympathizer.

DORPALEN, ANDREAS *Hindenburg and the Weimar Republic.* Princeton:
Princeton University Press, 1964.
Portrays the German surrender of power to the Nazis.

FEST, JOACHIM *Hitler.* New York: Harcourt Brace Jovanovich, 1974.
The most comprehensive biography of the Nazi leader.

FISCHER, LOUIS *The Soviets in World Affairs: A History of Relations
Between the Soviet Union and the Rest of the World, 1917–1929.*
Princeton: Princeton University Press, 1951.
Shows the techniques used by the Soviet Union and the
Comintern to subvert democratic governments during the 1920s.

HALPERIN, WILLIAM S. *Germany Tried Democracy.* New York: Norton,
1946.
A competent and conscientious survey of the Weimer Republic.

HUGHES, H. STUART *The United States and Italy.* Cambridge: Harvard
University Press, 1953.
A sensitive analysis of the rise of Mussolini and Italian Fascism
and the response of the United States.

JACKSON, GABRIEL *The Spanish Republic and the Civil War, 1931–
1939.* Princeton: Princeton University Press, 1965.

Analyzes the Spanish Civil War as a testing ground between the
forces of democracy and totalitarianism.

ROWSE, A. L. *Appeasement: A Study in Political Decline, 1933–1939.*
New York: Norton, 1961.
Brilliant portraits of Neville Chamberlain and Edouard Daladier.

SETON-WATSON, HUGH *Eastern Europe Between the Wars, 1918–1941.*
Cambridge: Cambridge University Press.
A fine exposition of the dependence of Eastern Europe and the
Balkan countries on the policies of the great European powers.

SHIRER, WILLIAM L. *The Rise and Fall of the Third Reich: A History
of Nazi Germany.* New York: Simon and Schuster, 1960.
An excellent popular account of the Nazi years.

TAYLOR, TELFORD *Munich.* New York: Doubleday, 1979.
The definitive work on the fateful Munich Conference.

TOYNBEE, ARNOLD *The World After the Peace Conference.* London:
Oxford University Press, 1925.
A succinct summary of the result of the postwar peace settlements.

WAITE, ROBERT *Adolf Hitler: The Psychopathic God.* New York: Basic
Books, 1977.
The best psychohistorical study of the German führer.

WALTERS, F. P. *A History of the League of Nations.* 2 vols. London:
Oxford University Press, 1952.
The definitive work on the League of Nations, by a British
scholar.

WHEELER-BENNETT, JOHN W. *Munich: Prologue to Tragedy.* New
York: Viking, 1948.
A fine account of the events leading up to the Nazi absorption
of Czechoslovakia.

Chapter 2
FRANKLIN D. ROOSEVELT: PROPHET AND PRINCE

BURNS, JAMES MACGREGOR *Roosevelt: The Lion and the Fox.* New
York: Harcourt, Brace, 1956.
Probably the definitive account of Roosevelt's first two terms.
Written by a master craftsman.

BURNS, JAMES MACGREGOR *Roosevelt: The Soldier of Freedom.* New
York: Harcourt Brace Jovanovich, 1970.
The finest book on Roosevelt the war leader. Meticulously
researched and superbly written.

CANTRIL, HADLEY, ed. *Public Opinion 1935–1946.* Princeton: Princeton University Press, 1951.
The most thorough study available on the swings of American
public opinion during the Roosevelt years.

CHURCHILL, WINSTON S. *The Second World War.* 6 vols. Boston: Houghton Mifflin, 1948–1953.
A remarkable historical and literary achievement by one of the great heroes of the Second World War.

CLEMENS, DIANE S. *Yalta.* New York: Oxford University Press, 1970.
The definitive account of the eight-day conference in the Crimea in February 1945, when Churchill, Roosevelt, and Stalin reshaped the world.

DALLEK, ROBERT *Franklin D. Roosevelt and American Foreign Policy, 1932–1945.* New York: Oxford University Press, 1979.
The central thesis of this superb study is that the cement that held together FDR's foreign policy was Adolf Hitler.

DIVINE, ROBERT A. *Roosevelt and World War II.* Baltimore: Johns Hopkins University Press, 1969.
One of the best character studies of Roosevelt the war leader.

DUROSELLE, JEAN-BAPTISTE *De Wilson à Roosevelt: Politique exterieure des Etats-Unis, 1913–1945.* Paris: Colin, 1960.
A superb comparison of Wilson's and Roosevelt's foreign policies, by a leading French scholar.

FEIS, HERBERT *Churchill, Roosevelt, Stalin.* Princeton: Princeton University Press, 1957.
A scholarly study focusing on the Teheran and Yalta conferences.

KOLKO, GABRIEL *The Politics of War.* New York: Random House, 1968.
A leading revisionist historian maintains that American capitalism is, by its very nature, expansionistic, and the Soviet Union is its victim.

MACMILLAN, HAROLD *The Blast of War.* London: Macmillan, 1967.
A British perspective of Roosevelt's war leadership, by a former prime minister.

PERKINS, FRANCES *The Roosevelt I Knew.* New York: Viking, 1946.
A moving personal memoir by FDR's secretary of labor and close friend.

ROGOW, ARNOLD A. *James Forrestal.* New York: Macmillan, 1963.
A psychohistorical account of the life and suicide of Roosevelt's secretary of war.

SHARP, SAMUEL L. *Poland: White Eagle on a Red Field.* Cambridge: Harvard University Press, 1953.
An authoritative account of Poland's fate between the great powers, including its disposition at Yalta.

SHERWOOD, ROBERT E. *Roosevelt and Hopkins.* New York: Harper, 1948.
The best account available of the relationship between Roosevelt and his closest adviser during the war years.

SMITH, GADDIS *American Diplomacy During the Second World War.* New York: John Wiley, 1965.
A good general overview, balanced and objective.

TSOU, TANG *America's Failure in China, 1941–1950.* Chicago: University of Chicago Press, 1963.
A definitive analysis—meticulously researched and fully documented—of an emotion-laden subject.

WILLIAMS, WILLIAM APPLEMAN *The Tragedy of American Diplomacy.* New York: Dell, 1962.
A leading Marxist perspective.

WILSON, THEODORE A. *The First Summit: Roosevelt and Churchill at Placenta Bay 1941.* Boston: Houghton Mifflin, 1969.
A crisply written account of the first encounter between Roosevelt and Churchill and of the drafting of the Atlantic charter.

WITTMER, FELIX *The Yalta Betrayal: Data on the Decline and Fall of Franklin D. Roosevelt.* New York: Caldwell, 1953.
Critics of FDR at Yalta will find ample ammunition here, but many of the "data" are of dubious authenticity.

WOHLSTETTER, ROBERTA *Pearl Harbor: Warning and Decision.* Stanford: Stanford University Press, 1962.
A prize-winning work that largely exonerates Roosevelt of lack of vigilance vis-à-vis Japan in the months before Pearl Harbor.

Interchapter: THE ORIGINS OF THE COLD WAR

ACHESON, DEAN *Present at the Creation.* New York: Norton, 1969.
The former secretary of state recalls the Marshall Plan, the creation of NATO, and the other American initiatives in Europe in the postwar world.

ALPEROVITZ, GAR *Atomic Diplomacy: Hiroshima and Potsdam.* New York: Vintage, 1967.
A leading revisionist argues that the United States, using its atomic monopoly, tried to push the Soviet Union out of Europe and thus precipitated the cold war.

BACKER, JOHN H. *The Decision to Divide Germany.* Durham, N.C.: Duke University Press, 1978.
This fine books shows that the division of Germany, by 1947, was not the result of a Soviet or American plot, but stemmed from "disjointed incrementalism" on both sides.

BRZEZINSKI, ZBIGNIEW K. *The Soviet Bloc: Unity and Conflict.* Cambridge: Harvard University Press, 1960.
An excellent description of political conditions within the eastern bloc during the cold war years.

COMPTON, JAMES V., ed. *America and the Origins of the Cold War.* Boston: Houghton Mifflin, 1972.
A useful compilation of different revisionist perspectives.

DAVIDSON, W. PHILLIPS *The Berlin Blockade.* Princeton: Princeton University Press, 1958.
A first-rate, blow-by-blow account of the 1948 Soviet blockade of Berlin and of the American airlift.

ETZOLD, THOMAS H., and GADDIS, JOHN L., eds. *Containment: Documents on American Policy and Strategy, 1945–1950.* New York: Columbia University Press, 1978.
Two excellent essays by the editors introduce a valuable collection of documents, most of which were only recently declassified.

FEIS, HERBERT *China Tangle.* Princeton: Princeton University Press, 1953.
A carefully researched account of American policy toward China during and after World War II.

GADDIS, JOHN L. *The United States and the Origins of the Cold War.* New York: Columbia University Press, 1972.
A thoughtful and balanced response to the revisionist attacks on America's postwar policy.

HALLE, LOUIS J. *The Cold War as History.* New York: Harper and Row, 1967.
Not eager to apportion blame, the author approaches the subject in a philosophical vein, almost as a Greek tragedy.

HARRIMAN, W. AVERELL *Special Envoy to Churchill and Stalin, 1941–1949.* New York: Random House, 1975.
An eminent presidential adviser and elder statesman reflects on the origins of the cold war.

HOLBORN, HAJO *The Political Collapse of Europe.* New York: Knopf, 1951.
A brilliant and sweeping analysis of Europe's decline in world affairs by a leading historian.

JONES, JOSEPH *The Fifteen Weeks.* New York: Viking, 1955.
A classic treatment of the conception and execution of the Truman Doctrine and Marshall Plan.

KENNAN, GEORGE F. ("X") "The Sources of Soviet Conduct," *Foreign Affairs,* July 1947.
This famous article, calling for the "long-term, patient, but firm and vigilant containment" of the Soviet Union became the basis of official policy during the Truman years.

KENNAN, GEORGE F. *Russia under Lenin and Stalin.* Boston: Little, Brown, 1961.
The best popular treatment of Soviet foreign policy, by a leading scholar-diplomat.

KENNAN, GEORGE F. *Memoirs, 1925–1950.* Boston: Little, Brown, 1967.
The reminiscences of an American ambassador during the cold war years.

MORGENTHAU, HANS J. *In Defense of the National Interest*. New York: Knopf, 1951.
A trenchant attack on "moralism" and "legalism" in America's postwar foreign policy.

SCHLESINGER, ARTHUR M. JR. "The Origins of the Cold War," *Foreign Affairs*, October 1967.
Both the Soviet Union and the United States are to blame, argues a leading historian in this first-rate, finely calibrated article.

WHITE, THEODORE H. *Fire in the Ashes*. New York: William Sloane Associates, 1953.
A splendid and often moving account of America's effort to rebuild a shattered Europe after 1945.

YERGIN, DANIEL *Shattered Peace: The Origins of the Cold War and the National Security State*. Boston: Houghton Mifflin, 1977.
One of the fairest, most scrupulously researched, and lucidly written interpretations of that controversial subject.

Chapter 3
KOREA 1950

BUNDY, MCGEORGE, ed. *The Pattern of Responsibility*. Boston: Houghton Mifflin, 1952.
A compilation of Secretary Acheson's speeches and congressional testimony.

BYRNES, JAMES F. *Speaking Frankly*. New York: Harper, 1947.
Truman's first secretary of state reflects on postwar policy.

DONOVAN, ROBERT J. *Conflict and Crisis*. New York: Norton, 1977.
The best available treatment of the Truman presidency during the years 1945–1948. A story splendidly told, including a great deal of new material.

FEIS, HERBERT *From Trust to Terror*. New York: Norton, 1970.
One of the best traditional treatments of the onset of the cold war, with special emphasis on the role of President Truman.

FLEMING, D. F. *The Cold War and Its Origins*, 1917–1960, 2 vols. New York: Doubleday, 1961.
The author places particular stress on Truman's anti-Communism and on his attitude toward Senator Joseph McCarthy.

GRIFFITH, SAMUEL B. *The Chinese People's Liberation Army*. New York: McGraw-Hill, 1967.
A first-rate analysis of Chinese military strategy, by a leading American military historian.

HAMMER, ELLEN J. *The Struggle for Indochina, 1940–1955*. Stanford: Stanford University Press, 1966.
A leading study of the French involvement in Indochina and Truman's shifting attitudes toward it.

MANCHESTER, WILLIAM *American Caesar*. Boston: Little, Brown, 1978.
A very comprehensive, balanced, and illuminating portrait of
MacArthur, the man and the general.

MCLELLAN, DAVID S. *Dean Acheson*. New York: Dodd, Mead, 1976.
A balanced, engrossing biography, rendering a favorable verdict
on Acheson's stewardship of American foreign policy.

MILLER, MERLE *Plain Speaking*. New York: Berkley, 1973.
An oral biography of Harry Truman that gives us the late
president's personal reflections on the men and events of his
time. Moving and authentic.

OGLESBY, CARL, and SCHAULL, RICHARD *Containment and Change*.
New York: Macmillan, 1967.
A leading revisionist interpretation of Harry Truman and
containment.

OSGOOD, ROBERT E. *NATO*. Chicago: University of Chicago Press,
1962.
A finely balanced analysis of NATO's inception and subsequent
evolution.

PAIGE, GLENN D. *The Korean Decision*. New York: Free Press, 1968.
A blow-by-blow account of Harry Truman's decision to repel the
North Korean attack in June 1950.

PANIKKAR, K. M. *In Two Chinas*. London: Allen and Unwin, 1955.
These memoirs by a leading Indian diplomat include some
fascinating vignettes of Chou En-lai during the 1950s.

RIDGWAY, MATTHEW B. *The Korean War*. New York: Doubleday, 1967.
MacArthur's successor in Korea tells his story.

SHERWIN, MARTIN J. *A World Destroyed*. New York: Knopf, 1975.
One of the finest assessments of the impact of the atomic bombs
on Soviet-American relations.

SPANIER, JOHN W. *The Truman-MacArthur Controversy and the Korean War*. New York: Norton, 1965.
A definitive study.

STOESSINGER, JOHN G. *Why Nations Go To War*. 2nd ed. New York:
St. Martin's, 1978.
A study of the outbreaks of six major wars in the twentieth
century, with emphasis on the personalities of national leaders.

TRUMAN, HARRY S. *Memoirs*. 2 vols. New York: New American Library,
1965.
The late president's own accounting to history. Uneven in
interest, but the ring of truth echoes throughout.

VINACKE, HAROLD M. *The United States and the Far East, 1945–1951*.
Stanford: Stanford University Press, 1952.
A very good brief account of Truman's policies in Asia.

WHITING, ALLEN S. *China Crosses the Yalu.* Stanford: Stanford University Press, 1960.
The definitive study of China's intervention in the Korean War.

WHITNEY, COURTNEY *MacArthur: His Rendezvous with History.* New York: Knopf, 1956.
MacArthur's side in the controversy with Truman is eloquently presented by one of the general's admirers.

WOLFERS, ARNOLD, ed. *Alliance Policy in the Cold War,* Baltimore: Johns Hopkins Press, 1959.
A sound analysis of the U.S.-NATO strategic relationship during the Truman years.

Interchapter: ROLLBACK AND RESPONSE

BRODIE, BERNARD *Strategy in the Missile Age.* Princeton: Princeton University Press, 1959.
An excellent primer on the strategic problems of deterrence, total war, and limited war.

DIVINE, ROBERT A. *Blowing on the Wind.* New York: Oxford University Press, 1978.
A first-rate analysis of the nuclear test ban debate during the years 1954–1960.

EISENHOWER, DWIGHT D. *Mandate for Change.* New York: Doubleday, 1963.
These presidential reflections are particularly interesting on Indochina and Ho Chi Minh in the mid-1950s.

FONTAINE, ANDRÉ *History of the Cold War: From the Korean War to the Present.* New York: Pantheon, 1969.
A French scholar's assessment of the rigidification of Soviet-American relations.

GARTHOFF, RAYMOND L. *Soviet Military Doctrine.* Glencoe, Ill.: Free Press, 1953.
A leading American strategic thinker assesses Soviet military doctrine during the 1950s.

GURTOV, MELVIN *The First Vietnam Crisis.* New York: Columbia University Press, 1967.
Definitive on the American dilemma whether or not to intervene in Indochina on France's side at the time of Dien Bien Phu.

KAHN, HERMAN *On Thermonuclear War.* Princeton: Princeton University Press, 1960.
A fearful scenario of a world after a thermonuclear exchange. An influential book.

KENNAN, GEORGE F. *Memoirs: 1950–1963.* Boston: Atlantic-Little, Brown, 1972.
A former ambassador to the Soviet Union reflects sensitively on the congealing of the cold war.

KISSINGER, HENRY A. *Nuclear Weapons and Foreign Policy*. New York: Harper, 1957. Abridged edition, New York: Anchor Books, 1958. This trenchant critique of America's all-or-nothing nuclear strategy introduced the concept of tactical nuclear war.

KISSINGER, HENRY A. *The Necessity of Choice*. New York: Anchor Books, 1961. A sequel to the author's earlier work, expressing a great deal more caution on limited nuclear war.

LEVINE, ROBERT A. *The Arms Debate*. Cambridge: Harvard University Press, 1963. Assesses the entire spectrum of military thinking in the United States during the 1950s.

MANDER, JOHN *Berlin: Hostage for the West*. Baltimore: Penguin, 1962. A thoughtful treatment of the post-1958 Berlin crisis.

OSGOOD, ROBERT E. *Limited War*. Chicago: University of Chicago Press, 1957. The definitive overall treatment of the subject.

RANDLE, ROBERT F. *Geneva 1954: The Settlement of the Indochina War*. Princeton: Princeton University Press, 1969. The definitive study.

SCHELLING, THOMAS C. *The Strategy of Conflict*. Cambridge: Harvard University Press, 1960. A brilliant, conceptually innovative approach to deterrence, based on bargaining and games theory. A seminal book.

SNYDER, GLENN H. *Deterrence and Defense*. Princeton: Princeton University Press, 1962. A leading behavioral approach to the subject.

SPEIER, HANS *Divided Berlin*. New York: Praeger, 1961. Particularly good on Soviet-American military jockeying over Berlin after 1958.

STEEL, RONALD *Pax Americana*. New York: Viking, 1967. An excellent liberal critique of U.S. foreign policy. Particularly good on the 1950s.

STRAUSZ-HUPÉ, ROBERT, et al. *Protracted Conflict*. New York: Harper, 1959. Advocates an aggressive "forward strategy" for the United States.

THOMPSON, KENNETH W. *Interpreters and Critics of the Cold War*. Washington, D.C.: University Press of America, 1978. Fine assessments of Walter Lippmann, Reinhold Niebuhr, Hans Morgenthau, and George F. Kennan by a scholar whose thinking has been influenced by all four.

WOLFERS, ARNOLD, ed. *Alliance Policy in the Cold War*. Baltimore: Johns Hopkins Press, 1959. A thoughtful evaluation of NATO during the 1950s.

Chapter 4
EVANGELISM AS FOREIGN POLICY:
JOHN FOSTER DULLES AND THE SUEZ CRISIS

DONOVAN, ROBERT J. *Eisenhower: The Inside Story*. New York: Harper, 1956.
According to the author, the president played a more active role in foreign policy than was generally believed at the time.

DULLES, ELEANOR LANSING *The Last Year*. New York: Harcourt Brace Jovanovich, 1963.
A moving portrait of John Foster Dulles's final illness and death, by his sister.

DULLES, JOHN FOSTER *War or Peace?* New York: Macmillan, 1950.
The author reflects on his role in government during the Truman years.

DULLES, JOHN FOSTER "A Policy of Boldness," *Life*, 19 May 1952.
The secretary of state to be announces the Republican party's new policy of rollback and liberation.

EDEN, ANTHONY *Full Circle*. London: Allen and Unwin, 1960.
Memoirs of the British leader who perceived Nasser as another Hitler and Suez as another Munich.

EISENHOWER, DWIGHT D. *Waging Peace*. New York: Doubleday, 1965.
A somewhat wooden memoir of the presidential years.

EMMETT, JOHN HUGHES *The Ordeal of Power*. New York: Atheneum, 1962.
A sensitive description of the relations between Eisenhower, Dulles, and the author who served as adviser to the president.

FINER, HERMAN *Dulles Over Suez*. Chicago: Quadrangle, 1964.
A devastating critique of Dulles's treatment of Britain and France during the Suez crisis.

GUHIN, MICHAEL *John Foster Dulles*. New York: Columbia University Press, 1972.
An articulate defense of Dulles's foreign policy as realistic rather than moralist.

HOOPES, TOWNSEND *The Devil and John Foster Dulles*. Boston: Atlantic-Little, Brown, 1975.
An excellent and comprehensive biography, particularly perceptive on Dulles's crusading moralist approach to foreign policy.

LOVE, KENNETH *Suez: The Twice Fought War*. New York: McGraw-Hill, 1960.
A good account of the military mistakes leading to the Suez debacle.

MACMILLAN, HAROLD *Riding the Storm: 1956–1959*. New York: Harper and Row, 1971.
A former British prime minister assesses his country's travail and decline after Suez.

MOSLEY, LEONARD *Dulles.* New York: Dial Press, 1978.
A very chatty portrait of the Dulles family.

NUTTING, ANTHONY *No End of a Lesson: The Story of Suez.* New York: Potter, 1967.
A profoundly critical version, by a former British government official.

NUTTING, ANTHONY *Nasser.* New York: Dutton, 1972.
An excellent biography by a British author who was closely acquainted with the Egyptian president.

PARMET, HERBERT S. *Eisenhower and the American Crusades.* New York: Macmillan, 1972.
Eisenhower's great strength, according to the author, was his talent for coordination and maneuver.

SAFRAN, NADAV *Israel: The Embattled Ally.* Cambridge: Harvard University Press, 1978.
Probably the definitive account of three decades of Israeli-American relations.

SHANNON, WILLIAM V. "Eisenhower as President," *Commentary,* October 1958.
A superb, highly critical account.

SHEPLEY, JAMES "Brinkmanship," *Life,* 16 January 1956.
This perceptive article on John Foster Dulles's foreign policy coined a phrase.

THOMAS, HUGH *Suez.* New York: Harper and Row, 1966.
A British scholar concludes that the Anglo-French expedition in Suez had few parallels in the history of military imbecility.

Interchapter: NEW FRONTIERS

ALMOND, GABRIEL A., and COLEMAN, JAMES S., eds. *The Politics of the Developing Areas.* Princeton: Princeton University Press, 1960.
A trailblazing and comprehensive study.

BARNETT, A. DOAK *Communist China and Asia: Challenge to American Foreign Policy.* New York: Harper, 1960.
A trenchant critique of United States policy, on the eve of the Kennedy administration, by a leading China scholar.

BRZEZINSKI, ZBIGNIEW K., and HUNTINGTON, SAMUEL P. *Political Power: U.S.A.–U.S.S.R.* New York: Viking, 1964.
One of the earliest comparative analyses of Soviet and American societies. Daring and innovative.

BUCHAN, ALASTAIR *NATO in the 1960's.* Rev. ed. New York: Praeger, 1963.
An excellent exploration of the dilemmas of nuclear sharing in NATO.

CAMPBELL, JOHN C. *The Defense of the Middle East.* New York: Praeger, 1961.

A first-rate, hard-headed analysis of United States strategic dilemmas in the Middle East.

CLUBB, EDMUND O. *China and Russia: The "Great Game."* New York: Columbia University Press, 1971.
A comprehensive historical account with a fine assessment of the implications of the Sino-Soviet split for the United States.

CREMEANS, CHARLES D. *The Arabs and the World.* New York: Praeger, 1963.
One of the most sensitive and psychologically acute studies available on the subject.

DEUTSCHER, ISAAC *The Great Contest: Russia and the West.* New York: Oxford University Press, 1960.
A thoughtful assessment by the author of leading works on Stalin and Trotsky.

EMERSON, RUPERT *From Empire to Nation.* Cambridge: Harvard University Press, 1960.
An early classic on the rise of the new nations in Asia and Africa.

ERIKSON, ERIK H. *Gandhi's Truth: On the Origins of Militant Nonviolence.* New York: Norton, 1969.
A brilliant psychohistorical portrait of Gandhi.

FALL, BERNARD *The Two Vietnams.* 2nd rev. ed. New York: Praeger, 1967.
One of the finest analyses of Vietnam, by a leading French observer. Particularly good on the difficulties confronting the United States in fighting a counterinsurgency war. A prophetic book.

GEORGE, ALEXANDER L. *The Limits of Coercive Diplomacy.* Boston: Little, Brown, 1971.
The author assesses Kennedy's diplomacy in Laos and Cuba, as well as the beginnings of the intervention in Vietnam.

HILSMAN, ROGER *To Move a Nation.* New York: Doubleday, 1967.
An affectionate memoir by a member of the Kennedy administration. Good insights on decision making.

KAHN, HERMAN *Thinking About the Unthinkable.* New York: Horizon, 1962.
A more readable though equally fearful sequal to the author's *On Thermonuclear War.*

KISSINGER, HENRY A. *The Troubled Partnership.* New York: Anchor Books, 1966.
A thoughtful critique of the United States position in NATO in the 1960s.

KLEIMAN, ROBERT *Atlantic Crisis.* New York: Norton, 1964.
A sharply critical survey of the Kennedy administration's policies toward the NATO countries.

LACOUTURE, JEAN *Vietnam Between Two Truces.* New York: Vintage Books, 1966.

Especially perceptive on the early American Vietnam involvement and on the Vietcong's relationship to Hanoi.

MOSELY, PHILIP E. *The Kremlin and World Politics*. New York: Vintage, 1960.
A leading Soviet scholar and negotiator paints a realistic picture of Soviet foreign policy.

RUSH, MYRON *Strategic Power and Soviet Foreign Policy*. Chicago: University of Chicago Press, 1966.
A perceptive account of Soviet nuclear diplomacy between 1957 and 1962.

SCHELLING, THOMAS C. *Arms and Influence*. New Haven: Yale University Press, 1966.
An impressive sequal to the author's *Strategy of Conflict*.

STEEL, RONALD *The End of Alliance*. New York: Delta Books, 1966.
The author traces the resurgence of Europe in the Atlantic Community of the 1960s.

THAYER, CHARLES W. *Guerrilla*. New York: New American Library, 1963.
One of the most thoughtful early analyses of guerrilla warfare.

Chapter 5
THE BRUSH WITH NUCLEAR HOLOCAUST: KENNEDY AND KHRUSHCHEV AND THE CUBAN MISSILE CRISIS OF 1962

ABEL, ELIE *The Missile Crisis*. New York: Bantam Books, 1966.
A well-written journalistic account.

ALLISON, GRAHAM T. *Essence of Decision: Explaining The Cuban Missile Crisis*. Boston: Little, Brown, 1971.
A behaviorally oriented analysis.

BARNET, RICHARD J. *Roots of War*. New York: Atheneum, 1972.
The cold war and Vietnam, in the author's view, were inherent in the domestic capitalist structure of the American national security state.

CRANKSHAW, EDWARD *Khrushchev*. New York: Viking, 1966.
An imaginative reconstruction of Khrushchev the man, party boss, and national leader.

DINERSTEIN, HERBERT S. *The Making of a Missile Crisis*. Baltimore: Johns Hopkins University Press, 1976.
Missile gaps and strategic imbalances are the major culprits.

GALBRAITH, JOHN K. *Ambassador's Journal*. Boston: Houghton Mifflin, 1969.
A lively memoir of the Kennedy years by the former ambassador to India.

HALBERSTAM, DAVID *The Best and the Brightest*. New York: Random House, 1969.
A gallery of portraits of the decision makers in Vietnam during the 1960s. An enormously important book.

HORELICK, ARNOLD L. "The Cuban Missile Crisis: An Analysis of Soviet Calculations and Behavior," *World Politics*, April 1964.
The definitive account of the Soviet side.

KENNEDY, JOHN F. *Profiles in Courage* New York: Harper, 1955.
Courage manifests itself mostly in adversity, the author concludes, when a man must stand alone.

KENNEDY, ROBERT F. *Thirteen Days*. New York: Norton, 1969.
An invaluable insight into crisis decision making at the highest level, by a major participant in the Cuban quarantine decision of 1962.

KHRUSHCHEV, NIKITA S. *Khrushchev Remembers: The Last Testament.* Boston: Little, Brown, 1974.
Surprisingly candid recollections by the ousted Soviet leader.

LANSDALE, EDWARD G. *In the Midst of War*. New York: Harper, 1972.
A self-serving memoir by Kennedy's ambassador to South Vietnam.

MCNAMARA, ROBERT S. *The Essence of Security*. New York: Harper, 1968.
Reflections by the former defense secretary, at times compelling and revealing.

PACHTER, HENRY M. *Collision Course*. New York: Praeger, 1963.
Most illuminating on the sequence of Khrushchev's telegrams to Kennedy during the missile crisis.

QUESTER, GEORGE H. *Nuclear Diplomacy*. New York: Dunellen, 1970.
An analysis of American foreign policy as determined by the deployment of nuclear arms.

SALINGER, PIERRE *With Kennedy*. New York: Doubleday, 1966.
The perspective of Kennedy's press secretary.

SCHLESINGER, ARTHUR M. *A Thousand Days*. Boston: Houghton Mifflin, 1965.
An immensely readable, deeply moving, personal memoir of JFK, by one of America's great historians.

SCHLESINGER, ARTHUR M., JR. *Robert Kennedy and His Times*. Boston: Houghton Mifflin, 1978.
"Thank God for Bobby," JFK exclaimed after the missile crisis. The author agrees. RFK's role in preventing an air strike against Cuba in 1962, apparently was crucial.

SORENSEN, THEODORE C. *Kennedy*. New York: Bantam Books, 1966.
A sensitive and affectionate portrait by a close friend and special assistant.

WALTON, RICHARD J. *The Remnants of Power*. New York: Coward-McCann, 1968.
A poignant account of the tragic last years of Adlai Stevenson as ambassador to the United Nations.

WEINTAL, EDWARD, and BARTLETT, CHARLES *Facing the Brink*. New York: Scribner's, 1967.
An excellent study of crisis diplomacy.

Interchapter: THE TWILIGHT OF BIPOLARITY

ASPREY, ROBERT B. *War in the Shadows: The Guerrilla in History.* New York: Doubleday, 1975.
A very useful, broadly conceived historical survey.

BARNDS, WILLIAM J. *India, Pakistan, and the Great Powers.* New York: Praeger, 1972.
The best available and most comprehensive general survey.

BLACK, C. E. *The Dynamics of Modernization.* New York: Harper and Row, 1966.
One of the finest available studies of the Western impact on the political and socioeconomic fabrics of Third World countries.

BRODIE, BERNARD *Escalation and the Nuclear Option.* Princeton: Princeton University Press, 1966.
One of the most thoughtful analyses of nuclear diplomacy and brinksmanship.

BRYAN, C. D. B. *Friendly Fire.* New York: Bantam, 1977.
This story of the death of one American soldier and the agony of one American family is one of the most searing illuminations of the Vietnam tragedy.

CAPUTO, PHILIP *A Rumor of War.* New York: Holt, Rinehart and Winston, 1977.
The best account of the Vietnam war from the point of view of the fighting man. A harrowing, personal record.

DRAPER, THEODORE *The Abuse of Power.* New York: Viking, 1967.
A trenchant critique of Johnson's penchant for military solutions in Vietnam and the Dominican Republic.

FITZGERALD, FRANCES *Fire in the Lake.* Boston: Little, Brown, 1972.
A superb account of the American impact on Vietnamese society. Poignant and disturbing.

GREENWOOD, TED *Making the MIRV: A Study of Defense Decision Making.* Cambridge: Ballinger, 1975.
A workmanlike, carefully researched study.

KNIGHTLEY, PHILLIP *The First Casualty, From the Crimea to Vietnam: The War Correspondent As Hero, Propagandist, and Myth Maker.* New York: Harcourt Brace Jovanovich, 1975.
A first-rate survey of the multi-faceted roles of the war correspondent. Compelling and informative.

LACOUTURE, JEAN *The Demigods: Charismatic Leadership in the Third World.* New York: Knopf, 1970.
Excellent on leadership elites in Africa and Asia during the 1960s.

MILLER, J. D. B. *The Politics of the Third World*. London: Oxford University Press, 1969.
An illuminating perspective by a British scholar.

NEUSTADT, RICHARD E. *Alliance Politics*. New York: Columbia University Press, 1970.
Excellent on the stresses and strains in NATO during the Johnson years.

OBERDORFER, DON *Tet*. New York: Doubleday, 1971.
A brisk account of the North Vietnamese offensive in February 1968, that finally convinced Lyndon Johnson that the war could not be won.

PAGET, JULLIAN *Counter-Insurgency Operations*. New York: Walker, 1967.
A useful survey of the American Special Forces and antiguerrilla operations.

PIKE, DOUGLAS *Vietcong*. Cambridge: Massachusetts Institute of Technology Press, 1966.
A definitive study of the Vietcong's structure and operations during the 1960s.

REEDY, GEORGE *The Twilight of the Presidency*. New York: World, 1970.
"No White House assistant can stay in the President's graces for any considerable period without renouncing his own ego," concludes this astute student of the imperial presidency.

REISCHAUER, EDWIN O. *The Japanese*. Cambridge: Harvard University Press, 1977.
The definitive work, by the former American ambassador and leading Japan authority.

SCHLESINGER, ARTHUR M., JR. *The Bitter Heritage: Vietnam and American Democracy, 1941–1966*. Boston: Houghton Mifflin, 1967.
A savage attack on Lyndon Johnson's Vietnam policy.

SCHLESINGER, ARTHUR M., JR. *The Imperial Presidency*. Boston: Houghton Mifflin, 1973.
A magisterial study tracing the growing power of the presidency vis-à-vis the Congress in the twentieth century. Scholarly, readable, and enormously important.

SHAPLEN, ROBERT *The Lost Revolution: U.S. in Vietnam 1946–1966*. New York: Harper, 1965.
One of the best, most balanced historical accounts of the American involvement.

SILVERT, KALMAN, ed. *The Americas in a Changing World*. New York: Quadrangle, 1975.
The best available survey of modern Latin America's relations with the United States.

WALLERSTEIN, IMMANUEL *Africa: The Politics of Unity.* New York: Random House, 1967.
A first-rate general study of African politics and the interplay of East and West.

Chapter 6
THE AMERICAN EMPIRE: LYNDON JOHNSON AND VIETNAM

ARENDT, HANNAH "Lying in Politics," in *Crises of the Republic.* New York: Harcourt Brace Jovanovich, 1972.
Sharp insights into the compulsive liar in political life.

AUSTIN, ANTHONY *The President's War.* Philadelphia: Lippincott, 1971.
The author concludes that Johnson deceived the American people and used the Tonkin Gulf episode as a pretext to widen the war.

COOPER, CHESTER *The Lost Crusade.* New York: Dodd, Mead, 1970.
The title tells the story.

ELLSBERG, DANIEL *Papers on the War.* New York: Simon and Schuster, 1972.
Reflections by the man who leaked the Pentagon Papers.

EVANS, ROWLAND, and NOVAK, ROBERT *Lyndon B. Johnson: The Exercise of Power.* New York: New American Library, 1966.
Captures the political essence of the man, senator, and president.

FULBRIGHT, J. WILLIAM *The Arrogance of Power.* New York: Vintage, 1967.
The former senator critizes the tendency of American policy makers to commit the United States beyond its powers to uphold these commitments. An influential book.

FURGURSON, ERNEST B. *Westmoreland: The Inevitable General.* Boston: Little, Brown, 1968.
Makes a dull man interesting.

GOLDMAN, ERIC F. *The Tragedy of Lyndon Johnson.* New York: Knopf, 1969.
A perceptive and empathic analysis of a man whose virtues, like his faults, were on a giant scale.

GRAFF, H. *The Tuesday Cabinet.* Englewood Cliffs, N.J.: Prentice-Hall, 1970.
How Johnson browbeat his cabinet at weekly sessions.

HAYES, HAROLD, ed. *Smiling Through the Apocalypse: Esquire's History of the Sixties.* New York: McCall's, 1970.
A balanced and readable profile of a turbulent decade.

HOOPES, TOWNSEND *The Limits of Intervention.* New York: McKay, 1969.
An insider's account of the mounting opposition to LBJ, resulting in the President's decision to suspend the bombing.

JOHNSON, HAYNES B., and GWERZTMAN, BERNARD M. *Fulbright: The Dissenter.* New York: Doubleday, 1968.
The best biography available on the chairman of the Senate's Committee on Foreign Relations in the 1960s.

JOHNSON, LADY BIRD *A White House Diary.* New York: Holt, Rinehart and Winston, 1970.
The memoirs of a completely loyal First Lady.

JOHNSON, LYNDON B. *The Vantage Point.* New York: Holt, Rinehart and Winston, 1971.
A somewhat wooden, posturing memoir of the presidential years.

KEARNS, DORIS *Lyndon Johnson and the American Dream.* New York: Signet, 1977.
A wrenchingly intimate psychohistorical portrait of a haunted man. Compelling and immensely valuable.

MORGENTHAU, HANS J. *A New Foreign Policy for the United States.* New York: Praeger, 1969.
A highly sophisticated critique of the kind of thinking that led the United States into Vietnam.

MORGENTHAU, HANS J. "The Difference Between the Politician and the Statesman," *Politics in the Twentieth Century.* Chicago: University of Chicago Press, 1971.
A leading opponent of the Vietnam war concludes that LBJ was no statesman.

The Pentagon Papers. As published by the *New York Times,* New York: Bantam, 1971.
"They could hang people for what's in here," said Robert McNamara on first reading these revelations about the conduct of the Vietnam war.

RASKIN, MARCUS G., and FALL, BERNARD B., eds. *The Vietnam Reader.* Rev. ed. New York: Vintage, 1968.
A useful collection of articles for and against the war.

SIDEY, HUGH *A Very Personal Presidency: Lyndon Johnson in the White House.* New York: Atheneum, 1968.
Highlights LBJ's tendency to personalize politics and foreign policy, especially the Vietnam war.

TREWHITT, HENRY L. *McNamara: His Ordeal in the Pentagon.* New York: Harper, 1971.
The author traces McNamara's spiritual journey from hawk to dove in Vietnam.

Interchapter: BEYOND VIETNAM

BADEAU, JOHN S. *The American Approach to the Arab World.* New York: Harper and Row, 1968.
A thoughtful, level-headed survey.

BLOOMFIELD, LINCOLN P. *In Search of American Foreign Policy*. New York: Oxford University Press, 1974.
Written in anguish over the Vietnam War, the author recommends a "humane use of power" for the United States.

BRZEZINSKI, ZBIGNIEW K. *Between Two Ages: America's Role in the Technetronic Era*. New York: Viking, 1970.
An interesting and rather original assessment of America's position in the world, by the future national security adviser.

CLOUGH, RALPH N. *East Asia and U.S. Security*. Washington, D.C.: The Brookings Institution, 1975.
A valuable scholarly analysis of the changing relationships of the United States with China, Japan, the Soviet Union, Korea, and Southeast Asia.

DORNBERG, JOHN *Brezhnev: The Masks of Power*. New York: Basic Books, 1974.
A competent biography of the Soviet leader.

FAIRBANK, JOHN K. *China Perceived: Images and Policies in Chinese-American Relations*. New York: Knopf, 1974.
The dean of American China scholars compresses his wisdom into this slim but profound volume.

FITZGERALD, C. P. *Mao Tse-tung and China*. New York: Holmes and Meier, 1976.
One of the most thoughtful and balanced biographies available.

FULBRIGHT, J. WILLIAM *The Crippled Giant*. New York: Vintage, 1972.
The Vietnam catastrophe crippled not only America's physical strength, but also her soul, in the senator's opinion.

GEORGE, ALEXANDER L., and SMOKE, RICHARD *Deterrence in American Foreign Policy*. New York: Columbia University Press, 1974.
An excellent series of case studies on the employment of deterrence strategy to different types of challenges.

GIBNEY, FRANK *Japan: The Fragile Superpower*. 2nd ed. New York: Norton, 1979.
One of the best analyses of modern Japan and its relations with the United States.

GOLDMAN, MARSHALL I. *Détente and Dollars: Doing Business With the Soviets*. New York: Basic Books, 1975.
A first-class, hard-headed analysis. The Soviets are tough bargainers, the author says, but once they make a deal, they stick to it.

HINTON, HAROLD C. *Three and a Half Powers*. Bloomington: Indiana University Press, 1975.
Explores the changing balance of power in Asia in the 1970s.

LAQUEUR, WALTER *Confrontation: The Middle East and World Politics*. New York: Quadrangle, 1974.
An eminently fair and solid survey.

MATES, LEO *Nonalignment: Theory and Current Policy.* New York: Oceana, 1972.
The perspective of a leading Yugoslav scholar.

PFALTZGRAFF, ROBERT L., JR. *The Atlantic Community.* New York: Van Nostrand Reinhold, 1969.
One of the best surveys of recent stresses and strains in NATO.

SALISBURY, HARRISON E. *War Between Russia and China.* New York: Norton, 1969.
A leading scholar-journalist concludes that a Sino-Soviet war is quite possible, even likely.

STOESSINGER, JOHN G. *The United Nations and the Superpowers.* 4th ed. New York: Random House, 1977.
An analysis, through case studies, of Soviet-American-Chinese interaction in the United Nations.

STOESSINGER, JOHN G. *Nations in Darkness: China, Russia, and America.* 3rd ed. New York: Random House, 1978.
A perceptual analysis of Sino-Soviet-American relations.

ULAM, ADAM *The Rivals: America and Russia Since World War II.* New York: Viking, 1971.
A comprehensive and balanced survey, by a leading Harvard scholar.

WHITE, RALPH K. *Nobody Wanted War.* New York: Doubleday, 1968.
An interesting psychological interpretation of Vietnam and other wars.

Chapter 7
KISSINGER AND NIXON: THE SEARCH
FOR A STABLE WORLD ORDER

BALL, GEORGE W. *Diplomacy for a Crowded World: An American Foreign Policy.* Boston: Atlantic-Little, Brown, 1976.
A trenchant critique of Kissinger's diplomacy, especially in the Middle East.

BASKIR, LAWRENCE M., and STRAUSS, WILLIAM A. *Chance and Circumstance: The Draft, The War, and the Vietnam Generation.* New York: Knopf, 1978.
The authors, high staff members on President Ford's clemency board, demonstrate that wealthy, well-connected men had many legal ways of avoiding combat service in Vietnam.

BRANDON, HENRY *The Retreat of American Power: The Inside Story of How Nixon and Kissinger Changed American Foreign Policy For Years to Come.* New York: Doubleday, 1973.
A British reporter concludes that "never before in American history have the intellectual and conceptual views of one man influenced American politics as have those of Dr. Kissinger."

COLLIER, BERNARD "The Road to Peking, or How Does This Kissinger Do It?" *New York Times Magazine*, 14 November 1971.
An excellent account of Kissinger's secret trip to China in July 1971.

FALLACI, ORIANA "Henry Kissinger, Women, Power, the War," (interview conducted on 4 November 1972). English version, *New York Post Weekend Magazine*, 23 December 1972.
A revealing interview showing Kissinger's perception of himself as a solo performer in foreign policy.

GRAUBARD, STEPHEN R. *Kissinger: Portrait of a Mind.* New York: Norton, 1973.
A very fine early intellectual biography.

HOFFMANN, STANLEY *Primacy or World Order.* New York: McGraw-Hill, 1978.
More than one-third of this *tour d'horizon* of American foreign policy is a sharply critical evaluation of the Kissinger era.

JOINER, HARRY M. *American Foreign Policy: The Kissinger Era.* Huntsville: Strode, 1978.
A general, uncritical survey based largely on Kissinger's public statements.

KALB, BERNARD, and KALB, MARVIN *Kissinger.* Boston: Little, Brown, 1974.
A favorable journalistic account ending with the Syrian-Israeli disengagement in 1974.

KISSINGER, HENRY A. *A World Restored.* Boston: Houghton Mifflin, 1957.
Kissinger's doctoral dissertation on the Congress of Vienna of 1815. The concluding chapter on the nature of statesmanship foreshadows the author's later conceptual approach to foreign policy.

KISSINGER, HENRY A. "The Vietnam Negotiations," *Foreign Affairs*, January 1969.
The author's ideas on "Vietnamization" on the eve of his appointment as Nixon's national security adviser.

KISSINGER, HENRY A. *American Foreign Policy.* 3rd ed. New York: Norton, 1977.
This revised volume comprises three essays published while the author was still at Harvard and fourteen of his most important public statements as a government official.

LANDAU, DAVID *Kissinger: The Uses of Power.* Boston: Houghton Mifflin, 1972.
A sensitive early assessment.

LAQUEUR, WALTER, and LUTTWAK, EDWARD N. "Kissinger and the Yom Kippur War," *Commentary*, September 1974.
A balanced and thoughtful assessment.

MAZLISH, BRUCE *Kissinger: The European Mind in American Foreign Policy.* New York: Basic Books, 1976.
The author of this thoroughly researched psychohistorical portrait concludes that Kissinger's character was too flawed to serve as a model for Americans.

NEWHOUSE, JOHN *Cold Dawn: The Story of SALT.* New York: Holt, Rinehart and Winston, 1973.
The definitive account of the SALT I negotiations culminating in the Moscow summit of 1972.

NIXON, RICHARD *RN: The Memoirs of Richard Nixon.* New York: Grosset and Dunlap, 1978.
Defensive, detailed, overlong, often tedious, and short on humor, insight, and larger historical perspective.

RESTON, JAMES "Partial Transcript of an Interview with Kissinger on the State of the Western World," *New York Times,* 13 October 1974.
Revealing on Kissinger's perception of his role as historian and statesman.

SHAWCROSS, WILLIAM *Sideshow: Kissinger, Nixon and the Destruction of Cambodia.* New York: Simon and Schuster, 1979.
A British journalist indicts Nixon and Kissinger for the deliberate expansion and prolongation of the Indochina war by the invasion of Cambodia.

SHEEHAN, EDWARD R. *The Arabs, Israelis and Kissinger.* New York: Reader's Digest Press, 1976.
The author claims to present a secret history of Kissinger's Middle East diplomacy. A useful and balanced study, with a great deal of information on Kissinger's "shuttle" diplomacy.

SNEPP, FRANK *Decent Interval.* New York: Random House, 1977.
A former CIA strategy analyst describes the period from the Paris Accords of January 1973 to the Communist victory in Vietnam in April 1975. A bitter, disturbing, and controversial book.

STOESSINGER, JOHN G. *Henry Kissinger: The Anguish of Power.* New York: Norton, 1976.
Explains the intimate connection between Kissinger the scholar and Kissinger the statesman. A favorable assessment.

SZULC, TAD *The Illusion of Peace: Foreign Policy in the Nixon Years.* New York: Viking, 1978.
A comprehensive, painstaking critique concluding with an indictment of the "extraordinary immorality" of the Nixon-Kissinger foreign policy. The best of the critical accounts available.

Interchapter: THE POSTIMPERIAL PRESIDENCY

BECKER, ABRAHAM S. *Military Expenditure Limitation for Arms Control.* Cambridge: Ballinger, 1977.

A carefully reasoned critique of military spending in the United states.

BERGSTEN, FRED C., HORST, THOMAS, and MORAN, THEODORE H. *American Multinationals and American Interests*. Washington: Brookings, 1978.
A comprehensive, original, and quite possibly definitive study. The authors deal with the subject case by case, shunning facile generalizations.

COLLINS, JOHN M. *American and Soviet Military Trends Since the Cuban Missile Crisis*. Washington: Center for Strategic International Studies, Georgetown University, 1978.
The author of this carefully researched and systematically argued book concludes that, for the United States, military trends are generally adverse and deterrence is being eroded.

COMMONER, BARRY *The Poverty of Power: Energy and the Economic Crisis*. New York: Knopf, 1976.
A superb analysis of the conservation versus growth debate, by a leading environmentalist.

DUGARD, JOHN *Human Rights and the South African Legal Order*. Princeton: Princeton University Press, 1978.
A probing analysis of South Africa's legal system in the light of its history, politics and culture. Special emphasis is placed on human rights.

GALLOWAY, THOMAS L. *Recognizing Foreign Governments: The Practice of the United States*. Washington: American Enterprise Institute, 1978.
Over the years, the author demonstrates, the United States has tried to avoid defining its relations with newly established governments in terms of recognition or nonrecognition.

HAYES, DENIS *Rays of Hope*. New York: Norton, 1977.
A powerfully argued case for solar energy.

HOGGART, RICHARD *An Idea and Its Servants: UNESCO From Within*. New York: Oxford University Press, 1978.
A fascinating insider's report including an excellent treatment of the disputes over human rights, Israeli membership, and American policy.

KLINGHOFFER, ARTHUR J. *The Soviet Union and International Oil Politics*. New York: Columbia University Press, 1977.
An excellent and most informative survey.

MARTIN, JOHN BARTLOW *United States Policy in the Caribbean*. Boulder: Westview Press, 1978.
The former ambassador to the Dominican Republic argues for a special Caribbean-United States relationship, based on "nonintervention in most times and at most places."

MOORE, BARNINGTON, JR. *Injustice: The Social Bases of Obedience and Revolt*. New York: Pantheon, 1978.

A brilliant social scientist concludes that true reciprocity is probably impossible in modern international society.

OKSENBERG, MICHEL, and OXNAM, ROBERT B. *Dragon and Eagle: United States China Relations, Past and Future*. New York: Basic Books, 1978.
Thirteen authors have contributed to this carefully conceived and unusually valuable symposium.

PALMER, BRUCE, JR. *Grand Strategy for the 1980's*. Washington: American Enterprise Institute, 1978.
Five retired military officers including the former chairman of the Joint Chiefs of Staff, Maxwell D. Taylor, criticize the Carter administration for its lack of a coherent national strategy.

PONCHAUD, FRANCOIS *Cambodia: Year Zero*. New York: Holt, Rinehart and Winston, 1978.
A conscientious, grief-stricken account, by an eyewitness of the Cambodia terror since 1975.

RUSTOW, DANKWART A., and MUGNO, JOHN F. *OPEC: Success and Prospects*. New York: New York University Press, 1976.
The best brief analysis available.

SAID, ABDUL AZIZ *Human Rights and World Order*. New York: Praeger, 1978.
A good collection of essays discussing the moral and practical problems facing the goal of advancing global human rights.

SAMPSON, ANTHONY *The Seven Sisters: The Great Oil Companies and the World They Made*. New York: Viking, 1975.
A very useful, popular treatment of the subject.

SPAGHT, MONROE E. *The Multinational Corporation*. New York: Columbia University Press, 1978.
The perspective of a director of the Royal Dutch-Shell Corporation.

SPANIER, JOHN *American Foreign Policy Since World War II*. 7th ed. New York: Praeger, 1977.
An excellent factual account.

VERNON, RAYMOND *Storm Over the Multinationals: The Real Issues*. Cambridge: Harvard University Press, 1977.
A crisp analysis of the dilemma of political control of multinational corporations.

WILLRICH, MASON *Energy and World Politics*. New York: Free Press, 1975.
A balanced, calm, and persuasive assessment.

WORTMAN, STERLING, and CUMMINGS, RALPH W., JR. *To Feed This World*. Baltimore: Johns Hopkins University Press, 1978.
Two agricultural specialists propose a strategy for attacking the problem at its source. One of the most thoughtful and humane analyses available.

Chapter 8
ETHICS IN A WORLD OF POWER: JIMMY CARTER
AND THE GLOBAL HUMAN-RIGHTS CAMPAIGN

BARBER, JAMES D. *The Presidential Character*. Rev. ed. Englewood Cliffs: Prentice-Hall, 1977.
The author diagnoses Jimmy Carter as an "active-positive" president.

CARTER, JIMMY *Why Not the Best?* Nashville: Broadman Press, 1975.
A not particularly revealing autobiography.

CARTER, JIMMY "Interview With Playboy," *Playboy*, November 1976.
The controversial interview setting forth Carter's views on sex, power, and religion.

FERGUSON, CLYDE, and COTTER, WILLIAM R. "South Africa: What Is To Be Done?", *Foreign Affairs*, January 1978.
The authors recommend that, in the dilemma of apartheid and human rights in South Africa, Jimmy Carter should steer a pragmatic middle course.

FRASER, DONALD M. "Freedom and Foreign Policy," *Foreign Policy*, Spring 1977.
The case for giving more active support to Carter's human-rights policy.

GASTIL, RAYMOND D. "A Comparative Survey of Freedom," *Freedom at Issue*, January–February 1977.
A country-by-country survey of the status of civil and political freedom in the world.

HEFLEY, JAMES, and HEFLEY, MARTI *The Church That Produced a President*. New York: Wyden, 1977.
A useful account of Jimmy Carter's spiritual roots in the Baptist church.

HOVEYDA, FEREYDOUN "Not All Clocks for Human Rights Are the Same," *New York Times*, 18 May 1977.
Iran's former representative to the United Nations argues that the United States must remember that other nations may have different definitions of human rights.

KUCHARSKY, DAVID *The Man from Plains: The Mind and Spirit of Jimmy Carter*. New York: Harper and Row, 1976.
Carter, in the author's view, believes that love and kindness mean a great deal in one-to-one relationships but not in dealing with structures and corporate groups.

LAFEBER, WALTER *The Panama Canal: The Crisis in Historical Perspective*. New York: Oxford University Press, 1978.
The best available background study for an understanding of Carter's renegotiation of the Panama Canal treaties.

MAZLISH, BRUCE, and DIAMOND, EDWIN "Thrice-Born: A Psychohistory of Jimmy Carter's Rebirth," *New York Times*, 30 August 1976.
A perceptive insight into Jimmy Carter's religious roots.

MOYERS, BILL "Interview With Jimmy Carter," 6 May 1976, on *USA: People and Politics,* produced for PBS by Wallace Westfeldt.
A revealing character sketch.

Newsweek "The Push for Human Rights," *Newsweek,* 20 June 1977.
A special report that looks at some of the most shocking human rights abuses around the world.

ROTHSCHILD, EMMA "Carter and Arms Sales," *New York Times,* 4 June 1978.
The author points up the inconsistency between Carter's advocacy of global human rights and his policy on arms sales.

SCHLESINGER, ARTHUR, JR. "Human Rights and the American Tradition," in *America and the World* 1978, *Foreign Affairs,* Extra Issue, 1979.
The most thoughtful and balanced assessment of the Carter human-rights campaign currently available.

TURNER, ROBERT W. "I'll Never Lie To You," *Jimmy Carter in His Own Words.* New York: Ballantine Books, 1976.
A useful compilation of the presidential candidate's public statements.

ULLMAN, RICHARD H. "Human Rights and Economic Power: The United States versus Idi Amin," *Foreign Affairs,* April 1978.
The author urges a trade boycott against Idi Amin's Uganda in the name of human rights.

VANCE, CYRUS "Human Rights and Foreign Policy," *Department of State Bulletin,* 23 May 1977.
The secretary of state outlines the Carter administration's human-rights objectives.

VOGELGESANG, SANDRA "What Price Principle? U.S. Policy and Human Rights," *Foreign Affairs,* July 1978.
An excellent overall assessment of Jimmy Carter's global human-rights campaign.

WITCOVER, JULES *Marathon.* New York: Viking, 1977.
An overlong and detailed account recording Jimmy Carter's campaign for the presidency.

WOOTEN, JAMES *Dasher.* New York: Summit, 1978.
A good popular biography of Jimmy Carter, by the White House correspondent for the *New York Times.*

Epilogue
THE "MIGHT-HAVE-BEENS" OF HISTORY

BOULDING, KENNETH *The Image.* Ann Arbor: University of Michigan Press, 1964.
A pioneering study of the role of perception in modern society.

CANTRIL, HADLEY *The Human Dimension: Experiences in Policy Research.* New Brunswick: Rutgers University Press, 1967.
A good behavioral study of the impact of personality on policy.

COTTAM, RICHARD W. *Foreign Policy Motivation.* Pittsburgh: University of Pittsburgh Press, 1977.
The author navigates the treacherous waters of motivation in foreign policy most skillfully.

FARRELL, JOHN C., and SMITH, ASA P., eds. *Image and Reality in World Politics.* New York: Columbia University Press, 1968.
A good collection of essays dealing with the gaps between images and realities in world politics.

FREUD, SIGMUND *Civilization and Its Discontents.* New York: Norton, 1961.
The prophetic classic about the strains of modern technological civilizations.

FROMM, ERICH *The Anatomy of Human Destructiveness.* New York: Holt, Rinehart and Winston, 1973.
Profound psychiatric case studies of leading Nazi personalities and their impact on German society.

HALPER, THOMAS *Foreign Policy Crises: Appearance and Reality in Decision Making.* Columbus: Charles Merrill, 1971.
Focuses on individuals in foreign policy crises that risked or involved war.

ISAAK, ROBERT A. *Individuals and World Politics.* North Scituate, Mass.: Duxbury Press, 1975.
A trailblazing study of the impact of eight national leaders on their countries and the world.

JANIS, IRVING *Victims of Groupthink.* Boston: Houghton Mifflin, 1972.
An excellent study of psychological conformity in groups in foreign policy crisis decisions.

JERVIS, ROBERT *Perception and Misperception in International Relations.* Princeton: Princeton University Press, 1976.
A first-class analysis for the sophisticated reader.

KELMAN, HERBERT, ed. *International Behavior: A Socio-Psychological Analysis.* New York: Holt, Rinehart and Winston, 1965.
A well-conceived collection of articles with a behavioral orientation.

KLINEBERG, OTTO *The Human Dimension in International Relations.* New York: Holt, Rinehart and Winston, 1964.
A thoughtful and sensitive introduction to the subject.

LIFTON, ROBERT J., and OLSON, ERIC *Explorations in Psychohistory.* New York: Simon and Schuster, 1975.
The best general introduction to the subject.

LORENZ, KONRAD *On Aggression.* New York: Harcourt, Brace and World, 1966.
A seminal book, by a pioneer in the field of animal behavior.

MASLOW, ABRAHAM *Motivation and Personality.* New York: Harper and Row, 1954.
A post-Freudian analysis, based on human needs and hierarchies.

MAZLISH, BRUCE "The Psychohistorical Approach," in *In Search of Nixon*. Baltimore: Penguin Books, 1973.
A competent character study.

MEYERHOFF, HANS "On Psychoanalysis and History," *Psychoanalysis and the Psychoanalytic Review*, Summer 1962.
A thoughtful essay pointing out the possibilities and limits of psychoanalytic method when applied to politics and history.

MILGRAM, STANLEY *Obedience to Authority*. New York: Harper and Row, 1969.
Demonstrates why some human beings are willing to obey authority even to the extent of torturing others to death.

RIVERA, JOSEPH DE *The Psychological Dimension of Foreign Policy*. Columbus: Charles Merrill, 1968.
A good general introduction to the subject.

SHAPIRO, DAVID *Neurotic Styles*. New York: Basic Books, 1965.
Provides excellent conceptual tools for an understanding of neurotic and pathologic styles in political leaders.

STOESSINGER, JOHN G. *The Might of Nations: World Politics in Our Time*. 6th ed. New York: Random House, 1979.
This book emphasizes the importance of personalities and misperceptions in world politics.

WALZER, MICHAEL *Just and Unjust Wars*. New York: Basic Books, 1977.
An original and highly sophisticated analysis of a number of wars, with emphasis on the moral dilemmas involved.

WICKER, TOM *JFK and LBJ: The Influence of Personality Upon Politics*. Baltimore: Penguin, 1968.
Two sensitive psychological portraits and a thoughtful comparative analysis.

Index